Selling
to the World

Also by L. Fargo Wells

EXPORTING: FROM START TO FINANCE, THIRD EDITION

Selling to the World

L. Fargo Wells

McGraw-Hill

New York   San Francisco   Washington, D.C.   Auckland   Bogotá
Caracas   Lisbon   London   Madrid   Mexico City   Milan
Montreal   New Delhi   San Juan   Singapore
Sydney   Tokyo   Toronto

Library of Congress Cataloging-in-Publication Data

Wells, L. Fargo.
    Selling to the world / L. Fargo Wells.
        p.   cm.
    Includes index.
    ISBN 0-07-069302-1
      1. Export marketing—United States—Handbooks, manuals, etc.
I. Title
  HF1416.5.W453   1996
  658.8'48—dc20
                                   96-12407
                                      CIP

McGraw-Hill

*A Division of The **McGraw·Hill** Companies*

1 2 3 4 5 6 7 8 9 0 DOC/DOC 9 0 1 0 9 8 7 6

ISBN 0-07-069302-1

*The sponsoring editor for this book was David Conti, the editing supervisor
was Caroline R. Levine, and the production supervisor was Suzanne W. B.
Rapcavage. It was set in Palatino by Priscilla Beer of McGraw-Hill's
Professional Book Group composition unit.*

Printed and bound by R. R. Donnelley & Sons Company.

McGraw-Hill books are available at special quantity discounts to use as
premiums and sales promotions, or for use in corporate training programs. For more information, please write to the Director of Special
Sales, McGraw-Hill, 11 West 19th Street, New York, NY 10011. Or contact your local bookstore.

This book is printed on recycled, acid-free paper containing
a minimum of 50 percent recycled de-inked fiber.

To Karin—

Contents

Preface   xiii
Acknowledgments   xv

Part 1. Getting Ready

POTENTIALS

1. **Bring the World to Your Doorstep—and Make Money Doing It**   **3**

   Should You Go "International"?   4
   Types of Export People   4
   Potential Export Conditions   5
   Potential Export Products   6
   Characteristics of Prime Target Countries   9
   Synergism—Maybe!   11
   The Case for Combined Import/Export Activity   12

2. **Preparing for the Export Venture**   **15**

   Setting Up a Home Office   15
   Getting Equipped   15
   Finding Help and Advice   16
   Getting on with It!   21

STRUCTURING

3. **Structure: Putting the Framework in Place**   **23**

   Establishing the New Business Structure   23
   Getting Government Licenses and Permits   27
   Finding Accounting and Bookkeeping Assistance   29
   Lining Up Legal Assistance for Import/Export   30
   Taking Out Insurance with a Foreign Accent   30
   Locating a Bank and an International Banker   31

BASIC STRATEGIES

4. **Determining Your Export/Import Strategies**   **35**

   Export Vehicles and How They Operate   35
   A Quantitative Analysis of All Exporters   39
   Import/Export: The General Trading Company   39
   Deciding Whether to Export Directly or Through an
     Intermediary   41

Selecting and Dealing with an EMC/ETC   42
Alternatives to Direct Export Distribution   44
Realistic Assessment of Resources   48
Your Final Assessment   52
The Business Plan as an Expression of Basic Strategy   52

DISTRIBUTION STRATEGIES

5. Who on Earth?   56

Dealing with the End User   56
Selling Through Retailers   57
Using an Agent/Representative   59
Selling Through a Distributor   61

Part 2. Exploring Territorial Strategies

THE ROADMAP

6. Where in the World?—The Western Hemisphere   69

Degree of Trading Difficulty Ratings   70
The Western Hemisphere   74
  North America   75
  Central America   79
  Caribbean   81
  South America   83

7. Where in the World?—Europe and Africa   89

Europe   89
  Western Europe   89
  Central Europe   97
  Eastern Europe   101
Africa   104
  North Africa   106
  West Africa   109
  East Africa   111
  Central Africa   111
  Southern Africa   112

8. Where in the World?—Asia and the Pacific   114

Asia   114
  Southwest Asia (Middle East)   114
  Southern Asia   120
  Siberia and Central Asia   121
  East Asia   123
  Southeast Asia   130
Australia   134

Oceania—the Independent Pacific Islands   135
Antartica   135

Part 3. International Selling and Promotion

SELLING TACTICS AND SEARCHING FOR LEADS

9. Introducing Your Product Overseas   139

Key Points in Overseas Sales Communication   139
The Fax Revolution   142
Objectives in the Introductory Phase   143
Finding the Names and Leads for Initial Overseas Contacts   144
Nonfederal Trade Facilitation Assistance   147
Contact Sources from the Private Sector   147

RESPONSE AND QUOTATION

10. Responding to Overseas Sales Inquiries   149

Sorting Out the Inquiries   149
Prompt and Appropriate Responses   149
Sending Samples   150
Terms of Payment   151
Shipping Terms   152
Pricing and Price Lists   155
Pro Forma Invoices: The Ultimate Quotation   159
Caveats   161

TRAVELING

11. Selling Overseas   163

Strategies for the First Trip   164
Travel Tips   164
Traveling with Samples   167
Overseas Promotion   169
Trade Fairs, Trade Missions, and Catalog Exhibitions   171

Part 4. Transacting Foreign Trade

THE EXPORT PROCESS

12. The Anatomy of an Export Transaction   177

Negotiating for a Profit   178
Using Your Bank and Banker   179
Finding a Freight Forwarder   181
Handling the Documentary Side of a Transaction   182
Timing Is Everything   191

Checklist of Minimum Terms   192
Export Contracts and Purchase Orders   193
Specifications, Performance Standards, and Inspections   196
Collecting Payment   197

THE IMPORT PROCESS

13. Preparing for an Import Transaction   199

Preimport Preparation   199
Clearing Customs—Formal Entry   204
Clearing Customs—Informal Entry   206
The 1994 Customs Modernization Act   208
Import Quotas   208
Marking and Labeling   209
Restricted and/or Licensed Import Products   210
Drawbacks   210
The Custom House Broker   211

GETTING PAID

14. Letters of Credit and Payment Terms: Definitions and Strategies   214

Open Account   214
Documentary Collections   217
Letters of Credit   219
Wire Transfers and Advance Payment   242

EXPORT FINANCE

15. An Introduction to Export/Import Finance   243

Working Capital Financing   244
Trade Finance   245
Countertrade   248

PROTECTING PROFITS

16. Insuring Your Import/Export Business   251

Commercial Risks on Foreign Accounts Receivable   250
Political Risks on Foreign Accounts Receivable   252
Sources of Foreign Credit Information   253
Credit Insurance on Foreign Accounts Receivable   254

Part 5. Public Sector Programs

GETTING HELP TO THE MARKETPLACE

17. Government Support for Export Marketing   267

International Trade Administration   268

Department of Agriculture   277
Small Business Administration   282
Agency for International Development   284
Trade and Development Agency   287
Assistance from State and Nonfederal Governmental Units   288

HELP WITH EXPORT FINANCING

18. Government Export Finance Support   289

The Small Business Administration   289
The Export-Import Bank of the United States   291
Overseas Private Investment Corporation   294
Foreign Sales Corporations   295
State-Based Export Finance Support   296

AVOIDING PROBLEMS

19. U.S. and International Trade Regulations   297

Intellectual Property Rights   297
Export Licensing   302
Antiboycott Regulations   307
Foreign Corrupt Practices Act   308

Appendixes

A. Export Help "800" Numbers   310

B. Metric and English Table of Measurement
Equivalents   311

C. Eximbank Regional Offices   313

D. Eximbank City/State Programs   314

E. Public and Private Export Related Organizations 318

F. Export Reference Books   321

Export Marketing and International Trade   321
Cultures and Customs, and Export Sale Negotiations   322
Letters of Credit, Documentation, and Shipping   323
Research and Statistics   324
Dictionaries, Directories, and Encyclopedias   324

G. Export Periodicals, Magazines, and Publications 325

Index   327

Preface

The purpose of this book is to explain how small firms and individuals can learn to export their products or services quickly and successfully. The text is equally appropriate for the small manufacturer making a product in an industrial park and the independent exporter operating from his or her home. Both are entrepreneurs at heart. The company may be a manufacturer looking for extra sales to support existing fixed overhead or a firm convinced that its product will sell as well overseas as well as it does in this country. The individual may be an aerospace engineer whose promising career has come to an end with the close of the Cold War; a manager who finds a present career lacking challenge and eager to start a replacement career after hours; or simply a bright, independent-minded young person determined to see where exporting might lead.

In each case, this book will provide general initial strategies and minimize the possibility of false starts or errors as it guides the reader through the export/import process with a view to the fastest possible start-up. The book deals with the details of forms and technical issues only as they relate to specific instances. For general procedural matters, I urge that you acquire one of several basic reference books, such as the inexpensive U.S. Department of Commerce manual, *A Basic Guide to Exporting*, to refer to as you follow this narrative road map to world trade. My purpose is to help you focus on reasonable objectives—taking your personal background, available time, and financial resources, into account—and to guide you through the export process in a highly readable fashion.

The section of the text called "Where in the World?" takes a close look at the world through a trader's eyes. In three chapters—devoted to North and South America; Europe and Africa; Asia, Australia, and Oceania—the book presents a brief overview of the region's history, geography, and cultures from a *commercial perspective*. By integrating up-to-date trade facts with pertinent geopolitical background, these chapters will help you get a feel for the new global economy and its direct bearing on the choices facing your new export operation.

My own experience in the export/import field spans some 20 years. It has been broadened and deepened by the hard-won know-how of numerous business-people with whom I have exchanged information and anecdotes over the years. And it has been tempered by the questions, reactions, and opinions of the hundreds of individuals and companies I have worked with during that time, whether simply as a private consultant, or as Director of California's Export Finance Office, or while establishing America's first Small Business Export Development Center for the State of California and the U.S. Small Business Administration.

It is my hope that this guidebook will help make your export/import experience as stimulating, productive, and successful as my own has been.

Acknowledgments

I wish to thank again the experts and professionals to whom we turned for assistance in co-authoring the initial export reference book, *Exporting from Start to Finance,* Third Edition, McGraw-Hill, New York, 1996. Their technical knowledge was used in an abridged fashion, when called for, in the process of writing *Selling to the World.* Included among this group were:

Richard Barovick

Michael R. Doram

Stanley W. Epstein

William Filbert

Irene Fisher

Hugh Grigsby

Endy Hoffman

John R. Liebman

Robert D. Martini

Louis Monoz

William Norman

James R. Phillips

James Schill

Donald F. Schmoll

L. Stroh

A special thanks to Kenneth W. Waymire of Kenneth W. Waymire and Associates and retired Assistant Treasurer, Foreign Trade Services, Mattel Inc.; and attorney S. Richard Shostak of Stein, Shostak, Shostak & O'Hara, for their help in presenting the import process, a subject first addressed in these pages.

I would also like to acknowledge again the many excellent articles in the magazines *Export Today, The Exporter, Business America, International Business,* and *Trade & Culture,* which helped keep me current on general export information.

L. Fargo Wells

PART 1
Getting Ready

1
Bring the World to Your Doorstep

—and Make Money Doing It

"Bringing the world to your doorstep" is our way of saying that international trade can be successfully undertaken by small firms. What's more, it can be done with a reasonable expectation of tangible results in the short term and significant improvement in profits and sales in the long term. This introduction to international trade emphasizes export rather than import, because export is the starting point for most companies and traders unless their aim is offshore contract manufacturing. Bear in mind, however, as we discuss export, that the same rules apply to import, because (with the exception of import arrival and customs clearance) one activity is the flip side of the other. It's important to understand the basics of importing even if exporting is your primary interest right now, because export activity may lead to very profitable import opportunities.

This book assumes that you, the reader, either represent a small company manufacturing a proprietary product that has potential overseas, or that you are heading up an export management or trading company in the early stages of development. If you fall into the latter category, you face a somewhat more difficult task, as you must first find third parties with exportable products who are willing to cooperate in export development, including the creation of a pricing structure for the trading company that will make the overall effort a practical exercise.

As well as a hands-on discussion of ways to achieve a successful export business, you'll find numerous anecdotes in these pages detailing the setbacks, stumbling blocks, and frustrations that I and others have experienced as we learned the ropes in international trade. Hopefully, you'll be able to profit from our mistakes and apply the lessons we've learned before any problems arise. *Selling to the World* will help you find answers to many of your own questions—especially to the very important issue of how to make money as an international trader. This is not simply another compilation of facts about the nuts and bolts of exporting. It is a practical analysis of export/import trading, designed to help you minimize the time it takes to achieve a profitable level of trade.

You will, however, need a basic reference and guidebook and there are many of them available, including our own *Exporting from Start to Finance*,[1] which has been cited as one of the best of the comprehensive export books. But before buying that or any other book, we suggest a more compact and less expensive publication as your first export reference book: *A Basic Guide to Exporting*,[2] last published by the United States Department of Commerce in 1992 in cooperation with contributors from both the public and private sectors of the export community. This guide costs less than $10 and covers the basic elements of exporting and the public sector sources of assistance. Many changes of office and program names, addresses, and telephone numbers have taken place since that publishing, however. So for more current information on export support, call the Trade Information Center (TIC) at 1-800/USA-TRADE (800/872-8723) for the latest edition of a free booklet entitled *Export Programs: A Business Directory of U.S. Government Services*. The most recent printing at this writing was January 1995, but with the many changes now taking place as ordained by the 104th Congress, a 1996 version will probably be printed and will be very useful. We especially urge you to review the *Basic Guide to Exporting* and thereafter to use it as a reference from time to time as you read this book. The task of *Selling to the World* will be to bring those basic facts and procedures to life and into appropriate perspective so that you can see how they will work for you.

Should You Go International?

Let us answer that question by looking at the mix of factors involved, while keeping in mind that reliable sources tell us that, as of 1994, 26 percent of small-to-midsize businesses *do* export.

Types of Export People

Exporting is certainly not the dazzling and glamorous endeavor some would romance it to be. And, as in any career or effort, it will not be lucrative for all who try. It requires many repetitive procedures, whether within or outside an existing business, not the least of which is the continuing necessity of corresponding for response and selling purposes. Two other major requirements are a feeling for diplomacy, which includes sensitivity, patience, and an understanding of other cultures; and the ability to focus on details, a skill on which export transactions often depend, whatever the quality of the products involved. We'll consider all these areas, especially in connection with that concept and word *focus*, throughout this book. Exporting can be started with little capital, but doing a good job of follow-up, establishing overseas relationships, and meeting the demands of the export purchase agreement, contract, or letter of credit, require certain personality traits, in addition to both time and money. These traits are not often found in one person, whether he or she be the individual within the business responsible for its export development, or an individual trader and entrepreneur. To these personal traits one must add a high degree of determination to see that the more mundane details of international trade are nevertheless conscientiously performed until the export business grows to afford its own staff, after which routine chores can be delegated. It's wise to continually scrutinize your own personal attributes and available time, together with your available financial resources and product suitability, as you delve deeper into the export possibilities before you.

My first help, other than clerical, in our trading company was an individual dedicated to the notion of export selling and trading who later became a partner in the business as well. When he was able to convince me that the fastest way to offset his salary cost was to let him live in Japan for the first six months and establish our products on a face-to-face basis, it was tantamount to convincing me he also had all the attributes just mentioned, and he did. This was in the early 1970s and our first office was in the Osaka Grand Hotel. We were also one of the very first companies to export textiles to Japan. Today, considering costs there, I am not sure one could offset his room-and-board bill that quickly—to say nothing of his salary. But the man loved selling, and with no understanding of Japanese he especially loved the visual and nonverbal pantomimes and illustrations necessary to make Japanese with limited English understand and appreciate the value of the product he was offering.

Potential Export Conditions

What makes for a potential export situation or opportunity? The answer is not much different from what a marketing director would see in the U.S. market. Here is a list of some situations that come to mind:

- Utilitarian need.
- A clear price advantage over the foreign product (assuming that tariffs, hidden or otherwise, do not negate the advantage).
- Technological advantage (assuming that the target country can afford or needs advanced technology).

- Prior-generation technology exports to less advanced countries that can therefore be offered for less.

- Superior quality or design.

- Trendy styles, assuming that the target country sees the United States as a desirable leader in this area of styling. An example might be California sportswear or outdoor-living trends, admired by almost everyone that can afford them. France is a notable exception to appreciation of U.S. style trends other than blue jeans, a universal passion.

- New product or invention, but only if the need exists!

- Product or commodity shortage. These can represent good opportunities for the quick and fleet, but are often the most difficult to take advantage of for new export traders. The leads received from whatever source go to everyone in the trade, and after the regular suppliers are already or nearly sold out—so how does the newcomer find first-quality product? Worse, the potential customers are inquiring on an opportunistic basis and are not the end users. They very likely have no more knowledge about the product or commodity than the would-be trader, resulting in an unknowing buyer dealing with an unknowing seller—a recipe for disaster.

Potential Export Products

This may appear to be a restatement of the above comments, but it is not. There are basic characteristics that make some products easier to sell or more subject to successful export than others. An example would be products of high value relative to their weight and, more especially, to their bulk. If they occupy a great deal of space, they become excessively expensive to ship unless they are of very high value or unless they can be "knocked down" (compressed or folded, taken apart, and shipped flat) to a more practical shipping volume. Here are a few points that may provide clues when seeking good export products:

- Products that are readily knocked down (KD) to a very compact state.

- Products of sufficient monetary value to result in shipments of economic export size (over $10,000 per typical shipment, certainly over $5000, and preferably in the $25 to $50,000 range).

- Products that do not require much postsales service unless you anticipate overseas service branches or qualified and willing distributors.

- Products that are not excessively subject to breakage, spoilage, pilferage, and are not, therefore, excessively subject to claims. Claims are costly to settle, even when adequately insured, because buyers want what they ordered, not a monetary substitute paid months later by the insurance company.

- Products that are relatively easy to sample and that do not have so much variance season to season that expensive trips must be made to resell the new version or line. It is best if they can be well illustrated or described in catalog or brochure form and do not require individual viewing of each variation.

- Products that lend themselves to dramatic demonstration without requiring an unwieldy amount of equipment to do so.

- Products that have a good shelf life but that will also generate repeat sales, either by virtue of consumption or by word-of-mouth reputation.

- BUT MOST OF ALL, PRODUCTS THE CUSTOMERS WANT!

A prime area of both business and private consumer demand is products in the high-tech field. This is always one of the most buoyant segments of U.S. exports. Exports of all goods (no services included) rose to $512 billion in 1994, and high-tech exports continued to be the star performers. According to Stephen C. Messner, in his article, "The Special Challenge of High-Tech Exports," in *Export Today*,[3] PC software exports alone jumped 30 percent, to $2 billion, as early as 1992, and the trend has continued. To paraphrase Messner's article, the industry is a perfect example of export success for small and very small businesses, with many obtaining at least 30 percent of their sales from abroad. I personally know of several companies with total sales of under $1 million that are realizing over 60 percent of their business from exports.

There are downsides to the high-tech industry, however, because of short life cycles and often the need to provide after-sales support. Typically, high-tech characteristics include an ongoing and high investment (10 to 15 percent of sales) in research and development; they must therefore be concerned with intellectual property rights in the country of export. High-tech exporters sell highly engineered products to sophisticated customers and experience rapid product change. The United States is a leader in this area for several reasons: our world-class research; our government subsidies, largely indirect, stemming from our large expenditures on defense; our enormous home market; and our entrepreneurial culture.

Some key high-tech industries include: aircraft; computer hardware and software; pharmaceutical products; scientific/engineering equipment, instruments, and systems such as medical equipment, process control, and pollution control; and telecommunications. In these areas it is important to get close to customers, either to personally help them understand what will work best for them, or to find distributors who know the technologies involved sufficiently well to develop a close working relationship before and after the sale.

Services make up some 25 percent of all U.S. exports. The goods that constitute the other 75 percent can be roughly broken down into: manufactured products, agricultural commodities and extractables, or mining products. Table 1-1, which lists the top 30 exported goods for 1994, makes the predominance of high-tech products clear. But it's a little harder to determine which categories include the popular consumer export products. Some are ranked far below the top 30 products but still represent

Table 1-1. Top 30 U.S. Export Products for 1994
Categorized by SITC Code to Three Digits

Rank	SITC no.	Product(s)	$ Export value (in billions)
1	792	Aircraft & associated equipment	30.380
2	776	Electronic parts (e.g.,thermionic, cold cathode, photocathode valves, etc.)	26.459
3	784	Parts & accessories of motor vehicles	22.275
4	752	Auto. data processing mach., and units thereof	20.415
5	781	Motor cars and other motor vehicles	16.873
6	764	Telecommunication equip., N.E.S. & parts	14.799
7	759	Parts, etc., for office mach. & units thereof	14.013
8	874	Measuring/checking/analyzing inst., N.E.S.	11.710
9	713	Int. combustion piston engines & parts, N.E.S	8.400
10	714	Engines & motors, nonelectric & parts	8.333
11	770	Electrical mach. & apparatus, N.E.S.	8.274
12	772	Elec. apparatus for switch., protectg. circ.	7.294
13	723	Civil engineer. & contractors' plant & equip.	7.088
14	728	Machry, etc., specialized for particular ind.	6.694
15	898	Musical inst. & parts; records, tapes, etc.	6.263
16	971	Gold, nonmonetary (exc. ores & concentrates)	5.722
17	122	Tobacco, mfg.	5.421
18	641	Paper and paperboard	5.036
19	741	Heating and cooling equipment & parts	5.012
20	743	Pumps, air, or other gas compressors & fans	4.696
21	222	Oil seeds	4.688
22	782	Motor veh. for trnspt. of gds. & spec. purposes	4.375
23	872	Instr. & appls. for medical/dental purposes	4.311
24	598	Miscellaneous chemical products, N.E.S.[1]	4.212
25	044	Maize	4.197
26	699	Manufactures of base metal, N.E.S.[2]	4.154
27	892	Printed matter	4.086
28	041	Wheat	4.059
29	334	Oil (not crude) from petrol & bitum. minerals	4.032
30	891	Arms and ammunition	4.018

[1]SITC 598, "Miscellaneous chemical products," includes products as diverse as chemical elements and compounds; chemicals doped to use in electronics; chemical preparations; diagnostic or laboratory reagents, catalysts, etc.

[2]SITC 699, "Manufactures of base metal," includes everything from hinges, padlocks, and car springs; forged and stamped iron; steel chains; aluminum casting; to such household items as knitting needles.

SOURCE: Extracted from Bureau of Census Report FT925.

hundreds of millions of dollars of export business. Others are buried in the top 30 in the form of such things as auto accessories and parts, computer-related items, and musical instruments.

Characteristics of Prime Target Countries

There is almost no country in the world to which we do not sell something from the United States. Many are so limited or so difficult to sell to, however, that they aren't really worth an exporter's consideration. This is not to say you should deal only with rich countries or countries within a trade bloc of our own. After all, a country with rich potential for an exporter in one product area may be a zero for someone else. (We will look into this further in Chapter 6.)

For now, however, it may help to keep things in perspective if we take note of the top 10 export customers as of 1994:

Country	Total U.S. exports to (in billions)
Canada	$114.4
Japan	53.5
Mexico	50.8
United Kingdom	26.8
Germany	19.2
South Korea	18.0
Taiwan	17.1
France	13.6
Netherlands	12.6
Singapore	13.0

It is worth noting the dominance of Canada as the largest U.S. customer by more than double. Canada may not sound very exotic, but it is a logical and easy route for your first experience in selling outside the United States. For the third-party exporter it may be difficult to find a manufacturer client not already selling in Canada. But many small companies have no Canadian distribution, and if that is the case, you could make an instant hero of yourself. The next-largest customer, Japan, can be one of the toughest to sell to, unless consumers there actively want the product you're selling. The third customer, Mexico, can be a relatively quick and easy success if the product is right, especially in view of the North American Free Trade Agreement. The Mexican market will be better still as Mexico's current peso crisis subsides.

There are really three facets to the question of a country's export potential. The first is *financial* and can in turn be divided into:

1. Available disposable income
2. Available foreign exchange to pay in a currency usable by the exporter
3. Demographics indicating that the country has a sufficiently large upper or middle class to constitute a viable market for the product (even though statistics for the country as a whole might suggest that it is far too poor for anything but used clothing or subsidized food commodities).

The second facet is *cultural*. No matter how clearly the seller sees the potential market for its product or service, can that product or service find a place in the hearts of its would-be buyers? Once again, demographics should be examined, because there *may* be a hidden market.

In parts of the Middle East, there are very strict rules, based on the Koran, regarding women in general and behavior deemed sensual or indiscrete in particular. These rules of behavior for both men and women must be respected, and it is up to you, the trader, to discover them in advance. While perhaps neither as radical nor as seriously punishable when breeched, there are cultural rules, codes, and distinctions in every country that need to govern your behavior if you are to achieve success.

One typical Middle Eastern example involves the marketing of stylishly sensual lingerie in Saudi Arabia. There is, it turns out, quite a substantial market for this type of merchandise in the country, so long as those selling it are discrete and no illustrations of the merchandise are printed on the boxes or used in advertising.

I found myself uncomfortably close to jail for paying too little heed to these Islamic restrictions before I learned this lesson. While attending an apparel show sponsored by the U.S. Department of Commerce in the area, I displayed full-color blowups of the U.S. magazine advertising for my client's very elegant lacy lingerie. The items were in good taste but "revealing" and would be considered sexy by some. It seemed strange that our booth was so exceptionally busy and that we were passing out so much material in what I judged to be an area of limited potential for the range. I soon learned why. What I was doing was tantamount to passing out pornography. The police soon heard of our "success" and stormed the exhibition hall. They made a beeline for my booth, tore off my displays, and gave me a lecture that left me in no doubt about how much trouble I would have been in if the exhibition had not been under U.S. sponsorship.

Lacking appropriate and tasteful illustrations of the lingerie altogether proved a disadvantage, however, for the smart, or more export-oriented, competition had purposely created a completely different set of boxes, tags, and advertisements to circumvent this problem. (Interestingly, illustrations of sexy lingerie present no problem in Latin America, even though there too, a woman's modesty is closely guarded. But in Latin America, a photograph of such lingerie is perfectly acceptable so long as the model wearing it is an unknown third party. Furthermore, women in many Latin countries spend far more on their undergarments in proportion to outerwear than is typical in most countries.)

The third facet is the *utilitarian value* of the product when translated into the geography, climate, and lifestyle of a target country. Where industrial and commercial products are concerned, usefulness can be readily perceived, but with consumer products, no one can be absolutely sure, since rapidly changing trends in style, one-upmanship, prestige, and vanity play havoc with all predictions. It is not unusual to have astute and informed local businessmen convincingly pronounce a product contrary to the tastes or needs of the population, only to have another businessman with a positive attitude toward the product make a success of it against all odds.

Nevertheless, some logic should be applied in the initial stages of decision making, and this demands early consideration of such easily discernible factors as:

- Ability to pay, judged both on the internal creation of wealth in the country and its access to negotiable foreign exchange.

- Need for the product.

- Acceptance of the product or the product's ready adaptability to other cultures, languages, needs, and customs.

- Geographical relationship. No matter how universal a product's appeal may be, there *are* economic limitations on how many countries may be targeted for promotion when the costs of travel and promotion are considered. This also applies to special language, labeling, and packaging complications. Your own budget and time limitations will tell you how many world markets you can target, but common sense suggests that you concentrate on countries within those one or more world areas that are geographically and culturally related.

Synergism—Maybe!

The dictionary defines this very popular word as "the joint action of agents, which, when taken together, increase each other's effectiveness." This is often misunderstood to apply to marketing situations in which the buyer and seller have certain basic characteristics in common, which tend to enhance the product in the eyes of the buyer.

This can be a delicate subject, and I am sure some have taken offense on previous occasions when I have mentioned it. I refer to the not-uncommon assumption that, because of a shared ethnicity and/or skin color, faith and/or cultural heritage, the seller's success is assured. Nothing could be farther from the truth! While we have already pointed out that understanding the language, customs, and practices of your intended customers is an important asset and can clearly help your cause, it only does so when most of the other basic elements are in place. These include product, quality, and competitiveness, ability to sell and understand the customer's needs, ability to deliver, and a proven performance track record.

I have many times watched buyers and sellers negotiate across enormous ethnic and cultural divides. The groups they come from may possess ancient enmities, or even be involved in current conflicts. Yet in spite of those barriers, the negotiations go very well because one is selling what the other wants to buy. In other words, personal and cultural harmonies are far outweighed by commercial realities, and woe to the marketeer, domestic or international, who confuses the ability to "open doors" with the capacity to get signatures on the bottom line.

Real synergism relates to products and follow-on sales opportunities, not to the seller's identity, save where his or her sales skills are involved. It is always expensive to contact customers and service them, and especially so in the case of international sales. Therefore, one needs to consider products that relate to each other in terms of being purchased by the same or similar buyers or institutions, or products that add or relate to a primary product. (This is in keeping with the previous comment about focusing on countries that are geographically and culturally related to each other.)

The Case for Combined Import/Export Activity

A clear opportunity for synergism occurs when exporting to countries in which you have an opportunity to manufacture or procure parts or raw materials, or in which you may have specific import interests. With the growth of trade regionalism in today's international climate, a business venture that offers profits for both sides of the trade equation has an increasingly important advantage. You become "one of them" and are likely to receive favorable treatment accordingly, be it commercial, sovereign, or possibly both. Trading blocs are developing far faster than most would have imagined a few years ago. The example of the moment is the North American Free Trade Agreement (NAFTA), signed by Mexico, Canada, and the United States. There are also two or three major blocs in Latin America and Southeast Asia, to say nothing of the European Community. And we can expect to see further trade bloc developments in Eastern Europe and Asia.

Perhaps the best conditions for import/export are directly related to the cyclical nature of business. Because of the tendency for economic ups and downs to ripple around the world as a wave proceeds across the water, one side of an import/export business can help maintain profits during a sharp decline of the other. As business brightens in one area of the world and demand increases, a downturn in another area improves procurement opportunities and competitive pricing.

There are clearly economies of scale to be realized as a result of overlapping administrative expenses in such areas as documentary and shipping personnel. But far and away the most important economies probably come from overseas travel. Undertaken to further the export side of a business, such travel often leads to the discovery of excellent new products for import. Alert entrepreneurs have a chance to take advantage of such opportunities months before they are presented for sale in their own market by others.

> I will never forget a golden opportunity missed very early in my own export career when my then-partner and I discovered a newly designed office furniture caster in Denmark in 1970. We both recognized its value but made only a half-hearted effort to preestablish distribution and sales, in part because our minds were on export and in part because of fear of straining our limited financial resources at the time. Had we been otherwise oriented, that single item would probably have exceeded our total export volume for the next decade. If you look at the caster on the office chair in which you may now be sitting, the odds are at least 50/50 that you will see the design, if not the make, I am referring to. Yet then, the manufacturer would have been very happy to give us exclusive rights in this country in exchange for a very modest beginning inventory plus some of the follow-on orders any reasonable effort would have surely produced.

The Case Against Combined Import/Export Activity

While there are economies of scale to be found in combining importing and exporting and you will certainly encounter import opportunities if you are an alert exporter, there are also important potential disadvantages to a combined operation.

With the exception of the Export Administration Act as it concerns products requiring licenses and the antiboycott restrictions (the latter being almost exclusively confined to Middle Eastern country exports), our government in the main encourages and sustains exporters. Other regulations, like the Shipper's Export Declaration (SED) are minimal and can mainly be handled by a competent freight forwarder. In contrast, our government, like most others, is not interested in helping prospective *importers,* but is very determined to collect all import tariffs due. In fact, it often seems that customs law is the one area of our legal system where you are assumed guilty until proven innocent. There are many regulations and processing exercises involved in importing, although a good customs-house broker can steer you cleanly around such obstacles. (We will review this in more detail in the introduction and overview to importing in Chapter 13.)

There are other things to consider before becoming too enchanted with undertaking import activities in tandem with a new export business. One of them returns to the central issue of *focus* already mentioned. No matter how excellent the concept, it may be impossible to stretch your time and financial resources to both efforts without diminishing the potential results of each.

The issue of time is important, and we add a note concerning finances. Importing takes more capital up front because it is the importer who must put up the letter of credit in advance. This requires cash or the equivalent, except in cases where a company has a well-established credit line. Then, after importation, you are faced with the freight and duty bill, which must be paid before the merchandise even leaves the port of entry. Next come distribution and transportation costs, plus probably an open accounts receivable for at least 30 days. All things considered, the capital for the transaction will be tied up for at least 90 days. The actual time involved may be somewhat reduced in the case of air shipments, but it can also be a good deal longer—especially if your order must be custom-produced and the production time required is significant.

The good news is that imports are also much easier to finance than exports. The reason is simple: bankers feel that they have control over an important piece of collateral in the case of imports—namely, the goods being imported. They can effectively track them and maintain control until actual distribution is made to the retailer or end user.

So much for the preliminaries and the question of whether or not to go international. If you have analyzed all the pros and cons and decided that you have the right product or service, the target buyers, the opportune market conditions, *and* the personal temperament to make a success of selling abroad, you're ready to move on to specifics.

Endnotes

1. L. Fargo Wells and Karin B. Dulat, *Exporting from Start to Finance,* Liberty Hall Press of McGraw-Hill, Third Edition, New York, 1996.

2. U.S. Department of Commerce, *A Basic Guide to Exporting,* U.S. Department of Commerce, Washington, D.C., 1992.

3. Stephen C. Messner, "The Special Challenge of High-Tech Exports," *Export Today,* April 1993.

2
Preparing for the Export Venture

The next few paragraphs are addressed to readers who are planning to set up an export/import office in their own homes. As we make suggestions for equipment for such an office, we ask the forbearance of those with established businesses.

Setting Up a Home Office

Try to select an area for your office that is as far removed as possible from interfering noises and distractions. It is also wise to have your equipment and files in a room that can be safe from small, exploring hands that might destroy fax transmissions or computer files in your absence. A genuinely private area, or at least one that is set aside by mutual understanding, does more than offer escape from external interference. It provides an internal signal that you are now ready to shut out the daily routines and go to work.

As with any desk work area, be sure you have the best possible lighting and seating because it is very likely that you'll be using this space when you've already completed a busy daily schedule and you'll need the most supportive possible conditions for optimum effort. The days of failed savings and loan institutions and corporate downsizing have created some really marvelous bargains in office furniture from specialists in the used office-equipment business. Quality furniture that once would have been beyond the reach of even generous start-up budgets is now available at prices almost anyone can afford. Taking advantage of this opportunity to enjoy a little extra comfort will give you a "carrot" to make the best use of your home office. Lastly, be sure to top off these purchases with a file cabinet or, at the least, a good temporary fiberboard file for start-up purposes.

Getting Equipped

The electronic revolution has completely changed international trade to the small- or low-budget operation's great advantage. Communication with the rest of the world by fax has made the exploration of opportunities and leads so much faster and less expensive that your chances of success in international trade are substantially improved. If your budget is really restricted, count the fax and a small computer as near-necessities, even if they must also be purchased used. Virtually every business anywhere in the world owns or has access to a fax, even though the inadequate phone service in some parts of the third world and in parts of the former USSR makes them a less-than-perfect instrument for communication with these areas. If you are very active in one of these locations, it may be necessary to use telex communication when speed and reliability are needed. Such problems are so exceptional however, that we suggest you temporarily arrange for a public telex number contact until you are sure of the need. Leave the much-larger initial and operational costs of a telex to a time when it is clearly essential. If your budget allows, you will find that a dedicated telephone line will markedly improve reliable fax reception.

Today, at very modest prices, computers can be found that offer more computing power, information storage, and access than midsize companies could afford only a decade or so ago. The computer can send your facsimile transmissions, access trade databases, prepare invoices and quotations, and keep the business accounts—to say nothing of being the world's greatest typewriter. A computer with good software can prepare everything from handsome brochures and customized letters to mass mailings merged with individually selected names and addresses from large direct-mail lists. Of course the catch is that, if purchased separately, the software packages can cost more than the computer itself. Shop carefully for special packages or used-computers that include a word processing program and probably a modem. Word processing software is usually the most expensive to buy from scratch but is often to be found in used computers or even as part of an IBM-compatible component package and new-package brand-name deals. Instructions for major software applications are available as separate books at booklike prices. Small-business accounting packages (the largest seller of which continues to be the Quicken version) are available for well under $100. A typewriter for forms and individual addresses will help round out your communication needs.

There will be other items for which you will discover a need but they can be acquired within even the most modest expense budget as the need arises. Don't forget to purchase a very good, *up-to-date* map of the world. This, together with a good postage scale and international postage chart, is something the already equipped small manufacturer may also need.

Finding Help and Advice

As we have already explained, there is a lot of help and advice available on how to export and where to find export leads, making export an easier starting point for your venture into international trade than import. Whereas the former U.S. Department of Commerce (DOC) published a myriad of documents and books on exporting (still more are published by the Small Business Administration, or SBA), I am aware of only one available government guide on importing. It is published by the Department of the Treasury, United States Customs Service and is entitled *Importing into the United States*. This is hardly an importing-made-easy book capable of luring people into the field (as is the case with the DOC's new-to-export books), but it is a fairly complete statement of the technical side of importing.[1] Once you have gotten the goods into the country, however, a raft of publications on marketing and distribution are available to you through your local library and colleges. You'll find a selected list of export/import reading and reference books in Appendixes F and G of this book.)

Seminars

In addition to these publications, there are numerous types of seminars and classes open to you. Many seminars are held on a for-profit basis by the private sector and many more by volunteers as fund-raising events for export and allied trade associations and similar organizations. The seminars conducted by trade associations, chambers of commerce, and colleges are usually less expensive than those staged by professional seminar organizations. Seminars are conducted by the United States and Foreign Commercial Service (US&FCS), the SBA and its Small Business Development Centers (SBDC), your state's department of commerce or international trade service, and your local port authority trade promotion department. They are usually available at no cost or at minimal cost. Such seminars often include some information on the subject of importing. (See the list of telephone numbers in Appendix A for additional sources of export assistance.)

Federal Assistance

Before further discussing the government agencies that can help you undertake an export strategy or continue an ongoing effort, we should address a series of dramatic changes taking place in late 1995 as the draft of this book is being readied for printing. The prime federal source for export promotion and research support for many years has been the Department of Commerce (DOC), through its International Trade Administration (ITA). The leadership of the 104th Congress, however, in its determination to shrink the size of the federal government, selected Commerce as its first target, and it is possible that Congress might be successful in its quest. But even so, most of the DOC's important international trade functions, bureaus, and offices will continue to exist somewhere in some form. The ITA could be moved to the office of the United States Trade Representative (USTR), as proposed, and there known as the International Trade Office (ITO). Most of the ITA's programs and services would then continue from that location, including the key unit for gathering overseas commercial intelligence, the overseas Commercial Service offices, (the new, informal name for what has been known as the U.S. and Foreign and Commercial Service, or US&FCS). The reader may be forced at times to do some research to locate a particular function, office, address, or phone number as and when a reorganization occurs. Other associated changes will be addressed as the subject arises. (More can be found on this matter in Chapter 17, which covers all government sources for international trade assistance.)

In 1994 the federal export assistance agencies began to coordinate with each other to create one-stop service centers for export information and help in export matters. These centers are called U.S. Export Assistance Centers and go under the acronym of USEAC. USEACs are staffed with personnel from the U.S. Export/Import Bank (Eximbank) for financing information, the US&FCS from ITA (by whatever name) for export promotion and trade information and assistance, and the SBA for small-business assistance in the areas of trade promotion, export working capital, and asset financing. In 1996 there should be at least 15 such centers in operation, and if there is one near you, the SBA or the ITA's district office can advise you of its location. One of these centers would be a good place to go for initial orientation and information. The value of the assistance you receive there will depend on how well prepared you are for an export venture.

Choosing Your Key Sources

Telling would-be exporters where to spend their time and money is very difficult, and it is nearly impossible to say which sources of advice will be the best and most productive for you. Often the first key to entry into this world of information and help is your own and your firm's "export readiness." Those less ready will receive suggestions as to the best place for preliminary information, such as a Center for International Trade at a nearby college or university or a Small Business Development Center (SBDC). Some of the agencies will refer you elsewhere if they feel you are not well enough informed to be ready for export. An accurate determination of your state of readiness can usually be obtained at one of the new USEACs. If there is not one near you, the next-best place to start might be the SBA or one of their SBDCs. We suggest picking and choosing from among these suggestions with great care, for besides the time and cost factor, sizing up your best options can be a bit like the blind man feeling the body of an elephant—very hard to know where the subject matter presented fits into the overall scheme of things. Some may wish to follow up by attending an international business course at a nearby community college or university. Such courses, usually offered at minimal cost, will also give you some idea of the more specialized courses you can take to fulfill particular needs or interests. Where you live will naturally have a bearing on how much is available. Port cities usually have a steady agenda of programs. In this, they are closely followed by the larger commercial or inland port cities, such as Chicago. Every state has at least one ITA office and SBA office; most have several. You can find a current directory for your state in the *Basic Guide to Exporting.*

While on the subject of SBA and SBDC help, it is worth mentioning that if you are new to business management as well as new to exporting or importing, you should check into the basic business management consulting that both agencies provide at no cost and the many excellent books both offer on a wide range of business subjects both domestic and foreign. The SBA's Service Corps of Retired Executives (SCORE) has saved many a businessperson with hands-on help and advice. SCORE is completely staffed by volunteers who have had their own successful businesses or upper-management positions prior to retirement and are dedicated to helping others succeed in business. With luck, you may find one whose past experience has included international activities.

This excellent array of material is only the beginning. In fact, one of your most important early decisions must be determining when to cease the emphasis on reading and study and pursue a *focused plan of action.* Premature action before understanding the basics will, of course, lead to a lot of unnecessary wheel-spinning and wasted time and expense. But too much study and too many seminars will put a brake on your will and enthusiasm to get on with it (to say nothing of depleting your capital).

Seminars, courses, and reading are key to rapidly shaping your export skills. But after arming oneself to a reasonable degree with background and operational information, your next step should be to seek out one-on-one advice and information. Such personal assistance can be found through chambers of commerce, through export organization memberships (including the ITA's District Export Councils), and best of all, via personal references to active exporters. You will find many of them dedicated to increasing our nation's exports and willing to give their time and energy to discussing ways of pursuing your own export objectives. If you are a manufacturer or have an established domestic product distribution, you will find such exporters especially cooperative. But if you are an export wanna-be, be sure you do not waste their time and goodwill on a vaguely defined "fishing expedition" based only on unformed or ill-formed ideas. Get your act together and have a well-devised plan with some possible alternatives before you seek out such valuable one-on-one advice. You will get far more out of the time spent and will more likely be encouraged to return.

In my own experience of counseling budding exporters, the most frustrating moments have been spent with people who just "wanted to export" and possibly had attended a novice seminar or two but had read or studied very little. Sometimes they had a notion of what country they wanted to do business with (often with less-than-valid reasons) or were thinking about selling some generic product (from children's clothing to polishing wax or industrial supplies), but that was about as far as their planning had gone. They came seeking instant advice that would solve all their problems, provide them with a solid business plan, and make them rich. If anyone could so readily provide that information, he or she would surely be on the list of the country's wealthiest individuals.

In contrast, some of my most satisfying consulting moments have been with people who already had an exportable product, who were focused on a valid and well-conceived idea, or who had specific skills or knowledge that I could help them interpret and transform into an export scheme with a reasonable potential for success. Such entrepreneurs bring out the best and most creative in me—and in whomever they discuss international trade options with. They profit greatly from the time they spend with others and, in return, give their counselors the satisfaction of assisting in the birth of a new enterprise and, at the same time, being of service to our national economic interest.

One of my own most rewarding sessions as an export counselor involved a young man who had been in business with his father. After the older man's death, the son decided to go into international business. He showed me an acceptable range of commercial and home-use solvents and special additives of a type I had seen successfully promoted abroad, especially in Latin America. They didn't seem especially exciting, but it was a reasonable opportunity. I asked him more details about his present business because I was interested in knowing whether it could provide adequate support during what I anticipated would be a fairly lengthy time before his export business reached sufficient volume and profit to support him.

His answer astounded me. He and his father had been the chief suppliers of smoke and haze machines for special effects in the movie industry. They had distributed some other special-effect equipment also, and one of their biggest items was a small and relatively inexpensive machine for creating smoke effects on the smallest stage or even in amateur situations. He admitted that they had sold many abroad, which was what had made him think export would be an interesting pursuit in the first place. I urged him to throw his other catalogs away and concentrate on what he knew best. He had contacts all over the world, and many of the users of such equipment came to special trade shows or professional gatherings on the West Coast every year anyway. Exports could multiply his domestic business manyfold, he could easily become a major force in a small niche market, especially if a few related products could be added to this range. Small frogs can be very happy and wealthy in small ponds. He took my advice and achieved success beyond both our expectations, reaching foreign sales volumes he had only dreamt of.

The story above illustrates a key caveat for international trading: *Try to deal in products you understand and know, or be sure you learn about them fast.* Another caveat in international trade is to sell only to those who know something about what they are buying. A potentially dangerous situation always exists in selling to an unknowing buyer; this becomes explosive when the seller is also uninformed.

Getting on with It!

When writing about export development, one must walk a fine line between making it sound too complex and difficult or too simple and easy. Personally, I believe that someone proposing to present himself or herself as a professional exporter, especially a third-party exporter, should aspire to obtain professional-level skills at the outset. Moreover, I think that such an individual should understand the operational, marketing, and financial techniques of foreign trade and promotion because the business will be largely a one-man or one-woman show in the early days.

In the case of a small manufacturer, however, I prefer to err on the side of simplification and make it as easy as possible. If you have a product you really believe in, if it is already selling in this country, and if and there is no obvious reason why at least some other countries should not appreciate it—jump in! Some initial work and research must be done to avoid wasting money, but an aggressive individual can make rapid headway by getting some appointments lined up and just going over there and *doing* it. Forget language problems; find a good freight forwarder for the operational side and a cooperative bank with an international department, and you may well be amazed at the results you can achieve in global competition in the next six months to a year. I know firms doing 50 to 60 percent of their total business overseas who have started in just this fashion. Even a novice exporter should be doing some "real time" export marketing in the course of honing his or her export skills.

Marketing is a creative exercise. Marketing internationally demands even more creativity, especially when you are working within limited budgets. You must first establish human relationships, both with those supplying your resources and with your new or potential customers. You must be able to state a reason to buy your product or service persuasively and succinctly, because you or your buyers will be communicating in a second language with possibly only rudimentary second-language skills. We make this point early on, because if you cannot develop creative as well as practical plans that encourage interest from others, you may lack a key ingredient for ultimate success.

To get an idea of just how creative an exercise this should be when practiced at its best, read *Passport to Prosperity: Tales of a Yankee Trader*, by Jack Nadel.[2] It is a 250-page paperback written by a very successful entrepreneur and international trader. It is good, inspirational reading in terms of getting the creative marketing and selling juices flowing, but dwells not at all on the mechanics of international trade. Nadel was not interested in the mechanics—he just sold and promoted wherever in the world he could find an interested customer. His sales and margins were large enough and his resulting profits large enough to make staff afford-able, and he attracted colleagues who were more than willing to take care of the details for him.

Endnotes

1. *Importing into the United States*, Department of the Treasury, Custom Publication No. 504A, U.S. Government Printing Office, Washington, D.C.

2. Jack Nadel, *Passport to Prosperity*, MMS Publishing, Los Angeles, 1989.

3
Structure
Putting the Framework in Place

We begin by addressing some of the essential structural matters that every new businessperson must face in order to get up and running. Some would call this simply "getting your ducks in a row." After years of consulting in start-up situations, however, I have found that the answers are not as obvious and straightforward as people assume. Note: Readers presently in business may want to skip the following pages on business structure and go directly to "Lining up Legal Assistance" and "Insurance with a Foreign Accent" (pages 30–31).

Establishing the New Business Structure

What follows is a summary of basic information about setting up the fundamental legal structures and formats for your future business. It is based on the questions start-up businesses most often ask.

Sole Proprietorship

For an individual who wants to keep the business small and simple, the sole proprietorship is the easiest and least regulated business format to use. The sole proprietor has exclusive responsibility and control regardless of the number of employees. The sole proprietor is personally liable for all claims, taxes, and debts against the business as well as for any injuries caused by, or to, his or her employees during their employment. Such a business owner is entitled to all profits generated by the business, which must then be included in total on the proprietor's individual income tax return (Schedule C, Form 1040). If there are substantive assets, including home equities, this form of business has obvious disadvantages in this litigious age.

Except when using your own name as the primary element in your business name, as in "Robert Jones Enterprises" or "William Smith

Associates," the sole proprietorship has to file a Fictitious Business Name Statement, also known as a d/b/a (doing business as). In some states this is done through the office of the secretary of state or the local county clerk's office, while in others no more is required than to advertise the adoption of the name in a legal newspaper or a local newspaper's notices section. This is the case in California, where no list is kept of unincorporated business names, and only your own efforts can determine whether the same name is already being used. In such states, therefore, you are at risk of being sued to change your name if the prior user chooses to bring suit. It is necessary that you check your own state's rules on this issue. Definitive answers can be obtained through the services of an attorney, or by contacting the state department of commerce or the office of the secretary of state.

General Partnership

A general partnership of two or more is easily set up because it too requires only that the fictitious name selected for business purposes be advertised and possibly registered. In general, what applies to the use of fictitious names by proprietorships applies here as well. Again, you should check with your own state officials. The important part of a partnership is to have a clear agreement among all partners stating each person's specific management duties and rights, draws, and profit sharing together with a means and procedure for one or all to withdraw from the partnership. A partnership, unless otherwise agreed to, terminates upon the death, disability, or withdrawal of anyone of the general partners.

It is best to have an attorney draw up this agreement. When complete, it should include references to:

- Duration of the agreement
- How business expenses will be handled
- The authority and duty of each partner
- How draws or salaries will be dispensed
- If and how a partnership interest may be sold—probably utilizing a buy/sell agreement
- How the partnership will be dissolved in whole or in part in case of death
- Any specific required or prohibited acts
- The rules of arbitration in case of disputes
- How absence and disability will be dealt with

Each partner is an agent for the partnership and can act individually for the partnership in almost all areas, including hiring employees, borrowing money, or conducting business operations. The agreement as to duties is an interpartnership agreement which a partner may be penalized in some way for disregarding. But this does not alter the fact that the firm is liable for any commitment or performance requirement to a third party incurred or undertaken by such a partner.

A partnership is not a separate legal entity even though it is required to report its income on a separate, informational tax return (Form 1065). Each partner's share of the profits and losses must be included on that partner's individual tax return (Form 1040). The important thing to keep in mind is that each partner is personally liable, just as in a sole proprietorship, for *all* debts and taxes of the partnership—regardless of his or her proportionate share—to the extent that personal assets can be subject to attachment and liquidation if the partnership itself cannot satisfy the creditor's claims. Be aware also that there is such a thing as a *nominal partner*—a person who is not a party to the agreement but who gives or permits the impression of being a partner and who is also liable therefore.

Limited Partnership

For individuals wanting to invest in a partnership with little risk to their personal assets beyond the investment itself, the limited partnership offers protection. A limited partner is not usually allowed to participate in the management of the business, which must have at least one or more general partners who assume full personal responsibility for obligations beyond the partnership assets (as in a simple partnership or proprietorship). In California the state's Revised Limited Partnership Act requires that these partnerships file a certificate of limited partnership with the secretary of state's office. Be sure to check for the rules and costs in your state.

The Corporation

Although in some areas do-it-yourself forms are available, it's best to get an attorney to take care of the formalities of setting up a corporation. The purpose of this section is simply to help you decide whether creating a corporation is practical for your business plan at this juncture. The main disadvantage to a corporate structure is the initial cost which, including attorney fees, is usually between $2000 and $3000. (At least this is the case in California, which also imposes a minimum annual income tax of $800 whether the corporation shows a profit or a loss. Be sure to check the rules in your state.)

The primary purpose for creating a private or closely held corporation is usually to limit personal liability for the debts and liabilities of the business. This is true for judgments that may be brought against the company for any number of reasons. It is also true for general obligations, such as accounts payable, to the extent that suppliers extend unsecured credit to the corporation. In the case of suppliers of capital equipment, most will take a lien on the equipment of a new or small corporation just as they would in the case of a proprietorship or partnership. Lenders almost always demand personal asset guarantees of all the substantive owners, at least to the extent of the majority of the total shares. To this extent there is no such thing as limited liability. In the event of default, the capital equipment will be repossessed and the shareholders guaranteeing the loans will be liable to the extent of their personal assets under the terms of the guarantee, regardless of percentage of ownership (just as in a partnership). Therefore, until the corporation develops real financial strength in the form of liquid collateral and a track record of profits, there is little difference in terms of risk except in the case of liability judgments, taxes, and so forth.

A corporation is a separate legal entity and is a more structured form of business than a partnership. It can continue to function even without the existence of the original ownership or other key individuals. This is a factor that appeals to lenders and other investors. Even so, lenders may want to be the beneficiaries of "key man" insurance on the one or two persons in the company without whom it could not function so that they will not have to count on profits from future operations to pay off the amount of the loans outstanding.

In terms of different approaches to taxation, a corporation offers the most flexibility. This is particularly true of the so-called subchapter S corporation, a hybrid form of corporation wherein the federal government permits the profits and losses to pass through the corporation to the shareholders in total and then be taxed on each shareholder's individual income tax as in a partnership. There are restrictions, such as how many shareholders are permitted, but the purpose is to avoid double taxation. This occurs when the corporation is taxed on its profits (after shareholder/officer salaries) and then the profits distributed as dividends are taxed again as part of the shareholder's personal income. Discuss this with your accountant. Forming a subchapter S corporation may or may not be to your advantage, depending on the outside income of the incorporators and the earning prospects of the proposed corporation.

If you are going to work merely for sales or brokerage commissions from your home, or even if you are going to operate on a buy/sell basis, one transaction at a time, it may be much better not to spend limited financial resources on corporate formation and the additional accounting and busy work a corporation creates. If you have little to lose in terms of tangible assets, this is even more the case. As the business develops it is always possible to incorporate as certain points are reached. One such point is the hiring of your first regular employee; another occurs when you wish to bring in new equity from outside or develop a profit-sharing plan with your employees; still another arrives when a meaningful equity base or net worth is reached and you need to borrow some serious money.

In the main, partnerships are to be regarded with suspicion except under ideal circumstances, with ideal partners, when there are really valid reasons not to incorporate. Even then, it is a decision best discussed with an accountant and your attorney.

Getting Government Licenses and Permits

I am often asked about the licenses and permits needed to start a business. In the case of an export sales company, as a one-person, start-up, unincorporated business with a low profile, the answer is "Just about nothing." This answer will depend, of course, on your activities, location, and the city or county in which you are operating your home-based business. Let's quickly review them at the various levels of government.

Federal Requirements

In general, the federal government does not require permits or licenses for an import or export company. It is interested and involved in the description and value of the products you export and the destinations to which they are shipped. It may also want to know about certain buyer requests or conditions of sale or shipment (primarily concerning the Middle East relative to U.S. antiboycott regulations). These export licensing regulations by product are controlled under the Export Administration Regulations (EAR) established by the Export Administration Act.

If you are exporting a restricted substance or a product that requires an export license under the EAR, such as advanced technology products or arms, nuclear products, dangerous drugs and narcotics, alcoholic beverages, or other products regulated by a particular agency or department, you will need a validated license for that product or permission, however expressed, by the governing agency or department. You can ask a freight forwarder (whose services you will need anyway) to tell you when and how much help you should seek in the area of export licensing, or when antiboycott compliance may be at stake. Licensing and antiboycott regulations are discussed in Chapter 19 in greater detail. The role of the freight forwarders is described in Chapter 12.

The federal government is equally interested in the description, value, and origin of the goods and services you *import*. It also has a keen interest in collecting any tariffs and duties due. No import permits are required until it comes time to clear the incoming merchandise through U.S. Customs and pay whatever tariffs may be due. As in exporting, certain products require special licenses or processing. (Full details on the import clearance process are given in Chapter 13.)

Beyond these issues, the federal government's interest is chiefly in income taxes and employment taxes. When you are ready to hire employees, write to the Internal Revenue Service for a *Circular-E Employee Tax Guide* and apply for an employer identification number.

State Requirements

Every state has different laws and regulations, of course, but, in general, the state is primarily interested in control of businesses impacting public health and safety, fiduciary or financial institutions, businesses with a potential for fraud, and services requiring professional training. One common exception concerns alcoholic beverages and drugs whose import the state coordinates with U.S. Customs. Otherwise, it is unlikely that any state permits or licenses will be required. The chief interest will again be in state income taxes, sales, or use taxes (if destined for export these taxes do not usually apply) and, if you have employees, their unemployment and workmen's compensation insurance, assorted other employment related taxes, and state income tax withholdings.

In most states with a sales or use tax, it is necessary to obtain some sort of resale certificate. This certificate exempts you from paying sales tax to your supplier if you are buying for resale. It then becomes your responsibility to collect and remit the sales tax, except that merchandise exported is almost always exempt. A report of some kind will likely be required, even though you exported 100 percent of your wholesale purchases. Call your nearest state office building for the correct sources and phone numbers to check this out.

County Requirements

If your home or business is located within a city, there is less likelihood that any county permit is required. However, if you are not within the city, then county zoning and "use" restrictions will apply and a phone call to the county seat is appropriate. If you are working within your home and do not intend to have employees, foot traffic, commercial storage, or trucks, it's probably best to make a blind inquiry because if you have no visible profile or existence no one is likely to care one way or the other what you do. If you have a separate business address or any of the above elements, it becomes another matter. Nonetheless, unless your situation involves the zoning board in a dispute over the definition and extent of commercial activities within a residential or agricultural area, any county permit you need to get is likely to amount to nothing more than an annual permit at a modest fee.

City Requirements

Most of the foregoing remarks about county licenses and permits apply to city licenses and permits as well. Some cities have separate sales tax levies, but these are usually collected through the state process. Within the confines of a city certain zoning and business permit regulations and fees often apply. Where taxes for both city and county are concerned, however, there are rarely any special requirements for import/export businesses. A phone call is still the best insurance in each case, however.

Finding Accounting and Bookkeeping Assistance

In no field of business is the maintenance of good records more vital than in international trade. One reason is the EAR regulations, already described, which place most of the burden for proving yourself in compliance squarely on your documentary and accounting records. The same holds true for imports relative to duties, tariffs, and unlawful entries. Another reason for good records is the detailed buyer requirements demanded for each specific transaction, especially in the case of letters of credit.

Unless you have some experience in this area, it may be wise to employ a bookkeeping service or an accountant. With the excellent bookkeeping software available for your computer, you can keep most of the original entry records yourself with a little initial assistance. This will minimize the costs involved in having a bookkeeper or accountant make up the tax and payroll reports. However, it's important to select someone at the outset so they can suggest what records to keep and how to avoid unnecessary demands on his or her time at the end of each accounting period or at tax time. If you can do most of the clerical procedures yourself, consider and price the relative cost of a bookkeeper compared to a Certified Public Accounting (CPA) firm. Often there is little difference, and the accountant may be able to give you more definitive advice on everything from cash management and cashflows to income tax planning. Some bookkeepers are also quite well informed on these issues, especially where small businesses are concerned.

A "compilation" report and income tax filing based on your own well-maintained figures is all you need initially. No small business or start-up needs the kind of audit statement that requires a CPA to research and check your assets and liabilities and confirm your procedures. As your company grows and you need a bank line of bank credit, more will be demanded of you, and the demand may begin with a review statement. Such a statement requires certain procedural checks. But it is much less expensive than the audit mentioned above, which can be very costly because the CPA bears substantial liability if the audit proves erroneous and misleads lenders.

Lining Up Legal Assistance
for Import/Export

Without question, attorneys are expensive, but they can also spell the difference between disaster and success. Starting up as a sole proprietor, you might be able to avoid using an attorney and, if there is not too much at stake, get by by simply adapting form contracts for supplier and distributor agreements. (*Exporting from Start to Finance* and *Export/Import Procedures and Documentation,* among others listed in Appendix F3, contain such samples.) No one can actually recommend this course of action, however, so be aware that you are proceeding at your own risk. Your success will depend on your ability to construct clear language and express fairly the intentions of both parties. Should something come up that does require legal advice or help, try to select an attorney who has had commercial experience in international law. A good place to start might be to take advantage of the Small Business Administration's (SBA) Export Legal Assistance Network (ELAN). This program offers free initial consultations with attorneys having international experience. See the SBA segment in Chapter 17 for more information. At this stage you do not necessarily need a specialist who does nothing but foreign trade litigation. Rather, you more likely require a good commercial lawyer who understands at least the special problems that go with overseas distributors and agents and knows when to use the services of a foreign counterpart or other specialist. Unless you are fighting a claim dispute with a carrier, there is no need for an admiralty lawyer. But in the event that you face a carrier who seems to be unjustly denying a claim, a specialist in this arcane area of the law can be worth his or her weight in gold. I have seen situations where it took no more than a letter from an admiralty lawyer or an attorney experienced in freight claims to persuade a carrier to pay when it had previously been adamant that it was not responsible.

There is usually no charge for an introductory session with an attorney, so use the opportunity to ask the right questions, including fees and the hourly rate. Advise your prospective attorney what your business consists of and what legal problems you anticipate, if any. Listen to his or her responses and suggestions very carefully.

Taking Out Insurance with
a Foreign Accent

Assuming that you are starting an export business as a sideline or replacement for your present career, a word of caution is in order. Insofar as it is clear you are doing business in your home, claims relating to your business, such as equipment theft or damage and personal injury, may well not be covered by your homeowner's policy, no matter how broad its coverage is. Certainly, business assets such as inventory will not be covered.

You may wish to discuss this with your home insurance agent first. It is well to understand special business coverage, such as property insurance for equipment and inventory, business auto insurance, use and occupancy, errors and omission, liability insurance, product liability (whose cost is virtually out of reach for small businesses), and workers' compensation insurance if you have employees. Insurance can become a major expense, so before taking it out, consider what you have to lose and the possibilities of an insured event occurring, and weigh those factors against the cost. Also, determine the kinds of insurable events that a special business policy does and does not cover for your international business. For example, what are the benefits covered by your health insurance policy, should you be taken ill overseas?

Of special interest to exporters and importers is transportation insurance specifically designed for international trade—that is, marine and air cargo insurance, usually lumped together under a marine policy. Credit insurance for commercial and political risk coverage on foreign accounts receivable constitutes a second special insurance for foreign sales. Both items will be covered in detail in Chapter 16. There are one or two points you should be aware of right away in your preliminary consideration of these forms of insurance. The best bet for cargo insurance is a door-to-door marine policy covering air and ocean and all intermediary modes of transportation. However, such a policy comes with a high premium, especially if the exporter has no track record. Therefore, it is better to let freight forwarders cover it under their own policies. They must add a surcharge, but in most circumstances it is the more practical solution until your export/import business develops.

For smaller and new businesses, foreign credit insurance is most readily available through the U.S. Export-Import Bank (formerly from the Foreign Credit Insurance Association, or FCIA). Such insurance is not necessary if you plan to deal only with letter of credit terms. However, sooner or later, competition may force you to do otherwise in some cases, so at your first opportunity contact Eximbank Insurance for your own education. Eximbank's headquarters are in Washington, D.C., and they have regional offices in Chicago, Houston, Los Angeles (El Segundo), Miami, and New York. Any one of these offices will be happy to explain small-business and new-to-export policies in detail. They can sell you a policy directly or refer you to a specialty insurance broker handling this policy. Most general insurance agents neither write it nor understand it. (See Appendixes C and D as well as Chapter 16 on risk management.)

Locating a Bank and an International Banker

This may be one of the most difficult challenges of all those discussed. Banks are famous for not being particularly interested in small businesses, especially if they are only recently formed, lack a profitable track record, or are primarily engaged in export. In fact, if several of these just-mentioned conditions apply to you, you may find it extremely difficult to locate a supportive banker, let alone a supportive, qualified, *international* banker. Worse, their services cannot be purchased, as you would those of a lawyer or accountant; or even be linked to commissions, as in the case of an insurance agent. Banks provide most of their services or extend credit because they feel you have future promise, perceive little present risk, and are satisfied that you are already making enough of a contribu-tion to their profits through your domestic business to want to keep you as a customer. Most banks with international divisions are happy enough to take care of your documentary needs and procedures because they charge substantial fees for these services, which are purely operational and have little to do with the credit risk side of banking.

The good news is that there is a wonderful program designed to help you locate banks equipped for international business in your region and help you find out exactly what services they offer, as well as the type and size of businesses they are happy to serve. It is a free service called Access to Export Capital, or AXCAP, sponsored by the Bankers Association for Foreign Trade (BAFT). It maintains a nationwide database of over 215 organizations and processes up to 50 calls a week from busi-nesses seeking trade finance services from appropriate banks. Call the program administrator on their hotline at 800/49AXCAP (492-9227) and they will fax you a list of such banks in your area and will also advise the banks of your interest, which serves as an introduction.

It may also encourage you to know that banks *can* be persuaded to accommodate your export financing needs if assistance can be found from public sector export support agencies. The Small Business Administration's Office of International Trade has a newly revised and streamlined Export Working Capital Program that is related to a similar program of Eximbank's, which is also available to established businesses. Some of the states also have excellent export finance programs, the largest of which is California's Export Finance Office, or CEFO (which I had the pleasure of establishing). CEFO continues to offer hundreds of new or small companies help in financing exports, resulting in the cre-ation of 24,000 jobs after only 10 years of operation. A number of other states conduct such programs, including Florida, Kansas, Maryland, Minnesota, and the Port of New York/New Jersey. Several others are hoping to start their own soon. Depending on their exact design, such programs can lend or provide guarantees and guidance to businesses that cannot initially obtain export financing on their own; they do so by relying in part on the underlying transaction. Other states and port authorities have advisory councils to help seek export financing, and still others offer small business loan or guarantee programs that, while not necessarily structured strictly for export, can nevertheless be helpful.

(Details about export financing and these support agencies will be discussed in Chapters 17 and 18.)

Once you find a supportive international banker, its network, expertise, and skills can provide very important and timely information and help throughout your entire export career. Some banks are even in a position to help with foreign contacts or information through their overseas network of branches or correspondents. For these reasons cultivating a banker as a friend and mentor may be one of your most important steps as a new-to-export business. As with any friend, you must be straightforward, honest, and cooperative in your dealings with your banker, in addition to meeting your obligations. The banker is a person you should talk to at the earliest stages of anticipating a need for help, advice, or financing—not after you are already committed or locked in, or possibly in big trouble. Knowing what your banker can, cannot, and will not do can save you a lot of grief. A preliminary draft of your business plan as discussed in Chapter 4 will probably lead to a clearer understanding of your parameters.

As for which bank and banker you should seek, there *is* an ideal, but the ideal must be tempered by what you can realistically find. In terms of banks, unless you have an existing relationship, it is unlikely you will get real cooperation from the larger banks with extended international offices around the world, and you probably don't need them. Large banks' delivery costs for international trade services are very high, especially for smaller transactions. As a result, such banks are usually hesitant to offer smaller firms trade finance services, except for the purely fee-based documentary services.

The perfect international bank would be an organization with worldwide branches, all containing excellent documentary departments (referred to as *backrooms*), an interest in and familiarity with your range of product and targeted world regions, and an experienced international loan officer who is personally interested in you and your company and with whom you share a rapport. In the absence of such a paragon, you will probably be very fortunate to find an individual banker in a smaller bank that has a good range of correspondent banks overseas and that really supports its international specialist. If you are very fortunate, the bank may have some willingness to support transaction-based financing, especially with public sector support. *Transaction-based financing* relies first on the proceeds from the transaction itself, such as very high grade or insured foreign accounts receivable or letters of credit. This is followed by heavy reliance on the ability of the exporter to perform as required to obtain payment under the letters of credit.

Perhaps, because your base of activity is in a smaller city, you may not find a bank that meets even a few of these criteria. In that case, you will have to rely on any bank that knows you and is willing to act as your agent, by submitting documents for collection and handling various other matters through the nearest correspondent bank with an international operations department. This will add a bit to your documentary fees, but the convenience and availability of some help from the local bank should be well worth it. Perhaps you can get the bank's SBA loan department interested in utilizing SBA's working capital program or your state's program if it has one. In discussing these issues with your bank, try to get acquainted with the officer most familiar with international trade and letters of credit; you will need the assistance of such a person even though the bank may not have an official international division. The letter of credit is a primary international credit instrument which is also used in domestic banking, and most well-trained bankers are familiar with it.

4
Determining Your Export/Import Strategies

In Chapter 1 we discussed possibilities and *potentials* for exporting and importing. In Chapter 2 the prime subject was *discovery*—finding help and advice and focusing on your objectives. Chapter 3 covered *structuring* your business framework and establishing necessary ongoing sources of advice and assistance. Now let's look at *how* to engage in international trade—that is, at the fundamental *strategies* open to you.

The first strategic issue to decide is which export vehicle you will use. It doesn't matter whether your export vehicle is organized as a corporation, a proprietorship, or a partnership; the choice of vehicle is a question of function and strategy, not structure.

Export Vehicles and How They Operate

Exporting Manufacturers

This term describes any manufacturer exporting all or part of its product line, whether the manufacturer is a prime manufacturer, or an original equipment manufacturer (OEM).

Exporting Distributors

This term describes any conventional domestic wholesaler, distributor, or mail-order firm doing a significant percentage of its total business in exports.

Export Management and Trading Companies

The export/import entrepreneurial trader has existed under various names since the dawn of commerce. In this country today, third party, or independent international trade intermediaries, represent a somewhat undernourished industry, but they nevertheless offer an important source for generating foreign exchange and balancing exports and imports in the majority of countries of the world. In the United States, trade intermediaries are most commonly known as Export Management Companies (EMCs) and Export Trading Companies (ETCs) although they appear in many hybrid forms. Recognition of their potential is slowly developing in this country, and was first evidenced by our federal government in the Export Trading Company Act of 1982 and the Office of Export Trading Company Affairs established under that act. It is to the small or start-up EMC/ETC, as well as to the small manufacturer interested in starting export activities or expanding present infrequent or casual exports, that this book is addressed. Both are probably managed by archetypical entrepreneurs who represent a major opportunity for American export expansion. Export intermediaries are often among the most driven of human beings. A colleague of mine likes to say that export selling is similar to narcotics. The first sale feels good, but from then on each successive sale is merely the next fix.

The Export Management Company. The export management company, or EMC, acts as the export arm in certain foreign territories on behalf of one or more U.S. manufacturers. It helps them establish an overseas market for their products, usually on an exclusive basis for the territory in question. Take note that the exclusive feature, albeit a very important element to an EMC, need not apply worldwide. In fact, except for the very largest EMCs, it would be wise to seek only that portion of the world that an EMC can economically serve and for which the EMC is most qualified, expanding the territory only after experiencing mutually satisfying results from the initial territory. The export management company maintains close contact with its clients and is supply-driven. Relationships with manufacturers are important to the success of this type of company, but good contacts and relationships with overseas distributors are also key factors.

Export management companies may take title to the goods they sell, making a profit on the markup, or they may charge a commission, depending on the type of products they are handling, the nature of the overseas market, and the manufacturer-client's needs. Some export management companies also work on a retainer basis, especially if they are providing significant training and advice to their client or are undertaking substantial up-front marketing. The EMC that takes title to the product it sells enjoys far more control over its business because it can exercise greater discretion as to selling terms and credit policies. It also can better manage the interrelationships of its supplier clients and overseas customers. This is not to say, however, that the EMC's customers should become a closely guarded secret if the EMC and the supplier have a good initial understanding as well as policies and prices that are fairly and properly established. Both sides of the EMC/supplier equation will function better with an open relationship, and the supplier will be more satisfied that the EMC is providing a valuable intermediary service. In fact, in some very successful relationships, the supplier does the shipping, although we would caution against this arrangement unless the supplier is fairly export sophisticated and has an export-oriented shipping department.

An EMC must face the fact that whatever the agreement, and no matter how historically successful, in the long run the very process of doing a good job in establishing overseas markets may well be the basis for losing a first-class supplier client. In the case of my own export management company, the relationship with my largest client lasted about 15 years—something of a record. Yet it finally moved its overseas sales in house when it came to understand these sales' importance and potential, and it could not be faulted for doing so.

The downside of that long relationship (and yet possibly one reason it lasted so long) was the supplier's consistent disinterest in its overall export sales, tactics, and strategies. This was best illustrated by the supplier's continued failure to help our firm solve the problems of adapting its product to foreign markets. The supplier's lack of interest in such issues as packaging and labeling naturally reduced its export sales potential and, in turn, our own trading profits. The greatest product range in the world will not yield export sales close to its full potential without the sincere cooperation of the supplier. Such a level of cooperation is subject to change as top management changes—a turn of events that is often unpredictable. The answer to this potential problem—as well as to the problem of unexpected changes in the product lines an EMC represents, is to be alert for new, related, but noncompetitive products to add to your product range. It is vital, of course, to maintain good relationships with current supplier clients; it is also important to develop good relationships with companies that can offer substitute products in the event of unforeseen changes.

The Export Trading Company.   In contrast, the export trading company, or ETC, is demand-driven and transaction-oriented. It can play many roles, but most often it acts as an independent distributor, responding to inquiries or sales leads and serving as a link between buyers and sellers to fulfill a need, complete a sale, or arrange a transaction. Put another way, ETCs identify what overseas customers want to buy and work with a variety of U.S. manufacturers to fulfill those requirements. In some cases, ETCs perform a sourcing function, shopping the U.S. markets for specific requests from overseas customers. Some ETC firms specialize in this particular role.

Most export trading companies take title to the products involved, but some of them work on a commission basis. They keep up with the markets they serve through regular travel, participation in trade shows in the United States and abroad, and working closely with distributors and customers. These activities imply the need for some degree of specialization to assure excellent skills in the product area. The successful ETC develops good commercial relationships with its suppliers and customers, though these relationships are neither as close nor as regular as an EMC's. ETCs do not ordinarily have exclusive product arrangements, but are often treated as preferred customers. Export trading companies rely on a reputation for knowledgeable and fair dealing with both customers and suppliers over a period of time, usually restricting themselves to definable product groupings. ETCs also often attend both domestic and overseas trade shows for networking, product information, and discovery purposes, though not as participants.

Dealing with a wider variety of sources or suppliers and on an ad hoc or demand basis, ETCs are more likely to be on their own where credit or financing issues are concerned and, unless credit is established, will probably be forced to pay in advance or on COD terms. ETCs' deals are often larger than EMCs' because they are searching for export leads, which tend to be of fair size if circulated in the usual foreign trade information channels. By contrast, EMCs are searching for customers, who often want smaller initial or trial orders. ETCs thus need a larger capitalization or at least a heavier utilization of trade finance than EMCs. The matter of taking title is often crucial, but need not be as capital-intensive as one would imagine if all the tools of trade finance and export banking are thoroughly understood and employed with the help of a qualified banker. The good news is that for this kind of business, export letters of credit and trade finance are more likely to be found.

Almost without meaning to, many EMCs and ETCs become a blend of each function as they respond to opportunities that present themselves. There is no problem with this as long as ethical issues are kept in perspective and EMC-client relationships are not violated.

The typical EMC or ETC is a small firm employing from two to 50 people, with the staff size in most cases at the lower end of the range. A DOC survey of EMCs and ETCs in 1989 indicated that over 60 percent of such firms reported employing six or fewer employees and only 15 percent reported employing 21 or more employees. Over one-third reported earnings under $1 million and another third reported earnings between $1 and $5 million. But there were also some reporting earnings as high as $500 million, so don't set your long-range goals too low or believe that major success is not achievable within this format. Reinforcing the concept of *focus* that is so important for the new exporter, this survey also indicated that the larger U.S. export intermediary firms typically have a clearly defined product range.

Other Export Intermediaries

There are many additional configurations of export structures. They are much less common, however, and when utilized, usually develop naturally out of an existing situation or to answer a specific need. Examples include U.S. military post exchange and commissary sales agents for manufacturers particularly interested in that sizeable market; specialized buying offices for overseas retailer clients; export merchants and remarketeers buying to their own specifications for specific markets they might serve; original equipment manufacturers (OEMs) or subcontractors desiring piggyback exporter operations by supplying customers around the world with components or accessories through prime manufacturers or contractors; and endless other special applications.

A Quantitative Analysis of All Exporters

The Exporter Magazine has continually analyzed exporter activity levels in cooperation with the Census Bureau since 1987. Its most current findings tell us a number of interesting things about these various groups of exporters in the United States:[1]

1. *Infrequent exporters.* Some 95,000 occasional exporting companies generally make 50 or fewer shipments per year, accounting for about 4 percent of recorded U.S. exports. The majority of these exporters are businesses doing less than $1 million in export sales, and all do under $2 million in exports.

2. *Frequent exporters.* Some 8000 consistently active exporting companies make an average of roughly 120 export shipments per year. They account for 11 percent of U.S. exports and have export sales in the range of $2 to $20 million. Most of the EMCs and ETCs fall into this category.

3. *Most-frequent exporters.* There are about 2000 companies that account for 82.5 percent of all U.S. exports. Their annual export sales are between $20 million and $2 billion.

Viewed from another perspective, the 8000 frequent exporters represent the prime target of the International Trade Administration (ITA). It is clear, however, that if the Small Business Association and the ITA made it easier for even a portion of the 95,000 infrequent exporters to increase their export shipments by a modest number, we would see a dramatic change in the volume of total U.S. exports. The two agencies already recognize, as we all should, that there is a great potential for export growth among small companies.

Import/Export: The General Trading Company

Chapter 1 touched on the pros and cons of combining import activities with export distribution for international trade entrepreneurs. That information, as well as the following comments, applies mainly to the independent or third-party exporter. The reader who owns or represents a manufacturer is probably interested primarily in arrangements concerning the import process as it would apply to importing goods manufactured offshore, raw materials, or components needed for the completion of a domestic manufacturing process.

If a start-up company is determined to pursue a trading company strategy, it's probably best to concentrate either on import *or* export in the beginning, unless the organization is superbly financed and has sufficient personnel and experience to be a *general trading company* or an *export/import establishment* in every sense of the term. Once an import or export track record is established, with sufficient experience gained and contacts established, opportunities on the other side of the international trade coin can be considered. Assume for the moment that you begin with export (which seems to most often be the case for start-up companies), and in the course of that activity recognize or discover both a supply and a readily accessible demand for some specific imported merchandise. This could be a marvelous opportunity. But if multiple customers must be found or inventory must be carried, it is doubtful that a smaller organization could find the time to perform one function without diminishing the potential of the other.

Consider the consequences of even a relatively brief delay in finding a buyer for the imported goods, or of having a sale you are counting on fall through—a fairly common scenario. You suddenly discover you have received a serious blow to your cashflow, and the suppliers who were starting to develop confidence in you become very unhappy. Your accounts payable start to age quickly and the opportunity for a new and promising export transaction withers because you are unable to finance the import transaction.

Unless entered into with careful planning and with all bases covered, adding varied product import activities to an export marketing enterprise can spell doom for a promising start-up business—and has occasionally done just that. It can be difficult to get letters of credit from your domestic buyers of the imported product even though it is usually necessary to put up letters of credit to the foreign supplier. Early enthusiasm or business conditions can change rapidly as promised orders from your U.S. customers fail to materialize.

When undertaken with adequate funds and in your own good time, however, import/export activities are a perfect example of synergy—that is, of one hand washing the other. I do not mean, therefore, to discourage the export/import idea, but rather to urge you to weigh carefully the increased risks and the *trebling* of cash needs that such a course entails, along with the strength of your personal contacts in the domestic open marketplace.

While still on the subject of imports, I might add that detailed suggestions for the procurement of overseas products are not provided in this book because of the great diversity of a process so dependent on the type of business and product being sought. As stated earlier, the best opportunities often stem from discoveries made in the course of export activities abroad. In addition, just as in this country, our trading partners have many organizations, both public and private, that have as one of their primary responsibilities assisting their countrymen to export. These include overseas trade associations, chambers of commerce in those countries whose products are of interest to you, and foreign consulates based in the United States. The latter can provide you with the names and addresses of these organizations.

Deciding Whether to Export Directly or Through an Intermediary

If you are a small manufacturer or wholesaler with a product that may sell abroad as well as here, your first major strategic decision must be whether to do it yourself or let someone with established contacts, travel schedules, and overseas activity in related products do all or part of it for you.

Exporting Through Domestic Intermediaries

The roles of the various kinds of exporters, including domestic intermediaries, have already been defined. The comments concerning the operations of an EMC or ETC are as useful to a supplier considering the use of an intermediary as they would be to a start-up EMC/ETC. For manufacturers considering domestic intermediaries as a viable choice, here are a few pros and cons to assist in the decision-making process:

The Advantages of Using a Domestic Intermediary

- Probably faster market entry
- A more consistent focus on exporting
- Lower out-of-pocket expenses
- An opportunity to learn procedures and customers
- Access to established expertise in export skills and strategy

The Disadvantages of Using a Domestic Intermediary

- Loss of control
- Competition from related products
- Possible buyer reluctance to deal with third-party intermediaries

- Possible added costs and/or higher selling prices
- Possible neglect of your product in favor of others

Not all of these advantages or disadvantages are relevant to every case, and in each situation there may be other factors to consider. On the other hand, careful selection and a well-designed supplier/exporter contract can overcome some of the disadvantages.

Selecting and Dealing with an EMC/ETC

If your decision is to undertake all or part of your export objectives using a qualified EMC/ETC, you can find one by advertising in a regional newspaper or business publication. There are also several directories and listings of export intermediaries. One is a database of over 12,000 firms which has been published annually by the DOC in cooperation with private sponsorship. It is known as the *Export Yellow Pages*.[2] This is the largest available compilation of EMC/ETCs and it continues to be reasonably current because of its frequent publication. Its categories include Export Services; Trading Companies (subcategorized into EMCs, ETCs, purchasing and sourcing services, equipment rental and leasing, and wholesalers/distributors); Technical Services; and interested or involved Exporting Producers, which are in turn further categorized by product. The supplier/manufacturers listed presumably want to make themselves available to overseas buyers and/or domestic intermediaries. Therefore, these names might be of interest to qualified EMCs seeking to represent certain product types in an area of the world in which the supplier or manufacturer may not be currently doing business. *The Export Yellow Pages* is available at no charge from your DOC District Office, sometimes from the SBA, and often at export trade events. If you are currently exporting, you may wish to have your own firm listed in the next edition. There are also several private publications (see Appendix F6). Among these are the *Directory of Leading Export Management Companies*, published by Bergano Book; the very new *Registry of Export Intermediaries*, published by SPC Marketing in cooperation with the National Association of Export Companies; the *Trading Company Sourcebook* published by International Business Affairs Corp; and the Export Yellow Pages.

If you are a manufacturer, you might seek recommendations for reliable EMCs in the area from your nearest DOC district office and possibly from the local SBA office as well. You might also try contacting other organizations that work regularly with the international community, such as nearby world trade centers, departments of commerce at both state and local levels, local international trade clubs, port authorities, freight forwarders, and possibly international banking officers.

In selecting an EMC, don't hesitate to check references relative to past performance, both as to product and territory of emphasis. The DOC district office in the region may be acquainted with intermediaries specializing in your field and be able to provide some informal suggestions. EMC/ETCs are typically highly leveraged in financial terms, so don't be surprised to find some with rather thin financial ratios in terms of debt to equity or assets to sales. The important thing is to be sure that they are paying their bills and have a history of performance, especially if they are going to be responsible for the financing and assume ownership of your products. A manufacturer does not need to give any single EMC the entire world as a territory; very few would be fully qualified everywhere. You should assess where you want your product sold and where the intermediary is strongest. *Do not* break up logical country groups, such as Central America or the Gulf states. This rule even applies to the European Union to some degree. At the very least, subgroups such as Scandinavia should be treated as one territory.

An EMC negotiating with a prospective client or a manufacturing supplier seeking an EMC should consider the following points when proposing an agreement:

- Duration and termination
- Territory and exclusivity
- Rights to undertake overseas PX and commissary sales
- Performance standards for both exporter and *supplier*
- Method of fixing EMC/ETC purchase price, if applicable
- Payment terms
- Transfer of title
- Delivery schedules (very important to the exporter)
- Market development expense
- Compensation, commission, or export pricing system
- Product liability
- After-sales service and/or return policy
- Arbitration

Do not make the initial contract duration too brief; export markets cannot be developed in six months by anyone. One year is the absolute practical minimum and two or three years might be preferable, although with such durations reasonable goals of some kind should be established to give the manufacturer an option for cancelling if it is clear that there is no export potential or there is a lack of "best effort." Be sure the agreement is equitable to both parties to assure maximum effort, performance, and results for each party to the agreement.

The reader wanting to function as an EMC or ETC should read any preceding remarks addressed to the manufacturer as a mirror reflecting what an EMC will face in the course of being selected by a manufacturer. (In some cases the reverse is true for suppliers.) Where the various other alternative domestic intermediaries are concerned, the same general rules for agreements with an interested supplier or manufacturer apply—adjusted, of course, for the many different special situations that such a union might represent.

Exporting Directly

Whether your company's role is that of an EMC/ETC exporting for others or that of a prime manufacturer, an original equipment manufacturer (OEM) or a wholesaler that has decided to export directly, the next logical step is the selection of the type, or types, of distribution channels. This decision will have a major bearing on the speed and success of your sales efforts. For this reason, the whole of Chapter 5 is devoted to the factors that must be considered in choosing the correct trade channels. The final decision will depend on what part of the world is under consideration. It may also be influenced by the responses to your initial presentation. Because this is an important decision that will have a long-term impact on your export history, it deserves careful attention. The initial plan and focus should be in place during the exploratory phase of your operation.

Alternatives to Direct Export Distribution

There are various reasons why a manufacturer might decide not to export its product to a certain region, even though it wants to do business overseas directly in most areas. So before proceeding to the subject of distribution channels, let's touch on a few further options or strategies that you should be aware of before committing yourself to a direct export program. The primary alternatives to direct distribution are:

Licensing and Franchising Agreements

More common than contract manufacturing is licensed manufacturing, with distribution and sales being the responsibility of the licensee. If you have a product in which design or technology is a major factor and for which the designs, know-how, or patents offer valuable consideration in terms of sales or profit opportunities to an otherwise qualified foreign manufacturer, licensing may be the most practical solution. Licensing is used even in situations where the consideration is little more than the use of a trademark, as in the case of some apparel lines. The reasons a company might consider licensing include: production limits; shipping or logistical problems; or the lack of sufficient staff or financial resources to conduct its own export operations. Licensing can be useful to a firm currently heavy on Research and Development, for instance, whose management feels it will be some time yet before it has the marketing and distribution skills and resources to match its technological skills. In such instances, the royalty from a good licensing arrangement can provide badly needed working capital with minimal investment of time or money. The franchising concept and purpose is similar to licensing, except that the product franchised is more often a service as opposed to a manufactured item.

The caveats are several. First and foremost is the fact that the relevant patents, design patents, and/or trademarks must be well established in this country and some protection available in the host country. The foreign manufacturer's country must have acceptable laws to protect these intellectual property rights so they can be reclaimed by the licensor at the end of the agreement term, or in the event of default for any reason by the licensee.

The next caveat is that a license or franchise agreement is not as easy and carefree as it may sound. The licensee wants lots of help and information. If such assistance is not forthcoming, the licensee usually starts a series of rationalizations that either result in minimal effort and royalty or in cutting all the corners of the agreement and the reported sales as much as possible. For a license to work, there must be a sincere and consistent rapport and communication between the licensee and licensor at a top executive level. However, be aware that in the act of creating a successful license relationship, one is also creating a competitor—not only in the host country, but possibly in one's own country at some point after the agreement has concluded.

Lest these caveats sound overly dark, keep in mind that licensing has been around for a long time, and there are many very satisfied practitioners of the procedure. The practice saves a lot of time and resources while often establishing a very nice cashflow, all of which can support a total focus on the domestic market or continued heavy R&D expenditures. At its best, it can also provide valuable cross-pollination of ideas, technology, or design between the licensee and licensor.

The following checklist may prove helpful in preliminary negotiations, whether your interest is in licensing or franchising. It appears courtesy of, and is adapted from, the *Management Export Information Manual* prepared by Richard E. Sherwood and Walter R. Thiel with contributions from many members of the Southern California District Export Council.

Checklist for License Contracts

1. Performance is the keystone of contracts. Take your time finding the licensee.

2. The span of the contract should be fixed but be sure to provide intermediate escape points from bad performance and options to renew for good performance.

3. Specify the national law governing the contract. You may want both parties to execute your contract in the United States.

4. Semantics may be a problem. Provide an official language of the contract. For technical products, you may want your own glossary of translated terms.

5. Provide for allocation of taxes during the life of the agreement and upon its termination.

6. Observe, and require that your licensee observe, all foreign government tax and administrative regulations.

7. Safeguard your patents and trademarks before you start to negotiate.

8. Use your own trademark if you can. You may want to do the manufacturing yourself at a later date. Consider this and similar goals and fit your licensing arrangement into long-range planning.

9. Specify who will take judicial and administrative action to protect property rights and who is to bear the costs.

10. Provide for review of changes in designs, techniques, parts, or procedures. Someone in the home office should be clearly responsible for keeping technical communication clear between you and the licensee.

11. The right to assign or sublicense should be exclusively yours.

12. Keep informed on de facto sublicensing assignment of responsibility by your licensee to others through subcontracts.

13. Waivers of conditions can undermine the strength of the contract. Careful surveillance should catch defaults before they occur.

14. Make sure you are getting the substance, not the shell, of your patents if you have to recapture them.

15. Guard your know-how. Consider substantial liquidated damages if nondisclosure requirements are violated.

16. Provide for careful indoctrination of know-how and reciprocal exchange of information on new developments.

17. Supplying know-how may involve key personnel; avoid tight schedules.

18. Do not brainwash your licensee by insisting on complete adherence to your own systems. Foreign needs may not match tolerance for quality.

19. Granting exclusive rights may limit your sales and profits and may also violate antitrust laws.

20. Leave the door open for amendments that will help counter new legal or trade factors.

21. Insert a reciprocal force majeure clause.

22. Leave the door open for renegotiation or rearrangements of the license should common markets or changes in common markets occur.

23. Let opportunity, not geography, shape sales boundaries.

24. Encourage, but watch, the antitrust aspects of compelling use of components, replacement parts, and accessories produced by or bought by you.

25. Arrange disclosure fees as advance royalties. You may be able to take advantage of treaties to generate high foreign source income at low foreign tax rates.

26. Royalties may be transitory; stock participation can yield more permanent values.

27. A sliding percentage royalty scale is usually desirable, but be sure a minimum yield is payable and that nonpayment or unsatisfactory performance gives you the right to cancel.

28. Reserve the right to cancel if you cannot get the cash in American dollars or a satisfactory equivalent.

29. Look into United States government guarantees.

30. Adequate protection means adequate inspection.

31. Interim production and sales reports are important; the right to independent audit is a safeguard.

32. Watch for financial danger signals; bail out before bankruptcy.

33. The warranty you or your licensee give today could haunt you in court tomorrow. Be sure to negate any warranties not specifically given by you.

34. Monitor your licensee's advertising because it can misrepresent your product and damage your name.

35. If you cannot reconcile your differences, consider providing arbitration as an alternative to court.

36. If you have to cancel, consider momentum. Provide adequate notice for termination and look out for damages payable because of abusive termination under foreign law.

37. Be careful of restrictive covenants.

38. Examine all prospective or existing licenses in light of American and foreign antitrust laws.

Contract Manufacturing

Production, supply limitations, or sheer bulk may lead some firms to have their product manufactured under contract arrangements with a qualified manufacturer in the overseas territory. Distribution of the product is then directed by a local distributor or a subsidiary or branch office of the U.S. company. The administrative, legal, and financial considerations related to this approach are beyond this book, just as are the following alternatives, but the possibilities are mentioned here to keep all the alternatives in perspective.

Joint Ventures and Strategic Alliances

These terms cover a broad array of relationships. At one end is the *joint venture*—an independent business entity set up by a U.S. firm and a foreign company to pursue a shared commercial goal. At the other is the *strategic alliance*—an agreement by a U.S. firm and a foreign company to work together toward a common and synergistic end.

Wholly Owned Subsidiaries or Branches

These vehicles for overseas commercial activity entail investing to a greater or lesser extent in a foreign enterprise. They are subject to the laws and legal system of the host country and frequently involve built-in restrictions in terms of repatriation of profits, minimum required native ownership, limitations on the ownership of real property, and so on. Developing countries, on the other hand, frequently offer foreign businesses actual incentives to encourage job creation and capital investment. This is also the aim of the world's various multilateral development banks which, in the case of many of the emerging democracies of Eastern Europe and the former states of the Soviet Union, have set up enterprise funds to help established outside firms finance the creation of new companies or buy moribund existing companies. Some such funds are multilateral and others are confined to this country.

Realistic Assessment of Resources

A realistic assessment of your available resources should include financial resources; human resources (both your staff and your own personal qualities, skills, experience, and available time); and production or supply resources. If you are starting up as an export entrepreneur—and especially if you are starting up as an EMC or ETC—you must force yourself to be brutally honest in taking this inventory. There is a strong tendency among new exporters to let enthusiasm win out over reality here.

Financial Resources

Exporting provides certain opportunities to stretch working capital because of the underlying nature of the transaction. This is especially true when the payment terms are very secure, as in the case of a letter of credit. Exports also can *increase* working capital needs, however, because under other than letter-of-credit terms there is a tendency for even the strongest firms in most countries to pay more slowly than the 30-day terms we are accustomed to in this country. (It tends to be more like 60 to 90 days.) Even without the additional time required for payment, the additional transit time often adds to the exporter's carrying cost. There are also higher operating expenses, such as foreign travel, special production requirements, and so on. Recognizing the most favorable payment terms that can be offered and the extent to which they may restrict your sales potential is part of your financial assessment.

Letters of credit do not solve all problems. They seem to offer the promise that merely presenting the device to a bank or lender obviates the need for normal credit resources—that the letter of credit will answer all credit requirements. Be advised that this is not the case, even though they can be very helpful in *supporting* your own credit through assigning the letter-of-credit proceeds to a lender. When third-party exporters can obtain and use a transferable letter of credit, it can substitute for the exporter's credit, but transferability is often not available. (Further details on letters of credit and various other means of financing trade are covered in Chapter 14.)

You can be sure that opportunities and attendant expenses will usually exceed resources faster in international business than in domestic affairs for the obvious reason that the whole world is a bigger, more expensive, and more time-consuming place in which to work, travel, and communicate than is any one of its parts.

Importers have an advantage here in terms of obtaining bank financing because the bank knows it can control the imported merchandise through liens and have it in the United States, where it can attach this collateral if necessary. When it sells to the ultimate buyer, they can still have a domestic receivable as security. By contrast, exports are leaving the country and passing into the hands of a foreign buyer over whom the bank has minimal or no control except in the case of letters of credit. The problem is, importers often need more financing to carry more inventory longer and also to carry domestic receivables that would seldom be supported by letters of credit.

Human Resources

In addition to an assessment of your own experience, skills, and knowledge, you must consider the expertise of your staff if one exists and the collective time available. In terms of knowledge and experience, remember that calamities in international trade are far more likely to occur when an unknowing seller is doing the selling. Your own knowledge and skills should not be a problem if you are a manufacturer, but if you are an EMC or an ETC, be sure that you, at least, understand the product you want to export. If you don't have present knowledge, select products about which you can quickly learn. Knowledge and experience need not hamper you in target countries if you take care to study the wealth of information available concerning customs and practices in any given area. What does matter is the export experience required, depending on the degree of trading difficulty in a given country or area. Trading difficulties and opportunities are taken up in Chapters 6, 7, and 8. Do not begin with the most difficult territories or deals; they may well overstretch your current human resources.

One always wants to grow, but if you have the appetite for single transaction "big deals" in third world countries, be sure to budget more than half of your time and expenses to building a steady business of lesser deals that pay the rent, and develop personal and staff expertise that will maintain the business as a consistently profitable venture.

More than one of my weekends or vacations was ruined, and more than one supplier's payment was delayed or regular piece of sustaining business neglected, while I was chasing a tempting "big deal," whether it was in tons or barrels of sugar, rice, cement, urea, or oil. These products were the favored big deals then, and most still are today. Pursuing these deals often meant forsaking the products we knew and understood and that we were known to be a source for. Negotiating a really large transaction looked terrific on the current month's profit and loss statement, but the result often simply strengthened the "fix" to pursue more big deals which only occasionally worked, leaving large splashes of red ink across the empty months. It took several years and many disappointments to learn this.

The lesson here is that as you look at export situations and export products, focus on opportunities that relate to things you know or can readily learn and handle, and that can be profitably undertaken on a scale commensurate with your resources. It is usually true that among those companies engaged in general trading that largely owe their success to the sheer selling and negotiating skills of their principals, many have focused on specialty markets such as Russia, Eastern Europe, Africa, or the Peoples Republic of China. This is a very high-risk approach, requiring substantial financial resources for sufficient staying power. One may have worked on the perfect deal for over a year, only to have it crumble with the stroke of a policy pen or a change of government.

The time-tested export successes I know firsthand are all rather prosaic businesses with a lot of product knowledge and skills. I am thinking of EMC/ETC operations that have made their owners a good income and sometimes personal fortunes over a period of time by concentrating on such everyday things as the following: aviation parts; swimming pool components and equipment; stage and film lighting equipment (advancing from there into television and motion picture production equipment); canned and processed food; hotel and restaurant specialty foods; frozen specialty meat cuts; medical equipment; computer parts and accessories; kitchen appliances; carpeting; home construction hardware; and yes, even lingerie.

Many manufacturers have followed success in the domestic market with success abroad by doing as thorough and careful a marketing job in receptive countries abroad as they did at home. Market-share concepts need not be confined to the United States. When this happens in a truly fruitful fashion it is usually because a key member of the firm, at a policy-making level, has concentrated his or her planning and hard work on the development of overseas markets.

I know of one such company that designs, licenses, and manufactures iron-on or heat-processed decals for T-shirts and other consumer applications. International sales became a cornerstone of the firm's business and finally consummated a licensing deal involving foreign as well as domestic markets that launched a giant step upward in company size. In the case of both the manufacturer and its traders, increasing international business developed out of existing links, skills, contacts, and long-term effort.

Supply or Supplier Resources

Supplier relationships should not be a problem for the original equipment manufacturer unless it is leaning too heavily on its suppliers for financing rather than on equity or long-term borrowing. When this is the case, it can very suddenly threaten a manufacturer's ability to perform. Problems also frequently arise in handling the larger individual orders that export business often generate and implementing the changes and special adaptations required for the export customer.

Sources are especially critical for third-party exporters. An EMC/ETC should not merely call up a supplier and get the price list and a vague assurance that the supplier is willing to sell. It's important that the supplier be a steady, consistent resource with a product you *know,* after thorough checking, to have the quality and characteristics appropriate for export. Your investigation should include checking out the supplier's reputation and ability to make timely and complete deliveries according to agreed-upon specifications. Sit down with policy-level management, if possible, and explain your objectives and needs. Don't be afraid to discuss special pricing in view of the expenses you can save them on advertising and distribution costs for product sold in the particular markets you are proposing. Do *not* discuss worldwide, but rather a realistic collection of countries for which you can make a believable and knowledgeable case.

Be certain to let the supplier know that you will need adequate product information and what must be done by each of you in the way of brochures, customer support, and other details. Then, work out an understandable agreement with sufficient clarity and detail that both parties know where each stands. Be sure its length of term gives you time to perform and prove yourself, and that when you do, they will be reasonably obliged to renew.

You do not necessarily need a detailed agreement in advance with everyone. In some cases, a letter of intent with a price list and, hopefully, adequate discounts, will suffice while you are exploring. But you *must* go to work with the assurance that you have reliable products at competitive prices that make room for an acceptable profit that you can *deliver*. You cannot fail to perform, or a bad reputation will precede you all too quickly.

Your Final Assessment

If you are honestly satisfied with the sum of these assessments of your resources and believe that they are based on reality, you do have a focus and a strategy and the beginning of what it takes to have a reasonable chance of success with your first efforts as a trader, distributor, or small manufacturer. That chance is all you will need or can ask—a reasonable risk, given proper resources, information, skills, and product or product sources. No one can be assured of success, but the odds favor you if you arrive at this point with a realistic understanding of your problems and objectives which, in turn, will permit you to husband your enthusiasm and resources until the export potential translates into export sales.

The Business Plan as an Expression of Basic Strategy

One reason the request for a business plan has struck terror into the hearts of many entrepreneurs is that it does require a detailed, fully thought out, realistic strategy such as we have been discussing. This is more planning than many of us like to commit to, but if you have given full consideration to these comments, you should now be close to forming a credible plan needing only the addition of a few formalities and some financial assumptions. Even if you are not relying on commercial lenders or private parties for financial support, putting together a business plan will solidify your strategies and help keep you on track as your business develops. It need not be elaborate, but it should be an honest and realistic document if it is to be of any value to you or to prospective lenders or investors. Even for an established small manufacturing company planning to enter the global market, a business plan focused entirely on its emerging international trade project will help maintain a balance with existing domestic activities and future plans. A budget for the new effort can help prevent unforeseen cashflow demands that might prove harmful to your existing business. SBA counseling can be useful in this area if you feel you need some help.

The plan can run to two or three pages or to 50, but it must include a budget that states where the money is coming from. For start-up entrepreneurs the budget can be simple, but for your own sake it should include your personal income and expenses in bulk with an affordable and realistic set-aside to support the expenses of the new business for at least a year until meaningful income can be generated. Very possibly, entrepreneurs of new EMC/ETCs should keep their day jobs for a while yet!

Here are the most basic elements to include in a business plan for export:

- How the product will be manufactured, adapted, or procured, or the service provided
- How the overseas market will be created
- How the product or service will be sold
- What the projected gross margin will be
- What the expenses will be, sorted out as to fixed and variable
- The profit margins projected
- The breakeven volume
- The total investment required
- The amount of additional money needed for start up of the business or the new division and where it will come from
- When the new capital or borrowed funds will be needed
- The repayment schedule for borrowed funds and the projected yield and return on equity funds
- How the loan will be serviced and amortized
- A summary of your own and your company's qualifications to make or procure the product or provide the service and administer the business—that is, to achieve the objectives stated above

Assembling these statements plus any others that come to your mind to fit special circumstances will force you to take a realistic and objective view. It permits you to think and rethink your strategies and identify your strengths and weaknesses while perceiving details you might otherwise overlook. A finished business plan can be an operating tool to help you plan, manage, and review your progress, whether you are anticipating using outside funds or not.

If the plan is intended to be used to attract outside money or interest, it will need to be dressed up a bit to round out and justify the answers to some of the above questions. For example:

The Summary:	If your business plan is very long it will need to be condensed into a two- or three-page executive summary as an introduction to arouse initial interest.
The Company:	Its structure, ownership, and history.
The Product:	What it is, why it is unique or in demand, and how it is distinguished from the competition. Explain any technology involved.
The Market:	The current size of the target market, based on market surveys, trends, distribution, and competition. Do you have a market-share percentage in mind?
Finance:	The source of the necessary equity capital and the sources and term of the proposed nonequity financing. How the borrowed funds will be repaid from projected revenues, profits, and cashflow. The longer the term of the loan, the more details and plans need to be provided. As part of this section you should include the capital expenditure budget, pro forma balance sheets, profit-and-loss statements, and cashflow projections, which are a key element of the business plan. Cashflow projections are not as difficult as commonly thought, but a carelessly prepared or obviously inaccurate projection can cost you confidence. Talk to your accountant or one of the SBA's SCORE advisors and/or see the SBA's free publication, *Understanding Cash Flow*. The National Business Association offers computer software, developed with the SBA's help, to make cashflow projections easier. Alternatively, your cashflow projections can be in a separate financial section if you have an accountant or the details warrant this expansion.
Appendices:	Include here supporting paperwork, exhibits, key correspondence, brochures or advertisements, reviews, contracts and agreements, licenses and permits, articles of incorporation, and so on.
Management:	The structure of the management team with its qualifications, experience, and interest in the company must be provided in great detail, including additional management and employees that must be added to accomplish the plan.

Promotional Plan: Your strategies to gain access to the market and the channels of distribution planned for the product.

Do not hesitate to seek help in this endeavor from advisors such as an accountant, an SBA advisor, or a nearby Small Business Development Center. Keep in mind that if you are seeking a loan, a prospective lender looks for a sound and convincingly realistic plan when considering the risks versus rewards relative to a loan for your company. Be sure you appear credible, practical, and committed. The degree of commitment is evidenced by such things as the direct risk you are assuming by virtue of your equity relative to your capital needs, plus your personal net worth or assets as a personal guarantee. In addition, they will be looking at your experience relative to the plan and the confidence you bring to the table. It is also a good idea to be prepared to show them that you have some alternative plans, should certain details not go according to your schedule or projections.

Endnotes

1. *The Exporter Magazine,* June 1990 and subsequent issues through 1994 covering Census figures, 1987–1993.
2. *The Export Yellow Pages* Department of Commerce and Venture Publishing, 1992. (Sold through the U.S. Department of Commerce District Offices.)

5
Who on Earth?

Distribution Strategies

Choosing the right channel of distribution from the start will save you time, money, and frustration in the long run. Once distributors or representatives are chosen and either have, or believe they have an exclusive commitment from you, it may well be expensive and troublesome to change your mind and appoint someone else. Therefore, take the time to carefully research the most appropriate distribution mechanism and to select the personnel or firm you wish to execute it, based on the customer you ultimately want to reach. As a manufacturer, even though you may have elected to use an EMC, it would still be beneficial to everyone concerned to take an interest in the choice of channels in key regions.

Let us examine the four basic channels for export sales and the considerations each should be given:

1. End user
2. Retailer
3. Agent
4. Distributor

Dealing with the End User

An end user can be either an individual, as in the case of consumer products, or a manufacturer, as in the case of a machine tool or an industrial solvent. In fact, during the introductory phase of a product, you will probably be contacted by end users with inquiries for more details on the product. But unless you are a specialist contemplating a direct-mail or house-to-house program, you should generally consider selling direct to end users only if they are established businesses, such as manufacturers needing high-value equipment or expensive machinery.

It may be that you intend to focus on direct sales because the product lends itself to project-size transactions of sufficient worth to merit your personal supervision. If so, you have several questions you must answer before undertaking business with the end user:

1. How will you handle installation or post-sales service problems with no agent or distributor and/or insufficient profit from the transaction to justify travel to the site?

2. How will you resolve difficulties early in the exploratory phase in determining a price for end users that will permit allowance for commission or profit margin for a future distributor, agent, or retailer?

3. How will you head off possible unforeseen repercussions from a single sale, such as its being premature relative to having filed for trademarks or patents? (Your own U.S. trademark may have been legally registered by others in certain foreign countries, including Japan, which will prevent you from the use of it in that country. In the case of patents, commercial sales, or even offering a product for sale in a country before applying for a patent, may injure your rights to secure that patent. You can learn more about the basics of patents and trademarks in Chapter 19.)

4. How can you ensure that the product will be properly used or installed in such a way as to enhance, not deter, the opportunities for future sales?

5. What are the appropriate sales terms, considering the urgent need for information about the buyer and the size of the sale, which might be prohibitively small for a letter of credit? A foreign credit report on the buyer can sometimes be the only answer to this question, which can take time—at least two weeks and often more. (The source of foreign credit reports will be discussed in Chapter 16. The problem concerning practical minimum values for letters of credit in view of minimum fees placing too much burden on the profit percentage is addressed in Chapter 14 on letters of credit.)

Selling Through Retailers

If you have a consumer product, selling directly to retailers may be a logical choice of channels, and in any event you may receive inquiries from retailers, even though you had in mind finding an agent or distributor. In this case, your first effort should be to find out something about the retail organization. It could be a single store proprietorship, or it could be a giant retail chain with a dominant market share in your product category. With rare exceptions, the very fact of selling to a single store foretells a long and tedious process of building up distribution and may be far from a final solution. On the other hand, dealing with a large store or chain may be all you could hope for. The key in selling directly to retailers is that the retailer should dominate in your product category. If the category is narrow or your product unique within that category, this one retailer could deliver a larger share of the market than you would have any right to expect. But the opposite may also be true, and you could find your product buried in a great clutter of like products with no one responsible for them or paying attention to them. The world's major department stores are among the most likely places for such a burial.

My experience in representing major apparel manufacturers around the world was that although the large retailers liked to dabble in our stylish and rather expensive merchandise, they seldom consistently purchased in real depth over a period of time and eventually contracted to have similar ranges made locally or took out a license with the U.S. firm for overseas manufacture. It was the boutiques and shops that really did the job of selling our line, but precious few of them had the kind of credit we could afford to ship against. By the same token, their orders, though frequent, were too small to make letters of credit practical. (In the chapter on credit and finance we will describe how we solved this problem.) The sum of many small orders can still produce a profitable, if tedious, business, but the strategy of how you do it will be different.

If retailers are the chosen channel, you need to exercise great care in determining what market the retailer represents. You must also be sure to employ discreet follow-up to be sure that your product is not buried. No matter how large the initial order is, or is promised to be after a first trial order, assume nothing and keep a close eye on developments, for no one is in the territory watching out for your interests. The rare exception mentioned previously of eventual success growing out of dealings with a small store occurs when the product presentation serves to arouse the interest of a top agent or distributor who otherwise might be too busy to be interested.

Success, on however small a scale, can be the key to getting really top representation in a country. With these shifting fortunes in mind, remember to structure your price direct to retailers high enough so that, if necessary, you can subsequently put the product in the hands of a distributor or representative without the need for major price adjustments. Here are some questions or cautions to consider when the retailer responds to your initial offering:

1. What is the nature and size of the retailer and what is its geographical coverage? The best initial source for the answer to this question is a World Traders Data Report (WTDR) which can be obtained through your nearest Department of Commerce District Office, and possibly via a foreign credit report as well. (We will discuss WTDRs further in the context of establishing credit for new customers in Chapter 15.)

2. What can you find out about the retailer you are dealing with, no matter how impressive the name? A credit report is a start and is neces-

sary for anything less than letter-of-credit terms. The WTDR may also help for this purpose because it takes into account size, reputation, and the nature of the products being sold. However, a retail store is a very public institution, and it may be that some contact in the country through your state foreign trade organization, or even a contact in the nearest U.S. trade consulate or US&FCS office, can informally provide at least some information.

3. Again, what are the appropriate sales terms—considering your need to be sure your pricing strategy accounts for future possible patterns or structures of distribution, such as a representative or distributor?

4. Avoid open-ended commitments that do not require some satisfactory performance level. Make a quantitative review of that level within a year or so.

Using an Agent/Representative

The function of a representative—often also called a *rep* or an *agent*—is to secure orders from customers and forward the orders on to the exporter. The exporter ships the orders direct to the customers, who are then responsible for payment directly to the exporter. (If the exporter or supplier is using an EMC or ETC, the payment will be made to one or the other depending on the EMC/ETC agreement.) It is strongly recommended that representatives have their duties clearly defined and restricted and be referred to as *representatives* or almost any name other than *agent*. This is because, depending on the legal system of the country, an "agent" may make binding contractual relationships in the name of his or her principal—a role that obviously represents a substantial risk.

While commissions, samples, and communication costs are the only direct expenses to be considered in the case of a representative, it should be kept in mind that the commissions will probably be higher than you anticipated. A commission that might please domestic salespeople here will very likely be inadequate in the mind of overseas representatives because they see a much more expensive landed product on their price list. Shipping costs, import handling, duties, and other miscellaneous costs make the imported product substantially more expensive than the factory or FOB price on which their commission is probably calculated. When representatives measure the value of their commission, it may appear to be very low as a percentage of the final wholesale or retail overseas price. If a representative has other comparable products in the same category that are manufactured locally (as is most often the case), the lower-percentage commission earned from the imported product may serve to dampen the representative's enthusiasm for promoting it over the lower priced domestic merchandise.

In considering representatives as a channel, you must also make some cost comparisons relative to representatives and distributors. Obviously a distributor needs to make a far greater profit margin than a representative's commission because of greater expenses. Distributors must factor in the payment of their own selling commissions, the financial costs of carrying inventory and credit, postsales obligations, and bad debts or the equivalent, which otherwise would be borne by the exporter or supplier. The process of choosing between a representative and a distributor should also include how many references or letters of credit there will be to deal with and how many defective-merchandise situations and after-sales service problems will have to be resolved. In theory, the commitment of a distributor—especially a stocking distributor, should be much greater than that of a representative, which is essentially only that of a salesperson. But the key words in this statement are "in theory." Distributors can't always be counted on to do all they are supposed to do. Good distributors can be very hard to find—at least until the product is proven and successful and in demand. During the trial phase, the possibly-more-tentative commitment of a representative may be all that is to be found.

In situations involving small distributors and representatives, it is well to remember that they are by no means always exclusively one or the other. For a wide variety of reasons, and especially depending on the terms and conditions offered, they may choose to act as a representative for one company and a distributor for another. Sometimes this flexibility can solve problems by compromise, as in the case of a distributor who is not yet prepared to carry inventory but who is prepared to act as a quasi-distributor by collecting orders until sufficient quantity is accumulated to make the import process economically practical. Thereafter, a combined order can be used for which the distributor is financially responsible and, after arrival, the distributor can be given responsibility for breaking out lots to the individual buyers. A representative can perform a similar function, but the exporter is then saddled with the responsibility of checking creditworthiness and extending terms to several foreign buyers who are often small and whose credit is difficult to check from overseas.

Assuming that the cost factors work out and you can afford a distributor, what should you look for? The ideal distributor: (1) carries an adequate inventory; (2) prices fairly; and (3) promotes your product with as much enthusiasm you would display for your product in this country. Unfortunately, this is not a perfect world, and perfect distributors are, like gems, rare. A good representative is superior to an uncommitted or less-than-satisfactory distributor every time, but the choice is seldom clear-cut. One can always move up to a distributor as market share increases and the product becomes well established and therefore a more desirable range to represent.

The choice can even be "none of the above," if the only way a competitive price can be maintained is by direct selling without representatives through retailers, in which case there are no distribution or commission costs. It can also be that the technical skills required are not to be found in any kind of representative and it is therefore better to price the product to include travel, installation, and follow-up by staff from your own domestic business location.

If a representative does seem to be a solution, or at least a start for your distribution process, here are some further questions to ask yourself:

1. What is the reputation of the representative, and is the profile of his or her present customers consistent with existing consumers of your product?

2. What other lines or products does the representative handle, and will their existence enhance your product's sales opportunities or compete with them? The answer will tell you whether the representative will be able to call on the same buyers or departments as for the products he or she currently represents.

If the answers to this last question are not positive, consider the possibility that the candidate will do nothing more than stow the product away to keep it from competing representatives. It is possible for representatives or agents to stall while minimizing sales for at least a year to suit their own purposes, and it may take a good deal more than a letter of dismissal to be rid of them. It is also possible that they are merely hoping to expand their range of contacts through your product and have nothing at present to offer in the way of new buyers. If, on the other hand, a representative seems qualified in terms of customers, reputation, and products represented and fits your needs, and you can answer one last question in the affirmative, a person-to-person meeting is called for:

3. Is the profit margin resulting from the present pricing sufficient to pay a commission, and, conversely, will this selling price, including commission, make a change over to a distributor arrangement more difficult if such an eventuality is considered?

Selling Through a Distributor

Selecting a distributor is a bit like a marriage of convenience. It is also the most difficult relationship from which to extract oneself. While a disgruntled representative can claim to have invested time and effort in building a product's acceptance in the market, a disgruntled distributor has the same claim plus a tangible investment in inventory and possibly capital equipment for servicing and transporting the product. For this reason alone, it may not be the right relationship to undertake as a starting point. It certainly will not be unless you are fully satisfied with the distributor's sincerity in desiring to promote your product and that organization can also demonstrate an ability to perform. As with a representative, I mention sincerity because it is not uncommon to have distributors claim product knowledge, experience, and enthusiasm they do not really have.

Distributors have also been known to take on a line merely to delay its legitimate introduction into the market. This is less likely if the distributor must first stock a meaningful inventory, and it is one good reason to require an opening inventory. In this connection, it is wise to let a distribution agreement become effective only on receipt of the agreed-upon opening order for inventory—and, most commonly, on receipt of a letter of credit to pay for it as well, even if subsequent orders will be available under less stringent credit terms.

On the subject of credit, do not omit examining the proposed distributor's credit even though irrevocable letter-of-credit terms are to be the standard method of payment indefinitely. This is because the distributor, as a continuing buyer, is representing to you that the firm can do a certain amount of business each year. But does it have the credit or the liquid collateral to permit opening this much in letters of credit? Whether it must put up cash to open a letter of credit or can do so against its credit line, the amount involved is finite, and if it is insufficient, the distributor will probably be unable to meet its distribution obligations. It is a common mistake to think that concerns about creditworthiness are eliminated because the payment terms will involve a letter of credit.

The key points to consider in contemplating a particular distributor are similar to those mentioned in considering an agent:

1. Reputation.

2. Present customer profile.

3. Current product lines.

4. Proposed pricing formula against your net price quote to the distributor. Does it seem to provide a fair and reasonable profit to the distributor and still be consistent with what you know to be common practice in a particular country? If there is insufficient profit, there will be little incentive to succeed; if the profit is too high, it is probable that neither you nor the distributor will succeed. Some exporters write the pricing formula into a distributor contract.

5. Financial resources and credit to be able to fulfill its commitment to you. Are the physical facilities necessary for performance in place? A WTDR report, or its equivalent, and a credit agency report are essential prior to signing any agreement.

6. Skills, personnel, and/or equipment necessary to handle any after-sales service for the product.

7. Business history. In this arrangement more than in any other, a good knowledge of the distributor's track record is essential to a sound decision.

This is a good moment to read a version of a basic distributor agreement from one of the sources mentioned in Appendix F3. It is also a good time to review Figure 5-1, courtesy of the *Basic Guide to Exporting*, which lists additional factors to consider when choosing a foreign representative or distributor.

After traveling the Middle East extensively on behalf of a consumer goods line, selling directly to retailers as well as through agents, I felt it was time to consider a distributor agreement with what seemed like a very substantial firm of good reputation, history, and size. I personally visited the operation, viewed inventories of several excellent European lines on hand, talked to management, and waited out endless meetings, delays, and frequent calls from the minarets to prayer. Feeling satisfied of a complete understanding, I left the costly sample line I had been carrying with our prospect, having initialed a preliminary draft of a good distribution agreement. Not only did I never sell the firm a penny's worth of merchandise, I was never able to get the money agreed on for the samples or even recover the samples themselves. Thankfully, planning, experience, and preparation usually paid off better than in this instance. I mention it here only to remind you that there are many surprises in this business despite the best-laid plans.

Figure 5-1. Factors to consider when choosing a foreign representative or distributor.

The following checklist should be tailored by each company to its own needs. Key factors vary significantly with the products and countries involved.

Size of sales force

- How many field sales personnel does the representative or distributor have?
- What are its short- and long-range expansion plans, if any?
- Would it need to expand to accommodate your account properly? If so, would it be willing to do so?

Sales record

- Has its sales growth been consistent? If not, why not? Try to determine sales volume for the past five years.
- What is its sales volume per outside salesperson?
- What are its sales objectives for next year? How were they determined?

(Continued)

Figure 5-1. (*Continued*)

Territorial analysis

- What territory does it now cover?
- Is it consistent with the coverage you desire? If not, is it able and willing to expand?
- Does it have any branch offices in the territory to be covered?
- If so, are they located where your sales prospects are greatest?
- Does it have any plans to open additional offices?

Product mix

- How many product lines does it represent?
- Are these product lines compatible with yours?
- Would there be any conflict of interest?
- Does it represent any other U.S. firms? If so, which ones?
- If necessary, would it be willing to alter its present product mix to accommodate yours?
- What would be the minimum sales volume needed to justify its handling your lines? Do its sales projections reflect this minimum figure? From what you know of the territory and the prospective representative or distributor, is its projection realistic?

Facilities and equipment

- Does it have adequate warehouse facilities?
- What is its method of stock control?
- Does it use computers? Are they compatible with yours?
- What communications facilities does it have (fax, modem, telex, etc.)?
- If your product requires servicing, is it equipped and qualified to do so? If not, is it willing to acquire the needed equipment and arrange for necessary training? To what extent will you have to share the training cost?
- If necessary and customary, is it willing to inventory repair parts and replacement items?

Marketing policies

- How is its sales staff compensated?
- Does it have special incentive or motivation programs?
- Does it use product managers to coordinate sales efforts for specific product lines?
- How does it monitor sales performance?
- How does it train its sales staff?
- Would it share expenses for sales personnel to attend factory-sponsored seminars?

Customer profile

- What kinds of customers is it currently contacting?
- Are its interests compatible with your product line?
- Who are its key accounts?
- What percentage of its total gross receipts do these key accounts represent?

Figure 5-1. (*Continued*) (*Source: A Basic Guide to Exporting, Department of Commerce.*)

Principals represented

- How many principals is it currently representing?
- Would you be its primary supplier?
- If not, what percentage of its total business would you represent? How does this percentage compare with other suppliers?

Promotional thrust

- Can it help you compile market research information to be used in making forecasts?
- What media does it use, if any, to promote sales?
- How much of its budget is allocated to advertising? How is it distributed among various principals?
- Will you be expected to contribute funds for promotional purposes? How will the amount be determined?
- If it uses direct mail, how many prospects are on its mailing list?
- What type of brochure does it use to describe its company and the products that it represents?
- If necessary, can it translate your advertising copy?

Thus far, I have treated each of the four types of basic sales channels as if they were interchangeable. In fact, it would be unlikely that you would receive inquiries from four different types of buyers or agents if your promotional material was properly focused. Furthermore, the answer at this initial stage of your particular product's introduction might be quite different from what it will be at some future time, when the product is established in comparable overseas areas and product demand puts you in a better negotiating position. What we have seen so far is the most basic of strategic considerations. We have not taken into account, for instance, the very important consideration of the country involved relative to the distribution channel.

The size and sophistication of the target market country will have a major impact on your preference of sales channels. A relatively small country with a major chain store may provide you with all the market exposure you could desire and may permit you to hold costs down by selling directly to the retailer. Such an arrangement would not work well in a large and complex market like Japan, whose multilevel wholesaling structure would give a well-established importer the best chance of success. However, that same complex structure can account for your product selling for 10 times your U.S. ex-factory wholesale price. To combat this expensive and cumbersome distribution nightmare in Japan (although it is improving), even small American companies are increasingly sending a key employee to Japan on at least a semipermanent basis to introduce the product vigorously and to expedite the process while seeking ways to minimize the number of distribution layers through which the product must filter. Partly as a result of our trade negotiations and partly out of underlying necessity, the much-discussed Japanese distribution system is experiencing reform in some product areas. (We'll take a look at the problems and obstacles to trade, or the lack of them, in all the regions of the world, starting in Chapter 6.)

Before making your final decisions on distribution strategies, ask many questions and don't fail to ask the staff in the U.S. commercial consulate office of the country as well as the ITA country desk officer in Washington, D.C. Gaining the experience of others can help you make your decisions even if your own final answers are quite different.

Determining distribution strategy can get very sophisticated and extensive in terms of market research, demographics, and variations of joint ventures, strategic alliances and company structures. The research can be home-grown or obtained from experts, as we have already pointed-ed out. The task of this book, however, is to help you get on with expediting your export sales as quickly as possible and to leave consideration of the more sophisticated and expensive strategies to when you may have both the time and the resources to pursue them.

PART 2

Exploring Territorial Strategies

6
Where in the World?

The Western Hemisphere

*Free trade, one of the greatest blessings which
a government can confer on a people, is in
almost every country unpopular.*
THOMAS BABINGTON MACAULEY, LORD MACAULEY
Essay, 1824

The rapid formation and increasing size of the world's trading blocs is an indication that free trade, at least on a regional basis, is more popular today than in Lord Macauley's time. It remains to be seen whether world-wide free trade is actually advancing or is instead becoming an enlarged and regionalized form of nationalism based on ethnicity and tribalism.

The purpose of the next three chapters is to take a new look at the world from a trader's point of view, with a special emphasis on today's trading blocs and trading opportunities. By integrating up-to-date trade facts with pertinent geopolitical background, these chapters will give you a sense of the present world's economic order as it directly relates to the export choices before you.

In writing this section of the text, I have found the book *Don't Know Much About Geography* by Kenneth C. Davis very useful, particularly in its ability to combine interesting facts and relationships with an extremely practical and readable geography lesson.[1] I acknowledge with thanks the many geographical references in the following pages that I originally found in his excellent work, and highly recommend it, along with an up-to-date map of the world, as you read these chapters. I also urge you to refer often to the World Order of Nations listings, in Tables 6.1, 7.1, 7.2, and 8.1.

As you explore the world's immense variety of markets, try to start thinking in terms of potential for your products, accessibility, and political stability. But remember, too, that both economic and political circumstances are subject to change at a moment's notice in many parts of the world. It is also important to bear in mind that special needs can make even the most unlikely targets a gold mine for particular products or services if approached at the critical time and under the right circumstances.

As I mentioned earlier, a trader's ability to interact successfully with certain peoples has little or nothing to do with the sharing of a common race, religion, ethnicity, or language. These superficial qualities are merely accessory qualifications for selling or trading in particular areas of the world. Your export or import products and sources and your physical and financial stamina, combined with your knowledge and experience, will be your ultimate determinants of success.

Degree of Trading Difficulty Ratings

To provide a baseline for assessing the relative difficulty of trading in various areas of the world, I have devised a Degree of Trading Difficulty (DTD) system with ratings from 1 to 10. Those countries presenting the least number of problems in terms of setting up *regular* channels of product distribution (in contrast to single or one-time-only sales) are rated 1 (the nearest thing to the relative simplicity of doing business domestically). Those receiving a rating of 9 present the maximum level of trade difficulty. A rating of 10 is reserved for any country our government considers unfriendly or even an enemy—declared or undeclared. In such cases, the U.S. government usually restricts or embargoes trade, or by means of licensing restrictions, prohibits trade on the grounds of terrorist activity.

The DTD rating system is informal and of my own devising. It should be taken only as a rough indicator of the overall effort or special difficulties you can expect in the course of marketing your products. I confess to exercising substantial license in applying the components on which the rating is based. They are all subject to broad estimates and will change as time marches on. The most crucial factors considered were import barriers—both acknowledged barriers, such as tariffs and others much less transparent—and country risk, in terms of political and economic stability, the level of civil unrest, foreign exchange, and country credit availability. Also taken into account were such factors as: internal distribution problems; per capita income; transportation problems; travel costs and personal risk; intellectual property rights protection; cultural obstacles; legal systems and government attitudes or regulations; availability of qualified importers; and use of English, at least as a secondary business language. These factors were then weighed against the relative sales potential of the specific country or region, in the case of smaller countries contiguous to each other. What could not be taken into consideration in this analysis were the continuously changing priorities of the sovereign governments, which can make funds, regulations, and red tape materialize or vanish overnight.

The DTD ratings view the country or the region from the standpoint of an exporter or trader, not from the standpoint of an international banker or lender or even a government export credit agency like the U.S. Export-Import Bank. After devising this DTD approach to rating countries and regions for trade purposes, I ran across a quotation from the book *Don't Know Much About Geography* that succinctly illustrates one element of our approach. Author Kenneth Davis quotes from Marco Polo's *Travels* (c. 1299) as this first China travel author describes his visit to the "island of Cipangu (modern-day Japan) and others in its vicinity," and speaks of the exotic spices and other items to be found there and in the other islands as follows: "It is impossible to estimate the value of the gold and other articles found in the islands; but their distance from the continent is so great, and the navigation attended with so much trouble and inconvenience, that the vessels engaged in the trade...do not reap large profits...." In other words, "Some business may not be worth the trouble." Helping you apply this principle judiciously is one of the things these chapters are all about.

Because our DTD ratings take into account political stability, country credit and debt, and foreign exchange availability, I have reviewed several services that would not normally be used by exporters. These sources provide detailed, periodic analyses of sovereign country credit ratings with input from many sources, including their own experience or that provided by a network they have developed. One especially useful provider of information on project and trade finance worldwide is the magazine *Euromoney*, which publishes "Country-Risk Rankings" several times a year for almost all the countries of the world.[2] (It is available in the business section of major libraries.) *Euromoney*'s March 1995 issue ranked 187 countries from 1 to 187. The magazine arrives at the rank by assigning a total score representing a sum of scores based on nine factors. Eight of them are each worth 10 points if perfect; the ninth, political risk (stability), is worth 20 points. (See note number 2 at the end of this chapter for further details.) Country-risk and country credit ratings will not mean much to most exporters or importers, because their first concern is the creditworthiness and/or reputation of the buyer or seller or the bank that issues or confirms the letter of credit. However, in a politically or financially unstable environment, confirmed or otherwise reliable letters of credit may be impossible to come by, and the buyer will probably have no access to foreign exchange. This can force the exporter to consider countertrade or barter, which is a great deal of trouble. Civil strife or military action can also keep a seller or manufacturer from performing. The result in any case is a lot more hassle in the business of trading internationally, so it has a real impact on the DTD rating.

The list of countries of the world in Table 6-1 in this chapter, and 7-1, 7-2, and 8-1 in Chapters 7 and 8, is not quite as obvious as one might first think. In part this is simply due to the many political changes taking place in the world almost monthly. It is due even more to the problems involved in making the economic and political facts of life relate in a logi-

Table 6-1. The Geographic/Political World Order of Nations: Western Hemisphere[1]

Areawide DTD	Country exception DTD[2]	Region and country	Trade bloc membership[3]
2		*North America*	
	1	Canada	NAFTA
	0	United States of America	NAFTA
	3.5	Mexico	NAFTA
5		*Central America*	
		Guatemala	CBI, CACM
		Belize	CBI, CC
	∧	Honduras	CBI, CACM
		El Salvador	CBI, CACM
	7–8	Nicaragua	CBI, CACM
	4	Costa Rica	CBI, CACM
		Panama	CBI
6		*Caribbean* (West Indies)	
		Bahamas	CBI, CC
		Turks & Caicos Islands (Britain)	CBI (eligible)
	10	Cuba	
		Cayman Islands (Britain)	CBI (eligible)
	∨	Jamaica	CBI, CC
	∧	Haiti[4] (shares Hispaniola Island)	
	∨	Dominican Republic (shares Hispaniola Island)	CBI
		Puerto Rico (U.S.A.)	
		Virgin Islands (U.S.A.)	
		British Virgin Islands (Britain)	
		Leeward Islands	
		Anguilla (Britain)	CBI (eligible)
	∧	St. Kitts-Nevis	CBI
	∧	Antigua & Barbuda	CBI
		Montserrat (Britain)	CBI
		Guadeloupe (France)	
		Windward Islands	
		Dominica	CBI
		Martinique (France)	
	∧	St. Lucia	CBI
	∧	St. Vincent & The Grenadines	CBI
		Barbados	CBI, CC
	∧	Grenada	CBI
	∨	Trinidad & Tobago	CBI, CC
	∨	Netherlands Antilles (the Netherlands)	CBI

Table 6-1. The Geographic/Political World Order of Nations
Western Hemisphere[1] (Continued)

Areawide DTD	Country exception DTD[2]	Region and country	Trade bloc membership[3]
4.5		*South America*	
		Venezuela	Andean
	8	Guyana	CBI, CC
	8	Suriname	CBI (eligible)
	^	French Guiana (France)	
	^	Columbia	Andean
		Ecuador	Andean
	^	Peru	Andean
	^	Bolivia	Andean
		Chile	
		Argentina	Mercosur
		Uruguay	Mercosur
	^	Paraguay	Mercosur
	v	Brazil	Mercosur

[1]The independent countries of the world are divided into the political and economic areas, starting with Canada in the Western Hemisphere, proceeding south through the hemisphere to South America, thereafter moving east to northern Europe, and so on. The broad, mostly continental, world areas are subdivided by regions or subregions in a north-to-south direction, with the individual countries listed in "belts" proceeding from east to west, beginning with the most northerly belt insofar as possible. Some deviations are required to accommodate trading blocs and irregular, overlapping geographical areas.

This system, in addition to assisting in the location of a given country, emphasizes the East/West nature of trade among equals and the North/South nature of trade with aid, or trade dependent on less expensive manufacturing labor in the South.

All independent republics, states, or nations are listed. Other deviations or additions made for clarity or for future developments are noted within the list, including dependencies which were included because of location on the mainland or because they represented a large landmass. In these cases, the mother country is given in parentheses.

[2]Where a country differs materially from the regional Degree of Trading Difficulty scale, it is indicated by a separate DTD rating for that country. Alternatively, when the difference is relatively not great, or adequate information is not available for a separate rating, the distinction is indicated by: a ^ for a greater DTD ranking (more difficult trading); and by a v for a lesser DTD ranking (easier trading).

[3]The full versions of the abbreviated trade bloc titles are as follows:
  NAFTA = North American Free Trade Association
  CBI = Caribbean Basin Initiative
  CACM = Central American Common Market
  CC = Caribbean Community or CARICOM
  Andean = Andean Pact Group
  Mercosur = Southern Common Market, or Southern Cone Group
[4]Indicates that the country is identified by the United Nations as one of the poorest nations in the world.

cal fashion to the world's geography and maps as we know them. It is difficult to find any two geographic or geopolitical authorities or their atlases that agree, even as to continents, much less borders, country names, spelling, and many other details. The final list, as shown in the tables, is based in some cases on the majority opinion, but in many cases it derives from observed commercial and marketing realities as they relate to the geographic blocs of countries, and especially to their own trading blocs and to travel problems. This is what underlies the pattern of listing the world's landmasses, starting in the Western Hemisphere with Canada and proceeding south to Chile and Argentina, and thence eastward to Europe. The same north-to-south process was used insofar as possible in listing the countries within the regional territorial divisions. (See Note 1, Table 6-1.)

It was not my initial intention to list all the countries of the world, especially those with little economic impact on trade or politics, but I finally did so, at least in the case of declared independent nations, states, or republics, because so many countries have a relationship to some trading bloc or trade pact in the world such as Brunei in the Association of Southeast Asian Nations (ASEAN) group or Iceland and Liechtenstein in the European Free Trade Association (EFTA). Dependencies or colonies are not listed unless they are part of an unbroken continental mass or relate to trade blocs or other groups through which they derive significance either directly or indirectly. The primary instance of this is in the Caribbean, where 12 of the 18 nonindependent entities are listed. In these instances I have indicated the home country in parentheses.

Omitted also are the free ports, even though they can form part of your worldwide marketing strategy. Margarita Isle off the coast of Venezuela is a good example. For high-tariff items such a port can be the primary means of distributing within the country itself and reaching some of the host countries' tourist traffic in the bargain. Check for such situations in your areas after you have established your primary targets.

All told, I have listed 192 declared independent countries, plus 17 dependencies or semidependencies. Notes at the ends of the World Order of Nations tables list 11 countries that are not members of the United Nations and another group of 21 countries that the UN defines as the poorest countries of the world. The latter group comprise *the Fourth World*—a newly coined phrase. The length of the total list illustrates the point that selectivity is required when choosing target countries.

The Western Hemisphere

To our neighbors in the Western Hemisphere go two-fifths of all U.S. exports. So it seems logical to begin at home, so to speak, in North

America, with our largest single market, Canada, followed by our southern neighbor in North America and or third-largest market, Mexico.

North America

Our northern neighbor, Canada, is our largest trading partner and by far our largest export customer. (We export less than half as much to Japan, our second largest customer.) Many U.S. firms think of Canada as an extension of the United States—just one or more additional regions of the domestic market base—rather than as an export market to be managed by their international divisions. This could be a major mistake. Not only does Canada represent a $115 billion market, it is, no less than the United States itself, a vast and very diversified country, and it is just as unlikely to be adequately served by one agent or distributor. If selected as a major target, Canada must be divided along geographic and demographic lines to achieve a suitable market share. And the size of the individual regions involved should be less a determining factor than such considerations as accessibility and travel time, customs, and population.

Erik Wicklund, in his book *International Marketing,* has a somewhat different way of approaching this issue.[3] He distinguishes between "centralized" and "decentralized" countries. Although he is using the terms in the context of an exporter's personal travel to the countries, the same reasoning tends to reinforce the idea that several distributors or agents may be necessary to represent a product. He uses as examples of *decentralized* countries: Canada, Germany, Italy, the Netherlands, Spain, Sweden, Switzerland, Brazil, Columbia, Australia, New Zealand, Japan, India, Turkey, Saudi Arabia, the United Arab Emirates, Nigeria, and South Africa. What all these countries have in common is neither physical nor economic size, but multiple commercial centers.

Wicklund maintains that *centralized* countries—in which a single visit to one city in the country may be sufficient—are: France, England, Norway, Denmark, Finland, Greece, Austria, Portugal, Egypt, Mexico, Argentina, Chile, Venezuela, South Korea, Thailand, Indonesia, Malaysia, Taiwan, and the Philippines. Again, you see there is little relationship to size or geography in this list. Germany is a prime example of a decentralized country and would almost certainly figure as a multimarket for firms pursuing maximum sales in that area. One the other hand, Mexico, although much larger, does virtually all its business in the huge commercial center of Mexico City, D.F.

Considering this, one would divide Canada into possibly five separate marketing regions to describe its great demographic diversity and industrial needs. These would be: British Columbia; the Middle Provinces; Ontario; Quebec; and the Maritimes. Quite different regions might be delineated, depending on a company's product and market-share expectations, but the differences among these particular five could not be more pronounced. Think of Quebec, speaking only the French language and more French than France itself, versus British Columbia, which seems almost like an extension of the state of Washington.

Geographically speaking, we have ignored Canada's Yukon and Northwest Territories, which reach north into the largely frozen Arctic Ocean and lie within the Arctic Circle. The state of Alaska abuts the western border of the Yukon and spreads westward, coming very close to Russia in the Bering Straits and not far from the Aleutian Islands of Alaska. The Northwest Territories include three of the world's 10 largest islands: Baffin, Victoria, and Ellesmere—all very northern, with Ellesmere lying largely within the Arctic Circle. The area itself does not mean much to the international trader, but the rich natural resources of northern Canada mean a great deal to them.

Canada is our largest trading partner, with over $243 billion of fairly balanced total import/export trade and $70 billion more than our very unbalanced second-largest trading partner, Japan. Besides being the sole possessor of the number 1 ranking in our Degree of Trading Difficulty (DTD) ratings, Canada was also our initial partner in the Free Trade Agreement (FTA), which now includes Mexico and has become the North American Free Trade Agreement (NAFTA). Despite some problems, our present free trade agreement with Canada has produced vastly increased trade and economic benefits for both nations. If there is any need for your product in Canada and distribution is not already established there, it is a good place to hone your export distribution skills. With virtually no foreign political risk, Canada is truly "the safe bet next door," as the magazine *Export Today* calls it.[4]

For the sake of consistency and order, as well as for importer readers, we include on our Western Hemisphere list the United States. Import distributors must divide the United States into one of several possible regional configurations if nationwide distribution is being sought, just as exporters need to divide Canada into regional markets. No serious effort to establish a U.S. market could be attempted from any single location, even though budget limitations might demand that only one or two regions could be exploited at any given time.

For traders in a large entity such as the United States, logistics can be a vital element to a business, and having import and export facilities and services—to say nothing of sources of information—immediately available and in juxtaposition—can be very important. For those whose imports involve subsequent exportation or even those whose imports must be held in inventory for meaningful periods of time, the availability of nearby Foreign Trade Zones (FTZs) or their foreign equivalents can be a money-saving factor as well.

Logically, our DTD rating for the United States has to be 0 because it is our home base and because doing business domestically is the standard against which all other countries or regions are measured, even though it may not always be that easy.

Our third-largest trading partner, Mexico, is also the third participant in NAFTA. According to the DOC in 1993, 85 percent of the overseas production of manufactured goods by foreign subsidiaries of U.S. companies is not in Mexico, but in industrialized, high-wage countries of the European Union, as well as in Canada, Japan, Australia, and New Zealand. Only the remaining 15 percent of overseas production is in low-wage areas such as the Asia-Pacific countries and Latin America. Although, as predicted, there will probably be *some* job loss to Mexico, this should only be a short-term effect and will be offset by jobs created through manufacturing for U.S. exports to Mexico. The unanticipated Mexican peso crisis of December 1994 makes it harder to predict the timing of the long-term effects of NAFTA. However, the early signs of a fairly fast recovery in Mexico and the continued strength of exports to Mexico (1995 exports were not anticipated to reflect any increase, and possibly a loss, over 1994, but nonetheless to show a substantial increase over pre-NAFTA 1993), help most economists stand by their original convictions that NAFTA will provide many new jobs in all three countries over the next five years.

When you consider the fact that the Mexican economy is just one-twentieth the size of the U.S. economy, and take a look at the favorable balance of trade in most product areas, it is clear that NAFTA will have far more effect on Mexico than it will on the United States. Economists believe that some of the industries expressing the greatest anxiety about job dislocation—among them, the automotive industry, agriculture, and possibly the textile industry—will actually experience a net gain after initial dislocations. It is acknowledged that Mexican clothing manufacturers crave U.S. textiles, and there are many great success stories among our agricultural exporters to Mexico. Telecommunications and infrastructure projects will surely gain, as will the service industries typified by financial services, insurance, and transportation. Intellectual property rights will be easier to control, which will be a major help to our high-tech industries.

On the other hand, while the crisis that might have occurred if NAFTA had not been consummated has been averted, NAFTA's possible failure to develop successfully and along the lines anticipated would have grave consequences for Mexico's promising, though currently shaky, political and economic future. There would be a real chance of a backlash that might even encourage an "anti-Yankee" syndrome. In the long run, a failed NAFTA would further destabilize Mexico. At the least it would mean real problems for Mexico's economy and its standard of living as Mexico struggles to overcome the economic and per capita income problems created by the peso devaluation. *Euromoney Magazine* ranks Mexico the fifty-second best risk out of 187 nations, down from forty-fourth prior to the crisis. Its country-risk ranking is superior to all of Latin America except Chile and Columbia. Eximbank, moreover, makes available credit insurance, loans, and guarantees to Mexico without restrictions for both short- and long-term transactions, except for the commercial risk represented by the individual buyer. What political risks there are, therefore, can be covered.

Mexico has long been our third-largest trading partner, and with its 20 million middle-class consumers, it surpassed Japan in 1992 to become our second-largest and fastest-growing export market for manufactured goods, even though Japan's total purchases exceeded Mexico's as a result of agriculture exports. Its consumers like U.S. labels and merchandise and spend 15 cents of each dollar of per capita income on U.S. goods compared to 2 cents in Japan and the European Union. Even though still surpassed by exports, imports from Mexico also set a record high in 1994. For the immediate future, however, imports are expected to rise faster than exports.

Despite the blame that former President Carlos Salinas de Gortari must accept today, many of Mexico's economic reforms were thanks to the Salinas administration, under which Mexico joined GATT and diligently worked to reduce tariffs, encourage investment, and promote trade with the United States. It is too bad that the closing portion of the Salinas presidency was so weakened by a number of factors, including corruption, symbolized by his chosen successor's assassination.

In terms of the export effort required, Mexico gets a 3.5 on the DTD rating. It might be a 3 but for the current crisis and social unrest. Many fail to realize what a huge nation Mexico is. With more than 81 million people, it has the world's eleventh-largest population—more than any European country. In terms of its economy, it is fifteenth in the world—larger than Taiwan or South Korea—and with bounteous natural resources, including oil. In addition, its *parallel economy*—that is, that portion of the nation's internal business done unofficially and without reports—amounts to over 25 percent of the official GDP figures according to an excellent new source of information on the subject, *Business International's Guide to Doing Business in Mexico*.[5] Mexico still falls short of fulfilling its potential, but the reformed government's new approach to economics and trade will provide substantial improvements. Privatization is proceeding swiftly, trade barriers are dropping rapidly, and intellectual property rights protection is improving.

For most export-minded companies, Mexico, as with most of Latin America, is a market of great potential, a potential now enhanced by the existence of NAFTA. Eventually, there is the possibility that the entire Western Hemisphere may become one giant trading region, unmatched elsewhere in the world, with an opportunity to make real progress toward a better balance of education, job opportunities, and middle-class wealth for our southern neighbors. It is a long-term vision, but such a development would go far to alleviate frictions and immigration problems, as well as help stabilize the impressive conversion to democratic forms of government that has already occurred in much of Latin America, albeit on a rather tenuous basis in some cases.

Central America

This bridge to South America has long been an area of turmoil and sudden reversals in both political and economic fortunes. Costa Rica has been an outstanding exception to this rule, with a well-established history of democracy and nonviolence. Coincidentally, it is our number 1 customer in the region. Elsewhere in Central America, public sector political risks are fairly high, though largely insurable, at least for the short term. Despite the risks, the region as a whole will always be one of our most natural markets and an important source of our tropical imports. The political and financial disasters that began in the early 1980s severely reduced our trade relationships, but that trend is reversing in response to a clear tilt toward democracy, despite occasional setbacks. Today, with the exception of Nicaragua, all of Central America can be viewed as a fruitful secondary export market. The pump-priming effect of infrastructure development can stimulate job creation in Central America in the course of improving a largely disastrous transportation system, which will aid both the internal and external trade economies. The growth of U.S. exports to nonindustrialized countries is reflected here most of all, with U.S. exports to Central American countries totalling $6.7 billion in 1994. This figure, which had doubled in size over a five-year period, represented our largest regional increase in the world. Imports kept pace during this period as well.

Collectively, the nations of Central America constitute one of our best export markets, whether considered in relation to landmass, population, or gross domestic product. This is because on a per capita basis they are strong users of U.S. products and U.S. brands. Costa Rica's annual consumption of U.S. products is $460 per capita, which exceeds that of European countries like France ($216) and the United Kingdom ($422), or good Asian customers like Japan and Korea, ranging lower still. It is also very much better than that of the large South American countries, where Argentinians buy $105 per capita and Brazilians a mere $37, for example.

Costa Rica's economy has sustained a 3 percent growth rate or better over the last few years. It is our largest customer in Central America and represents about 25 percent of our trade in the region. It is said to offer special opportunities in the areas of computers and peripherals, food processing equipment, and machine tools. Guatemala is also a frequently overlooked market, with a high per capita total consumption rate of $1268. It is our second-largest trading partner and the largest economy in Central America. However, the country's emphasis on agriculture, combined with a small but dominant ruling class, creates a narrow consumer base. The best opportunities are said to be in agricultural equipment, food processing equipment, air conditioning, and refrigeration.

Panama, another high per capita consumer of U.S. merchandise, is our third-largest trading partner in the region. Both Costa Rica and Panama are attracting U.S. investors, and Panama is unique in that it uses the U.S. dollar exclusively.

Depending on the country, many of the typical range of leading American exports worldwide are in demand. This range includes: building and construction materials, air conditioning, medical equipment, telecommunications, power generation equipment, textile and apparel machinery, computers and peripherals, agriculture equipment, food processing equipment, and consumer products. All the countries must be considered individually in spite of their small size and proximity, for they have widely varying cultures and characteristics that require differing marketing approaches, especially in the consumer product areas. In the poorer countries the emphasis should be on early-generation high-tech products and basic industrial machinery, typified by generating equipment.

The Central American Common Market (CACM—also called CAM by some), was originally formed in the 1960s to include Mexico, but it was never very effective and ceased to be operative as wars and revolution broke out in the 1980s. Reestablished in 1991, it no longer includes Mexico, which is currently focused on NAFTA, but it does include all the Central American countries except Panama and Belize.

Panama is exceptional in many ways, partly because it uses the U.S. dollar and partly because of the U.S. military influence emanating from the Canal Zone. Also, some Panamanians prefer to think of themselves as more related to South America than Central America. Belize, as a former British Colony, is culturally very different from the region and is also very small, with a population of only 200,000. CACM is reviving its active role and has already eliminated tariffs on 95 percent of its intertrade products. The remaining tariffs range from 5 to 20 percent, compared to some tariffs of over 100 percent prior to 1991. This tariff reduction represents a meaningful opportunity for American businessmen.

CACM's economic impact as a trading bloc or common market is limited, however, because it cannot exceed the sum of its parts. A vastly differing cluster of economic profiles also has its impact on CACM's future success. This is best illustrated by the broad variety of GNP per capita that ranges from $2580 in Panama to $580 and $360 respectively, in Honduras and Nicaragua.

Even though it is not part of CACM, Mexico can play a vital and trusted supporting role and help CACM achieve its most important function as a solidifying link in the hemispheric economic chain. It, together with the United States' Enterprise for the Americas Initiative (EAI) will hopefully encourage the formation of bilateral trade agreements throughout the hemisphere, still with the long-range objective of a Western Hemisphere free trade area.

Because of the small landmass involved, political unrest in one spot quickly spreads to many, so keeping a watchful eye on the political stability within the countries of your trade relationships in this area of the world will always be prudent. Payment conditions are critical and varied, as illustrated by *Euromoney*'s country-risk rankings. The magazine places Costa Rica at number 76, with most of the other countries ranging from 83 to 101. Nicaragua, Central America's poorest country, is number 165 out of 187.

We award our DTD rating of 5 to the region overall, with a range of 4 in the case of Costa Rica to 7 or 8 in the case of Nicaragua.

The Caribbean

This is a diverse and difficult area to understand. Its people speak several languages, depending on their particular colonial history, and represent a wide variety of economic interests and priorities. As with many of the less developed countries, each former colonial power left not only a language, but also a preference for certain associated products associated with it, especially in the case of France, England, and Spain. This factor should be taken into account, for some markets can be in very close proximity with an outwardly similar population and yet present a totally different challenge and range of preferences. Here, too, is a part of the world where one must look especially closely at specific products by country statistics to be sure that you are not misled by a country's import of parts brought in for labor intensive processes, such as sewing, and then exported again as finished product. The statistics sometimes seem to indicate an export or import activity where there is none, except for an intercompany transaction.

We have listed virtually all the primary islands of the Caribbean, even though 11 of the 24 listed are not independent states, nations, or republics. (The mother country is indicated in parentheses.) This seemed necessary to help make sense of the geography of this island region, which is dominated geographically by the Greater Antilles, beginning off the tip of Florida with the larger islands of Cuba and Jamaica, plus Haiti and the Dominican Republic on Hispaniola Island, and finally Puerto Rico. To the south and east lie the Lesser Antilles, including the Leeward and Windward Islands, composed of smaller islands where most of the colonies or dependencies are to be found, plus the Dutch-owned Netherlands Antilles, including primarily the islands of Curaçao and Aruba, as one circles back to the west off the coast of Venezuela. The overall region, including the Bahamas is sometimes referred to as the West Indies.

The Carribean represents $4.6 billion in manufactures' exports and $3.3 billion in the U.S. imports, making our trade with this area similar in size to that with Central America. If total exports are considered, the Caribbean totaled $6.3 billion in 1992, compared to $5.4 billion in Central America. Outside of Puerto Rico, which naturally is not included in foreign trade statistics, by far the highest level of business is with the Dominican Republic (in part as a result of interim manufacturing operations), followed by Jamaica and the Bahamas in weak second and third positions respectively. A much-larger-than-normal share of trade with the tourist-oriented islands is focused on hotel and restaurant supplies and tourist consumer goods. The native population largely lives in desperate poverty. Cuba was once the heart of the Caribbean trade and, hopefully, will be again someday after the fall of Castro who currently manages to sustain it as one of the few remaining bastions of hard-core Communism.

To our surprise, some consider the Dominican Republic to be an overlooked market. Its growth has been erratic and economic reforms slow or nonexistent, but its champions point out that the free trade zone manufacturing sector has grown dramatically, thanks in part to the Caribbean Basin Initiative (CBI). Furniture to serve the tourism industry, a growing demand for better medical equipment, and textile machinery for an expanding apparel industry are considered to be highlights.

As for Trading Pacts in the Caribbean, there is the Caribbean Community (CARICOM) composed of 11 English-speaking island countries, plus Guyana and Belize, although it is not likely that now or in the near future the organization will have much impact on world trade. Probably its primary purpose is to stimulate and simplify tourism in the area. Of considerably more importance today is the U.S. Caribbean Basin Initiative (CBI), which includes all of Central America, most of the Caribbean, and Guyana in South America. While not yet providing the economic benefits promised when first undertaken, it is making a difference through duty-free entry for many eligible products and tariff and financing preferences for others. It has served to increase trade and investment but falls short of its goals because of budget problems and the economics of U.S. regional politics relative to products such as sugar and textiles.

Needless to say, the commercial and political risks vary widely in this area, but between some with unstable political situations and the tiny size of so many, one must carefully review any credit risk in this area, just as in Central America. The country-risk rankings vary from 46 for the Bahamas to Cuba, nearly at the bottom with 183, to Antigua and Barbuda at 184. I give the area as a whole a 6 DTD rating because it represents such small individual markets and has so many sovereign credit problems. Keep in mind, however, that as in Central America, there are many businesses with excellent commercial credit ratings that need imports. Country risk is often a minor factor if the credit is very short term or

sight letters of credit are employed. This is not to say that the credit factor can be ignored, however. I remember very well a time in the mid-
1970s when some funds deposited for us against an open account were
frozen by Costa Rica's central bank. It was almost two years before they
were released.

South America

Latin America, including Central America, has a population of nearly 400
million people. Prior to 1980, the area relied heavily on the United States
for its industrial and automotive imports and a good percentage of its
imported consumer products. (Brazil and, to a lesser degree, Argentina
were less dependent on the United States than most other Latin
American nations, partly because of their more dominant European heritage. Consequently, they were more protective of their local industries
than most of South America. To a lesser extent this remains true today,
even though, thanks in part to the maturing of the trade bloc, Mercosur,
the two countries have undertaken major reforms to open their markets.)
In any event, South America overall was long a very comfortable place
for U.S. manufacturing and represented one of our best markets for manufactured goods. Regrettably, its promise in terms of market opportunities was always clouded by unreliable governments. While there continue to be economic and political problems in South America, it is
encouraging that each of the 12 independent countries now boasts a pop-
ularly elected government, even though the present state of affairs in
Venezuela brings that happy state of affairs into question. French Guiana
is still governed from France.

In the early 1980s, as Latin debt became such an overwhelming problem that foreign exchange was simply not available, U.S. traders collectively left the market and then forgot to return. The Japanese, however,
did not forget how well we had done there, and today it is difficult to
find American cars in all of South or Central America. In the last few
years, Latin America has been the source of much of our export growth,
although not in the automotive field. Despite economic and political ups
and downs, the overall trend has been toward democratic and economic
reform, including a lot of privatization. Inflation has been one of the
biggest challenges, and it has been met with various degrees of success,
but overall the results have been astounding. The ultimate success story
belongs to Argentina which went from well over 3000 percent inflation in
1989 to virtually no inflation today. As a nation, the United States must
maintain and increase its market share and penetration in South America
or risk losing our most natural long-term export market and a dominant
role in what is essentially our home trading bloc. As individuals,
Americans may not see South America as their first target market. But
they should consider it very seriously as their second or third target mar-

ket, both in terms of long-range interests and in terms of sales potential.

Merchandise exports to South America exceeded $30.3 billion in 1994. This figure, though much less than the $50.8 billion in exports to Mexico alone, indicates that it is a very significant and promising market. The U.S. National Export Strategy has targeted Brazil and Argentina as two of its 10 "big emerging markets" worldwide.

A major contributor to the overall strength of South America as a trading partner is the region's most active and successful trading bloc, Mercosur, sometimes referred to as the Southern Common Market or the Southern Cone Group of countries. Mercosur includes Argentina, Uruguay, Paraguay, and Brazil. Many people believe that Chile will ultimately join the group. Mercosur planned to reduce external tariffs to a range of 0 to 20 percent by 1995. Under pressure from its largest and most dominate member, Brazil, a partial reversal of these reductions took place as a result of the flood of imports and inflationary pressures created by the December 1994, Mexican peso crisis.

Mercosur's combined population amounts to more than 200 million people and its combined GDP, which is still growing rapidly, to more than $1 trillion. The bloc now represents half the total Latin American market and is one of the world's biggest trade groups. It should be noted that Mercosur considers trade with Europe to be vital, and in fact its trade with the European Union slightly exceeds that with its second-largest trade partner, the United States. The four members' internal trade has also grown rapidly, thanks to a nearly zero internal tariff. The formation of a really active and growing trading bloc such as Mercosur can mean a great deal to an exporter in terms of expanding the effectiveness and efficiency of a given distributor. Of course, it can also complicate geographical exclusivity arrangements.

Brazil still has political and economic problems, but it is the largest trading partner the United States has in the region. Brazil is our biggest supplier, selling $8.7 billion in goods to the United States, compared to $30.3 billion for all the rest of South America. It is also our largest buyer of export merchandise at $8.7 billion. Our exports to Brazil have increased 70 percent in the last five years, with major increases coming in the last two years, and Brazilians still cannot get enough computer product imports. Brazil's country-risk rating is improving and now stands at number 58 out of 187 nations.

Market reforms initiated under the administration of President Fernando Collar de Mello and broadened under the Fernando Henrique Cardoso administration have succeeded in keeping inflation under control. Tariffs were down to an average of 14 percent and continued to drop until the Mexican peso crisis. Franchising and licensing has expanded, with liberalized rules for remittance of royalties, and foreign investment is increasing rapidly. Import certificates are readily issued, a fact especially welcome in the case of computer products, which, along with many high-tech products, constitute the best market opportunities for the United States in this sophisticated marketplace. There is still concern over Brazil's treatment of intellectual property rights and it is one of three countries singled out for this abuse by the U.S. Trade Representative's Office (USTR).

Spanish is spoken throughout the countries of South America, with four exceptions. The first three are the relatively small colonial-heritage nations on the northeast cost: Guiana, where French is spoken, Suriname, where the language is Dutch, and Guyana, whose residents speak English. The fourth exception to the rule is Brazil, where the language is Portuguese. More people speak Portuguese than any other language in South America because there are more Brazilians than any other nationality in the 12 remaining countries of South America.

Argentina, for a long time something of an economic basket case, is now one of the dynamic economic darlings of South America. It is our third-biggest customer in South America and in 1992 was by far the fastest-growing, too, with a 58 percent increase in exports. Inflation appears to be under control at 19 percent (compared to over 3000 percent in the late 1980s), trade barriers are falling and are nearly gone altogether. Investment is welcomed and many state-owned companies have been, and continue to be, privatized. Argentina credits much of its current success to the very substantial tariff reductions among its neighbors as a result of the success of the Mercosur trade bloc. American businesses may not be as well entrenched in Argentina as in Venezuela, for example, but they are starting to make inroads on their Brazilian and European competition. American consumer brand names are well accepted in the stores and it is much easier to do business in the country these days, especially with the government. There is no tariff on imported capital goods, and all tariffs are reasonable in the remaining areas.

Uruguay, like Paraguay, is a fraction of Brazil's size and economic strength, but is doing well as a service and financial center. Its financial sectors are among the most modern and free on the continent. Uruguay is reported to have one of the best-educated populations in South America. Paraguay is more backward and less educated than the other Mercosur countries. However, it is very open to foreign capital and is a free market economy.

The Andean Pact Group, formed in 1969 and the oldest of the Latin trade agreement groups, represents over 92 million people but has not developed as well as expected. It was recently revitalized more along trading lines, but just as its overall foreign investment and trade seemed to be blossoming, its largest member, Venezuela, slipped into financial crisis. Other trade pact groups, such as NAFTA, Mercosur, and the Caribbean group may make the Andean Group obsolete if its members cannot pull together soon. It is presently composed of Venezuela, Colombia, Ecuador, Bolivia, and Peru.

Venezuela, which has the largest economy of the Andean Group but not the largest population, was South America's second-largest buyer of U.S. manufactured exports. However, continuing economic deterioration under authoritarian leadership that took power in a 1992 coup have caused it to sink to fourth place. Its 1994 GDP growth rate was slightly negative, and its poor showing threatens the long-term success of the Andean Pact Group. Earlier reforms and privatization have stalled, and inflation, which dropped from the 80 percent range in the late 1980s, is now very much on the rise again as Venezuela's financial system approaches collapse. Communications can be a problem, and the country is weak where intellectual property rights are concerned. There continue to be severe economic inequities between rich and poor which is placing a strain on stability. Venezuela's *Euromoney* country-risk ranking has fallen from 51 in 1992 to 67 in early 1995. It is therefore surprising that many U.S. firms that have invested in the country expect to stay on for what they feel will be an eventual turnaround and do not seem to be as concerned as one might expect.

Colombia is now the third-largest U.S. customer in South America (very close in exports to Argentina), thanks to having had some huge increases in export purchases in recent years. Inflation is coming down and in 1994 was expected to be in the 20 percent range. It is in good standing with the world financial community, with the second-best country-risk rating in South America to prove it. It has had an ongoing economic liberalization program since 1990, and tariffs have been consolidated into four groups: 5, 10, 15, and 20 percent. Unfortunately, because of drug problems, it is still wise to check for U.S. State Department travel advisories before visiting the country.

In the case of Peru, while there are still some concerns, most observers believe they will resolve in the foreseeable future. Consequently, Peru is a current favorite for increased U.S. investment in Latin America, with a GDP growth rate that is the best of the Andean Group. The regional debt crisis is diminishing, and financiers are generally bullish on the area. Many companies are being privatized, and the economy is strengthening as inflation subsides from 7000 percent to at least workable levels in the range of 50 percent. Country risk is dramatically improved, with a *Euromoney* ranking of 93, down from 128 in 1992. But for its size and GDP, Peru is not a very exciting export market at $1.4 billion. Ecuador is smaller still, but with similar export and import figures, and Bolivia has a relatively tiny economy and imports very little from the United States.

Chile remains the wild card in South America's trading bloc alliances, belonging to neither Mercosur nor the Andean Pact Group. It can afford to be independent for the time being, with its great natural resources and its advanced state of economic reform. Chile is considered the best economy in South America. Its country-risk rating is accordingly ranked first among all Latin countries at 39 and carries an equally favorable assessment for its future potential. It is also considered free of corruption and one of the easiest countries in which to do business. Chile is seen as a safe and stable haven for foreign direct investment, in part as a result of a growing GDP and falling inflation. Privatization is complete, and the country seeks bilateral trade agreements while expressing a desire to support the U.S. Enterprise for America Initiative (EAI). Chile's agreement with Mexico has led to a 49 percent two-way trade increase. Foreign countries have the same legal rights as domestic companies in Chile, and tariffs are down to 11 percent. A free trade agreement with the United States is a possibility; it could reduce tariffs to zero by 1998.

South America is now taking its trading alliances very seriously. Most of them have as a prime objective the elimination of tariffs within the bloc. In addition to Mercosur and the Andean Group, there is the Latin American Integration Association (LAIA), which includes the 10 largest economies of South America, plus Mexico. (It excludes Central America.) LAIA was formed as an instrument to assist the organization of bilateral and multilateral tariff agreements, rather than as a trade bloc unto itself. It has been only moderately active. Trading blocs will increasingly affect marketing strategies for South America. Except for Guyana, a former British colony, Suriname, a Dutch territory, and French Guiana, which France considers a part of France, every country in South America is affiliated with one trade group or another. More trading groups are already in a negotiation and formation process.

In summary, while the newcomer will find many more surprises in South America than in Canada or Western Europe, it may just be that some of the disincentives to exporters and their importers are more transparent than in the case of some of our more sophisticated trading partners. South America represents a key area for international trade and can either be a foundation stone for any worldwide market approach or sufficient unto itself. Don't let political risk rankings overcome a logical and reasoned interest in the region. As is true of most of Latin America, and even the Caribbean, good solid repeat business is being carried on every day, and ways are being found to secure or ensure the regular business. It is recommended that business be done through confirmed letters of credit in most cases, if at all possible, except in very well-established situations. If not, consider the fact that in most countries Eximbank or other insurance is available if the business continuity and/or magnitude warrants it. All things considered, we give South America as a region our DTD rating of 4.5. As in most regions, there are diversities, such as the drug-based crime problems and accompanying travel risks in Colombia that might raise it to a 5, or the current political and financial instability in Venezuela that would raise it to a 5 or above, if not soon corrected.

Compare the current import/export statistics and growth rates for this region to some others in Europe and elsewhere that often receive so much more attention, and you will see why we say that in some ways

South America is one of our best, easiest, and most natural trading regions. Large increases are occurring in the short term, and for much of the area the long-term future is very bright right here in our own Western Hemisphere. So, go north *and* south young man and woman!—to paraphrase Horace Greeley's famous statement of many years ago.

Endnotes

1. Kenneth C. Davis, *Don't Know Much About Geography*, William Morrow, New York, 1992.

2. *Euromoney*, Euromoney Publications, PLC, Nestor House, Playhouse Yard, London, EC4Y 5EX. Note that the country risk rankings published by *Euromoney* include the following factors, each worth 10 points if perfect, except for the factor of political risk which is worth 20 points. The factors considered are (1) economic performance; (2) political risk; (3) various debt ratios as used by bankers in all forms of lending; (4) access to three basic forms of sovereign credit—bank, trade finance, and long-term finance; (5) forfaiting (a medium-term form of trade finance) discount rate; (6) credit rating (based on the rating by Standard & Poor's or Moody's for lenders considering a medium- or long-term loan to the country on the country's signature alone); and (7) debt in default or rescheduled. It is not necessary to understand all that goes into the rank, and we only mention it to indicate the complexity of analyzing country risk. For speed and comprehension, when referring to these rankings, I often do so by specifying one of the four quartiles into which I divided the 169 rankings, the first quartile being 1 through 42, and so forth. It is interesting to observe that after the first quartile countries, the forty-third and most of those in the three remaining quartiles score zero on the credit rating factor because their Moody credit rating is below BB—which is normally the minimum required to secure medium-term sovereign bank credit without collateral.

3. *International Marketing*, Erik Wicklund, McGraw-Hill, New York, 19XX.

4. *Export Today*, June 1993,

5. Gray Newman and Anna Szterenfeld, *Business International's Guide to Doing Business in Mexico*, New York, McGraw-Hill, Inc., 1993.

7
Where in the World?

Europe and Africa

Europe

Western Europe

EFTA and EU. The countries listed in Table 7-1 as being part of Western Europe include all those with membership in the European Free Trade Agreement (EFTA) or the European Union (EU). The European Union, it should be explained, has only been known by that name since 1993 when, following the Treaty of Maastricht, the members of the European Community (EC) adopted the new appellation to indicate the more binding nature of their association. While the word *Union* has caused some debate, just as the treaty itself continues to do, the EU clearly stretches the boundaries of Western Europe as they are understood today and will stretch them still further in the future.

Western Europe is composed entirely of either EU or EFTA countries and, with the exception of Greece, Finland, and Iceland, no countries from other geographic designations are members of the EU or EFTA. Iceland, which is an EFTA nation, has been shoehorned into our Western Europe list. Some geographers include Iceland as part of Scandinavia because it was formerly a Danish colony and is therefore Scandinavian by language group as well as by general global location. In any case, Iceland is of very minor economic significance, importing only $119 million from the U.S. Of even less significance is another island, Greenland, a Danish territory and the largest island in the world north of Iceland, with a population under 50,000. I mention Greenland under the overall heading of "Europe"—just as I included Antarctica in the overall list of countries—in a spirit of inclusivity, because it cannot be overlooked on the world map.

Table 7-1. The Geographic/Political World Order of Nations:
Europe

Areawide DTD	Country exception DTD[1]	Region and country	Trade bloc membership[2]
		Greenland[3] (Denmark)	
2.5		*Western Europe*	
		Scandinavia	
	∧	Iceland[4]	EFTA
		Norway	EFTA
		Sweden	EU
	∧	Finland[5] (politically)	EU
		Denmark	EU
		Ireland	EU
	∨	United Kingdom (British Isles)	EU
		Jersey (Britain)	
		Guernsey (Britain)	
		France	EU
		Monaco	
		Netherlands	EU
		Luxembourg } Benelux Countries	EU
		Belgium	EU
		Germany	EU
		Switzerland[6]	EFTA
		Liechtenstein	EFTA
		Austria	EU
		Portugal	EU
		Andorra[6]	
		Spain	EU
		Gibraltar (Britain)	
	∧	Italy	EU
		Vatican City[6]	
		San Marino	
		Malta (Island)	
	3.5	Greece[7] (politically)	EU
5		*Central Europe*	
	3	Finland (geographically)	EU
		Baltic States	
		Estonia	
	∧	Latvia	
	∧	Lithuania	
	∨	Poland	
	∨	Czech Republic	
		Slovakia	
		Hungary	
		Balkan States	
		Slovenia	
	6	Croatia	
	8	Bosnia and Herzogovina[8]	
	8	Serbia and Montenegro (de facto Yugoslavia)[9]	
	7	Macedonia[6,10]	

Table 7-1. The Geographic/Political World Order of Nations:
Europe (Continued)

Areawide DTD	Country exception DTD[1]	Region and country	Trade bloc membership[2]
		Balkan States (*Continued*)	
	6	Albania	
	^	Romania	
	^	Bulgaria	
	3.5	Greece (geographically)	EU
	4	Turkey[11] (an EU candidate)	ECO
6–8		*Eastern Europe*	
	6	Russia[12] (European portion)	
	^	Belarus	
		Ukraine	
		Moldova	
		Caucasus region	
		Georgia[6]	
		Armenia[6]	
		Azerbaijan	ECO

[1]Where a country differs materially from the regional Degree of Trading Difficulty scale, it is indicated by a separate DTD rating for that country. Alternatively, when the difference is not so great or adequate information is not available for a separate rating, the distinction is indicated by: a ^ for a greater DTD ranking (more difficult trading); and by a v for a lesser DTD ranking (easier trading).

[2]The full versions of all the abbreviated trade bloc titles are as follows:
EFTA = European Free Trade Association
EU = European Union
ECO = Economic Cooperation Organization

[3]Greenland, important only for its landmass, certainly not its economic impact or its population of 52,000 people, is the world's largest island, or its second-largest if one considers Australia to be an island rather than a continent, as some do. Greenland is the closest landmass of consequence to the North Pole and, of course, forms part of the boundary of the Arctic Ocean, together with the most northern portions of Siberia and Canada's northern islands. We have listed it under the European heading only because it is a territory of Denmark, but it could arguably be held to be more in the Western Hemisphere.

[4]Iceland is an island and is not part of Scandinavia, but by virtue of its former status as a Danish territory and because of its culture and language, geographers often include it with the Scandinavian countries.

[5]Finland is another country sometimes arbitrarily included in Scandinavia as a Nordic country, even though it is not on the Scandinavian Peninsula. It is in many ways Scandinavian in culture and politics. It is also a member of EU. It makes use of two languages: Swedish and Finnish. Finland shares a border with Russia and has very close economic ties to it, having served as a primary trade link between East and West during the Cold War. It was even once a Russian territory. It is also seen, however, as a Baltic nation, along with the three NIS Baltic nations of Estonia, Latvia, and Lithuania. I have therefore shown Finland in both the Western Europe and Central Europe categories, but for trading purposes have ranked it as part of Western Europe and the EU.

[6]Independent nations or states not members of the United Nations.

(Continued)

Table 7-1. The Geographic/Political World Order of Nations:
Europe (Continued)

---

[7]Greece, because of its role as a cradle of Western Civilization, because of the Mediterranean heritage it shares with Portugal, Spain, and Italy, and because of its membership in the EU, seems more oriented to Western Europe and is therefore ranked with the countries of Western Europe. It cannot, however, seem to free itself from its relations and conflicts with the Balkans—as evidenced by the present concerns over Macedonia—nor liberate itself from its problems with Turkey. Geographically, it cannot escape the Balkan Peninsula and shares its border with Turkey (which also occupies a small segment of the Balkan Peninsula). I have therefore shown Greece a second time under Central Europe, even though it is not so ranked for trading.

[8]Bosnia and Herzegovina was the focus of the Dayton Agreement of 1995 which attempted to settle the wars in the Balkans. The settlement created one country in theory but of two entities—the Herzegovina portion being recognized as the Federation of Bosnia and Herzegovina, composed of Bosnian Muslims and the Bosian Croats, the latter being primarily Roman Catholic. The remaining portion is called the Republic of Srpska and is composed of Bosnian Serbs, primarily of the Orthodox Church. Although Croatia (Roman Catholic) was at times involved in the fighting in this area, the Croatian borders remained much as they were defined as a province within the former Yugoslavia.

[9]Serbia and Montenegro is officially known as the Federal Republic of Yugoslavia but is more often referred to under the name of Serbia or Serbia and Montenegro. The Serbs of this region are closely related and comfortable with the Montenegrans. It most nearly represents Yugoslavia of the pre-Balkan War period.

[10]Macedonia is not yet recognized as an independent nation by a majority of countries and as of early 1996 is officially listed by the U.S. Department of State as the "Former Yugoslav Republic of Macedonia." It is most generally thought that it will continue its independence and its ultimate name will be something like New Macedonia.

[11]Turkey is the bridge between Asia and Western/Central Europe. The seat of the old Ottoman Empire, Istanbul (formerly Constantinople and one-time seat of Christianity) on the European side is the gateway on the Bosporus, connecting the Black Sea with the Aegean and Mediterranean Seas. To the east of the Bosporus begins Asia Minor, a term less used today, which we consider part of Southwest Asia, or the Middle East, this is where I have placed Turkey for purposes of ranking its DTD. Given Turkey's foothold in Europe on the west side of the Bosporus and its candidacy for the EU, I have also listed it with the countries of Western Europe, even though it is a very eastern nation for that body in political and geographic terms.

[12]Russia, even now, continues to be the one country decisively spanning both Europe and Asia, with ports on the Baltic for access to the Atlantic Ocean and Vladivostok in the Sea of Japan for the Pacific. It cannot be contained within the normal landmass definitions unless you choose to call the continent *Eurasia,* as some do, in place of defining both Europe and Asia as two separate continents, which they once were. The Ural Mountains, the Ural River, and the Caspian Sea are usually considered the demarcation between European Russia and Siberian Russia. The fact is, the Ural mountains were formed by what must have been a gigantic collision of the Asian and European continental plates. For purposes of this list, we have listed Russia once as European Russia and again as Siberian Russia under East Asia.

Geographically, Greece is a bit of an anomaly as an EU member, even though economically it makes more sense to include Greece than it does to include Portugal. From the standpoint of location only, Greece would seem to belong with the Balkan countries of Central Europe. But given its historical role as the birthplace of Western Civilization and its long involvement in Western European politics and trade, Greece's membership in the EU seems less strange. The same might be said of Finland as a member of EFTA. In many ways it is Scandinavian, or at least Nordic, but it is a former Russian territory abutting Russia's northwestern border directly east of Sweden and Norway across the Gulf of Bothnia. Swedish and Finnish are both considered its native languages, although Finnish is a Uralic language primarily related to Estonian in the Baltics and, more remotely, to Hungarian. In the case of both Greece and Finland, I have solved the problem of where to place them by listing them twice—once as part of Western Europe and once as part of Central Europe.

A final exception and explanation is called for in the case of Jersey and Guernsey in the Channel Islands. Lying between England and France, near Cherbourg, they are semi-dependencies of Great Britain but have their own legislature and a separate administrative, fiscal, and legal system. This permits them to benefit independently from their role as offshore money centers, free of any EU constraints by virtue of a treaty negotiated at the time of Great Britain's entry into the EU. They are enjoying considerable success in this regard and each boasts a substantial number of registered international corporations: about 30,000 in Jersey and 16,000 in Guernsey. They are in competition with tax haven counterparts like Luxembourg, Liechtenstein, Gibraltar, and Monaco, the Isle of Man, the Cayman Islands, and the Virgin Islands.

The remaining EFTA countries are potentially future members of the EU. Switzerland is concerned, as always, about its historical neutrality, and, as of 1993, has declined membership. Former EFTA members Austria, Sweden, and Finland once had concerns about joining the NATO-oriented EU. However, with the Cold War behind us, these countries joined the EU in 1995, bringing its membership to 15. Hesitation about joining the EU was understandable in the case of Finland because of its ethnic, geographic, and trade ties to Russia, and because, like Austria, it had served a special role as a commercial bridge between the West and Eastern Europe during the Cold War. Both countries maintain a delicate balancing act to keep Russia's friendship. Norway, while continuing to agonize over potential membership, declined the option by popular vote on 1995. Liechtenstein's only international trade commodity is money, so its financial neutrality is foremost and it has therefore also declined to join the EU. For Iceland, EFTA membership is primarily a way of getting together with somebody—anybody. The EU problems created by a proposed common currency, the *ecu*, (proposed to become effective in 1999, with Germany, the Netherlands, and France as the first participants) and other matters contained in the agreement signed at Maastricht in January, 1993, had a good deal to do with complicating or postponing joining the EU.

Demand for Inclusion by Central and Eastern European Countries.
The EU's real problems will come with the growing demand for inclusion by the countries of Central and Eastern Europe. The Czech Republic and Slovakia, Hungary, Poland, Romania, and Bulgaria are all eager to become

participants. This possible-early-entry group would represent over 39 million people. In addition, Turkey, Malta, and Cyprus wish to join—accounting for another 61 million people. In total, the conceivable future EU population could well be 536 million people.

Russian Membership. This scenario does not include the possibility of Russian membership. In Russia's case, the EU hopes to confine future relations to a partnership and cooperative agreement as soon as stability permits. Russia's combined roles and its position straddling Europe and Asia (some would say *Eurasia*) make it an unlikely EU member, even in the EU's largest imaginable configuration. Some of the poorer and less stable countries, such as those in Central Europe, will settle for an "associate agreement," with an interim preparatory period of varying lengths depending on economic and financial status. This is already taking place. It appears that soon the common assumption, held until recently, that the EU is an entity of Western Europe will have to be discarded and concerns as to what is and is not Western Europe will no longer be pertinent.

In all probability, the more countries the EU embraces, the less likely it becomes that it will ever achieve the very close "supranational" union, in terms of currency, law, and external politics, that its strongest supporters once cherished. As a result of some recent policy overreaching by EU leadership and resentment concerning Germany's insistence on high interest rates, hopes for the close bonding of EU fiscal policies previously anticipated have dimmed and popular support for a stronger union and a common currency has waned.

EU Market. The EU has overly dominated our commercial attention in recent years at the expense of other areas in the world, especially Asia and Latin America. The EU-15 (a term sometimes used to differentiate the former EU of 12 nations from the current composition of 15 with the addition of Finland, Austria, and Sweden) market is greater than the U.S. market but smaller than the NAFTA (North American) market. In 1994 total U.S. exports of goods to the EU-15 were $108 billion. Imports were $144 billion, with the balance of trade shifting slightly in favor of the EU as of 1994. The EU's GDP is $6.9 trillion—slightly larger than that of the U.S.—and its population is close to 370 million—110 million more than our own. While some worry that the EU will attempt to restrict external trade, that is most unlikely and would be very self-defeating for the EU. Of more importance will be its impact on marketing strategies in Europe, including distribution patterns and agreements. The Treaty of Rome, which is the foundation of the EU, prohibits exclusive distribution agreements within the EU in many cases, although smaller exporters should note there are *de minimis* exemptions waiving this restriction. (*De minimis* means that your product or market share may be too small to be of concern relative to pricing or other monopolistic practices.)

ISO 9000 Requirements. Another issue that will create some real problems for many newcomers to the market—or at least demand their careful attention—is the ISO 9000 EU standard testing and certification requirements for regulated products and services. These are intended eventually to cover many service providers and most manufactured product categories. The EU is making rapid progress in implementing them, and this is being done in cooperation with the International Organization for Standardization (ISU), including the American National Standards Institute (ANSI). A large portion of the standards are already well established. Hopefully, once agreed upon, they will have the effect of making at least this area of international trade rules and regulations more transparent and clearly understood, not only in Europe, but worldwide. A firm considering doing business in the EU on a meaningful scale—or any forward-looking firm, whether its business targets are domestic or foreign—should consider ISU certification. Many elements of it are said to have a very positive impact on profits and internal organization as well. Once you have met or exceeded the ISO 9000 standards, you will have a product technically acceptable almost anywhere in the world, including the United States, which continues to be an important contributor to the standards development. Call the DOC Single Internal Market Information Service (SIMIS), at 202/482-5276 (check this number with TIC), for a listing of business guides available. If you have the EU standards reference number for your product, call the American National Standards Institute, at 212/642-4900, to obtain copies of the standards, or ask your trade association.

Homogeneity of EU. One real danger of the evolving EU market is a tendency to assume that, because of its lack of cross-border rules and regulations, its lack of internal tariffs, and its adoption of common minimum standards, the EU will be a homogeneous market. Even with the present EU-15 nations, this is far from true. As the EU continues to grow it will become even less so, as a moment's study of the countries applying for membership will tell you. The demographics vary dramatically from Ireland to Greece and from Portugal to Finland. Even though the overall cost of marketing and distribution in Europe will be reduced, no single promotion package can be expected to do the job for the entire market.

Individual Countries. Let's now take a look at some of the individual countries on the Western Europe list, beginning with the United Kingdom. Our fourth-largest customer worldwide, the U.K. is our largest EU customer, with $26.8 billion in total 1994 exports, which include every imaginable product range. Next is that economic giant, sometimes called the EU locomotive, Germany, with $19.2 billion in exports, but with less interest in the consumer goods area and more in high-tech products than the United Kingdom evidences. Even though Germany is the third-largest economy in the world, with a GDP of $1.9 trillion, the United States regularly experiences a substantial German trade deficit. This is in part because Germany is suffering from its enormous task of absorbing and privatizing the former East Germany, whose economy was extremely weak and inefficient. While the mechanics of this task are now largely complete, many of its social ramifications are still to be worked through.

With a fairly stable economy, France, also one of the major industrialized economies, has had better success in recent years than most of its European neighbors. In 1995, however, it experienced a series of strikes and other problems as it attempted to diminish its budget deficits and increase its monetary strengths in preparation for the EU common currency adjustments. U. S. exports to France in 1994 were $13.6 billion and imports were $17.3 billion.

The Netherlands, a major distribution center for Europe and a major customer at $13.6 billion, is followed by Belgium/Luxembourg at $11.1 billion. Belgium is the home of Brussels, the capital of the EU. Luxembourg is a very good market for upscale consumer goods. The smallest customer in the EU is Greece, at under $830 million in 1994. Even though its economy is struggling, its country-risk ranking falls well within the first quartile, and it has considerable potential for exporters involved in its major infrastructure projects. Portugal is another place where the United States is enjoying good business with infrastructure project exports as the country successfully labors to establish its role as a full-fledged member of the EU. U.S. exports to Portugal increased by a dramatic 29 percent in 1992 and have continued to grow. Austria has an extremely high per capita GDP of $21,000. Besides being a good market in its own right for computer software, electronics, and industrial chemicals, it is an important staging area for business with Central and Eastern Europe, which have long been Austria's commercial specialty.

Scandinavia's economics were not very good overall in 1993–1994, and that was reflected in our sharply declining exports to the area. Norway, the country that surprised and upset many of its neighbors by voting to decline membership in the EU, has shown some recent economic improvement. Finland also has been doing better, while Sweden, our largest customer in Scandinavia at $2.5 billion, has commenced a reform process and is embracing freer trade that should pay off in the long run. As of today, however, its economy and trade remain disappointing.

Summary.   In summary, even though exports to Western Europe in total have been stagnant or even declined in some countries in the last few years, the EU and all of Western Europe is our largest cohesive market in terms of being relatively easy to access and understand. Overall, therefore, Europe receives a DTD rating of 2.5 or 3. Considered separately, the United Kingdom, Germany, and the Netherlands would each merit a 2. These ratings assume that the stagnant or downtrading areas will reverse this trend in the normal course of business cycles. All the nations of Western Europe are considered excellent in terms of country risk and fall within the first quartile of *Euromoney*'s rankings, ranging from Luxembourg at number 1 to Italy at 22 and Greece at 39.

Of course, the problems encountered will vary by product and competition as always, and will partly be governed by culture. Even at the heart of the very Western EU culture, it can readily be seen that it is easier to sell in the English-speaking United Kingdom than it is in Italy. Scandinavian countries are much more amenable to Californian color schemes and outdoor styles than many other Europeans, for example. Germany is usually intrigued by most American styling in consumer products but often does not approve of our quality. France is often resistant to things American, from clothing to wine, although in recent years the French have become hooked on some of America's teen and young fashion fads and athletic-related clothing. To repeat: the countries of Europe, whether members of the EU, participants in EFTA, or independents, have widely differing market characteristics, and you must analyze each one separately just as carefully as you would have done before there was an EU.

Central Europe

As we look at Central Europe, composed primarily of former USSR satellite states, we begin to see a much greater degree of difficulty for international trade in general and exports to the region in particular. Greece and Finland, already discussed as EU members in the context of Western Europe, will not be considered here.

Poland, the Czech Republic, Slovakia, Hungary, and Estonia represent the best of Central Europe economically. At the other end of the spectrum are impoverished Albania and the war-torn fragments of the former Yugoslavia. Bosnia and Herzogovina, Serbia and Montenegro, and Croatia are prime examples, among too many in the world, of internecine strife born of ethnic and religious differences. Hopefully, the tide of tribal hate that engulfed the Serbs, Muslims, and Croats for four bloody years will now subside as the U.S.–brokered Dayton Peace Agreement takes hold. In this traditionally fractious area of Europe, however—as well as in many other hotspots throughout the world—the best products for export are probably armaments—not a subject for this book.

Commercial Opportunities in Central Europe.   Apart from the Balkans, there are many good commercial opportunities in Central Europe if a way can be found around the problems of distribution, logistics, and payment. Exporting to Poland, the Czech Republic, Slovakia, and Hungary can be a reasonable process because good banking and monetary structures are in place or have begun to take shape. Poland (one of the U.S. National Export Strategy's "big emerging market" targets), is the largest country in population and land area of the former satellite countries. In 1990 it embarked on a severe and rapid economic reform process, and it has paid off. Poland's outlook is good, although many people were disappointed by the Solidarity Party's defeat in the 1995 elections. Except for Russia, Poland is our largest customer by far in Central and Eastern Europe, purchasing about $625 million in U.S merchandise. It continues to achieve steady progress in terms of underlying economic strength, even though national wages and income remain low. The astonishing rise of a very diverse and entrepreneurial small business sector in Poland is one of the most encouraging signs of renewal. Consumer goods are among typical U.S. export products, but U.S. exporters face stiff competition as a result of Poland's tariff preference agreement with the EU. This, incidentally, is a trend our U.S. Trade Representative (USTR) negotiators must ultimately resolve in the case of many Central and Eastern European nations.

Trade fairs are a tool, increasingly available in this area, for presenting products in the marketplace. The American Business Center in Warsaw has been established to help small and midsize U.S businesses gain a foothold. Although it is not a large market, Poland, like much of the region, promises an important long-term future in terms of U.S. exports.

Romania. The second, but much smaller, export market of Central Europe in 1994 was Romania, a pleasant surprise in view of Romania's recent history and its closed borders. It was not until 1989 that it toppled one of the most isolated, confining, and repressive dictatorships in European history. Romania is the only Central European country with a Latin language and culture much more related to Italy and France than its neighbors, even though, alone among Latin countries of the world a majority of its population adheres to the Orthodox Church. Romania's recent history of repression has meant that it has not long been a target of foreign investment, unlike many of its neighbors which attracted foreign interest by undertaking some reform during the 1980s. Described as a Byzantine environment, Romania remains a difficult country to do business in, both because of its complex bureaucracy and because bribery and corruption continue to be a way of life in government. Nonetheless, there have been sweeping reforms in politics and the economy. Nearly 4000 state-owned companies were scheduled for privatization in 1995, for example, and the inflation rate, reduced from 300 percent in 1993 to 60 percent in 1994, was continuing to fall. Perhaps it should not be so surprising, therefore, to find Romania doing more business with the U.S. than do countries like Czechoslovakia and Hungary, with much more advanced financial and economic systems. It is amazing to find this small country importing $337 million in U.S. products in 1994. Its worldwide export/import trade grew at a rate exceeding 33 percent in the first half of 1995 and over half of that trade was done with the EU. With foreign investment now developing, Romania offers far more potential than one would expect, given its status as a difficult market.[1]

Hungary and the Czech Republic.   Hungary is the third-largest market after Poland and the most industrialized among its neighbors. The country's limited foreign debt relative to most of Central Europe makes credit more available. It is considered a good potential market for U.S. exports, which stood at $309 million in 1994. Hungary offers one of the most Western-like financial and commercial environments in Central and Eastern Europe. As is the case in so much of this area, the top potential products are high-tech, pollution control, and telecommunications equipment, but agricultural equipment, food processing equipment, and consumer goods may be added to the usual Central Europe list. The next-largest customer in the area is the Czech Republic, which would have been in second place but for its peaceful break with Slovakia in 1993. The breakup, however, will eventually prove to be more important for its future potential than its present sales or purchases.

The Baltic States.   The Baltic states again offer more potential than existing business, but they will be among the first to straighten out their problems if their known energies and past economic and political history of independence are anything to go on. This should be of special interest to companies seeking to invest in Central Europe, for the Baltic states represent a labor pool of hardworking and entrepreneurial people with a pre-Soviet institutional memory. Lithuania and Latvia have already signed agreements leading to associate membership in the EU, but Estonia has proved to have such an exceptionally advanced economic structure that it will be permitted to forego the usual transition period and be accepted as an associate member as soon as the agreement is ratified by all the parliaments involved.

Albania.   Albania, with its abundance of natural resources, has been an exceptionally closed and backward country, and it is therefore surprising to see it open its doors as quickly as it has to foreign investment. It is taking an aggressive approach to replace its outdated technology and equipment. This development is especially noteworthy, given Albania's severe shortage of foreign exchange and low per capita GDP. Considering the nature of the long civil war among the former territories of Yugoslavia, even with the success of the U.S.–brokered peace, it will be some time before any kind of normal commercial activity will be able to take place in that general region. Special situations will arise, but it clearly remains an area of danger as of 1996, and most observers would recommend staying away from the area for some time to come.

Risk Level and DTD Rating.   The country-risk levels obviously are much higher in Central than in Western Europe, with the Czech Republic, at number 35, being the best risk. The Czech Republic's place near the bottom of the first quartile is followed by Slovenia at the top of the second quartile and then by Hungary, Slovakia, Estonia, Romania, and Poland, with Bulgaria at the bottom of that quartile. The remainder fall into the third and even fourth quartile of rankings to include the countries consumed by civil war, which cannot even be ranked.

In terms of the DTD rating, it's a mixed bag, but I would have to rate the region as a 6 overall and thereafter assign 4–5 to the top group of states, a 6–7 to the more backward countries at peace, and 8–9 to the recent war zones.

Countertrade Techniques. With many of these countries, countertrade techniques or equally time-consuming financial arrangements are often necessary, but care must be taken that the country involved has countertrade products that will readily sell abroad. Aside from countertrade, (a whole subject unto itself, but briefly reviewed in Chapter 14), some of the exports to soft-currency countries filter through a series of intermediate currency countries by degree. Thus, they might be sold first to Hungarian traders for U.S. dollars and then resold to traders in a country like Bulgaria, which has a softer currency; the currency must be one that the Hungarian buyers/sellers can use in regular business activities in Bulgaria. A portion of this same shipment may be recycled in the same way to less and less stable currencies, so that the U.S. exporter may have indirectly reached markets that could not otherwise have been considered.

Investments. Where investments are concerned, there are many funds supported by the United States as well as by multilateral funds set up to encourage restructuring of business and production capacities. They include the following enterprise funds: Polish-American; Czech-American; Slovak-American; Bulgarian-American; Hungarian-American; and Baltic-American. Should peace ever come to the former Yugoslavia, it is expected that more hyphenated enterprise funds will be formed. Call the Trade Information Center (TIC) at 1-800-USA-TRADE for current names and addresses. Multilaterally, the World Bank supports funding for the purchase of Eastern European companies being privatized. This was the case when Germany began to privatize former East German companies. Eximbank is trying to help bring order and encourage commerce with some high-risk insurance underwriting on commercial paper and receivables, but it changes from day to day, and insurance is definitely not available for all countries. Central Europe is also an area in which the U.S. Overseas Private Investment Corporation (OPIC) is active and helpful in insuring, lending, and in some cases, even taking temporary equity positions. Here, too, the U.S. Agency for International Development (AID) is active.

Central Europe is an area in which great care as well as creativity is necessary. To get up-to-date information on available sources of help, call DOC's Eastern European Business and Information Center (EEBIC) in Washington, D.C. at 202/482-5745, and/or the Business Information

Service for the Newly Independent States (BISNIS) at 202/482-3145. If the numbers have changed, again check with TIC. Check also the frequently updated Export Hotline. (See Appendix A.)

Eastern Europe

Russia.   The list of Eastern European countries starts, of course, with Russia—and more particularly with European Russia which extends from Russia's western border in Europe eastward to the Ural Mountains, where the continents of Europe and Asia meet. The European portion of Russia encompasses about one-third or less of Russia's total territory; the remainder is located in Asia and is essentially composed of extremely resource-rich Siberia.

Newly Independent States.   After Russia, the balance of Eastern Europe is composed entirely of the former European provinces of the USSR, now referred to as the Newly Independent States (NIS). Although Russia would prefer that most of the NIS would agree to be part of the Commonwealth of Independent States (CIS), many of these new entities appear to be very skeptical or even hostile toward the CIS concept—even toward Russia itself—and are declining the honor. The European NIS (as differentiated from the Muslim-dominated NIS of Central Asia) include: Belarus (Byelorussia), the Ukraine, and Moldova, plus the Caucasus region south of the Caucasus Mountains between the Black Sea and the Caspian Sea. The Caucasus NIS countries include: Georgia, Armenia, and Azerbaijan. They are not all good neighbors, nor even settled as to political orientation, and they are rife with pockets of disputed ethnic rights, as in Armenia.

Russia is having some trouble holding onto the NIS entities (and in some cases to its own dissident republics, as in the case of Chechenya). Nonetheless, if it simply kept all of Siberia and recovered its equilibrium—and few claim that it won't—its span of territory, from the Atlantic regions to the Pacific, would qualify it as a mighty economic force. For Russia to develop both its European and Siberian components—which together occupy one-eighth of the world's landmass—it must be capable of dealing with many trading blocs and establishing close commercial ties in both Asia and Europe.

Russian Federation.   Russia, or the Russian Federation, is even now an important U.S. trading partner, buying $2.6 billion of U.S. exports and selling $3.4 billion to the United States. The federation has 150 million citizens and possesses a large share of the world's remaining resources, mainly in Siberia. Russia's weakness lies in the threat posed by its outlying provinces, which are made up of many diverse and separate ethnic groups. It isn't difficult to imagine these provinces observing the new-found independence among the NIS and concluding that such independence might be theirs to enjoy as well.

Wheat and other agricultural commodities have traditionally made up a large portion of U.S. exports to Russia. Presently, however, there is heavy demand for technology and equipment. This is expected to continue, with future increases coming in vehicles, clothing, footwear, household appliances, and similar consumer goods, including prefabricated housing. Russia's development of its huge oil and other underground natural resources has stimulated U.S. service exports in specialized engineering areas and related equipment.

Commercial centers are taking shape in many areas away from Moscow, such as Kiev, St. Petersburg, and Vladivostok. While economic trends can change rapidly, given the political uncertainties surrounding President Boris Yeltsin, Russia remains a very large country with a huge civil service trained in political objectives that tend to be self-sustaining. It is hard to know, however, what impact the underlying popular yearning for a return to some form of communism will have on this self-sustaining bureaucracy. Regardless of headline-making changes in leadership and policy, most believe a way will be found for reform to go on. It is too late now to stop the basic changes that have been set in motion; it is rather a question of speed and degree.

As with the DOC, the usual U.S. and multilateral financial agencies are at work in this area as well. Among them are Eximbank, the Overseas Private Investment Corporation (OPIC), the Trade and Development Agency (TDA) and the Agency for International Development (AID). These agencies are prepared to assist with grants and feasibility studies, investment insurance, credit support, and a host of other schemes.

Exclusive of Russia itself, all the former Soviet Republics mentioned here as part of Eastern Europe combined represent total exports of well under $500 million. The Ukraine and Belarus have been disappointing in terms of turnaround time and reform progress. Of course, political realities have brought some things to a near halt, just as in the Caucasus. The Ukraine, the second-largest NIS, with a population of 52 million and a land area similar to that of France, was supposedly less progressive, but more stable, although that distinction is now in question. It is, however, by far the largest buyer of U.S. goods of $181 million in 1994. Belarus produces machine tools, chemicals, and electronics, but is also one of the most polluted and contaminated of the NIS. The pollution arises from the use of peat for industrial fuel; the fallout from Chernobyl provides the nuclear contamination. Moldova is largely made up of ethnic Romanians and is drawn to the possibility of reunion with Romania. The leading state in the Caucasus, Georgia, possessing fewer resources but a much greater degree of sophistication, has also been a disappointment; but it is the second largest importer of U.S. goods among the European NIS. There is no question, however, that there is a great market potential there if peace can be maintained and reform with privatization continued.

The Department of Commerce is making a special effort to assist exporters in the NIS states as they are doing throughout Central and Eastern Europe. This includes the Business Information Service for the Newly Independent States (BISNIS), which is attempting to establish an Overseas Network to collect commercial intelligence and identify contacts to be published through BISNIS publications. BISNIS is also establishing a very focused intern group to serve exporters in this region. There is a Consortia of American Businesses in the NIS that will make matching grants up to $500,000 for business groups to establish a commercial presence. There is also a Market Development Cooperator Program that competitively provides up to $500,000 in matching funds over three years to trade associations in support of export of U.S. goods. And there are still-more specialized and focused programs. For information on all of this, telephone BISNIS: (202) 482-4655.

Given its political and economic chaos—to say nothing of several small wars—Eastern Europe must be seen as one of the most difficult and uncertain areas of the world in which to trade, even though it represents great potential. *Euromoney*'s country-risk assessments for most of these states are very low, placing the entire region in the fourth quartile. It may be surprising that among the NIS countries, Russia ranks slightly below Belarus and Armenia at 141, but such rankings can change rapidly for better or worse. On the positive side, Russia is clearly developing a substantial entrepreneurial class of accomplished business people. On the downside, there is the popular support for a return to a Communist-style government and/or extreme nationalism. Should this mood prevail in the 1996 elections, economic and political conditions would become very uncomfortable and unstable for some time to come. I show a DTD rating of 6 for Russia, depending on unfolding political developments there, which could drive it higher, and a 7 for most of the NIS states. With any solid trend toward stability, Russia's DTD rating would improve rapidly in view of its enormous size and potential.

Throughout the region, there is a desperate need for everything from luxuries to infrastructure necessities, but excruciatingly limited funds with which to pay. I speak not only of a paucity of hard currency in the Central Bank, but also of the poverty of the populace. By Western standards, the vast majority of Russians are very poor—poorer by far than the people of Central Europe. President Yeltsin's reform efforts, while well-intentioned, have left people poorer still, at least for the time being. Since the collapse of Russia's foreign trade bank Vneshekonombank at the end of 1991, letters of credit drawn on Russian banks have had little credibility unless confirmed in a financially strong country. Many commercial banks are reestablishing themselves, and Vneshekonombank eventually will. For now, however, only 10 percent of trade is facilitated by letters of credit, mostly drawn on U.S. banks, with the remainder split between barter and cash in advance.

If commercial contacts have been established in the former USSR, they may well extend to at least some of the other countries we have listed as part of Eastern Europe, where some fine opportunities no doubt exist for the skilled trader or the manufacturer of a product in specific demand. But this book is intended for the new-to-export firm or individual, and I urge you to think twice—no, many times—before spending precious time and expense cultivating business in such a climate when you could be doing so in more settled areas. The U.S. government, as well as the World Bank, the International Monetary Fund, and others, are trying to help but their assistance emphasizes infrastructure and investment—not the sort of things of interest to, or within the capability of, most new exporters. Eximbank is trying to insure letters of credit drawn on Russia's Foreign Trade Bank, provided there are sovereign guarantees. It is trying to do the same thing in the case of certain countries in Eastern and Central Europe, but the result so far is an on-again, off-again situation that cannot be relied upon until the moment of application for insurance or guarantee. You can readily understand, therefore, how critical credit support is from these agencies, and since it will be several years before any kind of real stability exists, you will find a "wait and see" attitude may serve you best.

Africa

A continent of almost 600 million people, divided up among 53 countries, presents a marketing challenge almost beyond the realm of possibility. This is compounded by the fact that U.S.-African trade, as a whole, represented merely $9 billion in U.S. exports in 1994, or 1.8 percent of total U.S. exports. To put this in perspective, tiny Central America almost equals this percentage, at 1.3 percent of total U.S. exports. Furthermore, of the total exports to Africa, 56 percent of the 1.8 percent was sold to two countries: South Africa and Egypt. Imports from Africa were somewhat greater, but of similar proportions. There are clearly significant and untapped opportunities in Africa if a commercial relationship can be established and thereafter truly fulfill its promise to grow. For example, franchising is felt to have a great future throughout Africa—and for good reason. This is because it provides what is so often missing: training and financing. As of now, however, 1994 exports are down nearly 10 percent from 1992.

In an article in *Export Today*, Michael Sudarkasa makes the suggestion that because of the fragmentation of the market into so many small countries, it makes sense to focus on the regional blocs of Africa and their regional trade shows.[2] Sudarkasa mentions the South Africa Customs Union (SACU), the South African Development Community (SADC), the Preferential Trade Area of East and Southern Africa (PTA), the Economic Community of West African States (ECOWAS), the Central African Customs and Economic Union (UDEAC), and the Maghreb Permanent Consultative Committee (MAGHREB). All of the countries served by such groups are noted in Table 7-2. Unfortunately, most of these "blocs" are very loosely organized and incohesive, and many are quite new.

Table 7-2. The Geographic/Political World Order of Nations:
Africa

Areawide DTD	Country exception DTD[1]	Region and country	Trade bloc membership[2]
6		*North Africa*	
		The Maghreb ("The West")	
	v	Morocco	AL
	^	Algeria	AL
		Tunisia	AL
	10	Libya	AL
	v	United Arab Republic (Egypt)[3]	AL
		Sub-Saharan Africa	
8		West Africa	
		Mauritania[4]	AL ECOWAS
		Mali	FZ ECOWAS
		Niger[4]	FZ ECOWAS
		Senegal	FZ ECOWAS
		Gambia[4]	ECOWAS
		Guinea-Bissau	ECOWAS
	v	Guinea	ECOWAS
		Sierra Leone[4]	ECOWAS
	^	Liberia	ECOWAS
	v	Côte d'Ivoire (Ivory Coast)	FZ ECOWAS
		Burkina Faso	FZ ECOWAS
	6.5	Ghana	ECOWAS
		Togo[4]	FZ ECOWAS
		Benin	FZ ECOWAS
	6.5	Nigeria	ECOWAS
8.5		East Africa	
	^	Sudan[4]	AL
	v	Ethiopia[4]	
	^	Somalia[4]	AL
		Djibouti	AL
8		Central Africa	
		Cameroon	FZ
		Chad	FZ
		Central African Republic	FZ
		Equatorial Guinea	FZ
	v	Gabon	FZ
		Congo	FZ
		Zaire	
	^	Uganda[4]	
	^	Rwanda	
		Burundi	
		Tanzania	
	6.5	Kenya	
		Angola	
		Malawi	
		Zambia	

(Continued)

Table 7-2. The Geographic/Political World Order of Nations:
Africa (Continued)

Areawide DTD	Country exception DTD[1]	Region and country	Trade bloc membership[2]
6		Southern Africa	
	^	Namibia	
		Botswana	
	v	Zimbabwe (formerly Rhodesia)	
	^	Mozambique[4]	
	^	Swaziland	
	4	South Africa	
		Lesotho	
9		African Islands of the Atlantic Ocean	
		Cape Verde[4]	
		Sao Tome & Principe[4]	
7		African Islands of the Indian Ocean	
	^	Seychelles	
	^	Comoros[4]	FZ
		Mauritius	
		Madagascar	

[1]Where a country differs materially from the regional Degree of Trading Difficulty scale, it is indicated by a separate DTD rating for that country. Alternatively, when the difference is so great or adequate information is not available for a separate rating, the distinction is indicated by: a ^ for a greater DTD ranking (more difficult trading); and by a v for a lesser DTD ranking (easier trading).

[2]The full versions of the abbreviated trade bloc titles are as follows:
AL = Arab League
ECOWAS = Economic Community of West African States
FZ = Franc Zone (Consists of 14 former colonies of France which maintain an integrated market with France that is tied to the French currency. While the currency of the colonies itself is not acceptable foreign exchange in trade and cannot be hedged, the same result can sometimes be accomplished by placing a contract on the equivalent sum in French francs.)

[3]The United Arab Republic (UAR), better known as Egypt, is clearly part of Africa, but as it includes the Suez Canal and the Sinai Peninsula, it is frequently thought of more in connection with the Middle East. Besides these geographical connections, the UAR is a member of the Arab League with close ties to the spirit and cultures of the Middle East. Egypt is a natural bridge between Africa and Southwest Asia, although it has not always been a very comfortable link between the two.

[4]The poorest nations of the world as identified by the United Nations.

North Africa

History. Much of what Africa and Europe have in common centers on North Africa. The Europeans colonized much of Africa in modern history, of course. But some 2000 years before that, a series of wars called the Punic Wars were fought between Rome and Carthage, capital of what is now Tunisia. During one, in a daring and famous military campaign, the

Carthaginian general, Hannibal, took his army and full baggage train, including elephants, through southern France and over the Alps to defeat the armies of Rome. But he was unable to consolidate the victory and was forced to return to Carthage to defend that city against Rome. Rome did finally sack Carthage after Hannibal's death in 146 B.C., with the result that Carthage became a province of the Roman Empire. The struggles and relationships between Egypt and the Greek and Roman empires, their generals, and their rulers make interesting reading. Later the Moors of North Africa conquered and ruled Spain for part of the eighth century. Finally, in the twenty-first century, the Allied North Africa campaigns to defeat Germany's Field Marshal Rommel in World War II were key to the ultimate Allied victory in the European Theater.

Geography. In terms of proximity, Northern Africa is very close to Europe, separated by a mere 12 miles of water, called the Strait of Gibraltar, from Spain and Portugal on the Iberian Peninsula. Of course, Egypt is also the southern bridge to Asia via the Suez Canal and the Sinai Peninsula. Although Africa is Africa, many people think of North Africa as part of the Middle East. This is especially true of the United Arab Republic (UAR), or Egypt, because of that country's intense involvement in Middle Eastern affairs, as well as its possession of the Sinai Peninsula which borders Israel and Jordan.

North Africa begins on the western Atlantic coast of Africa with the region known as the Maghreb, meaning "The West." The Maghreb includes Morocco (which now also occupies the country to its south, formerly known as Western Sahara), Algeria, Tunisia, and Libya. This amounts to all of North Africa except for Egypt. A large portion of North Africa is composed of the Sahara Desert, which extends from the Atlantic to the Red Sea and is by far the largest desert in the world (over 3.5 million square miles) as well as the hottest (its highest recorded temperature was 136°F). The Sahara desert system encompasses what are also known separately as the Libyan Desert, the Arabian Desert, and the Nubian Desert, the latter two being the area from the Nile to the Red Sea. Fringes of the Sahara extend south into Sub-Saharan Africa and into the next east/west belt of African countries, especially Mauritania and Sudan.

Trade. The United States has a very unbalanced trade relationship with Egypt, our biggest customer in North Africa. In 1994, that trade consisted of $2.8 billion in U.S. imports (largely of military equipment) and $593 million in exports to the U.S. With $1.2 billion in exports, Algeria is the second-largest U.S. trade partner in North Africa, followed by Morocco and Tunisia. Algeria's economy is in difficulty, not only because of debt-service problems, but also because the country is experiencing a mounting level of violence and resulting political instability. Travel cautions are in effect regarding Algeria, and one should check with the U.S. embassy before undertaking even essential travel there. In spite of this, Eximbank and OPIC have tried to remain active, but as of this writing, their cover is very limited and short-term only.

Egypt.   Egypt is a special story because, for political and military defense reasons, the U.S. State Department provides that country with massive support, just as it does Israel. Accordingly, a substantial portion of Egypt's imports from the United States represent purchases through the Foreign Military Sales (FMS) program, as opposed to general merchandise and equipment. The United States is, in turn, Egypt's leading trading partner. The country is doing many things in the name of internal economic reform, though in reality to satisfy World Bank and International Monetary Fund (IMF) demands. Egypt is currently facing many economic and social difficulties, many of which are fomented by Islamic fundamentalists.

Morocco and Tunisia.   In contrast to Algeria, Morocco and Tunisia are both very much open for business, with growth expected in a broad variety of products ranging from fishing boats to aircraft parts. Morocco, a Muslim country that has close ties to Europe—only 12 miles away across the Strait of Gibraltar—is successfully undertaking serious economic reforms but has been suffering from persistent drought. The DOC calls Tunisia a "model developing country," and Eximbank is open for guarantees and insurance there, with fewer restrictions than in Morocco. Tunisia has an important advantage in having duty-free access to EU markets for industrial products. Last—and least—of the North African nations is Libya, with whom we have no trade whatsoever. In response to that country's terrorist activities, the U.S. imposed a trade embargo on it, which is still ongoing.

In terms of *Euromoney*'s country-credit-risk rankings, the North African countries of Tunisia and Morocco are in fair shape—an achievement shared by few other countries in Africa—with rankings of 54 and 59 respectively. Egypt is ranked 73 and Algeria continues to slip, ranking 102 out of 187. Overall, North Africa—exclusive of Libya—receives a DTD rating of 6.

Sub-Saharan Africa

Sub-Saharan Africa begins with the east/west belt of countries below North Africa. The history of these nations is largely one of broken dreams, corruption, and poverty. The dreams developed as the bonds of colonialism were broken. Corruption has marked the rule of authoritarian leaders who have all too often been able to seize power in societies lacking a solid native civil service structure with an institutional memory. These grave problems have been compounded by tribalism and the existence of many nations too small for any hope of cooperation and mutual support. The result in all too many cases is a concentration of great wealth in the hands of a few and deepening poverty created by bankrupt, short-sighted fiscal and economic policies. In the May 25, 1993, edition of the *Los Angeles Times,* a feature on Sub-Saharan Africa stated that, according to UNICEF, African children will account for 39 percent of infant deaths worldwide by the year 2000. It also stated that by 2000 49.7 percent—up to 300 million people—of Sub-Sahara Africa will fall below the poverty line, compared to 47.8 percent today. Thirty-nine countries make up mainland Sub-Saharan Africa, and it is interesting to note that in its April 19, 1993, issue of *Business America,* the DOC was able to report on only six of them. Of the 21 countries listed as the poorest in the world by the United Nations, the majority are in Sub-Saharan Africa. I have designated them by means of footnote 4 in Table 7.2. Needless to say, there is little economic news to report in most of these countries, especially those in the grip of widespread turmoil and human suffering, such as Somalia, Liberia, Rwanda, and Angola.

On the other hand, and without regard to this darker view, the *Los Angeles Times*[3] in its August 4, 1994, edition makes a case for the many open- and closed-end mutual stock funds that are now investing in African companies and their stock—especially in the more promising Sub-Saharan countries other than South Africa. The article heralds such companies as the last frontier for investment. Some investments are even being made by prestigious firms like the Sloan Financial Group and Morgan Stanley & Co. If these investments pay off, we suspect it will be because the Republic of South Africa has led the way in the economic development of Sub-Saharan Africa. The specific countries mentioned in the *Los Angeles Times* article on the bullish investment community, besides South Africa, were Botswana, Ghana, Kenya, Mauritius, and Zimbabwe. These were also the countries where franchises were reported to have met with success.

West Africa

All the states in West Africa belong to the Economic Community of West African States (ECOWAS). Formed in 1975, it is the largest and oldest of the African trading blocs and encompasses 206 million people. One of its goals has been better public relations and trust in the world trading community as well as among its member nations. ECOWAS could be a force in the world of trade if its members can ever develop a sufficiently stable political and economic climate to allow it to take small steps toward its goals.

The first east/west belt of countries in West Africa consists of Mauritania, Mali, and Niger, none of which generate a significant amount of trade. Moving southward, the next east/west belt includes countries with more export potential. Nigeria (which used to be known as the Gold Coast) is by far the biggest user of U.S. goods in the group, at $509 million in 1994; it is followed by Ghana at $125 million. Nigeria used to import over $1 billion from the U.S. But that figure has fallen dramatically as a series of military rulers—in place since 1985—continue to plunder the economy and ruin the prospects of one of the most promising oil-rich nations of Africa. It is said that Nigeria's workforce is well trained and hardworking and trying to force the return of a civilian government, but today it seems little will change; the promised "democratic elections" have been set aside and tyranny continues. Even acknowledging that Nigeria is a corrupt and debt-ridden country, a surprising amount of trade does take place in this most populous state of the Sub-Sahara. The chief export opportunities offered by this country are airport and ground-support equipment, oil and gas field machinery and services, and telecommunications equipment—the favorite U.S. export product ranges everywhere in the world these days. But unless you have solid connections or overwhelming demand, combined with confirmed letters of credit from acceptable banks, it is better to postpone searching this area for business. What can be discouraging in Africa generally and in Nigeria particularly—is the presence of rampant fraud and deceit, much of it quite flagrant and unsophisticated to a knowledgeable exporter, but appealing enough to trap hundreds of normally careful businessmen.

My own export company has nearly one file drawer full of Nigerian correspondence—with no business to show for it. Today, I refuse even to respond to letters of inquiry from Nigeria—a rare exception to my rule on fast response. It simply wastes time and postage to no purpose. In the 1970s my company managed to gain access to a copy of a "not-for-public-distribution" list of names and addresses of bogus banks in Nigeria. It completely filled a medium-sized loose-leaf notebook!

The con artists continue to send unsolicited bank drafts to cash after shipment drawn on nonexistent banks. The same is true of letters of credit. Your own bank or its international correspondent can quickly advise you of the existence and relative strength of any such bank, and you should let it examine the document itself to see whether there *is* such a bank, should you continue to be tempted to pursue the "opportunity." Another famous and successful scam involves a letter stating that you are a well-known and respected person or firm with whom some bogus company would like to do business. Your reputation is excellent, so the firm can trust you to permit it to deposit some substantial funds in your bank account, if only you will provide it with the correct bank account numbers. If you do give the company the requested information, it will draw down your bank account. The DOC is well informed concerning this and other fraudulent schemes and can provide you with more details.

Overall, I can only give West Africa a DTD rating of 8. In spite of the frustrations that trade with Nigeria involves, its sheer potential might call for a 6.5 rating. A 6.5 also goes to the smaller but less risky Ghana. I must repeat that in West Africa, as in much of the rest of the continent, there are exceptions if a trader is well connected and knows the particular means that will generate real profits. But this is not likely to be the case for the newcomer.

East Africa

East Africa's Sudan, Somalia, and Djibouti have much unrest and little potential. The exception is Ethiopia, to which we export about $143 million. This represents a sharp decline from 1992, even considering that separate statistics are being kept for Eritrea, newly independent following its civil war with Ethiopia. Ethiopia was part of the Soviet bloc during the Cold War but now intends to privatize with a vengeance. At one time, many African governments were envious of the riches of Ethiopia.

Sudan, of course, is currently considered a terrorist supporter and is a very dangerous place for Americans. East Africa overall is a disaster area, as was clearly illustrated by the U.S. debacle in Somalia. The other nations of East Africa are little better off. In this region, the postcolonial experience has been especially cruel. The East African nations are all at the bottom of the fourth quartile of country-risk ranking. Warfare, starvation, and political instability all considered, I would assign this group a DTD of 8.5, unless possibly you are in the gray or black market armaments business, or are providing necessities through AID.

Central Africa

Conditions overall are somewhat better in Central Africa, but many of these countries, too, are on a sharply downward curve and a bit chaotic. Kenya, at $170 million, and Angola, at $197 million, were the only two countries to buy over $100 million worth of U.S. exports in 1994. Kenya is also one of those rare African nations to be found in the second quartile of the country-risk rankings. Zaire, which once offered promise, has become very unstable politically and economically, and U.S. exports to the country have dropped to just $33 million.

Many of Sub-Saharan Africa's trade channels are rooted in commercial and financial history of colonial Africa. A prime example is the so-called "Franc Zone." This zone consists of 14 former colonies of France in West, East, and Central Africa. (See Table 7-2, where all its members except for the Comoros Islands off the east coast of Africa, are designated by FZ.) The Franc Zone constitutes a single integrated market. Its importance to a U.S. exporter lies in the opportunity it offers you to hedge currency risks through the relationship of its currencies to the French franc. In Central Africa, as in so many other parts of Africa, many of the best export opportunities are tied to the U.S. AID organization or some of the other

United Nations organizations. The DTD scale registers an 8 for Central Africa—perhaps a little better if you have connections via Europe.

Southern Africa

Trade prospects brighten further as we move into Southern Africa. Zimbabwe, however, to which we exported $93 million in 1994, is sharply down from 1992. And Namibia, Africa's youngest nation, which became independent in 1990, and which was said to be following a very pragmatic and sensible economic course, has recently deteriorated some in terms of both political and economic stability. Zimbabwe, however, together with Botswana and Swaziland, are among the few African countries in the second quartile rankings for country risk.

It would have been difficult to predict the remarkable relative tranquility of the democratic elections in South Africa. It also points up the degree to which one or two men can change a situation that looked unchangeable. This would make one hopeful except for the knowledge that such men seem to be as often of evil intent as they are of good and practical intent. Until the embargo to encourage the elimination of apartheid was placed on South Africa in 1985, it was the brightest commercial spot in Africa, with a reliable financial system and a reasonably broad-based population possessing disposable income. The lifting of most federal trade restrictions (many state and local governments in the U.S. continued their own restrictions) on South Africa in 1991 resulted in immediate increases of U.S. exports and investments there. Today, exports are over $2.1 billion, with roughly equal imports. Based on this, and if the present rational course of government continues, the future for trade and foreign investment in South Africa looks exceedingly bright, even though the country itself still has many problems to solve. Continued success in turning things around in South Africa will make that country a key to better business throughout much of Sub-Saharan Africa and grant a better economic life to many other African countries and people. Its political-risk ranking has improved to 45 which puts South Africa just inside the first quartile with a very modest level of risk.

South Africa's ongoing success in putting apartheid behind it has some parallel with the experience of Zimbabwe as it transformed itself from the white settler state of Rhodesia. Zimbabwe's transition was not perfect, but it has avoided anarchy and may be regaining some of its former economic strength, although it has taken time and has not always followed a straight or easy path. It will be at least as hard, and very possibly much harder, to ensure a continued peaceful coexistence of interests in South Africa, given the time the wounds of apartheid have festered, and especially given the current "lost generation" of blacks. Let us hope all parties in South Africa continue to evidence the wisdom and effort that will be required to complete a peaceful and commercially viable transition. As of now, good judgment prevails as long as the radical factions on both the right and the left continue to be constrained. Actually, all of Sub-Saharan Africa shares in the hope for a peaceful and prosperous South Africa, which will have much to say about a recovery for large portions of the region.

To satisfy the curious, Madagascar, that huge island lying in the Indian Ocean off the coast of southeast Africa, is the world's fourth-largest island, with 1994 export purchases of $48 million and import sales to the U.S. of $60 million. The five remaining Atlantic and Indian Ocean islands associated with the African continent are included in our list of nations because they are independent and related to the African trade. But the only island of commercial significance is Mauritius, which is noted among developing countries for having established a thriving economy during the 1980s that attracted quality foreign investment. The U.S. exported $24 million to Mauritius in 1994, and it is a major source of imports at $234 million.

Overall, Southern Africa receives a DTD rating of 6, thanks in part to Zimbabwe's improvement and very largely to the revitalization of our relations with a renewed South Africa. On its own, South Africa deserves a 4.

It is always useful to remember that the African continent was a point of origin for man, and that its Mediterranean shores were one of the first cradles of Western civilization. It is also important to remember that the early European explorers who called Africa the "Dark Continent" did so in large part because of the mysteries of dealing in the continent, not simply because of its deep jungles. The term serves equally well today as a commercial description of Africa on a number of counts: poverty, political instability, fraud, and, in many countries, a very high percentage of available cash and GNP spent on armaments. This is true for such a large portion of the continent that it remains unwise to make this a target for export sales without very solid contacts, well-chosen products to meet real demands and needs, and considerable export trading experience or, alternatively, excellent sources of advice. Yet, under the right circumstance and with proper skills, Africa may indeed become a true frontier for the entrepreneur.

Endnotes

1. David Wingrove, "Boundless Byzantine Opportunity," *Trade & Culture*, September–October 1995.

2. Michael E. M. Sudarkasa, "Building Business on African Blocs," *Export Today*, April 1995.

3. Jojo Kumankumah, "Africa, the Last Frontier, Draws Blend of Bullish Investors," *Los Angeles Times*, August 4, 1994.

8
Where in the World?

Asia and the Pacific

Asia

Southwest Asia (The Middle East)

Southwest Asia is better known as, and more commonly called, "the Middle East," but as with Europe and Asia, there is some confusion as to where it begins or ends. The ever-changing political fortunes of the general area from ancient times to the present add to that confusion. At one time, much of Southwest Asia was dominated by the Persian Empire, which included all of present-day Iran, Turkey, and Afghanistan, as well as parts of Iraq, Egypt, and Pakistan. Subsequent empires in Southwest Asia included those of Alexander the Great, the Romans, the Muslims, the Byzantines, and the Ottomans. The boundaries of many of the nations in the region did not begin to take their present shape until after World War I. Politics aside, Turkey's Bosporus strait forms the dividing line geographically between Asia and Europe. On the European side, Istanbul, one of the world's most historic cities, becomes the approach to the bridge across that strait to the Continent of Asia via Asia Minor, which encompasses most of Asiatic Turkey. Istanbul was built on the site of ancient Byzantium by Constantine I in the fourth century and named Constantinople. Its purpose was to be the seat of Eastern Christianity, the religion to which Constantine had been converted. In 1453 Constantinople was captured by the Turks, a Muslim people. Constantinople then became the capital of the Turkish Ottoman Empire. When the modern republic of Turkey was formed in 1930, Ankara became its capital and Constantinople was renamed Istanbul. Modern

Turkey is the easternmost NATO country and continues to enjoy a strategic location as the crossroads between Europe, the Middle East, and the Newly Independent States (NIS) of the former Soviet Union. It is also worth noting that Turkey and Iran are the only two non-Arab Muslim states in the Middle East.

As mentioned in the segment on Africa, Egypt, while not part of the Middle East, forms both the border and the bridge from Africa to the Middle East and is politically very much a part of the Middle East and its affairs, along with the rest of what is known as the "Arab world." Besides all of North Africa, the Arab world includes most of Southwest Asia, excluding Iran, Turkey, and Israel plus Somalia, Sudan, Djibouti, and Mauritania in Sub-Saharan Africa.

Egypt's Suez Canal, the Red Sea, and that historic battleground, the Sinai Peninsula, are integral parts of the complex formula of the region. They are also the subject of the Camp David Treaty, which brought peace between Egypt and Israel, starting an interrelationship with the Middle Eastern world of Islam that continues its development to this day. It is hoped, and is increasingly possible, that the peace accords of 1993 between Israel and the Palestinians, and in 1994 between Israel and Jordan, will be followed by an Israeli/Syrian accord and ultimately by greater stability in the Middle East. How long will it take before there is a real sovereign nation within what was once an Ottoman Empire province called Palestine?

The growing power of Islamic fundamentalism should not be allowed to influence your decisions about where you can enjoy comfortable commercial relationships. In Iran and other countries dominated by radicalized forms of the Islamic faith, fundamentalism does represent a significant difficulty, not only because of its potential impact on political stability but also because of its prohibitions on the payment of interest. For most of our Muslim-dominated trading partners, however, Islamic fundamentalism remains a fringe movement and hopefully it will continue to be so.

Radical Islamic fundamentalism often coheres around a national leader who wants great power and takes advantage of the very apparent gaps between local standards of living and those in the West, and who makes much of the discrepancies and disappointing economic developments following the withdrawal of the former colonial powers. But Muslim countries are not necessarily backward in terms of economic basics. Besides our friends in the Gulf Cooperation Council, Turkey and Malaysia, in two very different parts of the world, are excellent examples of a thriving trade between Islamic buyers and Western sellers. You may have to change your styles and habits concerning time, working days, and holidays, but there is plenty of business being done with all the nations of Islam and a potential for much more. (See Table 8-1 for the listing of nations for this chapter.)

Table 8-1. The Geographic/Political World Order of Nations:
Asia and the Pacific

Areawide DTD	Country exception DTD[1]	Region and country	Trade bloc membership[2]
5		*Southwest Asia* (Middle East)	
	4	Turkey[3] (the Asian bridge to Europe)	ECO
		Cyprus [in dispute between Greece and Turkey]	
	4	Israel	
		Lebanon	AL
	7	Syria	AL
		Jordan	AL
	10	Iraq	AL
	8	Iran	ECO
	4	Saudi Arabia	AL GCC
	v	Kuwait	AL GCC
		Bahrain	AL GCC
		Qatar	AL GCC
	v	United Arab Emirates (UAE)	AL GCC
		Oman	AL GCC
	^	Yemen Arab Republic[4] (unified)	AL
7		*South Asia* (primarily the Indian Subcontinent)	
	8	Afghanistan[4]	
	6	Pakistan	ECO
	5	India	
		Nepal[4]	
		Bhutan[4]	
		Bangladesh	
		Sri Lanka (formerly Ceylon)	
		Maldive Islands[4]	
7–8		*Siberia and Central Asia*	
	7	Russia (Siberian portion)	
	8	Central Asian Newly Independent States (NIS)	
	v	Kazakhstan	
		Uzbekistan	ECO
	^	Kyrgyzstan	ECO
	^	Tajikistan	ECO
		Turkmenistan	ECO
	8	Mongolia (Mongolian Peoples Republic)	
3.5		*East Asia*	
	5	Peoples Republic of China (PRC, or Mainland China)	
	10	North Korea	
	4	South Korea	

Table 8-1. The Geographic/Political World Order of Nations:
Asia and the Pacific (Continued)

Areawide DTD	Country exception DTD[1]	Region and country	Trade bloc membership[2]
3.5		*East Asia (Cont.)*	
	3–4	Japan	
	3.5	Taiwan[5] (Republic of China on Formosa Island)	
	2	Hong Kong (Britain)	
		Southeast Asia	
		Indochinese peninsula	
	8	Myanmar (formerly Burma)	
	9	Laos[4]	
	6	Vietnam	
	4	Thailand	ASEAN
	9	Cambodia	
	4	Malaysia[6]	ASEAN
	3	Singapore	ASEAN
		Malay Archipelago	
	4	Philippines	ASEAN
	4	Malaysia[6] (shares Borneo Island)	ASEAN
		Brunei (shares Borneo Island)	ASEAN
	4	Indonesia (shares Borneo Island)	ASEAN
		Papua New Guinea (shares New Guinea Island with Indonesia)	
		Australasia	
	3	Australia	
	4	New Zealand	
6		*Oceania—the Independent Pacific Islands*	
		Federated States of Micronesia	
		Marshall Islands	
		Kiribati[5] (formerly Gilbert Islands)	
		Nauru[5]	
		Solomon Islands	
		Tuvalu[5] (formerly Ellice Islands)	
		Western Samoa[4]	
		Vanuatu (formerly New Hebrides)	
		Fiji	
		Tonga[5]	
		Antarctica	
		The Frozen Continent[7]	

[1]Where a country differs materially from the regional Degree of Trading Difficulty scale, it is indicated by a separate DTD rating for that country. Alternatively, when the difference is not so great, or adequate information is not available for a separate rating the distinction is indicated by: ^ for a greater DTD ranking (more difficult trading); and by a v for a lesser DTD ranking (easier trading).

Table 8-1. The Geographic/Political World Order of Nations:
Asia and the Pacific (Continued)

[2]The full versions of the abbreviated trade bloc titles are as follows:
ECO = Economic Cooperation Organization
AL = Arab League
GCC = Gulf Cooperation Council
ASEAN = Association of Southeast Asian Nations

[3]Turkey is the bridge between Asia and Western/Central Europe. The seat of the old Ottoman Empire, Istanbul (formerly Constantinople and one-time seat of Christianity), on the European side, is the gateway on the Bosporus connecting the Black Sea with the Aegean and Mediterranean seas. To the east of the Bosporus begins Asia Minor, a term less used today, which we consider part of Southwest Asia (more commonly thought of as the Middle East), and this is where we have placed Turkey for purposes of ranking its DTD. Given Turkey's foothold in Europe on the west side of the Bosporus and its candidacy for the EU, we have also listed it under Western Europe, even though it is a very Eastern nation in political and geographic terms.

[4]The poorest nations of the world as identified by the United Nations.

[5]Independent nations or states that are not members of the United Nations.

[6]Malaysia is rather unique in its almost even division between the mainland peninsula and Borneo Island in the Indian Ocean. For that reason we have listed it under both the Indochinese Peninsula and Malay Archipelago designations. However, since its capital of Kuala Lumpur lies on the peninsula, it is considered a peninsular nation.

[7]Antarctica is a permanently frozen continental landmass but has no permanent population, and is claimed by many countries even though, by common consent, it is shared for research by all interested countries. Note that, in contrast to this southern polar region, there is no land in the northern polar region to call an Arctic continent, only the Arctic Ocean, a substantial portion of which is also frozen year round.

Turkey, a country industrializing itself at a rapid rate, represents an outstanding opportunity for both trade and investment. Sales there have received a boost from major projects for which we are getting better support from Eximbank, as well as from suffering fewer unfair foreign government financial subsidies than in prior years. Turkey is one more country notable as much for its potential as for its present $2.8 billion in U.S. export purchases, which places it well up among our top 50 export customers. It has also harmonized its tariff system with the European Union and simplified its import restrictions with the EU in mind.

Turkey is a member of the Economic Cooperation Organization (ECO), a fledgling trading bloc of primarily Muslim states with a population in excess of 250 million, including Iran, Pakistan, and the former Soviet republics of Central Asia. Taken together with India, Azerbaijan, and Armenia, this may well become the "Asian Bloc." If such a bloc does take shape, it would represent a population of over one billion in a vast area potentially rich in minerals and agriculture. But it would also include many of the poorest nations in the world today, nations that are burdened with a built-in instability. The ECO includes over 40 percent of the world's roughly one billion Muslims. One-third of the bloc is made up of people speaking Turkic-based languages from the central Asian area that was known as Turkestan until it was conquered by the Russians in the nineteenth century. It is also an area of multiple territorial disputes, creating many flash points that may spoil the substantial potential it might represent.

Whether seen as a future member of the European Union or as the Asian bridge to Europe, Turkey is a key to many geopolitical questions and to trade development in the area. As with many customers in this part of the world, Turkey spends a large portion of its budget on military products. These purchases are included in the U.S. export sales figure, although many popular U.S. export products involving pollution control and telecommunications equipment are also major items.

Our financial relationship and political support for Israel is well known and includes a bilateral free trade agreement, which should keep the present level of trade at $5 billion in exports balanced by $5.2 billion in imports. This export level is second only to that for Saudi Arabia in the Middle East.

The Gulf Cooperation Council (GCC) is mainly composed of the Arabian Peninsula states bordering on the western shores of the Persian Gulf. It represents a population of only 23 million, but has a large collective disposable income. It includes the largest U.S. trading partner and export customer in the Middle East, Saudi Arabia, which spent $6 billion in imports and had $7.7 billion in oil exports in 1994 (though both figures were sharply down from 1992's).

As oil profits decline, the streets of Saudi Arabia and the other oil-rich states may no longer seem to be paved with gold, but it only takes a visit to their supermarkets or stores to see the consumer demand for Western goods. Anyone following the infrastructure projects there knows that there is still much to be done and that Americans can continue to play a major role, even though the opportunities may not be as great or our presence as dominant as in previous decades. No longer starved for imported goods or the completion of hundreds of infrastructure projects, Saudi Arabia nevertheless remains a top customer for many American products. Expect competition to be stiffer, however, especially in consumer products, where Saudi tastes more often than not run to European products.

Kuwait and the United Arab Emirates (U.A.E.) are our other best customers in the region, buying $1.2 and $1.6 billion respectively. Indeed, most countries in the Middle East except Iraq, which is under an embargo, would be considered good customers relative to their size. Excluding Turkey and Cyprus, our total exports to the Middle East in 1994 were $15.8 billion. Although imports were roughly equal, they were of little interest to traders other than U.S. oil importers.

The Middle East as a whole ranks fairly well in country-risk evaluation. In this regard, Israel leads, at number 30. The weak spots are Syria,

Iran, and Yemen, with Iraq near the very bottom, at 185 out of 187. The region is largely populated by buyers who have available foreign exchange dollars. Except for our continuing problems with Iran and Iraq, I give it a DTD rating of 5. If viewed separately, Turkey, Israel, and Saudi Arabia deserve a 4.

Southern Asia

This region is chiefly occupied by the subcontinent of India, which extends north to the ridges of the Himalayan mountain range. It is called a *subcontinent* because it is so clearly differentiated from the much larger main landmass of Asia and because its underlying geologic tectonic plates were once separate from Asia. Over millions of years they moved northward and collided with the Asian plate, creating the Himalayan mountain range in the process. The subcontinent is therefore the area south of the Himalayas, and includes Afghanistan, Pakistan, Nepal, Bhutan, and Bangladesh, in addition to India. India dominates South Asia economically and is the United States' thirty-fifth largest export customer, but sells us twice that sum. There exists an even greater U.S. trade deficit with Bangladesh, Pakistan, and Sri Lanka. In other words, we have a substantial trade deficit with this area of the world, fostered in part as a matter of policy in view of its urgent need for economic development. The dominance of imports from the region is created by heavy contract manufacturing for U.S. and other firms in areas like apparel and other low-cost labor-intensive products.

India is making sincere efforts at trade and economic reform in spite of recent political and social upheavals, including some backlash directed at U.S. corporations because of our high commercial profile. India has eliminated the two-tier exchange rate system, made the rupee fully convertible on trade accounts, and reduced tariffs. Still, the country continues to present certain difficulties as a customer in terms of currency availability, letter-of-credit opening delays, and similar problems. It is ranked fifty-first in the world for country risk. Substantial growth is developing as India enjoys an economic boom and rapid GDP growth as one of the world's most dynamic and growing consumer markets. Its middle class numbers 300 million out of a total population of 900 million. High-tech manufacturing, both independent and contract, is a major business sector for India, even though caution should be exercised where intellectual property rights are a concern. (India has been singled out by the U.S. Trade Representative [USTR] for denying effective intellectual property rights protection.) India is also attracting a great deal of foreign investment. Its weakness is a poor infrastructure, but the government is dedicated to improving this area.

This concern about improving infrastructure—and image—denotes a remarkable change from the early 1970s, when I can clearly remember boarding an Air India flight in the 1970s, bound for Kenya. I had only rupees for change, expecting to use them for beverages on the long flight. To my dismay, they would not sell me a drink to be paid for in rupees on India's own national airline—only dollars would do and no credit cards taken. It was a dry trip; and my only joy came from knocking Air India for years to come. But times have changed and I am told they are happy to sell you a drink for rupees these days.

Pakistan, an ECO member, is our next-best customer, although its $719 million in imports from the U.S. is about one-third of India's. Bangladesh and Sri Lanka are in the $200-million-export customer range and are surprisingly well regarded in terms of country risk for this part of the world, with a listing in the second-quartile ranks. The region also includes that disaster area, Afghanistan, with which we have virtually no trade and which ranks 186 out of 187 in country-risk status. Overall, we would give the region a rating of 7 because of the dominance of India which, by itself, would merit a 5.

Siberia and Central Asia

The next region in our global journey is perhaps the most difficult to quantify, both from a geographical point of view consistent with the regional listing method we have used, and from the standpoint of political relationships. I am sure the Russian people would justifiably take umbrage with even a theoretical separation of the country from its extremely valuable Siberian territory, especially given the independence of the former Soviet republics of Central Asia (now called the Newly Independent States, or NIS). Much of the region is difficult to imagine as "Asia," because Russian Siberia extends north to the Arctic Ocean and the NIS states extend far south through Central Asia to Turkmenistan on the Caspian Sea.

Why do we insist on mentally separating Siberia from Russia? Because Russia's political orientation in modern times is toward Europe, as is its fiscal and manufacturing interrelationship network, while Siberia's indigenous population is neither European nor of Slavic origin or speech, but rather is more typically Asiatic in terms of religious, cultural, and ethnic backgrounds. All of the Russian Federation contains more than 104 ethnic groups and 100 languages and stretches across 13 time zones, with the majority of this diversity located east of the Ural Mountains. Similarly dramatic differences between Russia and Siberia exist in their degree of industrial development, transportation, and distribution infrastructure. Of course there are many European (Slavic) Russians in Siberia, but the majority are there more in a colonial sense than as natives to the land. In fact, most of Russia, Siberia, and China, plus historic Persia, was conquered and ruled by the Mongols in the thirteenth century. The Mongolian Empire extended west to the Black Sea and the Arabian Peninsula, east to the Pacific, and south to the Himalayas.

Siberia can be divided into three parts: Western Siberia, or lowland plains area, Central Siberia or upland plateau area, and Far Eastern Siberia, which approaches within a few miles of our own Alaskan shores at its extremity on the Bering Strait. The eastern part of Siberia contains just over seven million people and is thought to contain close to half the world's natural resources. This great wealth of resources, and the port through which much of it could be shipped, Vladivostok, is much closer to other world powers such as China and Japan, than it is to Moscow. This juxtaposition, together with Russia's weakened and politically unstable condition today are two good reasons we like to consider Siberia separately as well as a part of Russia.

This combination of circumstances, including the lack of homogeneity between the European and Siberian portions of Russia, creates a potential flash point in today's geopolitics. Before the collapse of the USSR, the Chinese and the Japanese had become the Soviet's largest trading partners, thanks to their larger purchases from the USSR compared to those by the United States. A heavy share of the Asian trade was through Far Eastern Siberia, and both countries provided large trade credits, loans, and aid. It is clear that China and Japan will remain very active players in this area for both short- and long-term reasons and will provide stiff commercial competition, with government subsidization in key areas if necessary.

In the section on Europe, we mentioned that Russia's trade statistics and *Euromoney*'s country-risk rating placed the country at number 141 out of 187 because of its financial and political instability. That reference was to all of Russia, including Siberia. Because of its enormous wealth and other distinctions, Siberia is treated as a separate entity here only to achieve a clearer perspective. Nevertheless, even though Russia's relationship to its Asian neighbors represents quite a different economic and political connection than that with its Western neighbors, the fact remains that trade with Siberia is now and will continue to be trade with Russia for the foreseeable future.

On the other hand, although the Newly Independent States (NIS) of Central Asia do not lack for great natural resources and agricultural production (especially cotton), and they seek to make necessary economic reforms, trade with these five predominantly Muslim cultures is no longer trade with Russia. Rather it is trade with mostly landlocked countries whose independent political, economic, financial, and trade infrastructures are still somewhat embryonic and present many unique and vexing problems. In most respects, however, they have a more natural relationship with their neighbors to the south than they do with Russia. The U.S. DOC is opening offices in the territory and will undoubtedly be of help to the pioneering trader (but more often of help to investors seeking fresh opportunities). The best opportunities are said to be in the extraction and sale of natural resources, including oil, gas, coal, and nonferrous metals, an unlikely option for most of our readers. There may also be opportunities in agribusiness (including food processing), electronics, health and medical equipment, and environmental technology.

The trade statistics now available on the NIS states indicate that in 1994 the largest customers, Kazakhstan and Turkmenistan, purchased between $131 and $137 million each, with the remaining NIS nations buying from $6 to $90 million. These states were once restricted to selling vast supplies of oil, gas, gold, and uranium to the USSR at government fixed prices. Now that they are free to sell these riches on the open market, these and other NIS countries may present a very different picture in terms of financial strength. Mongolia, the only Central Asian country not a former state of the USSR, has a longer foreign trade history, but its export purchases have never exceeded $12 million (1991) and have fallen to $6 million in 1994. All but Kazakhstan of the NIS are members of that unlikely cooperative trading bloc of much potential, the ECO, which you will recall also includes nations as diverse as Turkey, Iran, and Pakistan.

Considering the vastness of Siberia and Central Asia, their lack of development, and their historical relationships to Russia and China, we can only give a DTD rating of 7–8 to the region. As is true of Siberian Russia (which is rated a 7), all the NIS country-risk ratings fall in the fourth quartile, as is that for Mongolia. Kazakstan, however, manages to achieve rank 129, which is in the lower portion of the third quartile.

East Asia

After reviewing the political stability and commercial prospects of Africa and Central Asia, moving into East Asia is like moving into the light. Without a doubt there is no more dynamic place on the face of the globe, with almost every East Asian country and most Southeast Asian countries contributing to that dynamism. (The sole exception is North Korea.) Experts estimate that the GDPs in Eastern and Southern Asia combined, excluding Japan, will more than double, from $5.5 trillion to $11.4 trillion, in the 12 years from 1993 to 2005. This compares favorably with the projected total world GDP growth for the same period of 53 percent, from $29.7 trillion to $45.5 trillion.

China, the world's fastest-growing major economy, represents a great opportunity for almost all ranks and categories of American business. David E. Moore, in an editorial in *International Business*, notes that the

United Nations already views it as the world's second-biggest economy in terms of purchasing power.[1] He states that DRI/McGraw-Hill forecasts growth in China's GNP at 8.2 percent over the 1993–1998 period compared to 3.1 percent for Japan and 2.6 percent for the U.S. Standard Chartered Bank estimates that the nonstate sector of mainland China's economy already produces 45 percent of its total industrial output and that, by the year 2000, there will be more than 30 million private enterprises—twice the current number—employing over 150 million people. On the downside, Mr. Moore's editorial points out that inflation is roughly 20 percent in the big cities, peasants are pillaging the rural countryside, and corruption is endemic in the bureaucracy and the military. The differences in job opportunities, personal income, and standard of living between cities within the designated enterprise zones and the vast rural areas of China are huge and make us wonder if the overall strategy will not require modification. Foreign investment is flooding into the country, based on present growth rates and anticipated future growth. This investment, excluding investment by Hong Kong and Macao, is led by U.S. companies, despite serious problems with government restrictions and the strategic maneuvering of conservatives within the ranks of China's leadership.

The five so-called special economic zones in southern China account for 14 percent of foreign investment in the country as a whole and 12 percent of its exports. They are primarily located in the provinces of Guangdong (directly north of and adjacent to Hong Kong), Fujian, Guangxi, and Hainan Island. The nearest mainland cities are Xiamen, Shantou, Zhuhai, and Shenzhen, besides Hainan Island. They have met with success in part because the inhabitants and players in these zones are exhibiting all the capacity for hard work, entrepreneurial spirit, and business acumen that seem to be so native to the Chinese. Those involved are also making good money and living a fast life. (Given their strong independent streak and shrewd business sense, it remains amazing that the Chinese were able to accept such a very dogmatic Communistic yoke for so long.) The zones were initially established by leader Deng Xiaoping as a desperate experiment to help China improve its then-deteriorating standard of living and catch up with the world after one too many cultural revolutions and great leaps forward. Recently, however, the zones have come under pressure because their high per capita income has created resentment in the much poorer interior provinces. The November 3, 1995, *Los Angeles Times* reported that Communist General Secretary Jiang Zemin denounced the scheme, and it suggested that some of the rules might be changed.

The lesson is that China traders must never forget that the state still does the planning, whether strategic or tactical, and that the planning is politically driven, which is how the commercial priorities are established. It is therefore necessary to understand the country's bureaucratic roles and procedures as well as any political trends that may affect your negotiations or objectives. The conclusion that is drawn by most China watchers is that the drive to what they call a socialist market economy (for which read "free market economy in designated industrial and economic zones or provinces") is nevertheless irreversible, regardless of leadership changes. However, in the short run there may well be some serious reversals in terms of human rights, opportunities for foreign investment, and business. Some of these symptoms appeared in late 1995. The question will be to what degree the leaders and planners can control the dissatisfaction created by living standard differentials between the peasants and others not involved in the current entrepreneurial rush.

The leading U.S. export products to China, which totaled $9.3 billion in 1994, are so diversified that it should encourage some further research by would-be China traders. U.S. exports include: aircraft and parts, cereals, cotton yarn and fabrics, machinery, fertilizer, iron and steel, plastics and resins, scientific and medical instruments, and wood and wood pulp. There is a market for consumer goods (Avon does just fine there), although not on the scale of the products mentioned above. But given a population of more than one and a quarter billion, a very small fragment of the market can mean really big sales figures. One of the problems with U.S. commercial relations with China is the huge and growing trade deficit, second only to Japan's, created by U.S. imports of $38.8 billion compared to $9.3 billion in exports. This creates friction between China and the United States, but there is hope that the USTR and other agencies will continue with a moderate and patient approach to correcting the deficit and avoid confrontations that might threaten China's most-favored nation status. It remains astonishing that China has managed to develop the buying power and economic growth it has in such a relatively short time especially in view of the ongoing ideological constraints.

In summary, China's commercial potential is huge, and even the immediate prospects are very substantial, but they require heavy-duty negotiating with some of the world's toughest and cleverest businesspeople, combined with long delays and red tape. Exceptions occur when Chinese entrepreneurs specifically target your firm and your product for reasons of their own. When that occurs, many things happen quickly that might otherwise seem impossible.

Experience has indicated that in high-tech areas the Chinese prefer to deal with small firms on the cutting edge. In our opinion this sometimes is the case because it is easier to acquire technology from a small firm that is anxious to please to complete the sale. In contrast, the larger, more sophisticated firms, like Hewlett Packard, understandably want to realize something for the technology transfer in addition to the product sale alone. There are also special problems with U.S. export licenses because there are still far more special restrictions on China than on most other countries.

In terms of *Euromoney*'s country risk, China is ranked number 42, near the bottom of the first quartile. Its letters of credit have been reliable, although occasionally delayed, and the Chinese will not permit them to be confirmed. There have, at times, been delays or problems because of foreign exchange shortages, but unless it is for a multimillion dollar deal, most feel safe with a letter of credit from the Central Bank or a lesser bank that is specifically approved to deal in dollar credits. I award China a DTD rating of 5, emphasizing the factors of future potential and rapid growth.

South Korea is another major customer, importing $18 billion in 1994, which places the country in sixth place on the list of best U.S. customers. The country has a not-unreasonable trade deficit, at least relative to China, Japan, and Taiwan. South Korea is one the four nations of East and Southeast Asia known as a *Tiger* because of its fast and aggressive economic growth. Even though South Korea's economy continues to grow, it has many negative trade imbalances of its own, and it fears a repeat of the rapid growth of imports in the late 1980s which then led to a severe "frugality campaign" designed to reduce nonessential imports and consumer goods. There are also prohibitions on many agriculture products. Subsequent negotiations have persuaded South Korea to abate this campaign, but it remains to be seen what the government really does. Many of South Korea's import restrictions are not transparent and therefore difficult to monitor on a government to government basis. While it is a major market with a bright future, it is not an easy market, and it has many hidden as well as announced trade barriers.

South Korea is ranked number 26 in *Euromoney*'s country-risk list, a good ranking for a newly industrialized country (NIC). I would rate it a 4 for Degree of Trading Difficulty.

North Korea is quite another story. It is suffering a U.S. trade embargo, besides being the very last ranked in terms of country risk, at 187. As Cuba begins to slip away from the Marxist fold, North Korea remains the only hardline, doctrinaire Marxist country left in the world. With Kim Jung Il, the son of its long standing dictator, Kim Il Sung, having assumed power after his father's death, North Korea has become even more of an enigma in terms of world peace. It may represent a still greater threat considering Kim Il Jung's possible geopolitical and nuclear ambitions. Many observers think that his ambitions are similar to his father's or worse and that they may even be more threatening because of the need for a crisis of some kind to take North Koreans' minds off their serious consumer shortages. But despite this unease and uncertainty, the prediction remains that, short of a nuclear standoff, the Asia-Pacific area will grow at twice the rate of either the EU or NAFTA blocs.

The leading developed industrial country of East Asia, Japan, is the second-largest economy in the world and the second-largest buyer of U.S. exports in 1994 at $53.5 billion—second only to Canada which purchased $114.4 billion. If manufactured exports alone are considered, however, Japan drops to the third-largest buyer of U.S exports, being exceeded in that category by Mexico. Unfortunately, the U.S. imported from Japan

$119.1 billion, producing by far our largest trade deficit, although most recently this negative trend has begun to decline. A key to our future economic success with Japan, as well as to the continued close political alliance between our two countries, may rest with the ability of the Japanese to force their government to make infrastructure improvements to benefit their living standards and real income. Such a tendency is increasingly evident, especially in the younger generation, aided in part by the USTR negotiations. These trends must be accompanied by more transparent import regulations, a streamlined distribution structure, and more retail competition. Some of these trends seem to be developing.

Japan hosts many excellent trade fairs for almost every range of merchandise, and the Japanese External Trade Organization (JETRO) really can be helpful to the newcomer to business in Japan. Its offices can be found in New York, San Francisco, Los Angeles, Chicago, Houston, Atlanta, and Denver. Japan is a very large market, and getting started there is a slow and time-consuming affair unless they seek out you and your product (a sourcing process at which Japanese businesspeople are masters). Short of being so fortunate, do not let the anecdotes of hidden trade barriers and structural impediments necessarily discourage you from trying. If, however, there prove to be significant barriers to the import of your product, hidden or otherwise, there is little you can do to overcome them unless you are very powerful or incredibly patient. Problems are not easy to recognize because there is no valid system for comparison with the success of a competitor or an industry. Careful review of the export development process at every step should nevertheless make any such roadblock detectable, in which case forget Japan for the time being and get on with other markets. If there are structural impediments, you may be able to enter the market, but you will probably have to settle for a much smaller market share than you deserve, although this can still be a very meaningful sales figure.

Japan is a huge market, requiring enormous expenditures in everything from travel to food and entertainment to office space to consultants and advertising. Advance research and a substantial budget are essential. Experienced business travelers tell me it now takes well over $500 per day to travel in Japan. Quality control is more important there than anywhere in the world, and a well-known and respected trademark or unique styling is very helpful; no country is more brand-conscious than Japan, whether in consumer goods or in commercial and industrial supplies. It is also critical to find the right distributor the first time out, since the Japanese hate "disorderly markets," which overlapping distributors or changes in distributors can lead to. To repeat, if you don't have the time or money and appropriate product to meet these challenges, it may be better to defer this market, however appealing, until you are ready. Currently, some key product ranges include pharmaceutical (caution—the Japanese equivalent of FDA approval can take years), medical equipment, computer software, and wood products. It has always been a great market for apparel, and especially for famous brands, forward fashions, and niche area products.

Japan is ranked number 2 in the world in *Euromoney*'s country-risk rankings, second only to Luxembourg. (The United States which once held the number 2 ranking, has now slipped to number 5, behind Switzerland and France.) As a rule, commercial risks are reasonable and Japanese businesses tend to be stable and to concentrate on long-term profits rather than on putting one another out of business. This is not to suggest that the country doesn't have its share of hustlers and highly leveraged start-up businesses. But whatever is said about the difficulties of doing business in Japan, it is far from impossible if you have a product that is acceptable to Japanese culture or industry and has no special barriers to overcome. For the small exporter with a product the country likes we would give Japan a DTD rating of 3. For a big business with a high profile, the difficulty rating would be 3.5 or 4, depending on the industrial/governmental politics that apply.

The Republic of China, or Taiwan, as most traders call it, is a somewhat different situation. Its trade barriers are more visible but its hidden barriers may be fewer. It is the second of the Four Tigers and is considered the most mature of the four. In fact, it is sufficiently mature that it is said to be starting to move from a manufacturing economy to a service economy, which, if true, makes the appellation of newly industrialized country (NIC) passé. Taiwan's total trade with the U.S., its most important trading partner, is the largest of the Tigers at $43.8 billion, of which $17.1 billion is in exports. This makes it our seventh-best customer but regrettably also our fifth largest trade deficit, which is nevertheless remarkable for so small an island country. One can well understand why mainland China insists that Taiwan must ultimately unify with it. As China's own development proceeds, there are no doubt commercial interests within Taiwan that will increasingly feel the same.

As Taiwan's economy matures, the country can afford to permit entry of more upscale consumer goods and sophisticated capital goods. Taiwan is also investing heavily in its infrastructure, and American companies have managed to be very competitive and relatively successful in the transportation, telecommunications, energy, and environmental protection areas. The latter will have further support through the United States–Asia Environmental Partnership (US-AEP). This partnership is intended to promote environmental protection and, at the same time, to encourage the many U.S. businesses involved in the engineering, technology, and manufacturing for this product sector through grants and other means of financial assistance. Taiwan's falling tariffs and acceptance of GATT should also improve U.S. export prospects.

On the downside, Taiwan has developed a large and slow-moving bureaucracy that is very difficult and frustrating to deal with. Your customers may have a problem obtaining import permits, for example. Taiwan has also become a very expensive place in which to do business and requires substantial research for success. Unfortunately, it offers limited protection for intellectual property rights, with improvements from the impact of 1992 legislation on this subject still to be determined. To enable the United States to recognize the mainland People's Republic of China (PRC), our government officially ended its recognition of the government of the Republic of China (Taiwan). As a result, instead of a U.S. embassy in Taiwan, we have an American Institute, and what would normally be the Taiwanese embassy in the United States is known as the Coordination Council for North American Affairs.

Taiwan enjoys a high ranking in terms of country risk. It is ranked fifteenth in the world and is also projected to be the eleventh-best in terms of *Euromoney*'s economic outlook projections for 1995–1996, an honor it shares in East Asia with Japan, which is projected to be third-best. On my DTD rating I give it a 3.5 and hope that the present direction continues, including a decline in tariffs and improvement in its intellectual property rights climate.

Hong Kong has been every entrepreneur's dream—few rules and no holds barred. The competition is intense, money flows like wine, and the commercial excitement in the air is intoxicating. Consider the fact that this tiny enclave imports from the United States $11.4 billion and in return exports $9.7 billion to us, making it our eleventh-largest customer even ahead of China itself. These figures include everything from airplanes to lingerie, with no tariffs, no permits, and virtually no regulations. Hong Kong's economy continues to grow at a rate in excess of 4 to 5 percent, and each Hong Kong resident spends an average of over $1,150 annually on U.S. products. Hong Kong infrastructure projects offer great opportunities, with the United States continuing to be the largest supplier of goods and services to the Hong Kong government. Hong Kong, now a British colony, will become part of China in 1997, just as Macao, a nearby Portuguese colony, will do in 1999. But except for occasional hiccups and some worry, relatively few firms have left or are changing their basic strategy; the frantic economic activity and investment continues apace despite some recent reports of capital outflow. This overall positive outlook is further borne out by Hong Kong's very consistent and favorable ranking in terms of country risk, which heavily weights the political risk factor, twenty-fourth among the nations of the world.

The trade figures quoted above must be tempered by the knowledge that Hong Kong is a backdoor to and from China, so that much merchandise that appears to be going into Hong Kong is in reality going to China, and vice versa. The upside to this, however, is that Hong Kong is a perfect area in which to seek out future business for the Chinese mainland, including future China distributors or partners. The myriad Hong Kong trade fairs are an excellent place for these activities. Hong Kong gets a

DTD rating of 2, for its freedom of economic action, its eagerness to do business, its large, high-income population, and its present and future as a door to one of the world's greatest potential markets. East Asia as a region is one of the strongest areas in terms of country-risk, with all nations of the region ranked in the top half of the first quartile (with the obvious exception of North Korea). To the region of East Asia as a whole I give a DTD rating of 3.5.

Southeast Asia

Southeast Asia is one more very strong and vibrant region in Asia, boasting some of the globe's highest growth rates. It is also a supplier of labor to the world, and to East Asia in particular. It is organized into the Association of South East Asian Nations (ASEAN). This is an active trade bloc that shows promise for continued development both in terms of political cooperation and in terms of internal tariff reduction. ASEAN includes Thailand, Malaysia, Singapore, Brunei, the Philippines, and Indonesia, with a combined population of 380 million—larger than the EU, although its combined 1993 GNP of about $445 billion is a fraction of the EU's more than $4 trillion. Collectively the ASEAN nations currently have by far the highest economic growth rate in the world. Except for the Philippines, which has suffered severe political and infrastructure problems, all these nations averaged growth levels in excess of 7 percent from 1988 through 1994.

By far the leading member of the ASEAN group—and of Southeast Asia, for that matter—is Singapore, one of the Four Tigers and the only Tiger outside East Asia. It is ranked number 8 among nations in terms of its country risk and also judged by *Euromoney* to have the world's best 1995–1996 economic outlook (an honor it has often held). As a customer for U.S. exports (our tenth-largest), it buys $13 billion and sells us $15.4 billion. The imports to the United States largely represent goods manufactured under U.S. purchase contracts in Singapore and elsewhere in Southeast Asia. (The same could be said of our imports from East Asia, especially in the case of Hong Kong, Korea, and Taiwan.) Singapore has long had the role of a regional trade channel for many kinds of purchases and services throughout the Southeast Asia region, although its neighbors are actively trying to discourage this practice so that their own agents and brokers can reap those distribution profits. It has done the most to establish itself as a regional services center and to develop its economy in the direction of becoming a more capital-intensive and higher value-added base. In fact, Singapore, like the other three Tigers and especially Hong Kong, is a classic example of national progression from a cottage industry base—usually textiles and apparel—to ever-more sophisticated manufactured goods with higher value-added input. Everyone can benefit from this progression, as the increasingly affluent population then buys more exports from the industrial nations, including the United States.

Future development in this industrial progression role has now passed to the remaining players in Southeast Asia. It is for this reason that the United States suffers a trade deficit in much of the region. Southeast Asia is a primary source of low-cost labor, and in turn the less developed countries' (LDC) trade surpluses permit them to gain in economic strength and per capita income—the only way we can ultimately encourage democracy and peaceful coexistence, as well as gain new customers with buying power.

The second-largest Southeast Asia trading partner of the United States is Malaysia, with $7 billion in export purchases and $14 billion in sales to this country. It has successfully industrialized itself and has only recently emerged as a middle-income country—a regularly occurring phenomenon in Asia, as we have noted. Per capita income has risen in the past two decades from $700 to $3613. It is indicative that, in 1996, a pair of office buildings will be completed in Kuala Lumpur that will be the world's tallest, even taller than the Chicago Sears Tower.

Another rising star, Thailand, is expected to be among the fastest-growing economies in the world in 1996. At the beginning of the 1980s, Thailand was primarily agriculturally oriented, but by the end of the decade, it was well on its way to industrialization. An area of special success in Thailand for American businesspeople has been franchising, an important component of our foreign investment and sales worldwide. One reason for U.S. franchising success in the country is Thailand's youthful population (60 percent are under 27 years of age), their propensity to spend, and their fondness for things American. The July 1993[2] issue of *International Business* states that Thailand offers a fine opportunity for small businesses, both because of the vast variety of goods and services needed there and because of the follow-up needs generated by the country's many infrastructure projects. However, the article adds that one should not expect it to be an easy place to do business. Its inclusion in the USTR list as one of three countries cited for failing to adequately protect intellectual property rights, such as trademarks and patents, is one example. Business is often difficult in countries going through such a transition phase. Singapore is probably a major exception in this regard.

The Philippines and Indonesia have similar trade figures where business with the United States is concerned, buying between $2.8 and $3.9 billion and selling between $5.7 and $6.5 billion. Much the healthier of the two, economically speaking, is Indonesia. Even so, Indonesia accounts for 60 percent of the ASEAN population but only one-third of its GNP. It is making progress, however, and has aggressively deregulated and attracted substantial foreign investment and U.S. suppliers in the area, all of whom expect substantial sales growth. This will include construction services and supplies, as Indonesia rapidly invests in an enlarged infrastructure. There are still, however, many regulations and legal problems that give Indonesia a reputation for being a relatively difficult place in which to do business or perform services.

In the case of the Philippines, the political corruption and infrastructure problems created by the Marcos regime, followed by the uncertainties and political instability of the Aquino presidency and the withdrawal of several U.S. defense bases, have kept the country from becoming a fifth Tiger and experiencing the economic success of its ASEAN neighbors. Although the situation is now improving, not long ago the lights could be expected to go out in Manila almost every afternoon by 2:00 P.M. or earlier for lack of adequate electrical generation and business regularly came to a halt in many buildings, especially when the reservoirs dropped after the rainy season. As a result there are thousands of electric generators in the city, but many do not serve the offices on the upper floors (making the Philippines a top customer for diesel-generator manufacturers). Not only were no new electric plants being built but some of the existing hydroelectric plants had ceased to be fully operational.

With the Philippines' current President Ferdinand Ramos gaining popularity and his administration's economic reforms taking a sound and businesslike approach to governing the country, both realities and expectations are changing. Privatization is proceeding, and the government-sponsored telecommunications monopoly, a major stumbling block, is being broken. Even now, foreign exchange availability is not a problem, and the country has a very sophisticated and reasonably aggressive banking system interested in supporting its small businesspeople and contractors. A few random indications of change are that inflation has been sharply reduced, the population has become more health- and environment-conscious, and imports of high-end apparel have risen 20 percent. Even with its problems, the Philippines purchased $3.9 billion in U.S. exports and sold us $5.7 billion in 1994.

With the exception of Brunei (whose 1994 exports were $376 million and which is said to have the highest per capita income in the world), Papua New Guinea (whose 1994 exports were just $65 million), and possibly Vietnam, the remaining nations of Southeast Asia are rather impoverished and undeveloped, mostly as a result of wars and revolutions. But considering the region's potential, they could someday be Tigers too.

Vietnam is definitely the best prospect among them and has many assets, many of them left over from its rather sophisticated colonial history. The country boasts a 90 percent multilingual literacy rate plus excellent natural resources in coal, oil, and gas. The United States has recently established some diplomatic relations and most of the embargo has been lifted—and none too soon, either, in view of many other nations' much earlier de facto removal of embargoes and their commercial activity there. As foreign investment funds from the International Monetary Fund (IMF) and World Bank pour into the country, changes are expected to occur rapidly. It is said that the World Bank is grossly underreporting the economy and its assets. For example, the DOC's Commercial Service reports that 87 percent of Vietnam's households own television sets, and that savings are far above official figures, presumably in mattress-type hiding places. The Vietnamese love American consumer products and many such goods began making their way into the country even before the embargo was lifted. It won't be easy, however, since foreign and especially Japanese competition is already there and will be very well established before U.S. business can position itself there with strength after U.S.-Vietnam trade agreements are reached and "most favored nation" (MFN) trade status is established.

Renewed fighting in Cambodia has had a chilling effect on business with that country, the best export opportunities for the time being are again through multilateral institution projects like the World Bank. The situation in Laos is similar, in terms of using Asian Development Bank and other programs to sell support materials for infrastructure projects. Myanmar (Burma) has some activity, including U.S. consumer goods, but most business is done through countertrade. The country's extremely repressive government and its human rights abuse record makes it a place to avoid for now.

Although not mentioned on a country-by-country basis, the best export product prospects are much the same throughout Southeast Asia—as they are in much of Asia, and indeed, throughout the world. It is a list composed of computers and peripherals; software; aircraft and parts; industrial chemicals; plastics and resins; paper, paperboard, and wood products; food processing equipment; medical equipment; environmental and pollution control products; and, most of all, telecommunications equipment. Drop a few products for each country and add one or two, but the list remains similar. The continuous theme and sales success standouts virtually worldwide, however, are computer-related products, medical equipment, and telecommunications. With the exception of the Philippines, the ASEAN nations rank quite well within the first quartile of the world in terms of country risk, and receive a DTD rating of 3.5. For Southeast Asia as a whole, the rating should be a 4 with a few notable exceptions, which make an overall rating difficult due to the broad differences.

It is hard to leave Asia without mentioning the 18-nation Asia-Pacific Economic Cooperation (APEC) group. Besides the entire North American representation of the United States, Canada, and Mexico, and Chile from South America, APEC includes Australia, Brunei, the People's Republic of China (PRC), Hong Kong, Indonesia, Japan, Korea, Malaysia, New Zealand, Papua New Guinea, the Philippines, Singapore, Taiwan (called for this purpose "Chinese Taipei"), and Thailand.

APEC is enjoying a greater level of sincere cooperative effort than was to be expected from what appears to be primarily a political showcase. While it cannot be considered a present or future trade bloc, it can encourage an existing trend of cooperation in trade growth and international investment, furthering the objectives of GATT and NAFTA. It might also help to forestall the kind of misunderstandings that lead to trade trend reversals.

Australasia

We are treating here Australia and New Zealand together as making up an entity of its own—Australasia—for in economic and business terms that is the most expeditious solution. Others would include in the group some of the neighboring Pacific islands, and still others insist Australia is a continent entirely to itself, which it technically is, or otherwise it must be considered by far the world's largest island.

Australia and New Zealand

Australia is unique in being both a country and an entire continent. It is a hospitable land and a very enjoyable place to do business, but it is not without its problems. Australia was our thirteenth-largest customer in 1994, with $9.8 billion, but suffered a severe trade deficit with the U.S. because it sold us only $3.2 billion. Its product needs are similar to those just named for much of Asia, with the addition of automotive parts and service equipment.

In spite of Australia's having one of the largest landmasses in the world, its population is highly concentrated in six cities. Sydney and Melbourne alone are home to more than one-third of the population—some six million of the country's 18 million people. This greatly simplifies marketing strategies.

Australia was once one of the most tariff-protected nations in the world, a mistake for which it has paid dearly. This policy resulted in a socialist-leaning government and a spoiled labor market, which in turn led to a lack of global competitiveness. It has taken the last five electoral terms—won by the Labor Party, a reformed liberal rather than conservative government—to start a major dismantling of trade barriers and a drive to compete with the rest of the world, although some serious trade barriers still remain. The country is still experiencing a lingering recession, but U.S. exports have continued to grow and U.S. traders feel very much at home in the Australian business and cultural environment. There are no exchange or financial controls to create problems and the United States is Australia's prime source of foreign investment. Australia is ranked seventeenth in the world in terms of country risk and I give it a DTD rating of 3, with sheer distance and travel time being the only constraining factors.

The similarities between New Zealand and Australia are as marked as the differences. Although the two countries are neighbors and both members of the British Commonwealth, the people of New Zealand tend to be very much a part of Great Britain, whereas the Australians are much more outgoing and American in style. New Zealand shares with Australia the curse of a history of high tariffs, although for quite different reasons. Australia wanted to be an "island unto itself" and manufacture or grow products to fill most of its own needs, resulting in very short and inefficient production runs that needed protection. New Zealand was an agricultural outpost or farm for Great Britain, specializing in sheep husbandry and very happy doing so until Britain joined the Common Market, forcing it to revoke the special trade privileges it had granted New Zealand in return for its dedicated-supplier role. The result created chaos in New Zealand that is only now being resolved with numerous economic reforms. These include privatization, for the country was also a rather socialized state.

New Zealand is a country in which it is very easy and pleasant to do business, but it is a very small market and of course a very distant one. It is ranked eighteenth in country risk and gets a 4 on our DTD ratings.

Oceania—the Independent Pacific Islands

These are lovely islands to visit, and if one can do some business in the process, one can hardly claim it to be anything but a success. In total, exports to these island are less than $400 million and imports a fraction of that. Clearly, much of the export is to support the tourist industry, which would have very little in terms of local supply except seafood and tropical fruit. Those exporters who do serve this area, however, are very crucial to the economy and tend to be specialists, as in food for the various hotels or procurement offices for the principal retail establishments on the islands. It is something of a fraternity, and while it can be a very good and profitable business, it will take some time and effort to get acquainted prior to breaking into it. The reason is the local buyers cannot risk enmity from their prime suppliers, to whom they owe their existence. Although widely varying in degrees of poverty or potential, a DTD rating of 6 would probably be generous, especially considering travel distances and difficulties, and miniscule market size.

Antarctica

This very large frozen continent on the southern axis of our world might be considered to have great political instability because many nations make many overlapping claims, yet all continue to cooperate in the name of science. No people, no problems, no business, no risk, no ratings!

Endnotes

1. David E. Moore, "China, the Superpower," editorial, *International Business*, American International Publishing Corp., Harrison, New York, August 1993.
2. John Clowley, "A Dragon in the Making," *International Business*, July 1993.

PART 3

International Selling and Promotion

9

Introducing Your Product Overseas

Because international business travel is a major expense, you must develop an interest in your product among potential customers before going abroad. This means that in the beginning you need to learn the procedures and the skills of direct-mail selling—which today often means direct-mail faxing. In fact, you will probably find that direct-mail selling and its follow-up correspondence will always be a critical part of your international business. Thus, mastering this skill is key to your future success.

Direct-mail selling is a business in itself of course, and any local library will have some excellent books on the subject. One recent book, written by William J. Bond for entrepreneurs wanting to get into the mail-order business, is called *Home-Based Mail Order*[1] and offers many basic rules for writing direct-mail letters and brochures. As an exporter writing to gain initial interest from importers, distributors, agents, and retailers abroad, your problems are specialized, of course, but you must still answer to the principles of gaining attention, telling your story with both power and brevity, and inviting immediate action. Even though you may have elected to use an export management company, you should get involved with its efforts to put together a direct mailing with promotional material. Your input can help make it a better mailing and improve the EMC's grasp of the product.

Key Points in Overseas Sales Communication

Keep It Simple, Clear, and Concise

Your initial contact will most likely be in English, which means it is probably not the mother tongue of your intended reader and therefore must be simple and easy to understand without sounding patronizing. It must also be interesting without relying on colloquialisms or innuendoes that might either be completely lost on your reader or worse, counterproductive. Always imagine yourself reading such material in Spanish or some other language you studied in school but have never lived with. This applies to both general and follow-up correspondence as well as to your introductory material.

Early in my own career I was fortunate to have a multilingual secretary who one day entered my office laughing. When asked why, she explained that she had just been taking dictation from my machine and I had used the phrase "ball-park figure,"—an expression we use without thinking twice. She reminded me that baseball is not a game common to every country and certainly not to the country I was addressing, so no one would have the faintest idea of what I was talking about. This is a good lesson to remember, even when conversing with overseas customers, for even though they may speak English quite fluently, it is doubtful they understand colloquialisms that seem so second nature to you.

We should digress at this point to discuss styles of correspondence and some pros and cons as to translating into the prospect's language versus corresponding in English. There is no general agreement on this issue. Naturally, if your business is going to focus on one or two language areas, you and others in management should speak and write easily in that tongue. Fluent communication in the language of your customers not only makes good business sense but gives you an important advantage. It's essential that your files and your proposals be in a language in which more than one member of the management team is fluent—and that means fluent in the business usage and customs of that language. If this is not practical, it is better to do business in English, so that all the staff involved can get into a file and learn everything necessary before responding to an inquiry. When translation does become necessary, as possibly in the case of an agreement or specifications, it can be attached to the English original. If you are targeting a number of companies or world regions, the odds are that the latter approach will best suit your efforts—at least initially.

Even when someone speaks a language well, he or she may miss important nuances or not realize the extent to which business usage differs from social usage. Failure to understand such things can more than outweigh the advantage gained by speaking the language. Here are some examples of various linguistic sensitivities and idiosyncrasies: Germans are extremely formal and fond of professional titles. The French tend to be rather formal and elaborate in their phrasing, very proud of their language, and quite offended when it is misused or when traditional linguistic courtesies are omitted. Russians are said to be very relaxed in their business correspondence styles, though they are especially appre-

ciative when others make an effort to use their language. The Japanese
are quite at ease with English, though their own style tends to be very
formal. (This is also true of Arabic-speakers.) Scandinavia and Latin
America are other areas in which speaking English seems to serve us
very well. If you should decide to use Spanish, don't try to do so in
Brazil. Brazilians speak Portuguese and are offended by the implication
that Spanish and Portuguese are somehow interchangeable. While they
may understand Spanish, they are proud of the fact that it has different
linguistic origins; many would rather be addressed in English than in
Spanish.

This recital of language differences is but a sample to emphasize the
added problems you can encounter if you elect to "do it their way." It is
one of our good fortunes to have a language that is so universally used in
international trade, and I would be cautious about throwing that advantage away unless you feel certain of real bottom line gains. Still, AT&T
thinks translating is important enough to have developed a translation
service for both telephonic and written communication in 140 languages.
They call it the *Language Line Service* and you can get more information
by calling 800/367-9559, extension 46. There are also many fine translation services in every major city.

Keep It Cost-Effective

This might be a corollary to the first point. Keeping your message simple
also keeps it brief and to the point. Postage has become an increasingly
expensive item and much more so for overseas mail. The question of
weight must be kept very much in mind and cannot be resolved by simply using tissue-thin paper—which tends to look cheap and does not present your product well. It is also vital to keep your message short if you
are sending your introduction by fax.

Make It Believable

Your reader is far away and should not get the feeling that he or she must
wade through a lot of puffery to get to the facts. Building confidence in
the unknown entity you represent is a major secret to success and
overblown claims are not the way that is done.

Be Specific

This is part of being believable. State the specifications, shipping weights,
and volumes and anything else about your product that will help your
readers determine whether it is practical for their purposes or customers
and whether its physical characteristics lend themselves to their shipping
and warehousing parameters.

Consider Your Audience

Try to picture the type of individual who will be making the decision about whether to buy your product, or who will be responsible for investigating your offer further. Imagine if you can that person's management level, work, and cultural surroundings as you reach out to them in your written message.

These are but a few of the most obvious things to be aware of in developing a promotion strategy that includes direct mail. Don't forget to maintain a healthy respect for your direct-mail output. In this country we have so much junk mail that we tend to demean its stature as a promotional tool, but the technique is much less well understood and used in most other parts of the world. It has been developed into a fine art here, so take advantage of one of our homegrown skills; your presentation may have far more impact than you might imagine from your domestic reactions. There is a lot to writing good copy, and unless you have had experience in this area, you will enhance your chances of success with a little self-education and/or some professional help. At the very least, let someone read your offerings who has had some experience in advertising and direct-mail copy writing and who can understand the benefits and use of the product you are promoting.

Should you be interested in further details, see my previous book, *Exporting from Start to Finance.*[2] In it you will find six chapters covering the subject of introducing and promoting your product overseas, including comments from leading writers and specialists in this area of expertise. You will also find, in Appendix F1 of this book, an extensive list of books on the subject of export marketing.

In the July 1993 issue of *International Business*,[3] writer Jerry DeMuth describes a clever strategy used by Admiral Screw Co., a $5 million screw manufacturer, to find overseas markets. Its marketers simply looked up their domestic customers in various directories to locate their foreign branches. They then contacted those overseas branches directly, with amazing results, and now do 25 percent of their business in exports. The article describes other firms taking a similar approach, also with excellent results.

The Fax Revolution

As we have already mentioned, the fax has been a major benefit to the exporter, not only saving postage, but speeding responses, which permits you to take an early reading on the effectiveness of your message and the interest in your product. You can get an idea of your chances of success on the current promotion in days instead of a month or two. Use it for all it's worth!

The fax should not, however, be overestimated. Effective use of facsimile transmission depends on the nature of the product you're promoting and how briefly you can make a good case for it. Don't impose on your prospects by sending lengthy transmissions that end up jamming in their machine or garbling at some point to everyone's frustration.

Use the fax as a means of determining interest *before* you send expensive brochures or free samples. Hold off on that generous impulse to offer free samples or catalogs in your direct-mail or fax presentations. Even if they themselves cost you little or nothing, sending them will be too expensive to sustain profitably at this stage of the sales effort (and remember, the world is full of people who seem to have nothing better to do than ask to see such material without having any genuine interest). You may need to invent some qualifying questions without being too obvious that you are screening. Unfortunately, it is only the rare exception when an entire initial transaction can be successfully consummated by fax.

Another caution regarding overreliance on fax transmissions relates to the odds that they have been received in readable condition—or received at all. In some respects the fax can be something of a "black hole"; there's no immediate way of telling whether—or how—it arrived. Therefore, it is wise to determine if the country involved has reliable telephone service. If it is questionable, as in much of Eastern Europe for example, your introduction may be better initiated by mail. Even in countries with good telephone service, I would not abandon further attempts to introduce yourself and your product by mail in the case of prime prospects that have not responded to your fax.

Objectives in the Introductory Phase

During the start-up phase you are probably not going to sell much besides samples (even if you are lucky). Your objective should be to get descriptive material and if practical, samples, into the hands of *qualified* buyers. During this phase, you should also begin developing a profile of your typical customers, with your first overseas sales trip in mind. It will help if you target your initial probe in areas where it will be practical for you to plan a trip. Export selling cannot be done at a profitable and sustainable level without travel. When you finally do take a trip, roughly 50 to 60 percent of your available appointment opportunities at any given stopover should be with prospects who have agreed to meet with you during your visit. So why spend the larger part of your presumably limited budget on introducing yourself in areas you can't afford to travel to at this time. Finally, don't expect to sell enough during the initial phase to pay for that necessary future sales trip—it won't happen, and you will need to have funds in reserve to take the trip.

Finding Names and Leads for Initial Overseas Contacts

Assuming that your direct-mail and promotion materials are written and ready to go, where do you send them? In Chapter 5 we discussed the main types of distribution channels open to you as an export operation. The next step is to obtain the specific names and addresses of the kind of firms or contacts you seek for each target area. To do this, you need to explore the various sources of categorized, and hopefully qualified, leads available to you. The sources you choose and the parameters for selection within those sources will not only determine the cost-effectiveness of your introduction, but very probably the whole future of your business. Fortunately, there is a wide variety of sophisticated and well-maintained databases—available from both public and private sector sources—out there to help you.

International Trade Office Contact Sources

A discussion with your trade specialist at the nearest DOC District Office is a good place to start. If a district office is not readily available, call a trade specialist at the Trade Information Center in Washington, D.C., on its free hotline number: 800/USA-TRADE (800/872-8723).

You will find that there are two basic products that the DOC's International Trade Administration (ITA) and its Commercial Service trade specialists will mention. The first is the computerized *Foreign Traders Index*, containing over 55,000 names and addresses of individuals and firms abroad that have expressed an interest in certain U.S. products. It is categorized by commodity and by country and provides the firm's contact name, address, telephone, latest year of contact, year established, number of employees and relative size, and the products it handles by name and by harmonized commodity number.

The Index is updated monthly on two CD-ROM disks known as the *National Trade Data Bank* (*NTDB*), which also collects export promotion and international trade data from 17 federal agencies on foreign market research, including those prepared by the Commercial Service and Foreign Agricultural Service (FAS), Census Bureau data on U.S. imports and exports by commodity and country, and the *CIA World Factbook*. The disks are updated monthly, and a personal copy can be obtained for $40 per monthly issue or $360 annually. The CD-ROMs are also available at over 900 federal depositary libraries nationwide. (The NTDB offerings are discussed in more detail in Chapter 17, both as to their full scope and their individual offerings.)

Allied with the Foreign Traders Index is the *Trade Opportunities Program* (TOP), which is very timely because it represents the inquiries or leads of the moment that are electronically transmitted daily. These are the leads that continue to build the Index as the older names are dropped off. This TOP information is posted on DOC's Economic Bulletin Board (EBB), which also posts the latest statistical releases from the Bureau of Census and several other federal agencies. The EBB can be accessed each day through a personal computer with a modem at a subscription cost of $35 per year, plus some modest access charges. A twin program is called EBB/FAX which permits your fax machine to receive the same data. These daily leads are also published in the *Journal of Commerce* as well as through other, private trade information services, depending on your area.

The final product of this series is the *Export Contact List Service* (ECLS). This currently costs 25 cents for each prospective overseas customer name on a printed list or mail-ready on gummed labels. It is selectively drawn, based on the screening criteria you provide, from names in the Foreign Traders Index, augmented and screened by input from the Commercial Service officer in the country of interest.

The key DOC program for finding initial contacts in the form of agents or distributors seeks a few qualified names in the country or marketing region selected. This is the *Agent/Distributor Service* (*ADS*). The program is targeted to specific countries for a specific product or product range. The Commercial Service officers in the commercial section of the embassy or consulate in the city and country selected attempt to identify and solicit the active interest of up to six qualified prospects that have examined the literature and catalogs included with your request. This service currently costs $250 per country/product and can be very fruitful. Since this is a custom service, researched and prepared for you in the field, its effectiveness varies with the U.S. foreign office involved and their present staff and budget. Therefore, do not let a poor result discourage you from future work with the ADS or the Commercial Service in general and, conversely, do not let an excellent outcome lead you to expect miracles in each case. Sometimes the DOC trade specialist can give you an idea of which foreign offices are, or are not, currently providing satisfactory responses.

A somewhat more sophisticated, and definitely more expensive, service is offered under the name of *Customized Sales Survey*, a custom-tailored research service available from some foreign Commercial Service locations that goes into depth on marketing and foreign representation for individual products in selected countries. The resulting reports are based on field interviews and surveys relative to customers, competition, comparable products, applicable trade events, and other related information. The cost runs from $500 to $4000 per country.

Within the aegis of the DOC is a media contact mechanism called the *Commercial News USA*. This is an illustrated catalog-magazine distributed through U.S. embassies in 140 countries as well as to visitors at overseas trade events. Your advertisement in one issue of this publication, which produces 10 issues per year, is $250 for one-sixth of a page in a section appropriate to your industry or product. The magazine also has a special section for new products or products that it deems to have especially high export potential. This can be a very effective tool, producing a great number of inquiries for a relatively small cost. For the special section only certain products will be accepted as qualified according to the DOC guidelines.

There are other means for contacts through the DOC that come about through travel and overseas trade shows. These will be discussed in later chapters on travel and trade development. One, however, can be taken advantage of without overseas travel and at a relatively low cost, possibly in cooperation with your supplier. We refer to DOC's Foreign Buyer Program, in which the DOC encourages foreign buyers to attend selected U.S. trade shows in industries with high export potential. At these shows the DOC will ask the foreign buyers to register in a special area to make contact more accessible to you. It may also make these registration lists available later. If you, as an export management company, can get your supplier to display at such a show, you should also participate so that you can handle the foreign visitors at the booth. If you are a manufacturer taking part in the show, make sure that the person in charge of your new export division is there. In fact, at almost any U.S. show a supplier/manufacturer enters regardless of DOC participation, the EMC or export division should try being in attendance to handle the foreign contacts. They are all too often badly handled and poorly followed up by the domestic sales staff. It is usually easy to have the show management check its records on past foreign attendance.

The DOC *Catalog Missions* are also relatively inexpensive ways to make qualified, or at least well-targeted, contacts without traveling, if you find one that suits your product and target areas. The net results, however, usually match the much lower cost.

U.S. Department of Agriculture Trade Contact Sources

The Department of Agriculture's Foreign Agricultural Service (FAS) is similar in scope to the Department of Commerce's International Trade Administration and its Commercial Services, although FAS does not have district offices throughout the country for firsthand access. It does have a point of general access in Washington, D.C., however, known as the Trade Assistance and Promotion Office (TAPO), which will direct your inquiries to the best source and answer preliminary questions. TAPO can be reached by calling 202/720-7420 or by fax at 202/690-4374. Alternatively, you can also obtain preliminary information from the Trade Information Center (TIC) at 800/USA-TRADE. Because the entire FAS export program is detailed in Chapter 19, we will mention them only briefly here. The FAS groups its contact services under the name *AgExport Connections*. It has three specific services for overseas contacts which are:

1. *Trade Leads,* a service through which foreign buyer inquiries are sent in from the 80 FAS foreign offices and made available on the electronic bulletin boards, the *Journal of Commerce,* the AgExport fax connection, and the weekly *AgExport Trade Leads Bulletin.*

2. *Buyer Alert,* a weekly overseas newsletter intended to introduce food and agriculture products to foreign buyers. Exporters can prepare their product information and submit it to AgExport, where it will be edited and transmitted overseas for incorporation into a bulletin, newsletter, or fax at a modest fee.

3. *Foreign Buyer Lists,* a database of 20,000 foreign buyers of food and commodities. Lists are categorized by product and country and may be ordered for a specific commodity and country at $15 per list. The Foreign Traders Index in the NTDB contains the agricultural product buyer inquiries as well.

Nonfederal Trade Facilitation Assistance

State and local governments provide many services to exporters, and many have their own trade lead programs. State colleges and universities, as well as local chambers of commerce, export trade organizations, and nearby port authorities can also be a rich source of trade leads and many have well-established trade lead programs.

Contact Sources from the Private Sector

Mailing lists can be rented from private sources that are presorted by virtually any criteria and profile imaginable. The trick is to find the right source for you and to be sure of its lists' authenticity in terms of adequate testing. Libraries with a large business section will have directories providing names of direct-mail specialists, list suppliers and their databases, and catalogs that can lead you to the right suppliers. Ask your librarian for help. Industry trade associations and industry trade shows are another abundant source of such lists.

The foreign counterparts of U.S. trade associations are an excellent means of finding well-targeted prospects. The comparable domestic trade association often has the names of its own counterparts around the world. A publication called *Trade Directories of the World* contains a huge number of associations worldwide.[4] These directories will provide users of certain types of equipment common to their industry as well as the names of salespeople or sales organizations selling the products of the trade. A foreign trade association represents a highly targeted source of contacts and also provides some assurance of active involvement in the industry. Your own trade association may also be an excellent source for names as a result of international cooperation or from accumulated inquiries received from abroad.

There are private firms whose sole business is providing foreign mailing lists. Typical of these firms is Blytman International in Healdsburg, California. It offers lists sorted by type of business—retailers, wholesalers, manufacturers, agents, and distributors and so forth—as well as by country and product. Such companies try to keep their lists current and guarantee the names they provide by refunding if the mail is returned. But they do not refund your postage, which is the far greater cost, so use them with caution.

Another source that has come to my attention recently, but that I have not personally had experience with, is the *Standard Handbook of Industrial Distributors*.[5] At $95, it is relatively expensive, but claims to locate leading distributors, dealers, agents, and representatives by country and product. You will find other advertisements for similar publications, but they all share the problem of keeping current.

It sounds a bit odd or primitive, but the first private, nongovernment source for contacts that many exporters used was the yellow pages of overseas phone books. Probably as a last-minute resort, many business travelers still do, judging by the missing pages in hotel phone books. Many phone books of the major cities of the world can be found in your library and represent a fast and useful method of finding companies and services in your product category currently in business in specific cities of the world. It is a ploy so obvious that it is often overlooked, just as it is overlooked for domestic sourcing. Living in a major metropolitan area, I am often asked by new exporters for suggestions on how to source, or find this or that exotic item. I frequently suggest the *Thomas Register*, which is found in the library, or the *California Manufacturer's Register*, but add that first they might simply try looking in the telephone yellow pages of any major U.S. city. It's amazing how often this provides all the sources they need and then some.

Endnotes

1. William J. Bond, *Home-Based Mail Order*, Liberty Hall Press of McGraw-Hill, Inc., Blue Ridge Summit, Pennsylvania, 1990.
2. L. F. Wells and Karin B. Dulat, *Exporting from Start to Finance*, McGraw-Hill, New York, 1996.
3. Jerry DeMuth, "Stop-and-Go Exports," *International Business*, July 1993.
4. *Trade Directories of the World*, Croner Publications, Queens Village, New York.
5. *The Standard Handbook of Industrial Distributors*, Bergano Book, Fairfield, Connecticut, 1987.

10

Responding to Overseas Sales Inquiries

With the strategies set, the world in focus, and initial mailings and contacts made, it's time to attend to the business of selling. Responses to your initial product promotion have started to arrive, and your first reply and related decisions will begin to place flesh and sinew on the skeleton your export strategies have formed. Just as in the early stages of developing a domestic business, the future impact of decisions and policies established today will form parameters that may be difficult to alter in the future. As pointed out in Chapter 5 relative to distribution strategies, the selection by design or omission of one specific distribution channel may make it difficult to change to another, especially if the relative pricing scales have not been first carefully considered.

Sorting out the Inquiries

As the initial inquiries come in, consider what kind of agent or buyer the inquirer is and whether the channel that that entity represents will further your strategic plans. Will the price you quote to a single buyer or an agent provide sufficient margin to afford a distributor at a later date? Will a few quick sales made today serve to prove the value of your product or simply muddy the water in terms of finding an appropriate long-term distribution partner later on? If experienced after-sales service is critical, will today's sales, made without adequate on-site support, serve mainly to harm the product's reputation and history of reliability? And so on!

Prompt and Appropriate Responses

Whatever your decisions on such issues, try to make them conform to your preferred distribution channels and strategies. However, you need to maintain some flexibility for inquiries outside your chosen pattern, depending on the response level, because sincere interest from worthwhile contacts can be difficult to come by. Consider politely delaying your decision until more inquiries arrive and you better understand what is possible. Your reply—asking legitimate questions as to market and buyer qualifications or requesting more details as to the use or distribution plan for the product—is one example of such a delayed response. You will likely need a number of these qualification forms, so it might be wise to design a form asking the key questions, including those that will make it possible to obtain a World Trade Directory Report (WTDR) from DOC to determine the inquirer's relative size, product lines, number of employees, date established, and so on. The same is true for future commercial credit checks and/or trade references.

It is wise to try to maintain the highest possible level of interest during this period. To that end, try to have on hand some more detailed literature or a minisample that you can send along with your reply, both as a courtesy and to assure the inquirer of your genuine interest. Whatever you do, try to do it with dispatch—assuming that the inquiry appears to offer some potential. Be careful about prejudging the value of an inquiry or response based primarily on what you might be accustomed to in terms of U.S. business practices. Still, there are some clues that can indicate an inquiry of little merit, depending on the country from which it comes. You can expect a more sophisticated format in terms of letterhead and related details from a country like Germany than from a small country in Africa, for example. Somewhere in between these extremes are the business practices of Latin American and Eastern European countries. Even there, you will find wide differences between more commercially oriented countries, such as Venezuela, Brazil, or Argentina on the one hand and Paraguay on the other. More specifically, a handwritten letter without a letterhead from Germany might either be discarded or given a very brief, courteous reply, while a similar letter from a less sophisticated country might be given more serious consideration, at least until the first exchange is completed. Do not expect too much in the way of numbered street addresses; some countries, especially in the Middle East and Latin America, do not use specific street addresses. Instead, there may only be a reference to a district, a bridge, or a gate, plus a post office box number. Remember also that what might appear to be an unqualified respondent could actually be an interested party trying to communicate in a language he or she knows only slightly—a problem possibly compounded by a different alphabet with different characters. In such situations, many business letters are written by hand because typewriters with Roman characters can be expensive and hard to come by.

Sending Samples

Eventually, a customer's definite decision or degree of interest will be based on sampling the product. And in the case of some products, providing such samples can become a major cost in terms of both product and shipping expense, with the latter often being the largest of the two. Who pays? If the prospective overseas buyer seems to have a legitimate interest in the product and an apparent means of using, selling, or distributing it, you should be able to charge a minimal cost for the privilege of evaluating it. The sometimes-herculean task of clearing it through customs is definitely the buyer's task, but it is your responsibility to make this task as easy as possible. Whatever you decide as to charging for samples, it is in your own self-interest to keep the charge as low as possible for prospective buyers, with due regard for your own overhead. Be sure not to create a disincentive for new prospects by careless shipping, relative both to packaging and method. *In general, plan on shipping samples via courier or parcel post using a Form C1 customs declaration, even if it seems much more expensive than air or ocean routing.* Receiving something through the postal system or by direct courier delivery usually enables the recipient to avoid formal clearance through a seaport or airport. Such formal clearance tends to be time-consuming and aggravating. It can also entail the imposition of a well-established bribery schedule. More than the occasional sample shipment remains unclaimed for just these reasons. Lack of adequate research into ways to avoid these problems exposes your own lack of expertise and experience. The import reader should note this and take precautions to avoid similar blunders on the seller's behalf by providing and emphasizing advice as to the best means of shipping samples.

Firms in some countries seem to be in the business of acquiring free samples, which can easily ruin your export promotion budget. Most companies around the world understand this problem and are quite willing to pay for samples at a discount plus the costs of shipping, provided they have enough information, illustrations, and if possible, advance minisamples to adequately prejudge your offering. If such a minimal preliminary sampling or illustration cannot be developed, you will have to seek a solution that is recognizably fair and equitable, taking into consideration sample value, shipping costs, and the likelihood of a serious deal with the prospective buyer or agent. In some cases, postponement until the buyer can visit the United States or you can visit the buyer's country is the best and least expensive solution for all parties concerned.

Terms of Payment

Somewhere at this stage—besides the price list, which will be discussed later in this chapter—will come the issue of payment terms. Where samples are concerned, one of the most frequently discussed or requested terms is *free of charge*. This is, of course, a policy decision as well as a commonsense issue of budget items versus sales aggressiveness. For actual product (as opposed to samples), the primary terms of sales in order of least to greatest risk are:

1. Payment in Advance
2. Letter of Credit (LC)
   a. *Sight:* Payment by the bank more or less immediately after shipment and presentation of documents to the bank.
   b. *Usance:* Payment by the bank a specified number of days (usually 30 to 180) after sight presentation.
3. Documentary Collection
   a. *Documents against Presentation* (D/P): Payment by the consignee when the overseas collecting bank presents shipping documents, assuming that the consignee accepts and pays the draft.
   b. *Documents against Acceptance* (D/A): Payment by the consignee a given number of days after the overseas collecting bank presents shipping documents. The consignee accepts the shipment by signing the draft in favor of the shipper and agreeing to pay in the time stated therein.
4. *Open Account:* Payment based only on the buyer's creditworthiness and commitment to pay. This can be arranged in a variety of circumstances. In one variation, *consignment shipments,* the buyer agrees to pay after sale or collection. In another, involving *wire transfer,* payment is made within any time frame agreed to—when the goods are ready to ship, when they have been shipped, when they have arrived, or some number of days after their arrival. (See Fig. 14-1 for the parameters of consideration concerning payment terms.)

Shipping Terms

Another issue that will come up in the course of responding to inquiries—along with information regarding prices, delivery time required, and selling terms—will be the shipping responsibilities of the buyer and seller respectively. These can have a significant impact on the price as well as presenting favorable or unfavorable operational circumstances for the buyer. While this is another nuts-and-bolts subject, best left to your reference books and discussion with your freight forwarder, there are certain fundamental terms you should be familiar with.

I strongly recommend that you deal *only* with the most recently published version of international shipping terms as defined by the International Chamber of Commerce. This is the 1990 *Incoterms* update. It can be found in detail in *A Guide to Incoterms,* which makes an excellent reference item to have in your export library.[1] The new version encourages shippers to think of shipping terms in four groups designated by the first letter in the shipping term or acronym. The words enclosed in brackets [ ] are words I have added for clarification:

Group E   [Little or no accommodation by Seller]
EXW   Ex Works [factory] (named place)

Goods available only at seller's own premises, to be picked up and loaded on a conveyance or "stuffed" into the container at the buyer's expense, with all export arrangements being the buyer's responsibility except for whatever assistance in this endeavor is requested by the buyer. It is very difficult for the buyer to arrange shipment or understand the final cost under these terms in most cases.

Group F [Main carriage not paid, but Seller is responsible for delivery to Carrier]

FCA Free [in the hands of] CArrier (named place)

Used to avoid the confusion and inaccuracy of the former and very common FOB term for carriers other than waterborne vessels. *Thus, this is the shipping term to use in the case of overland shipments, shipments by air carrier or when the shipper is told to use a consolidator unable to provide a negotiable bill of lading.* FCA terms define the seller's responsibility to be discharged and the transport risks to transfer when the carrier or a named freight forwarder or its agent takes charge of the goods, not necessarily loaded onboard the plane or whatever other conveyance may be contemplated by the buyer.

FAS Free Alongside Ship (named port of shipment)

For waterborne shipments only. Less used today, except in certain trades and product types, because of the many special types of loading and containerization now available, and also because under this term the continuing mobility of the goods being exported is interrupted, exposing them to added hazards. The buyer, rather than the seller, must clear the goods for export and have them loaded onboard. In general, it is best to avoid use of this term.

FOB Free On Board (named port(s) of shipment)

This term also is restricted to *waterborne shipments*. It is a very ancient term, but one of the most commonly used. The issues of seller and buyer responsibilities are very well defined, and the buyer's responsibilities end and the risks transfer when the goods "cross the ship's rails." The seller accepts all responsibility for export arrangements, subject again to the requests of the buyer. For this reason the buyer will often find it acceptable to name several alternate ports, "any U.S. East (West) Coast port," or even "any U.S. port" to aid the seller in finding the first, fastest, or cheapest combination of overland and marine transportation. This term is usually the closest to the point of origin that letters of credit call for because the bill of lading is the preferred instruments for negotiating a letter. The buyer's bank will discourage inland terms which require truck bills of lading or dock receipts and other such less verifiable and nonnegotiable documents.

Group C	[Main carriage paid by Seller but without risk of loss after shipment or delivery]
CFR	Cost [of merchandise] and FReight (named port of destination)

For waterborne freight only. This term for a widely used quotation basis relates to the former C&F term and has the same meaning, in that the price quotation adds the freight charges to the cost of the merchandise, including loading and export documentation or other incidental costs required to carry the goods to the port of the buyer's destination country. While the costs are therefore higher, the transfer of risk is the same as in the FOB quote, in that it changes as the goods cross the ship's rails at the port of shipment, **not** the port of destination.

CIF   Cost, Insurance & Freight (port of destination)

For waterborne freight only. This, too, is a widely used quotation, adding the cost of insurance as well as freight to the CFR price of the goods and making the shipper responsible for obtaining the minimal or basic insurance unless an underlying contract specifies a requirement to obtain broader coverage. In any event, the insurance policy becomes one of the documents required for collection.

CPT   Carriage Paid To (named place of destination)

The distinction here is similar to *FCA* compared to *FOB* in the F Group of terms. The quotation can apply to any form of carriage: air, water, overland or multimodal. The seller is obliged to clear the goods for export and pay shipping costs for the goods' arrival at a named point suitable to the buyer, such as an airport or some port or terminal arranged at which the buyer can receive the goods from the carrier. The transfer of risk or loss, however, occurs when the buyer hands the goods over to a suitable carrier or agent of the carrier, as in the FCA term.

CIP   Carriage & Insurance Paid To (named destination)

The same term as *CPT* above, except that insurance costs are added, with the same stipulations and transfer of risk point that applied to the addition of insurance to the *CFR* term to create the *CIF* term.

Group D	[Seller pays all freight and bears all risk until arrival of the goods at named destination]
DAF	Delivered At Frontier (named place)
DES	Delivered Ex Ship (named port of destination)
DEQ	Delivered Ex Quay (named port of destination)
DDU	Deliver Duty Unpaid (named place of destination)
DDP	Delivered Duty Paid (named place of destination)

All D Group terms share the concept that the seller pays all costs to place the goods at the disposal of the buyer at a named point, and bears all risks of loss until they are at the buyer's disposal, presumably "disposal" being more cleanly defined in the underlying contract. The terms would seldom be used except in the case of a project, usually one requiring installation and/or other duties requiring the seller to have employees or agents at the named place. Otherwise it would probably be an unwise or needlessly difficult shipping term for the seller to undertake.

Pricing and Price Lists

What should the export price be relevant to domestic prices? Naturally, this answer will vary broadly, depending on the competitive pressures that went into the domestic price and any discount schedules that may be attached to it. Assuming it to be competitive, firm, and the discounts transparent, the ex works (EXW) export price would ideally be no higher than the domestic price. If competition is sharp overseas or the producer feels a targeted market share will have to be "bought," then any costs built into the domestic price that don't need to be borne by export production should be excluded, such as consumer advertising and domestic sales commissions.

From the manufacturer's standpoint, when thinking of a direct export price, the first decision is whether export sales will be looked on as: (1) extra sales and profits that permit taking a lower percentage profit to assure those extra sales; (2) a regular sale at regular profit but with the price adjusted for any operational savings as a result of the activities and functions of the third-party exporter; or (3) an opportunistic extra sale at a bonus-profit level without any concern for long-range overseas market development. The latter approach used to be commonplace, but today most businesses realize that their international sales are a critical part of their total sales picture and they must sell overseas to meet their potential and to compete with their foreign counterparts who are selling to their U.S. customers. Opportunism and short-range thinking in export marketing can lead a firm into the same kind of trouble that such thinking tends to lead to in any endeavor.

Undercutting the domestic price is fine if doing so is seen as an initial tool to penetrate a new market. Alternatively, if the product is even more unusual abroad than it is in the United States, it may be able to carry more profit burden in overseas markets, but that is the exception today in the larger foreign markets. In Third-World markets there may even be an opportunity to expand profits on technological products that represent earlier generations of sophistication. While the less sophisticated and less expensive version may be difficult to sell in this country, less advanced countries often prefer and only need that version, permitting the manufacturer to extend the life cycle of earlier products, usually with manufacturing cost advantages based on production experience.

In the long run, and with the exceptions noted, it is usually best for the successful company to go with normal pricing standards and structures, because export marketing tends to carry a slightly higher cost than domestic operations for obvious reasons, even though in large export markets this is sometimes offset by larger transactions to fewer buyers. Therefore, after adjustments for duplicated or eliminated costs, most companies should start with their domestic cost-and-profit structures.

For the export management company, the issue of a discount is another matter. As an export manager, I have always felt that the price to the EMC should be the best domestic price, adjusted for the costs and overhead that will be replaced by the activities of third-party exporters or overseas distributors, such as travel and sales commissions. To this basic price must be added whatever shipping or other export-related direct costs will be borne by the exporter. If you are an export manager, this price cannot always be achieved. In my own business, I was able to negotiate a discount with manufacturers only when they shared my philosophy on this point.

Based on experience of 17 years in the export management role and five years' counseling exporters and reviewing their financial statements, I know that it is an exception when an export management firm can make much financial progress with a gross margin of less than 15 percent. Even this is on the low side if a very aggressive selling policy is followed. There are exceptions when the dollar volume is very high, when turnaround time is short, when the transaction is very simple and collected surely and quickly—as with a clean letter of credit—or some combination of these circumstances. But if conditions permit, 20 percent is a much better figure, and well-managed firms that maintain this percentage or better more consistently show growth in volume and net worth, which permits still more profit by creating the strength to seek still more sales increases.

To the extent that an EMC must add to the domestic price to achieve a margin permitting sufficient profit to sustain the sales and administration expenses necessary, both the product and the EMC will be handicapped. The overseas buyers in any major or sophisticated market will discover the price difference eventually, if not at once, and will constantly try to go around the export manager to obtain the U.S. pricing structure. Even more critical is the fact that any increase in the export price is greatly magnified as transportation costs, customs fees, and other costs or fees further enlarge the base price. In addition, intermediaries, including foreign wholesalers and retailers and the EMC itself, each add their percentage increases to an ever-growing base price. For this reason, at every step along the way including transportation costs, the supplier, manufacturer and/or EMC/ETC must be very cost-conscious if there is to be any hope of gaining a significant market. As an example, for some products in

Japan it used to be necessary to assume that the final retail price would be about 10 times the U.S. cost price.

There are many disincentives for a customer to import anything, regardless of an excellent factory price, given the existence of opportunities to get it domestically or, alternatively, to find a more accommodating exporter. Some of the chief annoyances are problems determining the final landed cost, managing the paperwork and documentation that goes with importing, and getting reliable and rapid answers. Good price lists, based on clearly defined terms, can overcome most of these obstacles in one stroke. How much effort they require on the exporter's part depends largely on the product and how many world areas you are trying to target and promote. Some products can be reasonably purchased by container load, whether in airborne or waterborne containers. In other instances, a single unit of the product, as in the case of machinery, can make an economical shipment. Some products package into neat master cartons of consistent weight and measure. Others are all over the place in terms of weight and/or measure and require break bulk or Less than Container Load (LCL) shipments much of the time. In such cases, you should try to determine some minimum or basic unit for which the weight or measure can be reasonably estimated and price accordingly.

Your prospects are more likely to respond if they can readily see what the price will be at some point. From this information they can quickly judge the landed price, based on their own experience and their own domestic sources of information. The closer your price can come to placing the merchandise in their own customs-house the better. The latter would be a CFR/CIF term for waterborne freight or a CPT/CIP term for all other means of transport. There is an advantage in knowing that your shipment will be insured and under what conditions, so you may prefer to include the cost of insurance, as in CIF and CIP terms. If there are too many destinations, you must then settle for FOB or FCA terms. In the case of air, you will have to figure the cost to airfreight and insure your merchandise to the nearest and best international airport. For waterborne freight, if you are targeting customers in both Western Europe and Asia, you may want to quote one price from East Coast ports and another from West Coast ports. It is very difficult for an importer to get information on the best internal U.S. freight costs and carriers. You don't have to prepare quotations for every area, just the key areas you have targeted, or those sufficiently representative in the various areas you target, so that the buyer can readily estimate the final cost. You can always state that quotes for other destinations and quantity ranges can be obtained on request. Do *not* attempt to quote a delivered price (D Group), for then you are taking over the importer's job. The importer is much better positioned to understand the transport situation in the country of import and minimize internal transport costs and tariffs than you can hope to be. This is the flip side of the explanation relative to the importance of you as the seller developing quotations that include your internal transport costs to the U.S. port of importation.

It is helpful to the buyer to be given the landed unit costs of your products. But when it comes to the export invoicing of the product, it must be done on the basis of ex-factory, FCA, or FOB pricing. This is because the tariff on the merchandise is usually levied on the U.S.–based price rather than on the higher landed cost including overseas (main carriage) transportation. Therefore, if you are leaving an extra margin to allow for shipping-cost estimates, build that safety margin into the factory price where it will remain confidential. If you are pricing by container loads or similar bulk unit, you can add the overseas transport costs more conveniently by quoting a total shipping cost sum. If you quote a destination price (i.e., CFR, CIF, CPT, CIP), your pro forma invoice must match the future export invoice and separately indicate any shipping costs that differ from the initial quotation of the CFR unit price you used for the price list. Your buyer needs to understand this. Otherwise, the buyer's customs office will penalize your customer by calculating tariffs on the higher freight-included price.

The distinction becomes still more critical if you choose to name a base price and offer discounts from that price based on quantity or on the type of buyer (e.g., end user, retailer, distributor, etc.). A discount structure attached to the price list can be a useful tool that eliminates the need for multiple price lists and adds flexibility. But with overseas transportation included as an integral part of a unit CIF or similar price, you will be the loser, because the discount will be inflated when applied to the added transportation cost as well. The transport-cost-inflated discount must be taken into consideration, even in the case of FOB and FCA pricing.

Export price lists may seem like a great deal of trouble, but they can make buyers much more receptive to your offers. They can also eliminate inquiries that might have required time and money on your part because the economic impracticalities based on minimum or landed costs will be readily apparent from the start. Once done, it will save a great deal of the time required to respond as the pace picks up. It will also serve to make you, the exporter, more aware of pricing and transportation obstacles that must be overcome. With today's computer software for databases, spreadsheets, and word processing, these price lists are comparatively easy to prepare and very simple to update or add to. Remember that it is not your ex-factory price, but the final landed, duty-paid price that will determine your product's success, so careful study of the lowest cost, combined with reliable means of transportation, is critical.

At some point in the response process the seller needs to figure the estimated costs based on the base price lists, the miscellaneous export processing costs, the financing costs where extended payment terms are involved, inland freight, overseas transportation (main carriage), and insurance. Gathering all these costs and/or estimates into one place in an

```
ORDER/REF. NO. _____   NAME _____   DATE _____

PAYMENT TERMS_____   SHIPPING TERMS _____

PRODUCT INFORMATION
Product _____   Schedule B No. _____
No. of units _____   Dimension _____ x ____ x _____
Units per master ctn ____   Cubic Measure _____ sq. in.
Net weight _____lbs ____kg   (per unit)    _____ sq. ft.
Gross weight _____lbs ____kg                _____ m²
Volume Weight (air)_____   Total measure _____

PRODUCT COST/CHARGES                    EST.COST  QUOTE
Cost per unit _____ x units _____  Total  _____  _____
Profit/Margin _____ % or $_____          _____  _____
Special labeling/translation                 _____  _____
Sales/Agent commission                       _____  _____

MISC. EXPORT COSTS
Export packing/container or truck loading    _____  _____
Financing cost, including L/C bank fees       _____  _____
Consular invoice/documentation                _____  _____
Inspection/certification fees                 _____  _____
* TOTAL FCA SELLER'S PLACE OF BUSINESS        _____  _____

HANDLING AND CARTAGE CHARGES
Unloading/loading (heavy lift)                _____  _____
Freight forwarding/courier charges            _____  _____
Inland freight to_____                _____  _____
Harbor Maintenance fee (.125% of FAS value)   _____  _____
* TOTAL FOB PORT or TOTAL FCA MAIN CARRIER             _____

FREIGHT CHARGES        CARRIER _____
Based on ___ weight ___ measure; ocean ____ air ____
Rate quoted _____ item (tariff) #_____
Quoted by _____ date _____
Surcharges included _____
Total freight charges                         _____  _____
* TOTAL CFR PORT OF DESTINATION               _____  _____

INSURANCE
Type of Coverage _____
Basis _____ Rate _____ Amount  _____  _____
War Risk @ $_____ rate per $100              _____  _____
* TOTAL CIF PORT OF DESTINATION               _____  _____
                                              ========
```

* The application of charges under the various INCOTERMS is only
approximate and typical, and not intended to be definitional.

Figure 10-1. Export quotation worksheet.

orderly manner can help prevent costly errors and wasted time. A form I
recommend is reproduced in Fig. 10-1.

Pro Forma Invoices: The Ultimate Quotation

In spite of detailed price lists and carefully crafted terms and conditions,
your customers may ask for a Pro Forma Invoice after they have made up

their minds to buy and after the payment, shipping, and delivery terms and conditions are more or less agreed upon. The purpose of a pro forma is to tell the buyer exactly how much the shipment will cost under final or offered terms and what the invoice will total and cover on arrival. It is a good way for both the buyer and seller to avoid future misunderstandings, and it is especially useful with larger shipments for which a letter of credit is to be opened. The pro forma can, and should, be so specific that it clarifies most details that might lead to amendments or letter of credit negotiating discrepancies. Merely giving an example of shipping costs combined with price lists does not constitute a pro forma. And until the buyer knows exactly what he or she wants, and roughly when, a pro forma should not be offered. When the major terms and conditions have been resolved and the buyer knows exactly what he or she wants—and when you know what can or cannot safely be promised and delivered—the pro forma can be properly prepared. Alternatively, the buyer may simply mail or fax a detailed purchase order, and if the seller can meet all the stated terms and conditions, the purchase order can be confirmed after being modified by whatever conditions the seller needs to add. Since the pro forma probably constitutes a legal offer, be sure it is limited as to the latest date for validity and how many days must be allowed for delivery from acceptance of the pro forma or the exporter's receipt of an appropriate letter of credit covering the order. Thus it might be stated on the face of the pro forma that the "Prices quoted herein are valid only until *mm/dd/yy*" (and possibly add "and are subject to change without notice prior to written acceptance"). Concerning delivery, a good phrase is: "Shipment cannot be effected sooner than ____ days from receipt of an acceptable letter of credit" (or, "signed acceptance of pro forma" if a letter of credit is not used). The delivery date is often critical and can vary dramatically according to the size or nature of a shipment.

Another question to be considered when providing a pro forma invoice is that of allowing a reasonable cushion for yourself when the quotation includes transportation costs. If you have underestimated the cost of the freight or related expenses as a result of underestimating the bulk or weight or because of a rate change, you will have to absorb that cost once a quote is made. If, on the contrary, you have made a little extra because of an overestimate or because of finding a better rate, you may wish to keep the difference to offset future instances of underestimation. This can be delicate, however, in terms of customer relations, for the bill of lading may detail all the shipping costs. In any case, it can be important, in terms of keeping the product as competitive as possible, for the buyer to know the actual FOB U.S. port cost for application of the tariff schedule as already mentioned. When in doubt, U.S. Customs here or elsewhere will claim the larger sum. Therefore, this allowance is best built into the Ex Works price. Then, if it really is not needed, it can provide a future opportunity for an incentive discount or a negotiated exchange for some better terms on your side. To repeat again, be sure the buyer understands that the discount only applies to the Ex Works value, or you will find yourself absorbing part of the transport cost.

When granting discounts, remember to apply them line-by-line, for otherwise the foreign customs office may not allow a bulk discount deducted at the bottom of the invoice for the purpose of tariff calculations. Allowing for possible extra delivery time or costs is a necessary precaution that applies to all areas of the quotation or pro forma: production time frames, shipping times, vessel availability, and documentation and letter of credit negotiation times. The documentation phase can be especially critical if legalized or consular invoices will be involved. (This will be explained in more detail later.)

Finally, if the sale is a major one and is thoroughly negotiated relative to the pro forma, it is a good idea to be very specific about the terms to be included (or not included) in the letter of credit. (In Chapter 14, you will find a checklist that you can use when detailing for your customer what would be an "acceptable" letter of credit.)

Caveats

Your initial sales inquiries or orders will often be accompanied by requests for exclusivity, agency, or distributorship contracts or other requests that might weigh heavily on you as you learn more about the inquirer and the overseas market. Without sounding uncooperative or arrogant, make every effort to stall such requests, while still giving the prospective buyer reason for continued interest. It's important to get the merchandise into someone's hands in the target market and determine the reaction, including making necessary adjustments to your pricing, packaging, or other basic elements of market development.

There are too many variables to provide specific examples here, but your response could well revolve around the idea that you'll informally avoid selling to others until you have had a reaction accompanied by selling estimates from the present correspondent—or that you will temporarily refrain from selling to others without prior consultation with the present correspondent—or words to that effect. Another gambit concerns delay until any trip you are currently planning to your market. A trip of this kind can be made more fruitful if you can meet with the buyer in question *after* that party has had some experience with the product or product samples. Of course, the most natural and understandable delaying response would mention the need for time to gather details about the inquirer and the market, but this may not buy enough time and is less likely to encourage the buyer to accept a shipment in the interim.

However you do it, the secret is to keep as many options open as possible unless you know that all your objectives are being met. If you have no preconception based on very good past experience or knowledge of the target market, stick to the rule of doing everything possible to maintain interest while waiting to find your best permanent channel. In some instances you might want to encourage preliminary sales, but it is quite possible that even these should be deferred to be assured of not creating what the Japanese like to call a "disorderly market." It is to your advantage that, surprisingly often, responses from a given country or region will arrive in roughly the same time frame.

If at all possible, wait to make your permanent agency or distributor appointments until you can visit the territory. Even after you have made such a visit, you must strike a balance between making the commitment for too short a term—which gives the distributor or buyer little incentive to make a real promotional commitment—and taking the risk of a long-term commitment that restricts you but places no burden on the distributor or agent. In this case, even though the importer is not performing, there is little you can do until the agreement expires, and even then there can be problems. Obviously, short terms with conditioned renewal based on performance is the first line of defense in this situation.

Endnote

1. *A Guide to Incoterms*, ICC Publishing, New York, 1990.

11
Selling Overseas

Your new export venture has now reached a stage where selling in person overseas should be considered. Any serious export sales effort will have to involve travel to the primary target countries sooner or later. This is ultimately necessary for several reasons:

1. To consider new agents/distributors or to review the performance and potential of existing representatives
2. To understand the nature and competitive stature of your direct customers or end users
3. To understand the marketplace, including its needs and problems, its future potential, and how you might improve your competitive position and market share
4. As evidence to your agents/distributors/customers of your interest and commitment to their region and its special needs

In short, to know and understand what you are doing and to establish the personal relationships essential to most endeavors.

Who will do the traveling, of course, depends on whether the product is to be represented by a third-party exporter overseas or by the company's own staff if it plans direct selling involvement. In the case of a smaller export management company, the traveler will almost surely be one of the principals. If it is to be a self-contained operation by the manufacturer/supplier, the decision about who does the traveling will depend on the company's management structure and the makeup of the new export division. The first trip to a major new region should include the equivalent of a vice president of marketing (or higher), plus the individual responsible for export sales. The leader should *not* be the domestic sales manager unless he or she is the *only* sales-related executive in the company. Overseas media promotion may or may not come later, but for now, settle for flying the company flag and getting to know the marketplace.

Strategies for the First Trip

One excellent plan for the first trip is to attend, without official participation, a major overseas trade fair featuring your industry. It should be a fair either held in one of your target countries or at least serving a substantial portion of potential buyers from such countries. Here, you should come to understand the customs and nature of your prospective customers, become acquainted with foreign distributors and salespeople for your type of product, and begin to discover the worldwide competition you will face. It may even be possible to leave business cards or brochures with buyers attending the show whom you meet in the halls, cafes, or meeting places. Aside from the travel costs themselves, expenses are minimal for registered show attendees, compared to the fees paid by the trade fair booth occupants. Never mind that you are not in there selling from the start—this strategy sharpens your focus and can easily spell earlier profitable sales in the long run. In fact, this is a good strategy as a first step in the initial development of your export plans and can be a net time saver because it serves to more clearly define your mission and objectives. Alternatively, you can schedule a trade show visit as part of your first export mission, so that the trip can combine exploration and learning with selling. Preliminary visits to trade fairs and shows will also help you determine where and when you are ready to consider the expense of full participation in an overseas show.

Much can be learned from visits to the domains of the users and sellers of your product. Go through the stores that relate to your products. Try to arrange a few plant visits, possibly with the help of your own trade association and your international banker. Your banker can help by asking for assistance from their overseas correspondent banks or branches. These activities do not preclude sales calls, but don't make the mistake of booking a full schedule of sales appointments. If you do, you may become completely caught up in selling without ever understanding who it is you are really trying to deal with and the underlying nature of your new market. This is one of several good reasons for a senior company officer who's responsible for long-range goals to lead the first few trips: it relieves some of the pressure on subordinates to produce instant results. Results are a fundamental goal, but they will more likely be achieved if you understand everything possible about the task and the players.

Travel Tips

Plan your trips well in advance and focus on the best prospect countries. It gives you a better chance for success and avoids a potentially serious waste of time and money. It is a painstaking process to organize an effective overseas travel schedule, especially when you are new to the territory and have no established customers. Time is required to arrange passports, visas, and itineraries, to say nothing of appointments. To begin with, ask your DOC district office for the listing, "World Commercial Holidays," which is published yearly in its *Business America* magazine. It can be very discouraging to find that much of the time planned for the visit to a key city is lost because all the businesses are closed. There may be entire months to avoid in some countries where, while open, most of the key executives are on holiday. This can be the case in France for the month of August, in Moslem countries for the extended observance of Ramadan and, to a degree, all the summer months in certain very hot countries (though this last condition has diminished in recent decades). Extended holidays or seasonal downtimes are one reason to avoid including too many different world regions in one trip. There is a common pattern within global regions of good and bad times to travel. Mixing these regions can make for an extremely complex itinerary. And one can get surprisingly out of touch with the business at home and with reality in general if the trip is too long. It is also true that foreign travel can be very taxing on your physical strength. (I was fortunate to have started my foreign travel days just as the Boeing 747 was introduced, which initially created a huge oversupply of seats, permitting consistently wonderful nights of rest stretched comfortably across the entire four or five seats of the middle section.)

They say that getting there can be half the fun, but in most cases it is also a big part of the cost. Having made the investment, don't cut your time schedules too tight. It is very difficult in most countries and most cities to schedule more than two appointments in the morning and two in the afternoon—at least until you know the territory and the local practices. Moving around a strange city that may or may not have actual street addresses or English-speaking taxi drivers, and dealing with prospects not fully fluent in your language, or the reverse, more than doubles the time that you would expect the same appointments to take in the United States. Any time left over can be well spent scheduling new appointments, which the country's U.S. Commercial Service offices may have been able to set up for you, or following up other referrals or leads that come your way. In addition, time for new appointments, follow-ups on initial appointments, and other unplanned meetings should always be allowed. Try to leave at least 25 percent, and possibly as much as 50 percent, of your time open in the early, exploratory trips. Even if some of this time remains unused, it's better than wasting valuable time trying to juggle an existing itinerary to permit a longer stay. When this happens, your days are spent not only trying to change travel and hotel arrangements, but also attempting to reschedule appointments at future stops. In fact, I suggest that you regularly avoid the temptation to make changes in your basic schedule. Such changes cost not only money and time, but also goodwill, because of the appointments you inevitably miss throughout the balance of your trip.

Even though the budget for your travel may be limited, try to let it be sufficient to permit staying in first-class business hotels, as distinguished from the still-more-expensive luxury hotels; as well as from the lower-cost tourist or smaller, second-class hotels. The atmosphere for meetings in the lobby of a good hotel is helpful; their multilingual communications and business services can be invaluable; and you yourself will be more relaxed and effective. There is also a prestige factor to consider if you can possibly afford it.

Speaking personally, I can recall one visit to Tokyo when I was feeling very budget-conscious. I had few ceremonial or public relations duties to perform, and I selected an economy business hotel primarily used by mid- to lower-level Japanese businessmen. The room was so small, I thought I was in a submarine, and for that matter, the units of the room were of prefabricated construction with door thresholds similar to bulkheads. As I was inspecting the room I tripped on one of these and literally fell into the tub. It was a depressing visit and definitely subpar in accomplishment. Conversely, on a few occasions I let myself be persuaded to use a luxury hotel which, as is typical, proved to be well out of the local business district, creating huge taxi bills and worse, becoming a major threat to my time schedules.

Try to brush up on at least some of the basic cultural nuances of the countries or regions you are about to visit—especially on those concerning the negotiating habits of businesspeople in the area. You'll find many books on the subject in your library, including the "Culture Grams" developed by Brigham State University. (A partial list of books on this subject will be found in Appendix F.)

In terms of the length of your foreign trips, one very real limitation, apart from stamina and budget, is the need to return to your home base to take care of follow-up correspondence and fulfill your promises concerning samples and other matters that you've made in the course of most trips. If there is no one at home to take care of this for you, based on your instructions en route, then you had better get home in time to execute them yourself before the notes you made in the course of the trip become too stale. Even if you do have efficient help that permits you to count on your instructions being followed with intelligence and customer perception, there usually are at least a few matters best taken care of personally.

Finally, save some travel budget for emergency trips. If something is going wrong, if a claim is being filed, an important new customer is upset or confused, or perhaps a chance arises to deal with a buyer you had only dreamt of selling to, a quick trip can be a very wise and cost-effective investment. I have seen situations involving a major claim or complaint, that could have been resolved or minimized by a personal visit and sufficient goodwill generated to leave a prospect for future business. Instead, only the direct cost of the trip was considered, so that after many letters, faxes, phone calls, and much hand wringing, the final cost of settlement exceeded the cost of a visit by a wide margin, but with no positive "good-news elements," such as a reassured customer who was impressed with your quick and thorough attention to the problem.

Traveling With Samples

Give a great deal of thought to the samples you plan to carry. If they are too few, you will find that the journey has mostly been a public relations trip that will have to be duplicated soon if meaningful business is to be done. If there are too many samples, you will waste a lot of time in showing them. Samples can represent a serious burden in terms of packing, unpacking, and physically carrying them around, to say nothing of the problems they add in clearing customs. Take only your best samples the first time; if they are well received, you'll have time enough later to enlarge the range after establishing customers and learning the circumstances and potential of the market. If the samples are clearly usable and have a significant value, you should consider a carnet, especially if you are traveling on a business visa. A carnet is a document that allows you to take samples into over 30 countries without paying duty on entry. It is issued by an international group, the ATA Carnet System, and requires a bond for 40 percent of the value to assure you will return to the United States with the samples. If you can make a case that the primary purpose of your trip is pleasure rather than business, and if your samples are compact and of little value in terms of practical use, I would suggest *not* displaying your carnet, even if you have obtained one. The reason is that it can often result in substantial time delays in terms of customs procedures, whereas if you are traveling on a tourist visa without a carnet, your samples will most often be considered part of your ordinary luggage. If foreign customs officers perceive that you may be bringing in saleable merchandise and could conceivably leave it in the country, you will be made to pay duty or the samples will be rendered unfit for sale. The trouble is, they will then be unfit for use as samples as well. This is a special danger in South and Central America. If you need a carnet or just feel safer having one, contact the U.S. Council of International Business, 1212 Avenue of the Americas, New York, New York, 10036. To make a final decision, you might also want to contact the country desk officer at the U.S. Department of Commerce in Washington, D.C. (See Appendix A for the telephone number of the appropriate country desk officer or check with TIC at USATRADE.) Remember to keep all the carnet documents and have them certified as you pass through customs on your return home. This is necessary if you are to recover the value of the bond posted.

Whatever else you decide about samples, be sure that the sales information and any specifications necessary are complete and accurate, and that you can put your hands on them in an instant. This includes weight and cubic measure information, packing details, quantity contained in 20- and 40-foot sea containers or air containers, if appropriate, and approximate cost by unit and by container shipment to the primary ports and/or airports in the countries or regions you will be visiting. Be sure you have construction and quality details down pat and are truly a fountain of information about your offerings. Some of the most devastating moments in my personal export selling career came when I was asked a question I should have known but could not answer. Imagine spending the time and money to travel halfway around the world to present a product you are not fully informed about! You will not only lose credibility; you will probably lose the sale. One of the attributes your overseas customers most appreciate is knowledge and the feeling that they are talking to someone who knows what he or she is selling—either because they want to learn and know about a product in which they have an interest, or because they know but want to be sure you do.

Never find yourself in the place of the newly hired carpet salesman for a large carpet company I know of. He embarked on a trip to the Middle East feeling he knew everything, but failed to convert his pricing and other information from square yards to square meters. No one thought for a moment he could be talking about square yards, a measure virtually unique to the United States, so all his price quotations were short by close to 20 percent. He did not learn of his blunder until the end of a long trip and never really recovered from the gaffe.

Be sure the samples are clean and fresh and presented in a fashion that is easy to understand and is as self-explanatory as possible, especially in view of language problems. You may be sick and tired of dragging the samples in and out of airports and taxis, but treat them as if they were made of gold when you are showing them to a buyer or agent. You are asking them to invest money, time, and effort in what you are showing.

It would be my recommendation to avoid leaving the samples you have carried into a country with a prospective agent or distributor you believe you are going to make a deal with. To begin with, doing so is illegal because in most cases a tariff would have been due on entry. In the second place, you may be giving your samples to someone who turns out to be far from perfect when you get home and do some more research, or who ultimately declines the deal or simply does not respond to further correspondence. With your sample line in the hands of a third party, it can be awkward when concluding an agreement later with a different entity in the same city or territory. Giving up your samples also seems to diminish your own perception of the product's value in the eyes of the agent. Doing so is a temptation, especially at the end of a trip, but it has never worked out to my benefit.

Overseas Promotion

Direct selling overseas can be in the form of regular trips abroad; direct mail—including more personal and targeted mail to present customers; media advertising; and trade fairs or similar events. Most of the suggestions for regular travel are like those we offered relative to the introductory trip, just as are those guidelines for continuing direct-mail efforts are like those for product introduction. But there are some differences and additions.

Regular Foreign Travel

As overseas travel becomes a regular event, the leadership on those initial exploratory trips will likely shift from the top company echelons to those directly responsible for sales in the export department. Just as is true at home, however, an occasional visit from the "brass" is appreciated. This is especially true if you want to develop the best international reputation. Many overseas firms feel that U.S. companies are not really serious about their international business and overseas customers. Based on past attitudes, there is some powerful justification for this belief, even though in today's world U.S. businesspeople largely have a very different attitude about export sales. Nonetheless, the belief lingers on. Therefore, if a vice president or higher-level executive makes a showing every year or so, it is a signal that the company plans on seriously seeking a share of the market. The buyer is therefore somewhat more assured of consistently good treatment and attention and of a continuing presence in the market by the manufacturer and its product. This is very important to your export customer, especially if after-sales service or trademarks are essential. Consistent attention and interest in maintaining relationships are the rule in our domestic market efforts, but this is not always true for our overseas efforts.

Direct Mail and Correspondence

Direct mail and correspondence are as vital to international trade as they are to domestic trade. We have already considered the elements that must be altered or emphasized in the case of overseas mail relative to product introduction. As the export effort matures, it should become increasingly possible to target your mailings with a rifle rather than a shotgun in terms of both subject and recipient, and possibly to compose at least key portions of the message in a language indigenous to the target area.

Frequent correspondence with your customers, agents, and distributors is even more important than in domestic trade, for reasons similar to those already discussed relative to visits by principal executives of the firm. Regular communication and fast response to inquiries helps overcome the gap created by distance and language differences, as well as the lingering feeling that Americans give less attention to overseas business.

Media Advertising

Media advertising is a viable means of continuing promotion, although if aimed at the consuming public it is an expensive and tricky process beyond the scope of most smaller businesses.

Trade Publications.   If media advertising can be narrowed to trade magazines read by salesmen and distributors, or professional publications read by practitioners within a field like medicine or dentistry, or the executives and managers in specific industries, it can be very cost-effective. A publication entitled *Trade Directories of the World* lists virtually every such publication and is a worthwhile addition to the export library in many firms.[1]

Government Supported Media.   Another very inexpensive choice is government-supported advertising media. Primarily this consists of the DOC publication *Commercial News USA* already mentioned. For about $250 this publication will advertise your product in the most appropriate of several categories: "New Product Information Service," "International Market Search," and "Worldwide Services Program." Hundreds of thousands of copies are sent in bulk to all overseas trade consulates or Commercial Service offices and distributed by them at no cost to the readers. I will testify that they usually get an excellent response, much of which is from well qualified buyers or agents. On a cost-per-response basis it is probably more effective than any other medium I am aware of. Some of the U.S. Commercial Service overseas offices are supplementing this magazine with publications for their specific territories. Also, states and other entities like port authorities produce publications that provide free or low-cost advertising to a very broad band of potential overseas customers. Our import readers should also seek the flip side version of such publications for their own new product searches.

Commercial Publications.   There are American trade publications and technical journals of an esoteric nature that can represent reasonably good advertising buys to reach targeted markets. One publisher of such material is Johnston International Publishing Corp., 25 Northwest Point Boulevard, Suite 800, Elk Grove Village, Illinois 60007. They produce two publications for overseas markets, *Export* and *Automobile and Truck International*. Another publication is *Showcase USA,* published bimonthly by Sell Overseas America, 2500 Artesia Boulevard, Redondo Beach, California 90278.

Trade Fairs, Trade Missions, and Catalog Exhibitions

There are a variety of international events of this type, some sponsored by private organizations and others by the DOC's ITA or Agriculture's Foreign Agriculture Service (FAS). These events can save you considerable expense over privately sponsored ones, but they are sometimes not too well conceived in terms of timing and audience or other marketing details, so they should be carefully studied before you sign up.

Catalog Show

The least expensive DOC event is the catalog show mentioned in Chapter 9. This type of show takes the catalogs of a firm in a particular industry area and contracts with some party familiar with the industry to supervise the display and use of these catalogs in a series of showings in a given world region. The inquiries relative to your particular catalog are forwarded on to you, sometimes with comment, for your own follow-up. It is inexpensive (under $500), but success is limited.

U.S. Government Organized Trade Missions and Trade Exhibits

Trade missions are exploratory events scheduled with the private sector and government officials in specified countries of a region for a particular industry. You will probably have some very interesting conversations and meetings that may or may not yield tangible results. You are very dependent on the government's scheduling and arrangements, but you will surely come away with a better knowledge of your product's potential in the region and possibly some genuinely interested prospects. The cost is in the $3000 to $6000 range, which is still much less than an important trade fair.

In the same fashion, the DOC organizes traveling trade exhibits in which they make arrangements in a few key cities of a world region for exhibit to the trade. The problem is, it is difficult for Commercial Service trade officers to keep out the public, and while such exhibits can be helpful and possibly even a perfect training ground for full-fledged trade fair participation, you should review the arrangements carefully. Costs are similar to the trade missions. States, too, will make such arrangements, and they, as well as the DOC and FAS, will also organize booth sharing within large private trade fairs. Obtain a copy of the DOC plans for the next year, as well as those for your state, and study them carefully. If one fits your parameters, it may give you an opportunity for exposure that you could not otherwise afford. If these traveling trade exhibits are not industry-specific, however, I would seriously question their value.

Industry-Organized Domestic Trade Fairs

Before turning to participation in overseas trade fairs, be sure to consider something you may have overlooked: trade fairs in your own backyard. We refer to the regular trade exhibitions carried on throughout this country by the trade associations representing various industries. Naturally, they are aimed at the U.S. domestic market, but if it is an industry whose products are popular overseas, you will find many foreign buyers at the show. Some such shows even have special registration for overseas buyers and will help you meet them and provide you with lists of their names and addresses. Attendees are often excellent prospects, and their attendance at a show thousands of miles away from home attests to their interest. Check with your own trade association or that of your supplier if you are an export management company. In the latter case, ask if you can help staff the booth to help with any foreign buyers who might happen by. Domestic salespeople are notorious for paying little attention to them. At least get the person in charge at the show to take and save their business cards for you to follow up on later, or better yet, make appointments for prospects to meet you while they are still in the city.

Overseas Trade Fairs

Now for the big events: foreign trade fairs. They are a big event because they can produce a great deal of business, but they are also a major expense. If there is no opportunity to share a booth through joint participation in DOC or FAS U.S. pavilions, or other entities, the cost, including travel, can easily range from $10,000 to $25,000 or more. In comparison, however, traveling abroad and making individual sales calls, even with a well-organized itinerary, to say nothing of "cold calls," in anything like the range of cities and countries that one would be exposed to in a major trade fair can be as expensive and requires a good deal more time. With this kind of expense at stake, you must choose your trade fairs very carefully, considering product range, buyer type, country of origin, and cost. If you are new to international selling, it would not be wise to enter the largest of the fairs that might pull buyers from almost around the world because it is unlikely that you'll be ready yet to serve and follow up on such broad areas. It might be better to begin with shows that appeal to a narrower geographical range of customers. When considering a given trade fair, ask questions within your industry and its trade associations; request the postshow reports, buyer and supplier profiles, and any other information available on previous fairs from the fair organizers. Ask the DOC for its recommendation on the fair and for possible DOC participation. If it is a show featuring seasonal merchandise held more than once a year, picking the right season in which to exhibit can make the difference between success and failure, because northern or southern hemisphere customers may find only the winter or summer versions of a particular merchandise range useful.

A decision to participate should be made six months or more ahead of time to obtain a good booth location and to allow time to make careful plans for the show and the trip you will probably want to arrange around it. Budget for modest entertainment, but don't let yourself get carried away. Besides the budget, there are many things to consider:

- Will you need translators, and what services in this regard and others are provided by the fair management?

- How do the fair management's charges compare to services available outside the show?

- What minimum decorations and furnishings will you need? They are expensive!

- Is it possible to get a product video presentation that can be done in several languages and can help you get your presentation off on the right foot quickly, saving time and sales lost due to language barriers?

- Can you make qualified direct-mail contacts announcing your presence at the show and stating where they can find you? Previous fair attendee lists are a good place to expand such contacts, and from these you can better target specific types of buyers from specific areas. Most fair organizers are pleased to provide such lists.

- Will there be preshow events, such as press conferences or technical symposiums, that will give you a chance to mention a new or unique product, or provide an opportunity for you to make one-on-one contacts?

- Has a competent freight forwarder been arranged to take care of getting your samples to the show, and do they have a good custom house broker as a subsidiary or agent to receive them at their destination? Usually the organizers will have someone designated for this service that you can rely on.

If you are planning a sales trip in connection with the show, I suggest you do so after the show to permit contact follow-up and so you will be fresh for the fair itself, with plenty of time before it starts to set up your booth and take care of last-minute problems. Even if you are planning to make a postshow trip, expect to stay a day or two in the vicinity of the fair afterward for follow-up calls or prospect meetings generated at the show. There will never be a better opportunity to make your investment pay off! You will remember your contacts interests or problems more clearly and they will still have their initial enthusiasm for your product.

Endnote

1. *Trade Directories of the World*, Croner Publications, New York,

PART 4
Transacting Foreign Trade

12

The Anatomy of an Export Transaction

This is a crucial chapter because many blossoming international traders arrive at this juncture, having completed most of the initial effort and planning necessary on behalf of their product, only to let enthusiasm breed carelessness. When the first solid sales opportunities come their way, they let various particulars slide by, forgetting that, as always, "the devil is in the details." The result is unfinished transactions, loss of profits, and damaged reputations. Forethought, negotiating tactics grounded in solid knowledge and research, and careful attention to the many details involved in every transaction is the only way to guard against this scenario.

It's important to remember that there will always be some new roadblock or potential glitch lurking in the shadows to destroy your profit—and possibly even threaten you with a major loss. Since my first objective in this book is to help you move into the channels of international commerce as quickly and profitably as possible, my emphasis is on leading you to the most readily available and usable sources of assistance for foreign traders in the United States and helping you make the best use of them. It's vital to know when and where to ask the right questions concerning the paperwork, documents, formalities, and schedules relating to your shipment. The mechanics of following detailed instructions to complete the relevant documents or utilizing schedules will largely be left for you to learn from studying the actual document and its attached explanation as the need and circumstances arise. Mostly, you will be letting professionals, such as freight forwarders or bank documentary personnel, complete the final details for you, at least initially. These specialists can also prompt you to provide the information you will have to provide to let them do the job right. Export involves an entirely different language and lexicon that will probably seem strange to you. Some of the words or phrases have a different meaning than you might assume because international shipping and trade enjoys an ancient heritage of language and customs. The underlying nomenclature of the trade has changed little over the centuries, even though new styles, equipment, and developments now overlay the fundamentals.

Should you be interested in learning a great deal about import/export documentation, there are several current publications that emphasize detailed explanation, including *Export-Import* by Joseph A. Zodl.[1] A more seminarlike process is used in a well-organized, step-by-step description of the export process entitled *Developing Skills for International Trade,* by JuDee Benton.[2] The latter book is further enhanced by excellent student workbooks to supplement the learning process.

Negotiating for a Profit

It feels great to make an export sale! It's good for your ego, good for your export track record or the outside supplier who might be involved, and good for the outlook of your new business overseas. But first, was the sale consummated at a fair profit? It is your job to be sure you know and take into consideration all the cost elements in the transaction, including base price, commissions, final transportation costs, and possible postsales expenses—plus all the miscellaneous fees and finance-related costs that may only surface weeks or months later. As for the base price of the product, you may occasionally have to concede some of your profit for strategic purposes when moving into a market, but you will never, never "make it on volume." While a percentage margin that doesn't work for one product area or transaction size may well work successfully for another, most trading companies tend to seek a gross margin of about 15 to 20 percent. Although I do know of successful companies selling bulk goods as low as 5 percent, there are many more export management and trading companies that are growing and prospering because they have figured out how to gross 25 percent or more—especially if they incur overseas selling costs as needed to fulfill their mission.

As a small business starting an export effort, don't let yourself be deceived into thinking that all export sales will necessarily be larger than sales in your regular business (although many will be), or that export sales cost less to create (they cost more over the long haul). It's true that some domestic expense areas will not rise as exports rise and that some of your domestic expense structure will not benefit export sales, resulting in an expense "nut" that is quite different from that in your domestic operations. But it's also true, whether your firm is exporting directly or through an export management firm, that it is merely substituting one expense for another, and that possible reductions or increases in product cost will be offset by cost shifts in the exported product.

Just because one of your early export contacts that first interested you in exporting was a foreign distributor who seemed practically ready to snatch product away from you in its eagerness to acquire the line doesn't mean that all future sales will be as easy and therefore as inexpensive to initiate. New prospects may well become tougher and more expensive to discover and sell as you go forward into the foreign markets to *create* sales. In the same vein, pride that product is gracing the show windows of a store in some glamorous foreign capital will not necessarily be reflected in your net profit. So, should you find that your prospective buyer's negotiating strategy is to appeal to your pride or vanity as a way of getting you to give too much of your margin away, pinch yourself. It's going to make it just that much harder to adjust to a fair price at a later date. On the other hand, if continuing sales of the product are your objective, it is nowhere more true than in export distribution that *in really solid deals both sides must have a fair deal.* As in most businesses, the cost of doing the first transaction is sufficiently high to make it unlikely you will make a true net profit on it if indirect expenses are considered. The real profit usually comes from repeat sales, and to realize those sales, the price must be right and the buyer or distributor reasonably content with the arrangements. And always remember that profit presupposes getting paid in full.

Put a sharp pencil to calculating these altered expense structures and cost shifts to better understand just what latitude for negotiation you do have and what it takes to create a net profit, so that exporting is a satisfying, long-term success. Don't forget to anticipate the possibility of changing distribution channels and the effect that such changes may have on future product pricing and export distribution costs. Exporting is interesting, but not unless you make money doing it!

Using Your Bank and Banker

Chapters 3 and 4 urged you to make a concerted search for an appropriate bank and a qualified international banker and outlined the kind of business plan you would need to put together to secure his or her assistance in pursuing your objectives. Hopefully, you are satisfied with the results of your search, because you are now going to need that bank for documentary work relative to your new transactions, and possibly for some form of working capital or trade financing. If you have even come close to finding the ideal banker I described in Chapter 3, you should take the time to consult that person as soon as an important sale or project looms as a possibility—and well in advance of negotiating the deal if working capital will be a concern.

Why? You may have learned that the transaction is too big for your financial capacity, even though you know how to fill the order and are going to have an irrevocable letter of credit assuring you of payment.

Many businesspeople think that a letter of credit is all they need; why shouldn't a bank lend them whatever money is required? No matter how "clean" and secure the letter of credit is, there remains a long list of reasons why there still may be far more risk than most banks wish to accommodate unless an exporter has a proven track record of having profitably completed similar transactions involving similar manufactures, installations, and processes. Furthermore, you must provide evidence your underlying equity and working capital can absorb the loss and repay the loan, even if the letter of credit expires unused. The catalog of possible misfortunes leading to that possibility will not fit in this chapter, but the list begins with wars and strikes and ends with third-party suppliers, fires, illnesses, and misjudged timetables.

If your banker will not cooperate, there may be alternatives, such as going after a smaller piece of the transaction, taking in a partner for the particular deal or project, or possibly even working with the buyer to structure the transaction in such a way that you can satisfactorily complete it after all. Your primary supplier can also be the solution if you are a third-party exporter and the supplier will provide the necessary financial support through open account credit with an assignment of proceeds or similar arrangements. Profitably completing a smaller transaction or sharing the profit is much better for your future business and present profitability than losing money and the confidence of your customer, your banker, and any other support areas you may be relying on for future assistance.

On the other hand, the transaction may be feasible but require some special support, for which your banker could make suggestions for finding help, such as the third-party public sector guarantor for export finance support offered by the Small Business Administration, Eximbank, and some states. Or perhaps the deal is not that big, just tricky, and your banker can suggest ways for negotiating payment or construction of the letter of credit to permit the bank to be of more financial help than would otherwise be possible. This can include ideas for transferability, progress payments, and similar working capital boosters. It is also possible that merely stretching out the time frames for production or procurement can make the transaction work.

Your banker can provide information in advance on the relative strength of the foreign issuing bank for the letter of credit, thus easing problems for the ultimate negotiation or assignment of the letter. (Chapter 14 covers many of these terms in more detail.) It may be that, by insisting on a "confirmed" letter of credit, the bank can give you support that would not otherwise be possible. The whole idea is to make the bank your partner and get the highest level of assistance and support from it, not just for this deal, but the next and the next. Banks call this relationship *banking,* but the burden of maintaining a useful relationship always proves to rest more with the client than with the bank. We will go further into this vital subject as we discuss letters of credit, trade finance, and risk protection in later chapters.

Finding a Freight Forwarder

The next key to satisfactorily completing an export transaction will depend on the very specialized profession of a freight forwarder. The forwarder is regulated and certified to take care of export shipments. In contrast, the custom house broker, or customs broker, is licensed to specialize in shepherding imported merchandise through customs. (See Chapter 13.) In practice, most larger brokers and forwarders combine the two functions as two separate divisions within one business entity. In theory you can handle export or import goods directly. But unless you have expert in-house staff, you'll need professional help, except on those occasions when you are shipping via parcel post or exporting through carrier or transport agents who offer at least portions of the forwarder's service in connection with the carriage.

Here is a list of the export services a freight forwarder may offer, depending on the circumstances. It may:

- Advise you concerning the various means of transportation and routes
- Research the most favorable transport rates
- Offer current information on special conditions in the country of destination, port facilities, and foreign customs regulations
- Make suggestions regarding the export license required (though it cannot be held responsible)
- Arrange inland freight and warehousing if necessary, both in this country and in the destination country
- Receive and consolidate merchandise for shipment and delivery to the carrier
- Arrange for special crating and packing
- Make the booking on a carrier for the voyage or flight and arrange for necessary shipping containers
- Supervise on-loading of the shipment
- Obtain the clean bill of lading or air waybill according to the terms and conditions of the shipper's letter of instruction (SLI) and/or the letter of credit
- Prepare the shippers' export declaration (SED) for the Bureau of Census's statistical needs and for customs clearance of your export license

- Obtain all the necessary documents, either to create a shipment that can legally bind the buyer or to conform to the terms of a letter of credit

- Arrange for transit insurance, often through the forwarder's own master policy

- Prepare the documentation and present it to the bank for collection against documents or for negotiation under a letter of credit

- Deliver documents to the exporter's office at any point in the shipping process when the exporter wishes to assume control

- Follow up on the fate of the shipment at the foreign destination or at any transfer point in between

- File any necessary transport claims

- Handle fax and telex communications and provide messenger service during the course of the export shipping and collection process

- Assist you in tracking and reporting the harbor usage fees which are collected by U.S. Customs

While most forwarders are capable of handling all of these duties and possibly others, it is wise to keep a watchful eye on the process and handle or directly oversee some of the details yourself, initially as a learning process, and later on to maintain an overview of these vital services. Some of the functions are regularly provided as part of the basic forwarding fee; others are charged as utilized. Among the latter are messenger service and other out-of-pocket costs. Still others not regularly required are itemized additions to the basic fee. The thing to keep in mind as you gain your own expertise is that the people who work for the forwarder are very human and have good days, bad days, and busy days. They *can* make mistakes!

Forwarders can also save you money by sharing the special rates they receive because of the freight volume they handle. They can often also obtain cargo space when it's in short supply because of their ongoing business relationship with the carriers and through their functions as a freight consolidator. My suggestion is to search for a good forwarder who seems to take an interest in you and then work closely with it—which sometimes means not changing the forwarder every time a slightly better rate is offered by a competitor. This is not to say that you shouldn't do some checking of rates on your own to be sure that you are getting competitive rates and service overall.

Handling the Documentary Side of a Transaction

Paperwork is something the international trader must learn to live with! Here are the most essential documents to expect in virtually all trade transactions, import or export. Although others designed to fit special situations or needs will surface from time to time, you'll have ample opportunity to learn about them as the need or situations arise.

Commercial Invoice

This is of first importance, and normally differs little from the invoice you would send to any domestic customer. If a special form is required, such as the Canadians' customs invoice for shipments over CD$1200—which in their mind is in lieu of a commercial invoice—it will probably say so in the letter of credit or your buyer will tell you so in order to facilitate clearing of the goods through customs at their destination. The same is true of "legalized" consular invoices. Your forwarder has reference books to check for such special requirements.

Be careful that the way transportation is charged or sent for collection conforms to the shipping terms originally agreed to or specified by your buyer and duly noted on your invoice. (See the list of Incoterms and other relative comments in Chapter 10.) If you did not change the buyer's originally specified terms, those *are* the terms agreed to, even if you did not understand them fully at the time.

Unless a certificate of origin was also among the documents named, you may be asked to certify on the face of the invoice that it is a "true and correct invoice" and that "the goods are of U.S. origin," or that they "were manufactured in the U.S.A.," as the case may be. Some exporters stamp and sign a certification to this effect on every invoice, just in case it will help clear the goods at the other end. If you do this, be sure that the two statements are stamped separately, so that "U.S. origin" does not appear on goods not really made or originating here. The consequences can be serious, and it is easy for clerical help to stamp without thinking.

Finally, recheck your pro forma invoice, if you provided one, to be sure that the commercial invoice conforms to what you stated and your buyer accepted. (Reread the section on pro formas in Chapter 10, including the comments about foreign customs treatment of freight and discounts and the importance of providing any discounts on each item rather than in bulk at the bottom of the invoice.)

Consular Invoice

When the import regulations in the buyer's country are not satisfied with an invoice certified on its face to be "true and correct" or "of U.S.A. origin," it may specify a consular invoice. This is a regular commercial invoice "legalized" at the consulate or embassy. In some cases the Arab chamber of commerce is specified as an acceptable entity for legalization in lieu of a consular invoice. There is usually a nominal fee for such legal-

ization, but occasionally one hears of really significant fees or even outra-
geous fees for this service, so it is well to check with your forwarder or
the consulate in question as to both fee and the time needed to accomplish legalization. Since it must usually be the final invoice, including
shipping details, it can add substantially to the time required for document preparation prior to letter of credit negotiation, this can pose a real
threat to your schedule when the latest shipping date or validity date is
at hand. Check well in advance with your forwarder or others, preferably
before accepting the letter of credit as drawn, and then plan on forwarding the documents by a messenger service with receipt acknowledged.
This requirement applies mostly in the Middle East, Latin America, and
Africa, but it is also required in various small countries elsewhere around
the world.

Certificate of Origin

This is another invoice-related requirement that is usually accommodat-
ed on the invoice itself and for which many exporters insert a statement
as a matter of course. However, some buyers, and some countries, require
that a separate certificate be signed and notarized by your own chamber
of commerce. In active export centers the chamber will have forms. You
can also buy them from a business forms supplier like Apperson or
through your stationer.

In the case of Mexico and Canada, relative to NAFTA, or in the case of
the U.S.–Israel Free Trade Agreement, determining U.S. origin in accordance with the sometimes-intricate trade agreement formulas can
become complicated and will require a special form. Check with your
forwarder, the U.S. Department of Commerce, or the appropriate consulate.

Packing List

This is a term easily misunderstood, because what so many American
firms call a packing list is little more than a slip of paper stating the number of cartons or is actually a weigh bill. An export packing list (like the
genuine article in domestic trade) needs to state exactly what is packed in
each individually numbered carton. If a different number of widgets is
packed in several different boxes, you must make sure the box and packing list indicate just how many widgets there are in each. If you are a
third-party exporter, you may find it difficult to convince your supplier
of the importance of such a packing list, but you had better do so or you
will jeopardize your future business and customer goodwill. Most custom house inspectors require these lists so that they can more readily
spot check a shipment's contents for tariff assessment and illegal entries
without opening and inspecting each package.

This is a lesson I learned the hard way many years ago and very early in my export management career. It was the first shipment to Japan for my then-largest client, a major line of lingerie. This was one of those companies that did not perceive a need for detailed packing lists at the time—or any packing list or slip at all, for that matter. When my representative in Japan explained to me at home how necessary it was to have a packing list by carton to get through Japanese customs without major difficulties and delays, the goods were already at the U.S. port without the packing list I had requested. There was no way at that point that I could create such a record, and the latest shipping date on the letter of credit was upon me. My solution—and, I hasten to add, not a very good one—was to take all the bras, panties, slips, and nightgowns out of their many, many boxes and dump them all into a one giant wooden carton I had made that was about the size of a coffin. Thus my packing slip and invoice were in agreement as to being all in one carton only. The problem is, it took weeks for Japanese customs to sort it all out and check it against the invoice, and the buyers could hardly have been called satisfied customers. It was very nearly the end of my Japanese market. I finally found a new trading company for whom I did a much better job, and the line ultimately became very successful in Japan. It's good story now, but it wasn't then.

Bills of Lading

There are three basic bills of lading (BLs), plus some hybrids which, although less precise, are still designed to indicate the fact of shipment and the special terms and conditions of carriage. The three basic types are: (1) ocean bill of lading; (2) air waybill; (3) truck or rail bill of lading. Each is distinctly different from the others, and the fundamental differences as well as the carrier's varying liability should be understood. Some can be modified by virtue of being "short form" or "long form." The hybrid bill of lading goes by a variety of names, but probably the most proper all-inclusive name would be a "combined transport bill of lading," or simply "transport documents." There can also be something called "house bill of lading" and "NVOCC bill of lading," which are also transport documents.

Ocean Bill of Lading.   This is a negotiable document for ocean shipments, and is issued by the carrier in the form of a carriage contract. It indicates that the shipment is "clean onboard" (a named vessel), meaning that it has passed over the named ship's rails in good order, or with damage as noted if not "clean." The bill of lading is often actually prepared by the freight forwarder and sent for processing and checking by the steamship line. It is normally made up in three originals, any one of which could be used to claim title, plus numerous duplicates marked "copy—not negotiable." In an earlier era the two extra originals were sent on separate vessels to permit ultimate title transfer in case one or more of the vessels met with disaster.

Because of this history the ocean bill of lading continues to be a means of passing title. The key words for this purpose are "direct," or "straight," and "negotiable." A "negotiable" bill of lading (by virtue of the words "to order," or "to order of shipper," where the consignee's name is called for) is normally used in connection with a letter of credit or documentary collection, and indicates that the bill of lading is intended to be used as the means by which title is to be transferred. The title remains with the shipper until the shipper endorses the bill of lading after issue by the carrier, at which point the title rests with whoever is in possession of the original bill of lading. With such a negotiable document, the carrier would only release the merchandise to the buyer against an original bill of lading. The letter of credit, or collection instruction, will stipulate whether the bills are to be endorsed "in blank" or to the order of a third party, such as the paying bank under a letter of credit. If, instead, they were endorsed over to the consignee or the applicant of the letter of credit, that party might obtain the merchandise if coming into the possession of an original, even though the letter of credit negotiation contained discrepancies or was otherwise in dispute.

A "direct" or "straight" bill of lading would be used in the case of goods shipped under some form of open account terms. The buyer's name is provided in the space calling for the name of the consignee, and title passes when the bill of lading is issued and signed by the carrier.

It should be noted that the ocean bills of lading are not issued to the shipper until the vessel has steamed out of the port of embarkation. Be prepared to pay all ocean freight charges before receiving the bills of lading unless a credit line is arranged in advance with the steamship company or the freight forwarder. Even then, it will probably take at least three days before they are delivered, and it can take as many as 10 days. With increasing use of computers and electronic data interchange, such time lags continue to diminish, however.

Air Waybill. This is prepared by the air freight forwarder from information on the invoice and the packing list—subject to review by the air carrier, of course. While it also serves the shipper as the shipping contract and a receipt for the goods, it is never a negotiable instrument and is not used to transfer title. Therefore, it is usually made out to the consignee, but in some circumstances may be made out to a third party. This would be the case if the merchandise were to be sent under documentary collection terms (see Chapter 14). In that case, it would best be made out to the collecting bank, although its permission should be obtained in advance. Not doing so makes it more likely that the air waybills could fall into the consignee's hands, who could then simply go to the airport and pick up the goods, defeating the purpose of a documentary collection. An alternative is to arrange for an agent working on your behalf to be the temporary consignee. The agent could be the foreign office or correspondent of your freight forwarder. In either case, a notify party should be named so that whomever the third party has named as consignee will know who is ultimately supposed to pay for and receive the goods.

Truck or Rail Bill of Lading. This is an ordinary transport document used for domestic business and similar to air waybills. It can be an international trade document, in the case of shipments to Mexico or Canada. It is usually nonnegotiable and made out to the consignee. It is possible, however, to construct them as negotiable instruments by making them out "to order." In the case of Mexico, there have been restrictions on American trucks crossing the border. Therefore, the goods are shipped to the border—delivered at frontier (DAF)—in the care of the buyer's forwarder, who can make arrangements for the border crossing and then onward to the consignee. Possibly your forwarder has a Mexican subsidiary or partner who can arrange for the goods to be turned over to the buyer's agent. It must still be documented as an export shipment. Be sure to take the new NAFTA regulations into account.

With Canada, normal truck and rail traffic proceeds in and out of the country just as with domestic trade, but it still must clear Canadian customs like any other international shipment. Again, check the NAFTA regulations regarding origin and other special arrangements.

Combined Transport Bill of Lading. This is a bill of lading for intermodal transport and designed to permit shipment of a container load by rail, truck, or inland waterway to a port, and from there on board a vessel. The journey may even extend to unloading abroad and continue from there to a foreign inland point for final delivery, or some lesser combination of carriage events. When merchandise is shipped across the United States from the West Coast to an East or Gulf Coast port (or vice versa), intermodal transport is called a landbridge, or minilandbridge. From an inland city to a port, it may be called a microlandbridge.

At one time, such a bill of lading could not have qualified for a letter of credit, but today they represent an accepted form of transport that is becoming more important every day, with letters-of-credit rules and formats increasingly designed to permit their use. Utilizing this service can save both time and shipping costs, as well as permit the shipper to collect against a letter of credit under such a "through bill of lading" without waiting for the cross-country transit to reach a port where an ocean bill of lading can be obtained. Finding the route and obtaining a good rate for such sophisticated arrangements is a job that most exporters rely on professionals for help with. Landbridges and through bills of lading are so specialized that you have good reason to utilize professional help, and you should also check your bank's international department to confirm that the letter of credit you request is drawn to permit such arrangements. Intermodal shipments are forcing some into the practice of providing *four* original bills of lading to handle all the carriers involved. Of course, if you are located inland or regularly ship from both coasts, intermodalism can be an extremely valuable standard operating procedure.

House or NVOCC Bill of Lading. This is an ocean bill of lading prepared and issued by the freight forwarder, by the air freight consolidator, or by a non-vessel operating common carrier (NVOCC), which may also be a freight forwarder. They are considered bills of lading acceptable for negotiation under a typical letter of credit, provided that the issuer purports to be an agent of the carrier and is accepted as such. (And, as a general rule, they are.) However, if you are shipping under letter-of-credit terms and a freight consolidator or NVOCC will be issuing a house or NVOCC bill of lading or air waybill not issued by the carrier or an agent accepted as representing the carrier, it is best and safest to request that the letter of credit specify "house bills of lading" acceptable in the case of an air freight consolidator, or NVOCC bills of lading acceptable, in the case of ocean shipments. Failing that, be sure to mention to the advising bank's export letter-of-credit department exactly what form of bill of lading you will be receiving and find out whether they consider it acceptable in the case of the credit you are holding.

Do not let these minor extra arrangements or precautions deter you from using air consolidators and NVOCCs. They are only a bit cumbersome on the occasion of the first shipment. In fact, we want to emphasize that the use of consolidators and NVOCCs, who buy shipping and container space wholesale and sell it at retail on specific routes, can save you and your buyer substantial transportation costs, especially if you ship in less than container loads, but they must be selected with care.

Shipper's Export Declaration

The Shipper's Export Declaration (SED), commonly referred to as an ExDec in the trade, is a document required for all exports over $2500 (except for some shipments to Canada) and is routinely handled and filled out by your forwarder. (See Fig. 12-1). The easiest place for the forwarder to get most of the information for the SED is from the Shipper's Letter of Instructions (SLI), a form you must complete that is provided to you by your forwarder. The SED also contains any export license information the product and/or destination may require, an issue that must be determined well in advance of the shipment itself. (The subject of export licensing is discussed in Chapter 17 under Government Stumbling Blocks.) The license itself does not go with the shipment, but is retained by the exporter with shipments recorded against it until the license is exhausted or expired.

A copy of the SED is presented to the carrier by the forwarder and the original is filed with the Department of Commerce for use by the Bureau of Census for statistical purposes and by U.S. Customs and the Bureau of

FORM **7525-V** (1-1-88)

U.S. DEPARTMENT OF COMMERCE · BUREAU OF THE CENSUS · INTERNATIONAL TRADE ADMINISTRATION

SHIPPER'S EXPORT DECLARATION

OMB No. 0607-0018

1a EXPORTER *(Name and address including ZIP code)*		2 DATE OF EXPORTATION	3 BILL OF LADING/AIR WAYBILL NO.
	ZIP CODE		

b EXPORTER'S EIN (IRS) NUMBER

c PARTIES TO TRANSACTION
☐ Related ☐ Non-related

4a ULTIMATE CONSIGNEE

b INTERMEDIATE CONSIGNEE

5 FORWARDING AGENT

6 POINT (STATE) OF ORIGIN OR FTZ NO	7 COUNTRY OF ULTIMATE DESTINATION

8 LOADING PIER *(Vessel only)*	9 MODE OF TRANSPORT *(Specify)*
10 EXPORTING CARRIER	11 PORT OF EXPORT
12 PORT OF UNLOADING *(Vessel and air only)*	13 CONTAINERIZED *(Vessel only)* ☐ Yes ☐ No

14 SCHEDULE B DESCRIPTION OF COMMODITIES *(Use columns 17-19)*

15 MARKS, NOS. AND KINDS OF PACKAGES

D/F (16)	SCHEDULE B NUMBER (17)	CHECK DIGIT	QUANTITY - SCHEDULE B UNIT(S) (18)	SHIPPING WEIGHT *(Kilos)* (19)		VALUE (U.S. dollars, omit cents) *(Selling price or cost if not sold)* (20)

21 VALIDATED LICENSE NO./GENERAL LICENSE SYMBOL

22 ECCN *(When required)*

23 Duly Authorized officer or employee

The exporter authorizes the forwarder named above to act as forwarding agent for export control and customs purposes

24 I certify that all statements made and all information contained herein are true and correct and that I have read and understand the instructions for preparation of this document, set

Figure 12-1. Sample shipper's export declaration.

Export Administration (BXA) for administration of the Export Administration Regulations. There are severe civil and/or criminal penalties for failing to file the SED or misstating information on the declaration.

Insurance Certificate or Special Policy

If the terms of sale call for the seller to arrange for insurance, as in CIF and CIP terms, the exporter must provide proof of insurance by means of a certificate. If a documentary collection is involved, it will probably call for a "special policy," which stands on its own for the claimant and becomes one of the documents required for negotiation of the letter of credit. The easiest way of obtaining this certificate, or policy, is through your freight forwarder's blanket marine policy (which will also include air coverage, even though it is called a "marine" policy). As you become more active as an exporter, you may take out your own blanket policy or buy policies as required directly from your marine insurance agent. Although technically the terms may require less than full coverage, it is safest to take out full-coverage warehouse-to-warehouse type insurance, including all risks. The normal procedure is to take out cover for 110 percent of CIF value. Be sure to discuss this with your forwarder.

Draft

Do not overlook the draft (also called a Bill of Exchange), which is the mechanism that triggers payment in documentary transactions such as letters of credit (L/C), documents against payment (D/P), and documents against acceptance (D/A). The draft is essentially a check or order to pay drawn against the paying bank (drawee) by the exporter (drawer) and *signed by the exporter*. In the case of a draft used with a letter of credit, a specific bank is usually named as payee, while in documentary collections, the buyer is named as payee.

Other Documents

There are many special-purpose documents, depending on the product being shipped, certain project contractual obligations, shipping conditions, and so forth. These documents cannot all be discussed here, nor would there be much value in doing so. A few of the more common examples include:

Phytosanitary Certificate.   This document requires a preshipment inspection conducted by the U.S. Department of Agriculture. It is necessary when shipping plants, plant materials, or fruits and vegetables to most countries. It certifies that the product shipped conforms with the quarantine import regulations of the foreign country involved.

Inspection Certificate. This is the certificate a buyer may request to ensure that the goods conform to the original order as to specifications, quantity, and quality. This is a reasonable request, and the certificate is readily obtainable if the inspector is a qualified, impartial third party. If not, as in the case of a buyer-controlled inspection, care must be taken to avoid arbitrary frustration of a contract, purchase order, or letter of credit. (Refer to our discussion of inspections later in this chapter.)

Dock or Warehouse Receipts. These can become primary documents in the case of Free Alongside Ship (FAS) terms, or when the goods will have to be temporarily stored in a bonded warehouse at some point in the transaction.

Postal Export Shipment Forms. These forms are supplied by the post office. Form Number 2966 is used for sending small packages of samples, advertising material, and so forth. If the shipment value exceeds $2500 or requires a validated or other specific license, other documents, such as the Shippers Export Declaration, must also be provided. You should always have someone check restrictions or procedures in the country of destination on the occasion of first-time shipments.

Timing Is Everything

We have explored the role of your banker and freight forwarder as keys to building the structure of your transaction. We have looked at the various fundamental documents that serve as the skeleton of your transactions. Now it's time to discuss the flesh and sinew of your transactions.

Don't ever underestimate the importance of your timetable in every export transaction or project. It is the central factor in their successful conclusion. The clock starts ticking from the moment you first make a firm offer. Timing can make or break your deal and surely can be the difference between profit and loss. The word *timetable* refers to many elements and conditions, some of which may be fixed in time while others have to float against a variety of conditions. When discussing pro forma invoices and other firm quotations in Chapter 10, I emphasized the time line for delivery as representing that critical period from formal acceptance or receipt of the letter of credit (which is the controlling instrument if it is used) to delivery of the goods according to the conditions specified in the shipping terms. As we have learned, the conditions referred to can be anything from your factory or warehouse to the "ship's rails" to a foreign frontier or city. You cannot control when the buyer will accept an offer, except as to the validity dates you put on the offer or pro forma, and even then you will find that buyers often pay this detail little heed. On the other hand, it is risky to start acquiring inventory or product or begin a custom manufacturing process until the acceptance is final. If a letter of credit is to be issued on execution of the order, product preparation should start when the letter is in hand. For you to do otherwise, requires that your buyer be reliable, creditworthy, and known to you. Even then, there are added degrees of risk exposure, depending on the size and custom nature of the transaction.

Before negotiations or firm offers ever begin, you must develop a conservative timetable for inventory and supplies delivery, manufacturing cycle time, and transport and transport connections. This should include attention to the time gap from one ocean sailing availability to the next. To get to some of the less accessible ports in the world can actually take months, not weeks or days. A requirement that a specific ocean carrier be used can extend this time line still further, so that if one connection is missed by a day, the entire timetable changes by weeks.

The same is true of the manufacturing and labeling process. Even when standard products are being ordered, special coloring, labeling, or other treatment can throw what seems to be a very reliable production schedule into chaos. Another delay may result from what appears to be a harmless requirement for preshipment inspection. This can become a nightmare if there aren't clear rules governing the timing of such inspections and/or a waiver for them if that timing is not adhered to and included as part of the inspection requirement. (A few specific suggestions to avoid that problem are mentioned in the section on inspections further on in this chapter.)

Your timetable proceeds from acceptance through collection. Timely collection of the proceeds of the transaction may have a great deal to do with your continuing ability to export in terms of maintaining credibility through on-time payment to your suppliers or lender. Besides delivering and shipping, you must *collect*; this is the critical moment for all concerned. After shipping, you must be sure to include in your timetable the time needed to obtain bills of lading from your carrier (which can take as many as 10 days in the case of an ocean carrier, and even longer if the ship is held up in port for repairs or because of a strike). After the bill of lading is obtained, it may still take a day or two to complete the documentation, even assuming you have obtained the necessary invoice legalization and have requested the required certificate of origin from a chamber of commerce.

Timing can also play a role if something goes wrong with the shipment or the overseas installation process. A potential or actual claim must be dealt with rapidly. Claims never improve with age! As we have said elsewhere, the cheapest airline ticket you ever buy may be the one you bought to visit your buyer the moment you heard of a claim or a problem.

Checklist of Minimum Terms

A wish list is not a checklist. All the obligations and responsibilities implicit in the various preshipment and postshipment inspection conditions, delivery dates, shipping terms, and payment terms are there by omission or commission whether you have discussed them and considered them or not. The most-often neglected of negotiable terms are the terms within the letter of credit. Exporters often simply assume that since the buyer has agreed to issue a letter of credit as the form of payment, everything is secure. What a disaster this can create! The letter of credit may come with inspection terms; usance terms (days beyond "sight" which must pass before the bank will transfer funds); documents for negotiation that you may be unable to obtain in a timely fashion; a letter of credit validity date that matches your earliest possible delivery and consequently allows no time for negotiation of the letter of credit; payment at counters overseas or in other than U.S. dollars; and so on and on. Worse yet, you may discover that even though your buyer promised to open a letter of credit, he or she failed to mention that this would be done some stated number of days *after* notification from you that the goods were ready to ship. Use a checklist for requesting a letter of credit. It might be well to study it for order or confirmations with payment terms other than letter of credit because many of the conditions apply to terms for any export order. (See Fig. 12-2, which provides a sample form.)

Letter of credit or not, it is critical that every term and/or condition be clearly stated. This includes the shipping terms based on 1990 Incoterms, payment terms, and all other conditions or merchandise specifications when necessary. Accepting the return of merchandise because of a misunderstanding as to its qualities or specifications is a good deal more trouble and expense after shipping it overseas—especially when it has already cleared foreign customs—than it is after a domestic delivery. If a letter of credit is involved, send the buyer the form suggested stating what must or must not be in the letter. It is best if, before the buyer unilaterally spells out the details of a proposed letter of credit or other terms and conditions, some exchange as to general terms and conditions takes place. As explained earlier regarding pro forma invoices, once the buyer has had his or her own way in drawing up the letter or order terms and conditions, you are placed in the position of negotiating to take provisions out, add others, or request letter of credit amendments—and all the latter at your own added expense.

Having finally established all terms and their meaning, do not forget to "finger read" the letter of credit when it arrives to be sure it conforms to your agreement or pro forma. (Use the checklist in Fig. 14-7 to help you, bearing in mind that no list can anticipate every potential glitch and headache.) The same care should be used in the case of purchase orders, contracts, or confirmations to the extent that one of those documents is to govern a transaction.

Export Contracts and Purchase Orders

Without getting into legal details, you should be aware that since 1988 the United States has been a signatory to the United Nations Convention

FORMAT FOR REQUESTING A LETTER OF CREDIT FROM OVERSEAS BUYERS

TO: _____ DATE: _____

Dear Overseas Buyer:

Regarding your purchase order number _____ dated _____, please ask that your bank issue an irrevocable commercial letter of credit according to the following terms and conditions.

Beneficiary: (exporter's name & address) _____

Requested Advising Bank: (name & address) _____
                                          telex _____ cable _____ Swift _____

Please open via air mail _____ teletransmission _____

In the amount of $_____. Payment to be effected in U.S. Dollars

Shipment and price quotations are _____ (ICC 350 Incoterm FOB, CIF, etc.) Destination _____

Payment Terms: The letter of credit must be payable at the counters of (name of bank) _____
OR: Letter of credit must be negotiable and payable at the counters of a bank in (city) _____

Draft(s) to be drawn at sight, or _____ days sight, or _____ days after the date of bill of lading. In the case of time drafts, discount charges are for the account of the ___ buyer ___ seller.

___ Please have letter of credit confirmed by _____ (Bank), OR ___ confirmation is not requested.
___ Please have letter of credit allow transfer.
___ Please have letter of credit state that NVOCC or House Bills of Lading are acceptable.

Documentary Requirements: The letter of credit funds should be available upon presentation of the following documents:
1. Signed Commercial Invoices 2. _____ 3._____ 4. (etc)

Shipment from _____ to _____

Partial shipments are _____ permitted, or _____ not permitted

Latest shipment date _____ Latest expiration date _____

_____ days after the date of shipment must be allowed for presentation of documents to the negotiating bank.

All banking charges in the U.S. are for the account of ___ buyer or ___ seller, all other charges for buyer's account.

Please ensure that the letter of credit is received by us _____ days before our agreed upon shipment date.
OR: The shipment date will be based on _____ days after our receipt of an acceptable letter of credit.

PLEASE NOTE: If you are unable to meet any of these terms and conditions, please contact us immediately, and prior to having the letter of credit issued. Any deviation from the above terms and conditions without our agreement, may result in a delay of the shipment until the letter of credit can be amended.

Sincerely,

Exporter

Figure 12-2. Format to request a letter of credit from your buyer.

on Contracts for the International Sale of Goods (CISG), also known as the Vienna Sales Convention. As of 1994, 35 countries have signed the convention—a large enough number to make it important to understand some of its basic implications. Where the United States is concerned, one important point is that when one contracting party is based here and the other is based in a country also a signatory, the contract will automatically be interpreted under the convention unless specifically stated otherwise, even if the contract is not in writing. This is called a "reservation." It is one of five points that a signatory nation may select when it signs the Vienna Convention, which allows each signatory to accept it under slightly different terms. Although much of the convention parallels our own U.S. Uniform Commercial Code (UCC), there are certain distinct differences. Some are as basic as defining quite differently what constitutes an offer, acceptance, fraud, revocability, and the period of time for discovery of a defect within which a valid claim can still be adjudicated.

Be sure to find out, when preparing an agreement, which countries are currently bound by the CISG and which of the five possible CISG "reservations" are operative. Unless you are dealing with an attorney who can provide current advice on the merits of using CISG, I suggest that, at least for the immediate future, you declare that until you are advised of any advantages it might offer, the contract be "subject to the UCC as adopted by *a named* state in this country and not to the United Nations CISG." This advice is especially applicable if you want to use a standard contract you're used to and don't want it to be subject to different interpretations of which you may not be fully aware. It would also be safe to use the above language even if you have not determined whether the other party is or is not from a signatory nation. Of course, there is always the possibility they may want to use the CISG, in which case you should pursue the matter with an attorney knowledgeable about the Vienna Convention.

Keep in mind that it is quite possible, nevertheless, to receive from customers belonging to a signatory nation, routine purchase orders that would be considered contracts falling under the CISG. In such cases, it would be neither productive or practical to engage in negotiations as to whose law and codes might apply. You should probably study the issue, therefore, to understand the key points as they affect orders or purchase contracts under the UCC and the CISG. For smaller, day-to-day business it is unlikely to be a problem either way, unless a serious dispute arises that can only be resolved in court.

In any case, be aware that as you make offers, distribute price lists, counter offers, and accept orders, you are actually engaging in a contractual process. It is important to think carefully about what you are doing to the extent that your offer or the customer's acceptance is about to affect the anatomy of the transaction.

Specifications, Performance Standards, and Inspections

Specifications, performance standards, and inspections have been mentioned in several earlier contexts and are not usually critical to a simple sale of a product that is "off the shelf" and can be examined in advance by the buyer. Specifications and performance standards are normally associated with a contract involving custom manufacturing or capital equipment. To the extent that you are faced with them, study the conditions carefully and be sure that, so long as you meet whatever standards or specifications are involved, you can reasonably control the integrity of your export project. If the object of the inspection is conformance to specifications, be sure that the specifications are very clearly set forth and understood by both parties to the contract. If it is a Third-World government Mandated Preshipment Inspection Program, determine exactly what will be inspected. The inspection process can even include your pricing relative to competitors' to be sure it is in line with something called a "world price." It is possible the inspection could be intended to ascertain that your gross profit does not exceed certain arbitrary limits.

As mentioned in the section on timing, you must use care that inspection requirements cannot be misused to frustrate your ability to make a timely shipment. As an example, if a letter of credit requires a document attesting to a satisfactory preshipment inspection by the buyer, what do you do if the buyer's inspector does not show up? You might negotiate that an additional document be required for the letter of credit, attesting to your notification to the buyer so many days in advance of a date certain that the goods will be ready for inspection. This, in turn, will permit a clause in the contract and letter of credit such as the following: "If the buyer's inspector has not arrived within *xx* days after said notification of inspection date, the requirement for a buyer's certificate of inspection is waived and shall replaced by a manufacturer's certificate stating that the goods meet the specifications (or standards)." The Chinese are famous for using the arrival of inspectors or trainees to delay delivery for their own purposes and reasons.

Inspections can be perfectly harmless and arise even in simple transactions, but if they do, be sure they occur prior to the goods leaving the United States and that they are done by an impartial inspection service—which can be accessed from anywhere in this country. There are three major inspection services: SGS International Quality Services, Bureau Veritas, and Intertek. The largest by far is SGS International Quality Services and as such is a division of U.S. Testing Company, Inc., in turn a part of SGS North America, Inc., which is a subsidiary to the parent SGS in Geneva, Switzerland. The company has hundreds of offices around this country and around the world, many determined by the product area in which they specialize. An SGS branch can usually be found in the phone book of any fair-sized city, but if not, its U.S. headquarters are located in New York as SGS North America, Inc., 42 Broadway, New York, New York 10004; phone: 212/482-8700.

To avoid the time, trouble, and expense of third-party inspection, buyers can often be satisfied with an agreement that the supplier will provide a certificate that the goods meet the specified standards, which is obviously better for the seller but also provides comfort to the buyer because it makes fraud easier to prove. A frequently used compromise solution to this is a 10 percent payment retention for a reasonable period after delivery until the shipment can be assembled, inspected, or operated to the buyer's satisfaction. Intuition, past experience, and common sense must be used to determine whether this will be acceptable.

Should installation or other postsales service and follow-up be necessary, be sure to carefully investigate the real cost of local labor, the costs of maintaining your domestic staff, and any travel costs your buyer may not be covering. Ask questions of others in your field and your trade organization. Check for special rules concerning expatriates in the country involved through the U.S. Department of Commerce country desks in Washington, D.C., and every other place you can possibly think of to question. Many firms have found conditions very different and far more expensive than their hosts have indicated during negotiations.

Collecting Payment

Clearly, getting paid is a vital part of every transaction's anatomy and, in fact, is a continuing subject of this book. In Chapters 14 and 15 you will discover the mechanics for getting paid in a timely fashion by means of letters of credit or documentary collections and also for insuring the transportation and credit risks to ensure being paid through the claim process for monies that you cannot realize through the collection process. Whether the terms of payment provide for the greater credit exposure of open account terms or are for the most comfortable and readily negotiated letter of credit, they can all work very well and serve their purposes, depending on a careful initial credit investigation process and an intelligent selection of terms offered. Thereafter, good follow-through will usually result in payment ultimately, so long as the seller ensures that the buyer is shipped what was ordered in a proper fashion and without damage; that the formal documentary procedures plus appropriate written and verbal communication is taken care of; and that discrete follow-up communication is implemented to remind the buyer of its obligations. Whether the steps to be taken are mechanical, as in the case of letters of credit, or involve communications designed to courteously but firmly remind open accounts to pay in a timely fashion, common sense and attention to detail will have a great deal to do with the happy and profitable conclusion of the transaction.

Alternatively, in the worst-case scenario—involving war, political upheaval, lack of foreign exchange in the buyer's country, buyer insolvency, buyer nonpayment or delinquency, ocean or air disasters, spoilage or damage en route—you must depend on the insurance you have taken out to cover the risks that threaten your timely receipt of payment. Usually the costs can be passed on without difficulty to the buyer. For commercial risks, a more discerning analysis must be undertaken; for insurance on these risks is not readily passed on to the buyer—at least not transparently. The strength of the buyer relative to the size of the buyer's account must also be considered. This is called "commercial risk." The political stability of the buyer's country, its economic soundness, and the possibilities of war or piracy make each payment-risk decision unique. Covering these risks is discussed in greater detail in Chapter 16.

The "end game," as it is called in chess, is getting the money, putting it in the bank, and realizing enough profit on the transaction to pay the bills, while increasing your company's net equity and working capital.

Endnotes

1. *Export-Import*, by Joseph A. Zodl, F&W Publications, Cincinnati, Ohio, 1992.
2. *Developing Skills for International Trade*; JuDee Benton, Team Export, Merced, California, 1993.

13
Preparing for an Import Transaction

Much of what can be said concerning international trade applies to both exporting and importing because one of these functions is required to bring about the other. For example, what is said about requesting letters of credit can be applied to the opening of a letter on the import side. You can make equally good use of this information whether you are the party ordering or the party offering; it's a matter of role reversal.

Of course, marketing a product domestically differs in many ways from establishing the product in a foreign market, but a discussion of general domestic marketing techniques is beyond the scope of this book. You will find a list of additional reading and reference books in the Appendix, however, that will give you some hints for making initial contacts useful for your export marketing campaigns. The reference books in question include global lists of trade associations and trade shows, directories of U.S. manufacturers and manufacturer's agents and retailers.

Preimport Preparation

The paperwork and entry process needed to clear imports into the United States is unique to the import function. It is also true that the U.S. Customs Service, a division of the U.S. Treasury Department, frequently reveals an underlying philosophy of "presumed guilty until proven innocent." This cannot be compared to anything in the Department of Commerce or Agriculture or the other government departments or institutions you might have come in contact with relative to your trading activities. Performing what is essentially a policing function, U.S. Customs officials are always actively looking for unlawful conduct, and the importer must keep this in mind at all times. If the Customs Service believes that an importer has been less than candid, it has been known to assess unrealistically large fines or levies and leave it to the importer to prove them unjustified. This might be easy enough to prove, but while the allegation of wrongdoing is pending, the small business facing such a penalty and/or levy may find a powerful rationale to agree on a settlement that will conclude the issue. Aside from needing the importation released, the accounting reserve provision required for the large threatened Customs obligation can have a chilling effect on a company's credit standing.

Many people believe that you must obtain some sort of general license to be an importer. On the contrary. Except for applying to the Customs Service for an importer's identification number—which will normally be your Social Security number if you are an individual, or the Federal Employer's Identification number if you are a firm—there are no specific import licenses necessary. There are, however, many questions that must be resolved, and for some products licenses or advance permits must be obtained before you can clear Customs. It follows, therefore, that you should know these special circumstances before making a firm commitment to buy.

Besides the routine procedures of entry, this chapter will touch on the areas you should study in some detail in the U.S. Customs Regulations and that you should discuss with your custom house broker. A license must be obtained in advance to import certain controlled substances, just as a license must be obtained to export certain goods to certain countries. For example, in the case of distilled spirits, wines, or malt beverages, a permit must be obtained from the Department of the Treasury's Bureau of Alcohol, Tobacco, and Firearms, which is involved in other import licensing activities as well. Products coming under the surveillance of the Food and Drug Administration and the Department of Agriculture (especially dairy products, fresh produce, livestock, meat and poultry, plants and seeds) are among those that have controls or limitations for import placed on them. This is also true of certain chemicals, textiles, and consumer goods. The general practice, and often stated in the purchase agreement, is that the seller will be responsible for all necessary export licenses and government filings. Even so, you will be well advised to do some research of your own to be sure the exporter can, in fact, complete and ship the proposed transaction.

This chapter assumes that you have negotiated prices, terms, shipping dates, and payment or letter-of-credit conditions. Now that you are in the buyer's role, don't forget all the clever techniques your export customers practiced on you, the seller, to obtain the best possible import terms. Also, be sure to factor into your anticipated selling price—in addition to Customs duties and import clearance costs and fees—other costs that did not concern you as an exporter, such as distribution transportation costs, warehousing, handling, and domestic marketing.

As a starting point for the import transaction, assume that the overseas seller has performed as agreed in shipping the goods and that you have

been notified of the arrival date and flight or voyage number of the shipment. You have accordingly advised the professional who is going to
help you with the import process. This is your customs broker (or custom
house broker). He or she must be notified of its imminent arrival and
given full details about the nature of the merchandise, including its country of origin and any quota information that may apply. Remember, the
customs broker is only there to *help* you. It is rarely the broker who is
penalized for incorrect or fraudulent customs entries: it is you. And as I
indicated at the outset, the Customs Service is not an entirely user-friend-
ly organization. If it should find a false or wrongful entry several years
after the event, the amount of the undervaluation, plus penalties, plus
interest could easily exceed the net worth of a business. Later in this
chapter I'll explain why the services of a customs broker are essential to
the small or neophyte importer, but here, the emphasis is on not relying
entirely on the broker. You yourself should learn about any special quotas, restrictions, or conditions that might attach to your import. It will be
impossible for the customs broker to give you the best assistance possible
if he or she is not fully informed about the nature of your transaction.

For these two reasons—your need to know and your need to inform—
it is clear that you must do some research yourself, so that you can help
minimize the chance of unforeseen problems in the customs shed. Let's
back up in time a bit to learn what preliminary investigation you should
do for the U.S. Customs side of the transaction even before you call your
customs broker. There are numerous exceptions to the basic import regulations and you must be informed about any rules that might pertain to
your shipment because of the nature of the product or its country of origin, quite apart from the tariff rate itself. We strongly recommend that
you start by obtaining the U.S. Customs Service's inexpensive but easy-
to-read and very useful booklet, *Importing into the United States*.[1] It not
only contains further details about the material covered here, but also
describes the exceptions to the general rules and specifies the import
products that might present special challenges or require advance
arrangements.

A phone call to your local U.S. Customs office can help you understand
in a *preliminary* way what problems and duty costs might hinder your
import efforts. (Be sure to be ready with an accurate product description,
including country of origin.) A binding tariff classification can be
obtained by writing any U.S. Customs district director. (The details for
proposing such a request are provided in Chapter 9 of *Importing into the
United States*.) You should also locate for ready availability the
Harmonized Tariff Schedule of the United States of America[2] (HTSUS) which
contains the duty rates and the *Customs Regulations of the United States of
America*[3] which provides the procedural requirements. The *Harmonized
Tariff Schedule*, or *HTSUS*, and the Regulations can be found in many
libraries and are available from the Government Printing Office for

around $75 each. If you can, try to assess it in cooperation with your customs broker. It requires some experience to use its classification system correctly, and mistakes in interpretation can be costly.

A study of the *HTSUS* introductory explanations will give you a fair idea of how to use it, but we provide here some information to put you on the right track. The Schedule is similar to the Harmonized Schedule B, which may be familiar to you as an exporter and which coordinates with the rest of the world's product classification system for international trade. Commodities are listed in groupings by content, as in Raw Materials, or by use, as in Complex Manufactured Goods. There are about 5000 article descriptions listed as 11 digit numbers. The first two digits relate to one of the 99 chapters in the *HTSUS* and are rebroken down into specific subheadings. The last two digits (Statistical Suffix) are for internal U.S. trade statistics and do not affect the dutiable rate determination. In turn, the chapters are grouped into 22 sections.

After you find the proper classification subheading, the first column will indicate the way the quantity of the product must be listed on the Customs Entry form—i.e., number (*No*), weight (*Kg*)—or if no unit needs to be listed, X. Although primarily for statistical purposes, the unit is sometimes used to compute the duty by number of items instead of on the basis of a percentage of the value. The remaining columns indicate the dutiable rate, depending on the country of origin. The first of these columns has two categories: *General* and *Special*. The next column is called the *Statutory Rate* column and always presents the highest rate (being the former 1930 tariff). Actually, it applies only to our more or less current enemies or unfriendly nations who do not enjoy Most Favored Nation (MFN) status. There are very few nations now in that category, but, as an example, had the U.S. taken away MFN status from China (PRC), all merchandise acknowledged to come from China would have been at the higher rates, and Hong Kong would have become unimaginably busy as the "place of recorded manufacturer" of an infinite variety of goods.

The rates shown in the *General* category applying to the MFN nations, represent the bulk of U.S. tariffs collected. Tariffs have continued to decline over the years, however, thanks to the General Agreement on Tariffs and Trade (GATT) to which the United States and most of its trading partners belong. The most recent General Agreement on Tariffs and Trade which resulted in major reductions, is known as the Uruguay Round. It was finally concluded in 1994 after eight years of difficult negotiations. The nations listed in the *Special* column are less-developed countries (LDCs) that are eligible for special treatment under the Generalized System of Preferences (GSP) status (whether members of GATT or not), or that are otherwise subject to special beneficial treatment—as are Canada or Mexico because of NAFTA; Israel under the U.S.–Israel Free Trade Agreement; and the Caribbean Basin Initiative countries. Goods from these countries very often enter duty-free. The

Special column lists exceptions only, so that if nothing is shown in that column, the *General*, or MFN status applies. The various *Special* categories are listed and grouped by a letter designation in the HTSUS. After the correct ad valorem rate is determined, that percentage is applied to the *Transaction Value* of the shipment.

To review this chapter, I called on a customs consultant whose background was with a very large importer with responsibility for all its Customs affairs. He takes an even stronger view than I do about the dangers of importing without sufficient homework or professional advice. He recommended that the importer should go to the library and review the Customs Modernization Acts of 1978 and 1994 and the Trade Agreements Act of 1979 to fully understand the penalties that can be imposed and the U.S. Customs approach to enforcing the Customs laws and regulations and auditing the entries. In the past, small importers acting in good faith have been less likely to be audited and their incorrect entries dealt harshly with than large, experienced importers whose staff experts should know better. However, this tendency cannot be relied on and, with the newly computerized means of auditing, being a small business may less and less often serve as a shield. Every importer, however small or new, must be familiar enough with the import requirements to ensure that there is compliance with the Customs Laws and Regulations.

The customs expert offered as a "bad example" a California manufacturer which had discovered that a major component of its finished product could be made for much less in Korea. Accordingly, the manufacturer loaned the Korean manufacturer the relevant tools and molds to use in the contract manufacturing arrangement in Korea. The value of those tools and molds thereby became a dutiable cost (an "assist") which had to be added to the Korean manufacturer's production charges. This can legally be calculated by one of three methods: (1) applying a proportionate value of the useful life of the tools and molds against each unit; (2) applying the entire cost to one entire shipment; or (3) allocating the cost over the number of units for which a firm order is in place. The best way in this case, however, proved to be to sell the molds to the Korean company so that the Koreans would include the tooling costs in their prices of the exported components. The California manufacturer had to be advised, however, to be certain that an "arm's length" price be placed on the tools and molds to avoid the very real danger of a "592" fraud penalty being applied in a subsequent audit.

A preliminary caution before I explain the clearing process itself: To clear your imports, a surety bond or a 100 percent cash collateral deposit must be established prior to making entry and taking possession of imports. The custom house broker hired to clear your imports usually plays the key role in providing your access to such a bond and, in some rare cases, may even permit your goods to enter under the broker's own continuous term bond. The main exception is in the case of informal entries of low-value shipments that can be sent by mail, as will subsequently be explained. In fact, I am assuming here that you will retain a customs broker (probably a department of the same firm handling your export forwarding), but we will nevertheless explain the basics of the process that you need to understand so you can ask the right questions and provide the right information. As this process becomes clear, you will most likely see the sound reasons for having a custom house broker's assistance.

Clearing Customs: Formal Entry

Initiation and Documentation

As the initial step in the import clearing process, someone must first evidence the right to make entry of the shipment. This must be done by the owner, consignee, or a licensed custom house broker. A negotiable bill of lading made out "to order," or an airway bill will do, but very commonly a "carrier's certificate," filled out by the carrier and indicating the owner or consignee, is used. For formal entry, documents must be filed within five days and include:

1. Evidence of the right to make entry, as described above.
2. Entry Manifest. (This is usually Customs Form 7533, but could be the Application and Special Permit for Immediate Delivery Customs Form 3461 in special situations, such as fresh produce, articles for a trade fair, or approved merchandise originating in Canada or Mexico for which a bond is on file.)
3. Commercial invoice (or alternatively, a pro forma invoice if the commercial invoice is not available).
4. Packing list (*with carton-by-carton marking and numbering*), if appropriate.
5. The importing entity's IRS number (Federal Identification Number for corporations or the Social Security number for individual responsibility).
6. Power of attorney for the broker who is to act for you.
7. Any other special documents required to establish the admissibility of the merchandise.

Examination, Inspection, and Valuation

The second stage of entry is the examination and valuation process, which is sometimes waived in part, but normally includes:

1. The valuation of the merchandise for customs purposes—called transaction value—and its dutiable status. Transaction value is based normally on FAS value (that is, on the total country of origin price, plus any selling commissions incurred by the buyer, such as packing costs; preexport inland transport; royalty; or buyer "assists," which include items like materials, components, tools and dies, or foreign engineering that are provided at the buyer's cost) paid or owed for the goods prior to export shipping costs or fees. Not included as costs for tariff calculation are overseas export air or ocean charges or subsequent transportation costs, forwarder's fees, and insurance costs.

2. Checking for proper markings on the merchandise as to country of origin and other labeling requirements.

3. Reviewing invoicing as to comparable value, description, and quantity.

4. Reviewing to determine that the correct classification was selected by the importer or the broker based on the *Harmonized Tariff Schedule of the United States (HTSUS)*.

5. Inspection for any prohibited items or items with special controls not declared.

Payment of Estimated Duty and Liquidation

When all the above has been found to be in order and accepted and any quota requirements met, Customs Entry Summary Form 7501 is completed and signed by the importer (or his or her agent) and the merchandise is released. The estimated duty must be paid within 10 working days. Note the term *estimated duty*. After all this processing, the end result in the case of a formal entry is only an estimate of duty owed for the entry. U.S. Customs has the right to increase or decrease the levy for up to one year from the date of entry, which is the reason a surety bond or 100 percent collateral must be posted, and is one of the key roles of the custom house broker. After one year or longer, considering extensions or suspensions of liquidations, the formal entry is finally considered closed, or "liquidated."

Therefore, at the beginning of the entry process, your customs broker should properly suggest, as part of the broker's normal functions, applying on your behalf for a single entry or continuous U.S. Customs bond through a reliable surety company. In doing so, the broker will be conducting business as an insurance agent and will add the cost of the bond to the overall import brokerage fee statement. While this is the norm, you are also entitled to procure such a bond through an agent of your own choosing from any U.S. Customs–approved surety, or alternatively, to post 100 percent cash collateral in lieu of a bond. Unless your company is well known to the customs broker, the broker will probably need references and financial statements or credit reports. In some exceptional situations, especially for the high transaction volume of border traffic with Mexico or Canada, and when the importer is well known to the customs broker, the broker may permit the use of his or her own continuous bond for the sake of speed and practicality. In any event, the broker will be very interested in your company history and credit rating, because his or her own reputation for integrity and judgment will be at stake. Should the entry be made in the broker's name under the broker's own bond, there will also be a direct financial responsibility to the broker.

Clearing Customs: Informal Entry

Informal entry, which can be used only for shipments under $1250, is a much simpler process and does not require the posting of a bond. When the U.S. Customs inspector looks at the goods, he or she will stamp the papers as cleared and you can leave with the merchandise after paying the duties. The duties assessed are final, so payment of the duty simultaneously amounts to "liquidation" as well. (Keep this in mind in terms of both time and expense when requesting small shipments, such as samples from overseas. Note, too, that this is equally true in reverse for your export customers and relates to my suggestion that you ship samples by parcel post.) Informal entry is a process you can negotiate without the help of a custom broker, but unless the shipment is a mail entry, handled through the post office, you are still advised to use a broker.

Informal Mail Entries

These are the easiest of all customs procedures and are regularly accomplished by the importer in person, especially in the case of samples. In most cases, the dutiable value must be under $1250 for merchandise that is not under quota or other special restrictions. A Customs Service Declaration Form C1 is obtainable at post offices worldwide because it is approved by the Universal Postal Union. It must be affixed to the outside of the package in the country of origin (or alternatively stamped MAY BE OPENED FOR CUSTOMS PURPOSES BEFORE DELIVERY) with a commercial invoice inside the package or firmly affixed to the exterior. The package should be stamped INVOICE INSIDE. Be sure to advise your sender of these details and follow them yourself if you are sending samples. A U.S. Customs officer prepares the informal entry and turns it over to the nearest post office which either notifies you of its arrival, or has a letter carrier bring it to you. The U.S. Customs processing fee is only $5 per package of dutiable mail, plus a nominal fee for the post office. Obviously, a good deal of time and money for fees is thus saved. On page 9 of *Importing into the United States* you will find a list of articles, many of them consumer goods, for which the regular $1250 limit is reduced to $250. We stress these details here because it so often does involve samples which can represent either the beginning of a harmonious relationship between buyer and seller or an aggravation that may lead to the samples simply being abandoned by the importer. You can minimize problems at your end by courteously suggesting all these details to your sender after double-checking with the U.S. Post Office. The sender may or may not be fully informed or may have forgotten the exact procedures.

Formal Mail Entries

When the merchandise value is $1250 or greater, or is subject to a quota or some other restriction, mail entry can still be accomplished, but you or your custom broker must be present and documents consisting of customs declaration, invoice, and packing slip must be available, preferably on the outside of the package. There is a good chance that even here you will find it economical to employ your custom broker.

Special Entries

All the informal entries described thus far are *consumption entries,* meaning that the duty is paid on the assumption that the goods will be sold and used in the United States. The opposite is usually true of the following so-called *special entries,* which are all designed to defer or preclude payment of the duty that would otherwise be due:

- *In-transit entry (IT).* For operations not near the port of entry and for those that wish to delay making consumption entry until the goods have been moved in bond to a U.S. Customs office nearer to the operation for easier handling of questions or problems in the clearing process.

- *Warehouse entry.* For storage in a bonded warehouse to defer payment of duty until withdrawn, when the withdrawal is made. If the goods are shipped directly to a foreign country from a bonded warehouse, duty is never paid.

- *Foreign trade zone (FTZ) entry.* Similar in purpose and use to a bonded warehouse except that display, sales, and manufacturing operations can take place in the U.S. FTZ while the duty is being deferred.

- *Temporary import under bond (TIB).* Permits bringing merchandise into the country for exhibition, trade shows, and similar purposes. Bonds are posted to guarantee that the duty will be paid if the goods are not subsequently sent back out of the country.

- *American Goods Returned (AGR).* For goods brought back to the United States free of duty for repair or at the conclusion of a consignment arrangement.

The 1994 Customs Modernization Act

Because of the increasing volume of imports and the ever-growing complexity of transportation choices and electronic data processing, Congress passed the Customs Modernization Act in 1994, which makes revolutionary changes in the U.S. Customs entry process. The objective was to take advantage of the opportunities for paperless entries and to give the overloaded customs process both an opportunity to modernize and streamline *and* a less rigid time frame in which to check for improper streamlined entry declarations. The result was the 1994 Act, which is now being implemented and worked out over a period of time. The custom house brokerage industry is profoundly interested in the Act and its administrative interpretations. The industry itself, therefore, is in a state of change and adaptation, because no one knows exactly when and how all the changes will be implemented. The Act will change methods and administrative procedures and probably lead to more extensive auditing. As mentioned earlier, the expert who reviewed this chapter thinks that the importer should review both Modernization Acts. The changes that develop under this Act will be modifications, which, for the most part, you will learn about from your broker and U.S. Customs on an ongoing basis, but there may be details in the Act pertaining to your particular situation or product that you should be forewarned about at the very outset of your import project.

Import Quotas

Quotas are a means of limiting excessive imports—usually to protect an infant industry or at the urging of an industry under import pressure, or sometimes truly for national self-interest. Sugar and cotton are the agricultural products most infamous for long-standing quota controls. Together with many dairy products, animal feeds, candies, chocolates, and peanuts, they represent the bulk of commodities and products under quota. Certain dairy products, including many cheeses, can be imported only with a license from the Department of Agriculture, even though the quotas are administered and collected by U.S. Customs. Textiles are the other principal product traditionally under quota protection. Textile quotas, like most quotas are administered by U.S. Customs, but are imposed on the basis of directives issued by the Committee for the

Implementation of Textile Agreements of the U.S. Department of Commerce. The commodities subject to quotas are detailed in *Importing into the United States* and may also be found in the *HTSUS*. For the most current information and status, consult your U.S. Customs Office, which can also provide you with the telephone number of the Quota Desk of U.S. Customs in Washington, D.C., where you may obtain a taped telephone or computer message as to the current status and nature of the quotas.

Essentially, there are two types of quotas:

1. *Absolute quotas.* Permit import without limit to a specified total quantity of the product or commodity from sources worldwide or, in some instances, from specified countries. The limitation is normally on a per annum basis. Absolute quota goods received too late must be diverted, returned, or stored in bond until the next quota period opens.

2. *Tariff-rate quotas.* Permit a fixed amount of the product or commodity to be imported each year at a specified, more favorable rate; thereafter all imports for the balance of the year are assessed a higher duty rate. Since the point at which the quota is filled can not be predetermined with any certainty, a bond must be posted at the higher rate and a final determination is made after all records are certain. In the case of either quota system, to learn the current status you must check with Customs; it keeps daily track of the status by computer. Reservations for quota cannot be made; your place in line is determined on the basis of first-in-the-entry-process, first-in-quota-standing.

Marking and Labeling

Already referred to as a subject of special attention in the course of the entry-inspection process, the regulations governing marking and labeling, including exemptions, are set forth in the Tariff Act and in *Customs Regulations of the United States.* Expect most articles to have some requirements regarding labeling—especially consumer products. The biggest exceptions are for bulk products and products the marking of which would be impossible. The law, the Regulations, and *Importing into the United States* list the exceptions. Note that in the case of consumer products, the labeling has to be done on the individual items or, ideally, on the retail package as a customer would most likely purchase it, not as it might arrive on dealers' shelves. Labeling requirements are detailed by many other government agencies and legislation. While U.S. Customs administers them all for Customs inspection purposes, they can refer you on to the appropriate agency for further particulars.

Restricted and/or Licensed Import Products

These products or categories are described in detail in *Importing into the United States,* which also indicates the agencies responsible for oversight or licensing, together with all the addresses you need to obtain full details on specific restrictions and/or licensing requirements. The best rule of thumb is this: Any article for which a license must be obtained to manufacture or resell an article, product, or commodity will require special arrangements or a license to import it. In the case of alcoholic beverages, U.S. Customs will restrict entries that do not meet the laws or standards of the state of destination.

Here is a list of merchandise categories requiring licensing or bearing restrictions:

Agricultural commodities

Alcoholic beverages

Arms, ammunition, radioactive materials

Consumer products (electrical appliances) relating to energy conservation

Consumer products with potential labeling or safety problems

Electronic products (sonic or electrical radiation exposure)

Foods, drugs, cosmetics, medical devices, and drug paraphernalia

Gold, silver, currency, and stamps

Motor vehicles (autos) and boats

Pesticides, toxics, and hazardous substances

Textile, wool, and fur products

Wildlife and pets

The following categories of merchandise are prohibited:

Counterfeit articles bearing trademarks, trade names, or copyrights; or which copy such marks with an intent to deceive or defraud

Obscene, immoral, or seditious matter

Products made by convicts or forced labor

Drawback

Having discussed all the procedures, regulations, and problems of importing and the duty which must often be paid for the privilege of doing so, we now come to the subject of recovering duties already paid. The purpose of *drawback,* as it is called, is to provide 99 percent relief to importers who must reexport the goods for any one of a variety of reasons, including the return of an import shipment, but most often because the imported goods are involved in, or become part of, a manufacturing process to produce goods subsequently exported.

There are two types of drawback:

1. *Direct identification drawback* refunds duties paid on identifiable imported merchandise that is partially or totally used in a manufacturing process within five years from date of importation, or exported in the same condition as imported.

2. *Substitution drawback* provides for refunds on imports in those cases where both domestic and imported merchandise of the same kind and quality (fungible) are used to manufacture or produce articles, some of which are subsequently exported. A drawback refund on exported finished product may be claimed in the same proportion that imported and domestic material is used, without regard to its being specifically identified, as long as both ingredients are freely substitutable.

Details on the drawback process are available in various U.S. Customs publications. It is a process involving much red tape, and there are specialists who can handle the procedure for a percentage of the recovery. If your business is going to be involved in much activity of this kind, free trade zones or bonded warehouses offer a much less complicated way to import, manufacture, and export without paying duties.

The Custom House Broker

As already mentioned, the custom house broker, or customs broker, is often merely the other arm or function of the freight forwarder, although each serves an entirely different need and has different experience and knowledge. The broker serves as the agent for the importer in dealing with the U.S. Customs Service. Custom house brokers handle the majority of the hundreds of thousands of formal entries through customs each year.

Simply reading this chapter will give you an idea of the range of their many essential services. One signal advantage of having a broker is his or her ability to substitute a custom house general-purpose bond for your company's cash collateral. This represents a major financial convenience. (Of course, the extent to which a custom broker will accept exposure to these risks will depend on your company's history and credit standing, especially in view of the usual one-year time frame between entry and liquidation.) Another great advantage of having a broker is being able to benefit from his or her familiarity and training in connection with the Harmonized Tariff Schedule classifications and their application to your imports. The use of a broker's expertise also extends to the U.S. Custom Service's many rules and regulations, as introduced to you here and in the book *Importing into the United States.* A broker can also save you valuable time by being handy to the inspection site and by making available to you the error-prevention information services and specialized databases that he or she subscribes to as a professional in the business.

But don't let these encouraging words lead you to forget what I emphasized earlier about the importance of doing research, investigation, and checking *on your own.* Just as with the Bureau of Export Administration's (BXA's) export licensing, it is still necessary that you become familiar with the general procedures and provisions affecting your range of products, because it is you who are ultimately responsible. You need such information, both to inform your broker and to finalize your import negotiations. You will be specializing in a limited range of products, and hopefully they will be products about which you have some expertise or with which you are at least very familiar. As I have said relative to exporting: If one of the parties to a transaction lacks knowledge concerning the product and international trade, the risk of loss increases. If both buyer and seller are lacking such knowledge, a financial disaster is very likely in the making.

Armed with a good, basic knowledge of the product, however, you can be much more assured of a profitable transaction, and you will be alert to those moments when you must promptly supply your broker with the essential accurate information needed to serve you well. Good advance data to the broker should not only provide particulars about the merchandise but also give specific information related to:

1. Estimated time of arrival and means of transportation, including voyage or flight

2. Possible need for expedited clearance through the immediate delivery process

3. Common and scientific or technical name of the products

4. Components, materials, or contents of the finished product

5. Type of packing used (assembled or knocked down, etc.)

6. All-inclusive FAS value as mentioned earlier under the section on Valuation

7. Country of origin

In addition to a customs broker's primary roles in clearing your imports through U.S. Customs, he or she will take care of much of the other footwork and logistics involved in seeing that your imports get where you need them to be for domestic distribution or processing. Last but not least, having an experienced customs broker on hand when the customs officer—who is often overworked and harassed—is ready to inspect or question is vital to the rapid and efficient processing of your shipments.

In Conclusion

Don't let the apparent red tape connected with clearing Customs discourage you. When the focus is on a specific product with which you are familiar, the problems become much simpler. Help is available, and if it's necessary to get a quick response as to probable tariffs on what you propose to import before settling on a broker, you can call the nearest U.S. Customs Service office, which will be listed under the U.S. Treasury Department in the federal section of most phone books. Before calling, it's a good idea to have a preliminary idea as to how the merchandise would classify by checking in the Harmonized Tariff Schedule (HTSUS). While it is true that U.S. Customs can be arbitrary and abrupt, its officers can also be very helpful to people who are new to the process. This is especially true if you have done your homework so that you understand the problem and can ask the right questions even though you don't yet know the solution.

Endnotes

1. *Importing into the United States,* U.S. Government Printing Office, Washington, D.C., 19XX.

2. *Harmonized Tariff Schedule of the United States of America,* U.S. Government Printing Office, Washington, D.C., 19XX.

3. *Customs Regulations of the United States of America,* U.S. Government Printing Office, Washington, D.C.

14
Letters of Credit and Payment Terms

Definitions and Strategies

As I pointed out in Chapter 10, determining the relative inherent risks of the various terms of payment is one of the exporter's first considerations when weighing up an initial response to export product inquiries. But, while risk must be one of the first considerations, there is also the issue of financing the sale in light of the proposed terms and the capital, which may be tied up in receivables and the related interest expense. These factors must in turn be weighed against the element of competitiveness. Your customers are probably as stretched for capital in their business as you are in yours, even though they may be larger operations. Terms can make a large difference in the convenience of doing business with you, including the ease of reordering your product. The convenience of doing business in a similar fashion as with a domestic firm can be a factor for you as the seller as well. Therefore, as we review the relative risk of different payment terms in greater detail, the competitive strategies and international trade techniques implicit in each separate term's use deserve at least equal attention. Before and after reading this chapter, it might be helpful to review Figure 14-1 on factors to consider in setting payment terms.

Open Account

This is a very broad term encompassing many variations and time frames. In essence, however, open account provides the greatest convenience and desirability to your customer and conversely subjects the exporter to the greatest risk. Remember, however, risk is relative. I would be more comfortable having an open account receivable payable net—30 days from a large multinational firm such as Siemens in Germany, for example, than an unconfirmed letter of credit from a small bank in a

Factor	Require a letter of credit	Consider a documentary collection		Consider an open account
		Presentation	Acceptance	
Customer quality	Uncertain	Acceptable	Good	Good credit and history
Relationship	New	Established	Established	Established
Nature of order	Custom	Regular production	Regular production	In stock
Political status *Buyer's country*	Unstable	Stable	Stable	Strong
Economic status *Country paying*	Unstable	Stable	Strong	Strong
Transaction size	Large to moderate*	Moderate	Moderate	Moderate to small**
Price volatility	A letter of credit protects against pressures to renegotiate underlying agreement or pricing			
Cashflow needs	A letter of credit provides the most positive and practical control over timing of payment			
Competition	If intense competition, the above suggested considerations might be shaded toward a less conservative response if financial circumstances permit			

*Under $5000 the L/C costs too much to open and negotiate unless the buyer is willing to pay all the costs on both sides. From $5000 to $10,000 it is questionable as to L/C costs relative to profit margins. See comments in the accompanying text.

**Large, moderate, and small are relative terms in relation to the seller's financial strength and the buyer's credit rating as used here, except in terms of dollar transaction size compared to negotiation and fee costs.

Figure 14-1. Factors to consider before setting payment terms.

high-risk country in Africa or Eastern Europe. In fact, I would not for a moment consider trading one for the other. Naturally, risk depends on the creditworthiness of your customer, the stability of the buyer's country, and your ability to access and correctly analyze the available credit information. For some potential buyers, this can be a complex and tricky task. By contrast, a banker can probably advise you in a moment as to the relative security of the issuing bank of a letter of credit.

There are many degrees of risk within the various forms of open account terms, and each can become increasingly chancy, even though commonly accepted in particular industries. One example is the *minimum-guarantee* condition used in fresh produce trading, in which the buyer guarantees to pay no less than a certain base amount so many days after receiving the shipment, plus a percentage of the difference between that figure—which might represent landed cost to the seller—and the price actually received in the open market. Consignment terms go even further by promising to pay only for what was sold and relying on contractual arrangements to deal with the balance. This can be a very iffy proposition when the export product is thousands of miles away in a strange land.

Open account terms are usually expressed as a payment due date, such as "net 10 days (or 30, 60, 90 days) from date of invoice." The determinant dates are usually the invoice date, the shipping date, or sometimes the receipt of goods date (ROG). The ROG determination method leaves too much to the interpretation of the overseas buyer as to when the merchandise was received, and therefore is the least-preferred from an accounting and an accounts-receivable-aging analysis standpoint. Unless it is a wire transfer situation, 10 days is usually allowed from the shipping or invoice date to allow for receipt of at least the invoice, or very possibly more days still if the goods are shipped by ocean freight. Beyond that, 30 or more days may be offered to accommodate the buyer and allow time to sell off the inventory before payment is due. When selling on open account terms you are relying on the buyer's integrity and creditworthiness, which can be difficult to establish initially, especially on the first transaction when it may be impossible to properly investigate the buyer's credit rating. Once a serious commercial relationship is established, open account may carry little more risk in a stable country than it would in the U.S., assuming equal financials, credit reports, creditworthiness, understanding, and the credit analyst's judgment.

When creditworthiness is judged in error and an overseas account becomes delinquent, it can be a long, costly, and difficult process to collect from overseas. Nevertheless, much of the world's international business is done on this basis, just as it is domestically. Wise and experienced sellers know their buyers payment history and financial standing, and so must you to make this a reasonable proposition. Obtaining credit information overseas is somewhat more difficult and definitely more time-consuming and expensive than it is domestically. In the case of sample shipments made under open account terms, one can assume that most balances due, except to firms that really want the product, will only clutter up the past due account list (and ultimately will probably be written off).

While open account terms offer meaningful competitive advantages to the seller in most cases, successful and profitable administration of this kind of credit requires both experience and knowledge, in addition to adequate financing. Depending on the customer list and the exporter's financing needs, open account terms may also require foreign accounts receivable insurance which, although expensive, can take some of the sting out of the inherent risks. Credit insurance for both commercial and political risks is available and will be addressed in the next chapter. Another point to consider is that few foreign customers really expect open account terms on initial transactions unless they are exceptionally large or prestigious. Even that exception varies by country because some of the largest trading organizations in the world routinely begin trading with a new supplier under letter-of-credit terms—in many cases for their own protection or because of government policy. This is especially true in a number of Asian countries.

Documentary Collections

Documentary collection terms represent a substantial improvement over open account terms from the standpoint of exporter protection, even though they still leave many opportunities for potential problems. Documentary collections also represent a much lower transaction expense than letters of credit, so long as a nasty event called *nonacceptance* does not occur. Nonacceptance occurs when, for whatever reason, the importer does not respond to a notice from the overseas collecting bank to appear, sign the draft, and claim the shipping documents. There is no responsibility on the part of the exporter's bank or the collecting bank to make the importer appear and sign, although both will cooperate in follow-up attempts—the report of which is known as an *advice of fate*. If the importer still does not appear, however, it is considered an abandoned shipment. The exporter's only recourse beyond personal contact with the import buyer is to sue and/or resell the goods elsewhere or have them shipped back. In the latter case, the exporter's minimum loss will be the round-trip freight and handling.

There are two forms of documentary collection, each representing a very different level of risk. Apart from the issue of risk, however, the advantages of either form of documentary collection over letters of credit are:

1. Lower collection expense
2. Simplicity of operation
3. Less risk that errors or oversight in the negotiation of a letter of credit will defeat the lower risk expected from letters

Documents Against Payment

Of the two forms of documentary collection, by far the most common and less risky to the seller is documents against payment (D/P). In the case of D/P, payment is made when the overseas collecting bank presents the bill of lading and/or other documents to the buyer, who thereupon signs and pays the sight draft presented along with the documents. The important point here is that the buyer must obtain the documents before the goods themselves can be claimed. Otherwise, the goods remain in the seller's title and possession until payment is received. This is similar to the familiar cash on delivery (COD) term used domestically, but COD is not a term used in foreign trade, with the possible exception of accommodation by some of the international courier firms in a form then called cash against documents (CAD). The latter, although less formal and rarely used, would call for cash or its equivalent to be paid on presentation of an invoice and shipping documents only.

In the case of D/P terms, the seller's bank is usually the conduit for the process, based on an instruction form completed by the exporter. A draft must be prepared, which, together with the invoice and shipping documents, will be "presented" by a "collecting" bank in the buyer's city to which the buyer, on "sighting" will have to pay the amount of the draft drawn. After this process is completed, the collecting bank will hand over the shipping documents to the buyer so that the buyer can then pick up the merchandise from the carrier. Thus, in theory at least, while there is no guarantee that the buyer will accept and pay on the arrival of the merchandise, the buyer cannot obtain the goods until they are paid for. This is satisfactory for goods shipped under negotiable bills of lading, as in the case of ocean freight. However, for air freight the documentary process does not function as well; here the buyer can obtain the goods simply by demanding them from the carrier because they would have to be consigned to the buyer on a nonnegotiable air waybill. To make documentary terms work for air shipments or any kind of shipment other than ocean freight, the goods must be consigned to a bank or other reliable third party that has agreed in advance to act in a referee (bailee) capacity and will hold the merchandise until the draft is signed and paid by the notify party. The foreign agent or correspondent of your freight forwarder is one such possibility, and the CAD terms described earlier might be applicable.

Documents Against Acceptance

Documents against acceptance (D/A) terms represent an identical process to D/P. The import buyer merely signs a time draft (similar to a postdated check) before receiving the documents—and, thereafter, the goods—creating an obligation known as a *trade acceptance*. This version of a documentary collection considerably expands the seller's risk because there is nothing to assure that the buyer will honor and pay the time draft when it comes due, even though the buyer has previously taken possession of the goods from the carrier. The draft states that the goods are "accepted" and due to be paid some number of days after that acceptance—usually somewhere in the range of 30 to 180 days. Here, too, if usance time is extended, the exporter must be sure it is so many days from an invoice or shipping date, rather than from "sight." The reason for this is that the buyer is the only one in a position to determine when "sighting" occurs since this is determined by the buyer's own actions. It is important to remember that it is not the bank's responsibility to collect at the prescribed time and that the seller remains entirely dependent on the creditworthiness of the buyer, who is in possession of the merchandise. The advantage of D/A over open account terms rests solely on the fact that if collection steps have to be taken, there is no question that the buyer accepted the merchandise—a fact that firmly establishes the validity of the debt.

Letters of Credit

Letters of credit (LCs) are a subject unto themselves and are dealt with, from the exporter's perspective, in great detail in my previous book, *Exporting: From Start to Finance,* as well as in many other books, articles, and seminars. Letters of credit come in many formats, to say nothing of an end-less variety of terms and conditions that allow them to be adapted to almost any circumstance. However, the first and most basic principle of a letter of credit is that it substitutes the credit of the issuing bank for the credit of the buyer, thereby protecting the seller from all commercial nonpayment risks on the part of the buyer so long as the seller meets the conditions set forth in the letter—not always as easily accomplished as one might assume. There is the matter of the bank's ability to pay and to obtain U.S. dollars, but assuming that the L/C was issued by a strong and reliable bank in a country without foreign exchange problems, that is an insignificant risk. If the issuing bank's reputation is poor or the country's monetary and/or political situation is unstable, the advising bank or your own banker can usually inform you about potential risks and help you assess the situation.

The second basic principle, almost as important, is the *irrevocable* feature of letters of credit. As the term implies, it assures the seller that the letter of credit will remain in force from issuance throughout its validity date and that the export order or project can be undertaken with assurance that the related shipment or project will be paid for so long as accomplished within the validity and shipping or performance dates stated in the letter. This will hold true regardless of any mood swings or thoughts of cancellation by the buyer. Every letter of credit today is automatically irrevocable unless clearly stated to be revocable (which is very, very rare). It is this second principle, therefore, in combination with the first, that provides both the certainty and opportunity to complete the transaction and be paid for it—making letters of credit very attractive to their beneficiaries.

There are two basic types of letters of credit, which serve two quite different purposes and may provide security for quite opposite beneficiaries. The first type is the transactional letter of credit that requires the beneficiary to ship certain goods or provide certain services. (See Figures. 14-2 and 14-3 for samples of typical letters of credit and accompanying point-by-point explanations.) The second type is the standby letter of credit. (See Figure 14-4 for a sample of a typical standby letter and accompanying point-by-point explanation.) It should be hoped by all

BANK OF AMERICA

TRADE FINANCE SERVICES #661
550 MONTGOMERY ST., SAN FRANCISCO, CA 94110
P.O. BOX 37020, SAN FRANCISCO, CA 94137

7

PLACE AND DATE OF ISSUE:
SAN FRANCISCO JUNE 7, 19XX

① IRREVOCABLE DOCUMENTARY CREDIT

NUMBER
078910

APPLICANT
ABC TOYS IMPORT INC.
300 MAIN STREET
SAN FRANCISCO, CA 94000

DATE AND PLACE OF EXPIRY:
AUGUST 15, 19XX IN HONG KONG

BENEFICIARY
XYZ TOYS EXPORT LTD
8TH FLOOR STONE BLDG.
45 KOWHAN ROAD
KOWLOON, HONG KONG

ADVISING BANK
BANK OF AMERICA
HONG KONG BRANCH

②

AMOUNT: U.S. 85,350.00 (EIGHTY FIVE
THOUSAND THREE HUNDRED FIFTY U.S. DOLLARS)

PARTIAL SHIPMENTS: PERMITTED
TRANSHIPMENTS: NOT PERMITTED

CREDIT AVAILABLE WITH ANY BANK

SHIPMENT
FROM HONG KONG
LATEST AUGUST 10, 19XX
FOR TRANSPORTATION TO
SAN FRANCISCO / BAY AREA

BY: NEGOTIATION
AGAINST DOCUMENTS DETAILED BELOW
AND BENEFICIARY'S DRAFTS
AT SIGHT ON US

③ THE LETTER OF CREDIT COVERS FULL INVOICE VALUE
DOCUMENTS REQUIRED:
1. SIGNED COMMERCIAL INVOICE IN DUPLICATE
2. MARINE AND WAR INSURANCE POLICY OR CERTIFICATE FOR 110% INVOICE VALUE IN DUPLICATE.
3. SOLE ORIGINAL CLEAN ON BOARD VESSEL MARINE BILL OF LADING, TO ORDER OF SHIPPER, BLANK ENDORSED, MARKED: "NOTIFY BUYERS AND S.F. CUSTOMERS CLEARING AGENT, 100 MAIN STREET, SAN FRANCISCO, CA 94000 AND FREIGHT PREPAID".
4. CERTIFICATE OF ORIGIN, FORM A WHERE APPLICABLE OR BENEFICIARY'S CERTIFICATE THAT NONE IS REQUIRED.
5. PACKING LIST.

MERCHANDISE DESCRIPTION:
INFLATABLE TOYS AND TOYS, C.I.F. SAN FRANCISCO / BAY AREA
CATALOGUE NO. 1234 25,000 PCS. @ U.S. $3.00 EACH
CATALOGUE NO. 6789 10,000 PCS. @ U.S. $1.035 EACH

DOCUMENTS MUST BE PRESENTED WITHIN 5 DAYS AFTER THE DATE OF ISSUANCE OF THE
SHIPPING DOCUMENT(S) BUT WITHIN THE VALIDITY OF THE CREDIT.

④ WE HEREBY ISSUE THIS DOCUMENTARY CREDIT IN YOUR FAVOUR. IT IS SUBJECT TO THE
UNIFORM CUSTOMS AND PRACTICE FOR DOCUMENTARY CREDITS (1983 REVISION INTERNATIONAL
CHAMBER OF COMMERCE, PARIS, FRANCE PUBLICATION NO. 400) AND ENGAGES US IN
ACCORDANCE WITH THE TERMS THEREOF. THE NUMBER AND THE DATE OF THE CREDIT AND THE
NAME OF OUR BANK MUST BE QUOTED ON ALL DRAFTS REQUIRED. IF THE CREDIT IS AVAILABLE
BY NEGOTIATION, EACH PRESENTATION MUST BE NOTED ON THE REVERSE OF THIS ADVICE BY
THE BANK WHERE THE CREDIT IS AVAILABLE.

ALL DOCUMENTS TO BE FORWARDED IN ONE COVER, BY AIRMAIL.
NEGOTIATING BANK CHARGES, IF ANY, ARE FOR ACCOUNT OF BENEFICIARY.
THE ADVISING BANK IS REQUESTED TO NOTIFY THE BENEFICIARY WITHOUT ADDING THEIR
CONFIRMATION.

SPECIMEN

Authorized counter signature   Authorized signature

Please examine this instrument carefully. If you are unable to comply with the terms or conditions, please communicate with your buyer to arrange
for an amendment. This procedure will facilitate prompt handling when documents are presented.

Figure 14-2. Sample of an irrevocable negotiation letter of credit. (*Courtesy Bank of America "International Services."*)

IRREVOCABLE
NEGOTIATION LETTER OF CREDIT

① This shows how the information on the application, is converted into the actual letter of credit.
An irrevocable letter of credit is one that cannot be canceled or revoked without the consent of all parties concerned and is the type of credit customarily used in international trade.

② A letter of credit can be available by payment with a designated bank, by acceptance with the drawee bank, by deferred payment or by negotiation. If available by negotiation, it can be with a designated bank or freely negotiable with any bank. In this case, XYZ Toys Exports Ltd. may present the draft and documents to the advising bank, Bank of America, Hong Kong branch or any bank in its locale. When the negotiating bank has examined the documents and determined that they are in order, the negotiating bank will pay the beneficiary and will claim reimbursement from the issuing bank.

③ The terms presented here coincide with the precise conditions stipulated by the importer, ABC Toys Import Inc., in the application for the commercial letter of credit.

④ This is the engagement clause. Bank of America agrees to honor a drawing in accordance with the provisions of the Uniform Customs and Practice for Documentary Credits. As is the case with most documentary credits, this credit is operated in accordance with the International Chamber of Commerce's Uniform Customs and Practice for Documentary Credits (1983 Revision International Chamber of Commerce Publication No. 400), which is recognized by banking communities in countries around the world.

⑤ Easily overlooked, this section of the credit asks the beneficiary to examine the letter of credit to see if it conforms to his contract and that he is able to perform under the credit. If the beneficiary must request an amendment to the original terms and conditions, he should communicate with the account party directly and ask for an amendment covering the point or points to be changed. The account party then must make an application to the issuing bank for an amendment.

Figure 14-2. (Continued)

```
TYPE ADM
TEST O TESTED 06/10/XX IN CALIFORNIA
FROM:/SR-10 BQEI FRPP
       BANQUE EMETTRICE INTERNATIONALE
       PARIS, FRANCE

TO:    /SO 10BOFAUS6SYXXX30330
       BANK OF AMERICA
       SAN FRANCISCO, CALIFORNIA

DATE: XX0610

::700 ISSUE OF A DOCUMENTARY CREDIT          ①

:27 PAGE NUMBER: 1 OF 1
:40A FORM OF DOC CREDIT:IRREVOCABLE
:20 DOC CREDIT NUMBER: 2264A
:31C ISSUE DATE: XX0610 10JUNXX
:31D EXPIRY DATE/LOCATION:
XX0905 05SEPXX
SAN FRANCISCO CAL
:50 APPLICANT/ACCOUNT PARTY:
COMPTOIR D'IMPORTATION DE PRODUITS ELECTRONIQUES
15 RUE GEORGES DUMAS (75009)
PARIS, FRANCE
:59 BENEFICIARY:
RANDALL COMPUTER INC.
350 10TH AVENUE, PALO ALTO, CALIF.
94303 U.S.A.
:32B AMOUNT
USD US DOLLARS 872,770.00
:39 DETAILS OF AMOUNT:
MAXIMUM
:41D AVAILABLE WITH/BY:
BANK OF AMERICA NT AND SA,
SAN FRANCISCO, CALIF.
BY ACCEPTANCE                               ②
:42 DRAFTS AT/DRAWN ON:
DRAFTS AT 90 DAYS SIGHT
DRAWN ON BANK OF AMERICA NT AND SA
SAN FRANCISCO CALIF.
:43P PARTIAL SHIPMENTS: PROHIBITED
:43T TRANSSHIPMENT: PROHIBITED
:44 SHIPMENT INSTRUCTIONS:
SHIPMENT FROM ANY AIRPORT IN U.S.A.
TO CHARLES DE GAULLE INTERNATIONAL AIRPORT, PARIS
DTD NOT LATER THAN AUGUST 25, 19XX
:45A COVERING SHIPMENT OF:
505 RANDALL MODEL 39 COMPUTERS
QUOTATION F.O.B. U.S.A. AIRPORT
ACCORDING TO PURCHASE ORDER NUMBER
6703 DATED 04/15/XX
:46A DOCUMENTS REQUIRED:
AIR WAYBILL, MARKED FREIGHT COLLECT CONSIGNED TO BANQUE EMETTRICE
INTERNATIONALE TO NOTIFY COMPTOIR D'IMPORTATION DE PRODUITS
ELECTRONIQUES, 15 RUE GEORGES DUMAS (75009)
PARIS, FRANCE
COMMERCIAL INVOICE IN ORIGINAL AND THREE COPIES,
PACKING LIST IN ORIGINAL AND THREE COPIES.
:47A ADD'L CONDITIONS:
BENEFICIARY MUST PRESENT THE DOCUMENTS LATEST 5
DAYS AFTER SHIPMENT DATE.
:49 CONFIRMATION INSTRUCTIONS: CONFIRM
:53D REIMBURSEMENT:
AT MATURITY DEBIT OUR ACCOUNT WITH YOU.
:78 INSTRUCTIONS TO PAY/ACCEPT/NEGOTIATING BK:

SEND DOCUMENTS IN ONE COVER BY COURRIER
:72 RECEIVER INFO:
BUYERS INSURE HERE, THIS CREDIT
DOES NOT REQUIRE IMPORT LICENCE.
ACKNOWLEDGE BY MAIL.
-AUT/7E5F
```

SPECIMEN

ORIGINAL
This letter of credit forms an integral part
of our attached advice and is recorded
under our reference N° 900000
BANK OF AMERICA
NATIONAL TRUST AND SAVINGS ASSOCIATION
Trade Finance Service #661
P. O. BOX 37020
San Francisco, CA 94137

AUTHORIZED SIGNATURE

Figure 14-3. Sample of an irrevocable acceptance letter of credit. (*Courtesy Bank of America "International Services."*)

CORRESPONDENT'S IRREVOCABLE ACCEPTANCE LETTER OF CREDIT

① A correspondent bank is a commercial bank in one city or country which agrees to handle certain transactions for a bank in another city or country. In this case, Banque Emettrice Internationale, the correspondent bank, has issued its letter of credit on behalf of the importer, Comptoir d'Importation de Produits Electroniques, which is their customer. This is a copy of the incoming telex we received from the issuing bank. It is authenticated by Bank of America. The telex follows the S.W.I.F.T. (Society for Worldwide Interbank Financial Telecommunications) format.

② An acceptance credit, also called a usance credit, is a letter of credit that provides for time drafts. The drawee bank, Bank of America-San Francisco, will accept the draft on presentation of the documents from Randall Computer Inc. on or before the expiration date. At maturity, Bank of America will receive reimbursement from the issuing bank, Banque Emettrice Internationale.

③ Under the conditions and terms of this letter of credit, drafts will be drawn on Bank of America-San Francisco, the confirming and accepting bank. This type of credit is known as a "time" or "usance" letter of credit. When the beneficiary presents the drafts and documents to the accepting bank, Bank of America-San Francisco, and the bank has determined that they are in order, that bank will stamp on the face of the draft the word "accepted" and will sign and date it (see page 30). The bank thus promises to pay the full amount of the draft at the determined future date and the accepted draft becomes a bankers' acceptance. If the beneficiary wants to receive payment earlier than 90 days after sight, the beneficiary can request the confirming/accepting bank to discount the U.S. dollar acceptance and pay the beneficiary an amount less than full face value. The discount equals the bank's maacceptance rate plus commission on th

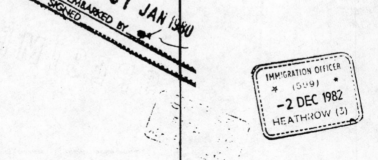

Figure 14-3. (Continued)

parties that this second type of L/C will not be negotiated, for the intent is that the beneficiary will only draw on the credit under circumstances such as nonperformance, failure to pay under the regular open account terms, or similar departures from the ordered course of events and contract. The beneficiary might be either the buyer or seller/provider.

BANK OF AMERICA

TRADE FINANCE SERVICES #661
550 MONTGOMERY ST., SAN FRANCISCO, CA 94110
P.O. BOX 37020, SAN FRANCISCO, CA 94137

7

PLACE AND DATE OF ISSUE: SAN FRANCISCO MAY 4, 19XX	① IRREVOCABLE DOCUMENTARY • NUMBER STANDBY CREDIT • 112345

DATE AND PLACE OF EXPIRY:
DECEMBER 31, 19XX IN SAN FRANCISCO

APPLICANT
POLYESTER PIPING CORPORATION
35 MAIN STREET
SAN FRANCISCO, CA 94116

BENEFICIARY
HONGKONG WATER & POWER AUTHORITY
GPO BOX 333
HONG KONG, HONG KONG

ADVISING BANK
BANK AMERICA
HONG KONG MAIN OFFICE #6055

AMOUNT: U.S. 3,500,000.00 (THREE MILLION
FIVE HUNDRED THOUSAND U.S. DOLLARS)

CREDIT AVAILABLE WITH US

BY: PAYMENT
AGAINST DOCUMENT DETAILED BELOW
AND BENEFICIARY'S DRAFTS
AT SIGHT ON US

② DOCUMENTS REQUIRED:
A LETTER FROM HONGKONG WATER & POWER AUTHORITY CERTIFYING THAT POLYESTER PIPING
CORPORATION HAS FAILED TO PERFORM AS REQUIRED UNDER PARAGRAPH 15 OF CONTRACT #78910
ENTERED INTO BETWEEN HONGKONG WATER & POWER AUTHORITY AND POLYESTER PIPING
CORPORATION FOR THE SUPPLY OF REINFORCED POLYESTER PIPE COUPLINGS AND THAT THE
AMOUNT DRAWN COVERS 50% OF THE CONTRACT PRICE.

SPECIAL CONDITION:
THIS CREDIT IS TO BE AUTOMATICALLY REDUCED BY 50% OF THE CONTRACT PRICE OF EACH
INVOICE AMOUNT OF THE RESPECTIVE PARTIAL SHIPMENTS UNDER BANK OF AMERICA, HONG KONG
MAIN OFFICE L/C #6055-1234, BANK OF AMERICA, SAN FRANCISCO REF. #001123.

WE HEREBY ISSUE THIS DOCUMENTARY CREDIT IN YOUR FAVOUR. IT IS SUBJECT TO THE
UNIFORM CUSTOMS AND PRACTICE FOR DOCUMENTARY CREDITS (1983 REVISION INTERNATIONAL
CHAMBER OF COMMERCE, PARIS, FRANCE PUBLICATION NO. 400) AND ENGAGES US IN
ACCORDANCE WITH THE TERMS THEREOF. THE NUMBER AND THE DATE OF THE CREDIT AND THE
NAME OF OUR BANK MUST BE QUOTED ON ALL DRAFTS REQUIRED.

ALL DOCUMENTS TO BE FORWARDED IN ONE COVER, BY AIRMAIL.
THE ADVISING BANK IS REQUESTED TO NOTIFY THE BENEFICIARY WITHOUT ADDING THEIR
CONFIRMATION. THEIR CHARGES, IF ANY, ARE FOR ACCOUNT OF BENEFICIARY.

Authorized counter signature   Authorized signature

Figure 14-4. Sample of an irrevocable standby letter of credit. (*Courtesy Bank of America "International Services."*)

IRREVOCABLE STANDBY LETTER OF CREDIT

① An irrevocable standby letter of credit is a letter of credit that cannot be changed or modified without the consent of all parties involved.

② These are the particular terms and conditions of the credit, as outlined in the application for the standby letter of credit on page 32. Hong Kong Water and Power Authority, the beneficiary, can draw drafts on Bank of America-San Francisco only when these conditions are fulfilled. The required document in this case is a written statement certifying that Polyester Piping Corporation has failed to perform according to the established terms and conditions of its contract.

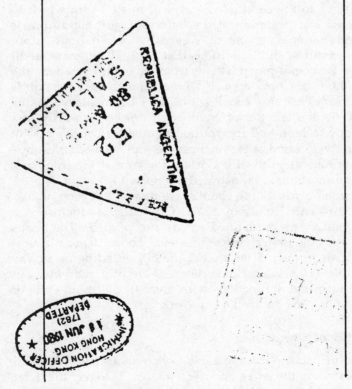

Figure 14-4. (Continued)

Transactional Letters of Credit

Because of the complexity and variety of letters of credit and because they play such an important and multifaceted role in international trade, the fundamental elements of these instruments need to be explained in some detail. It's essential that you become familiar with the basic mechanics and use of these instruments, understand what you are asking for and giving, learn what key clauses an L/C might include, and become aware of when to ask questions and seek further assistance. A more or less complete understanding of letters will only come with further study and experience. Consult your international banker if you expect to use the letter to support or enhance financing, and seek advice from your freight forwarder and/or banker relative to conforming to, and negotiating, the letter of credit.

Although an increasingly large amount of international trade is being accomplished on open account terms, the letter of credit continues to be by far the most commonly used form of secured or documentary payment, thanks to its twin advantages of reliance on a third-party bank's credit and certainty as to the conditions and time available in which to perform. The precise interpretation of the letter-of-credit conditions is governed by an international agreement, signed by most nations, stipulating the rules, procedures, and definitions that apply to letters of credit as they affect each principal party. The agreement is organized by the International Chamber of Commerce (ICC), and the current version is known as the Uniform Customs and Practice for Documentary Credits Number 500 (UCP–500). The letter of credit itself can be drawn up in a traditional hard-copy fashion and transmitted by mail or courier pouch; or it can be sent by well-tested telex; or it can be sent by a teletransmission system and format called SWIFT (Society for Worldwide Interbank Financial Telecommunications) as illustrated in Figure 14-3.

A key point to remember is that the banks issuing and advising or confirming L/Cs are governed solely by the L/C documents themselves, which include a good many predefined words and phrases. The banks are not concerned with the underlying agreements, contracts, or physical makeup of the shipment, merely with what the bill of lading or airway bill states it to be. Nevertheless, a skilled letter-of-credit practitioner can make the bank perform many functions with great flexibility in spite of the codifying definitions and stylized framework.

Parties to a Letter of Credit

In everyday terms, the prime parties to a letter of credit are the buyer and the seller, the bank issuing the letter, and the bank that is to pay the letter (which may or may not be one and the same). In either case, other banks that serve to transmit and handle the foreign letter of credit in the seller's country may also play an important role.

Buyer.   The *buyer* is the party opening the letter—normally referred to within a bank as the *account party, accountee,* or *applicant,* and is usually the actual importer.

Seller.   The *seller* is the exporter or shipper for whom the letter of credit was created and therefore is normally referred to as the *beneficiary.* The beneficiary is also sometimes technically called the *drawer* because of having prepared the draft for negotiation of the letter.

Opening Bank.   The *opening bank* is the bank that issues the letter of credit and on which the creditworthiness of the letter depends. It is also known as the *issuing bank.*

Advising Bank.   The *advising bank* is the bank in the exporter's country nominated by the issuing bank to advise the beneficiary of the letter and all its terms. A bank letter of credit is never sent directly to the beneficiary. It is always a bank-to-bank transaction. An advising bank does so *without any obligation on its part* except to verify that the transmission was legitimate in case it was teletransmitted. However, if the bank nominated to advise (usually a correspondent of the issuing bank) is aware that the issuing bank is a fraud or nonexistent, it would almost surely refuse the request to advise. It might also be requested to negotiate the letter or be nominated as the paying bank. In either role, the bank would still usually act without obligation. After having negotiated, or approved, the documents submitted as complete and accurate according to the letter's terms, the advising bank would then forward them to the issuing bank for approval to pay. Banks used to pay "with recourse" on behalf of the issuer if they were a correspondent bank with the issuing bank and had a credit balance account with it. Today, the money is seldom advanced to the beneficiary until a telex has been received by the negotiating or paying bank advising it to proceed.

Paying Bank.   The *paying bank* receives the essential draft, which must be drawn on the paying bank together with whatever other documents might be required under the letter's conditions. It may also be known, therefore, as the *drawee* or *drawee bank.* As such, it could be the opening or issuing bank, or it could be fulfilling an advising bank or negotiating bank role, but it will always be the paying bank if it is the *confirming bank.*

Confirming Bank.   The bank that advises the letter of credit might also *confirm* it and thereby substitute its credit for that of the issuing bank as far as the beneficiary is concerned. This means that if the confirming bank can find no problem with the documents submitted and negotiates and accepts the letter, it will pay the letter even if the issuing bank cannot or will not pay, or even if the country of the issuing bank closes off all transfer of foreign exchange. In contrast to an advising bank, a confirming bank becomes a primary party to the letter. Naturally, the buyer must pay more for such a letter because the confirming bank earns a larger fee by virtue of confirming rather than advising. Confirmation eliminates political and foreign exchange risk as well as any risks related to the issuing bank. The advantage of a domestic bank confirming the letter of credit in cases where the foreign issuing bank is strong and reliable and its country is stable, lies mainly in faster receipt of funds by the beneficiary, which is paid as soon as the letter is negotiated. For other than confirmed letters, some further delay will probably occur, so if cashflow is a problem, as it often is, a good suggestion is to call the advising bank's letter-of-credit department and ask just what the process and time frames will probably be. If there is an unstable political situation in the country of the issuing bank or its foreign exchange is tight, demanding a confirmed letter is the wisest course.

Key Phrases, Words, and Conditions

The following are words or phrases clearly defined in the most current internationally accepted Uniform Customs and Practices for Documentary Credits (UCP 500) or that have withstood the test of time and litigation. Some have a special meaning in connection with letters of credit and shipping transactions, and you must accept the usage for this purpose.

Discrepancy. Although never found in the letter itself, discrepancies are all too often discovered when negotiating a letter. A *discrepancy* is any deviation from the literal language set forth in the letter-of-credit conditions or documents required. If the negotiating bank discovers a discrepancy, it will automatically propose that the letter of credit be sent for collection, which leaves the applicant (buyer) in a position to determine whether to instruct the issuing bank to waive the discrepancy and pay, or refuse to pay. It is then up to the exporter to dispose of the goods or have them returned. If a potential discrepancy can be anticipated because of some condition that is impossible to meet, such as a shipping date or routing, the logical action is to request the amendment immediately in hopes of having it in hand prior to the shipping deadline. A discrepancy can be as minor and technical as failing to misspell your own firm's name as it was misspelled in the letter of credit. The alternative is to request an amendment, but since this costs time and money, it is easier to comply with the misspelling. Some discrepancies are readily corrected, but others cannot be. (This problem is discussed in the section on negotiating a letter of credit.)

Amendment. An *amendment* changes the terms of the letter or merely waives some term or condition that could not, or was not, met in the original letter. All primary parties to a letter—including the issuing and confirming bank, if there is one—must accept, or at least not reject, an amendment for it to be in effect. The buyer is under no obligation to create an amendment, and the seller need not accept an amendment. The seller should use care not to imply acceptance by tendering documents for negotiation before having rejected an unwanted amendment. The beneficiary may request an amendment through the banking channels. It may reinforce this request by contacting the buyer directly, but it is wise to use the bank channels as well. If the seller intends to reject an amendment, the advising bank should be notified at once.

Amendments are expensive and time-consuming. The seller pays for most amendments, which is a good reason to spell out your needs in advance to avoid unnecessary and increasingly expensive amendments. Review again the format for requesting the letter of credit. (See Figure 12-3.)

Assignment.   An *assignment* is the act of assigning a portion of the proceeds of a letter of credit to a third party—usually one or more of the suppliers relative to the export transaction. Unlike the situation in the case of a transferred letter of credit, when a supplier has an assignment, that supplier has no direct responsibilities under the letter. As the exporter and beneficiary, the exporter must perform according to the letter and successfully negotiate it, if either the exporter *or* the assignee are to be paid their respective shares of the proceeds. The bank holding the assigned letter of credit promises the assignee that its share of the proceeds realized will be remitted directly by the bank. The holder of an assignment of proceeds from a letter is therefore totally dependent on the exporter, which is why some suppliers refuse an assignment in lieu of prepayment, especially if they are not acquainted with, or do not have confidence in, the exporter. Another reason a supplier may not be interested in being paid through assignment is that, if other suppliers involved do not ship properly, the letter might not be usable, even though their own goods were properly delivered to the exporter and already out of their direct control. Unlike transferability, the letter of credit does not need to permit assignment. Domestic banks are not obliged to execute assignments but usually will, although they increasingly resist multiple assignments these days.

Transferable.   The term *transferable* refers to the act of transferring all of the seller's relevant obligations in a letter of credit to a second party supplier and in turn transferring a stated amount or percentage of the proceeds to this second beneficiary. The buyer's letter of credit must be specifically drawn to allow it to be transferable and a transferring bank nominated. (Some buyers prefer not to do this.) Transferability can be helpful when financing is not otherwise available, permitting the seller to complete the transaction according to the buyer's terms which might otherwise be impossible. The letter is by this means transferred to a second-party supplier who is able and willing to perform according to the terms of the letter. The transfer can be made in whole or in part, or in several parts, provided that other conditions or partial shipment requirements do not make the latter impossible. When possible under the conditions of the letter, the first beneficiary may have the negotiating bank substitute its documents for the documents of the second beneficiary to preserve the integrity of the direct relationship between the buyer and the seller. It can be quite tricky, however, to conceal the identities of the buyer and the actual supplier. In fact, it is sometimes impossible due to various requirements such as insuring conditions under CIF shipments or consular invoice requirements. If confidentiality is important, discuss the issue in detail with your banker in advance. Though banks usually do transfer letters of credit, they are not obliged to. Many banks resist doing so if more than one transferee is involved.

Revocable versus Irrevocable.   As of 1994 every letter of credit is *irrevocable* unless stated to be otherwise. I have never seen a *revocable* letter in my life and few people have, for it could only serve a very specialized purpose. If you ever receive one, bail out!

Confirmed versus Advised.   The meaning of the terms *confirmed* and *advised* have already been addressed relative to the advising or confirming bank's role. When requesting a letter of credit, it is advisable to state that it be paid "at the counters of" a U.S. bank, or better yet, at a bank in a named nearby major city. It is usually not practical to attempt to name the bank, because you will not know which issuing bank it will be or which banks in the area might be correspondents of the issuing bank.

Straight Credit versus Negotiation Credit.   If an L/C is stated to be a *straight* letter of credit, the letter must be negotiated and paid "at the counters of" the paying bank named on the draft as the drawee. If the L/C is stated to be a *negotiation* letter of credit, it can be negotiated through any bank in addition to the advising bank. Funds will still be disbursed, however, by the drawee, or paying bank. Technically, the negotiating bank could pay the exporter if they had a relationship with the paying bank, but only "with recourse"—meaning that they accept the exporter's creditworthiness and signed guarantee to repay in the event that the paying bank does not pay the negotiating bank as the UCP 500 obliges it to do, providing the documents are in order.

A negotiation letter can be important to an exporter located far from an active international center or from the bank at whose counters the payment will be made. An alternative, in the case of either straight or negotiation letters, is to have a local bank assist in reviewing the documents and submitting them to an authorized bank for the actual negotiation and/or payment, but in this case the local bank is acting, at whatever extra cost, as the exporter's agent, not as a party to the letter. Therefore any negotiation or advising fees and other fees will still be due to the nominated banks.

Sight versus Usance. The word *sight* as used in a letter of credit refers to the moment when the authorized negotiating bank has seen and accepted the documents after being sure they are all in order. A letter drawn *at sight* means just that—that the beneficiary is to be paid then or as soon as the funds can be transmitted from the paying bank, if the negotiating bank is not named as the paying bank. Although the money can be transmitted electronically in most cases, substantial delays can occur in the course of transmission if the documents must be sent overseas first.

A *usance*, sometimes called an "acceptance" letter of credit, provides for payment a certain number of days after sight, usually in 30-day increments up to 180 days. In this case, when the documents are negotiated, they are considered to be *accepted* and a *bankers acceptance* is substituted for cash in which the bank promises to pay the exporter after the specified number of days from sight indicated on the draft. This banker's acceptance can be converted to cash by discounting it with the bank creating the acceptance, or even with some other bank, so long as it is willing to do so. If the exporter plans to discount the draft, it is wise to check with the bank providing it to be sure it will, in fact, discount it. There are occasions when a bank will refuse to discount even though it is the bank's own obligation. Discounting is done at a very favorable interest rate—usually less than any interest rate at which you could possibly borrow—but there will also be a fixed fee discount charge in addition to the calculated discount.

Latest Shipping Date/Expiry Date. Either or both of these dates are a key to the exporter's ability to perform according to the terms of the letter and thus be able to collect the funds due. The *latest shipping date* is the latest date permitted to appear as the bill of lading date or whatever alternative transportation document is called for. If it is shipped at a later date, the letter has a discrepancy that cannot be corrected and the letter is therefore invalid, at least temporarily, and will be paid thereafter only on the express approval of the buyer or by amendment of the L/C. Understand that the bill of lading date is not necessarily the date the merchandise arrives at the point of embarkation, especially in the case of ocean freight. The ocean bill of lading will not be dated until the goods are physically on board the designated vessel and it is ready to sail. Not all letters show a latest shipping date; sometimes they show only an expiry date.

The *expiry date* is the latest date for validity of the letter of credit and is *always* part of a letter. The complete set of documents—(without discrepancies) for negotiation of the letter must be physically presented, complete with bills of lading, at the counters of the negotiating bank (not a bank that is acting as your agent to negotiate) on or before this expiry date. If this is not done, you have effectively shipped on open account, because it is not correctable, and you are entirely at the mercy of the accountee to waive the discrepancy and permit the issuing bank to pay under the letter. In some ways this is even worse than open account, for the element of mutual trust expressed in open account transactions is missing. You still have the right to sue the buyer for payment in the buyer's country, as in any commercial transaction, but the suit would be entirely outside the now-invalid letter of credit. The same is true if you miss the latest shipping date. If the letter includes a latest shipping date and it is an ocean shipment, you should make sure that that date precedes the expiry date by 10 to 14 days because it will likely take that long to obtain an ocean bill of lading and organize the documents for negotiation. If there is a shorter interval between the two dates, consider the earlier 10- to 14-day interval as your true latest shipping date to assure yourself of obtaining bills of lading and making other preparations for negotiation prior to the letter of credit expiry deadline, which takes precedence over the shipping deadline. Air waybills can usually be obtained within one day.

Clean on Board.   This term really stands for two conditions that must be met relative to a valid ocean bill of lading and that are therefore a "must" for negotiation. *Clean* refers to being without apparent damage to the merchandise or its packing or carton(s). If this is not the case, the ship's or other carrier's loading chief will note the damage on the bill of lading and it will thereafter not be considered "clean." Your forwarder should notify you in advance of that condition so it can be corrected, for otherwise it would be an uncorrectable discrepancy that would probably not be waived until after the buyer's inspection.

On board in ocean terminology means literally having "crossed the ships rails." If you are shipping FOB Vessel (FOB Port is considered to be the same thing), getting the goods onboard, including the cost of forwarding, will be at your expense. In the case of air, truck, or rail cargo, the onboard condition is satisfied when the goods are placed in the hands of the carrier or its agent.

Partial Shipments Allowed.   Letters of credit usually specify that partial shipments are, or are not, allowed. They *are* allowed if not stipulated otherwise. The allowing of partial shipments is important if you cannot be sure of a complete shipment because you are a third-party shipper (an export management or trading company, for instance) or because incomplete shipments are a frequent occurrence in your industry or business, as is the case in the textile industry. If partial shipments are not allowed, you might have a major discrepancy on your hands which, again, would place you at the mercy of the buyer. On the other hand, the buyer may be saying "partial shipments not allowed," simply to prevent a number of partial shipments going forward unnecessarily, because small shipments add greatly to the landed cost of goods due to minimum fees and other diseconomies. This legitimate buyer concern can be provided for in the letter by specifying the minimum size or number of shipments allowed. Some flexibility regarding minor shortages is allowed for merchandise that must be weighed or measured, in that the UCP 500 automatically provides for a 5 percent over or under allowance in terms of weight or measure. This flexibility does not apply to *unit counts,* such as items or cartons for which there is no modifying provision regarding what domestically you might consider minor "short shipments." Wording similar to "about" or "approximate" can help and will be discussed shortly. Also note that the overage allowance applies only to the bulk, not to the dollar value, which still cannot exceed the dollars specified in the letter. One more caveat: If partial shipments are specified in scheduled installments and any one installment is missed, the letter is invalid for that and *all future* installments unless stated otherwise or amended. In any case, if the negotiating bank notes any unauthorized shortage in the bill of lading or invoice, it will consider such a shortage a discrepancy.

To emphasize how critical these conditions can be, consider the $10,000-lesson I learned one day in the mid-1970s when I was shipping container loads of pant-weight fabric to one of Japan's largest trading companies. Since the product was textiles, the yardage almost never came within the over-and-under allowance provided and sometimes was delivered after the latest shipping date as well. I always requested an amendment but was usually told not to worry, in view of our "close working relationship." The buyer would always promise to accept the letter of credit immediately when it was forwarded for collection because of the discrepancy. Then one day the Japanese buyer awoke to the fact that it had more fabric in its warehouses than it would ever need, especially after an international political maneuver by then-President Richard Nixon that the Japanese subsequently named the *Nixon Shoku.* I had shipped a container load worth $70,000 of a fabric variously called "crinkle cloth," or "Indian cloth," among other names. It was woven so as to have closely spaced gathers or wrinkles in it and was very fashionable at the time. The trading company advised me that the shipment that had just arrived in Yokohama had too many crinkles. I protested and had them send me a cutting, which I had tested by a laboratory, along with the selling sample I had presented at the time the order was placed. They were identical and I so advised. At that point it was politely suggested that I should forget the tests, because although the shipment in dispute contained no letter-of-credit discrepancies, another shipment of $100,000 worth of denim, then on the water, did not meet the partial shipment allowance requirements and "might" be refused. It didn't matter that I had received the same assurances as in the past. It became crystal clear to me that unless I accepted return of the Indian cloth fabric, the container of denim would languish in Yokohama port. I had no choice but to accept the buyer's claim. In the end, I sold the "faulty" fabric at a loss to Levi Hong Kong, which made jeans of the disputed fabric and eventually sold those jeans to the same trading company. You can draw a number of conclusions from this tale.

About/Approximate.   When the words *about,* or *approximate* (or equivalent words) are used in a letter in reference to quantity, weight, measure, or value, the intent is to provide an allowance of 10 percent in any such specified quantity, weight, measure, or dollar value.

Transshipment.   The term *transshipment* refers to the act of off-loading the goods from one carrier to another. If there is no acceptable carrier that can provide a bill of lading from the port of origin to the port of destination, be certain the letter does not disallow transshipment. If nothing is said, it is presumed that transshipment is allowed. Off-loading should still be avoided if possible because of increased risk of damage and pilferage it incurs.

If operating letters of credit now seem very straightforward and protective, be aware there are many serpents lurking in the tall grass for the unsuspecting. One must understand the esoteric definitions and meanings *in advance* and be prepared to perform *exactly* according to the stated terms and conditions and request an amendment or extension if there is some question as to your ability to do so. From the importer's viewpoint, it is plain there are also hazards, the classic one being such total reliance on what the documents say that the beneficiary could fraudulently, but nevertheless successfully, negotiate a letter with documents claiming a shipment of engines which were, in fact, merely rocks in boxes.

With so many small details to consider, it is well to think in terms of checklists. Here is an abbreviated list to consider at the time of receiving the letter of credit, for it is much better to object or clarify *now* rather than on shipping day, which is too late, or even after work on the order has begun for the credit may contain conditions impossible to meet at any time. On receipt of letter of credit ask yourself the following questions:

- Is it irrevocable?
- Is the paying bank of good reputation and is the currency convertible in the event that the paying bank is overseas?
- Does it need to be confirmed in the United States?
- Is the seller's name and address spelled correctly and are there any other misspellings that might create discrepancies?
- Are the dollar amounts and quantities per your quotation?
- Is it at sight, or if a usance credit, is it as agreed?
- Are the shipping terms correct (e.g., FOB, CIF)?
- Are the documents required as agreed?
- Can you provide insurance as required?
- Are letter of credit fees and costs as agreed?
- Is there sufficient tolerance as to quantity (i.e., is the word *about* or an equivalent word necessary)?

- Is the merchandise correctly described?
- Are partial shipments allowed?
- Is transshipment allowed if necessary?
- Is there sufficient time to meet the latest shipping and negotiation timetable?
- Can you ship from the port of embarkation that is stated?
- Is the shipping destination as agreed and possible?
- Will the style and type of transport document you will receive from the carrier be acceptable (e.g., house bill of lading versus ocean onboard bills)?
- If a named vessel or carrier is stipulated, can you comply both as to availability and voyage timing?
- Do you have time to obtain the consular legalization and other certificates that are required?
- Are there inspection or mandatory PSI problems?
- Can you provide a packing list by carton?
- Can you meet marking and labeling requirements?
- If you need to ship on-deck, is this allowed?

Negotiating a Letter of Credit

The operative word here is *negotiating*. This is the word that makes a letter of credit something less than the "money in the bank" neophyte exporters believe it to be. Even though bankers give letters good credence as support for credit extensions, they still look to the assets of the borrower first. The obvious reason is that before negotiating the letter, the exporting beneficiary must have "performed." That is, the goods must have been shipped exactly as called for in the letter of credit—in the fashion described and within the time frame designated. The primary proof of this performance is the transportation document evidencing the shipment. A review of the primary transport document indicates the nature, weight, and number of cartons of the shipment, the points of embarkation and debarkation, the method of carriage, the insurance taken out, the date shipped, and possibly still more details. In addition, there are the insurance documents, the packing list, and the invoice. Each document called for in the letter must be exactly within the parameters it describes. (See Chapter 12 for details about these documents.)

The Ten Most Common Errors Made in Dealing With Letters of Credit. If you asked for the right terms in the letter of credit initially and then checked to make sure that the incoming credit was as agreed, there should be a minimum of problems in its negotiation. But errors do arise, and you are bound to have discrepancies on occasion; limiting those to 20 percent of the negotiations would be a better-than-average performance. As a study by the Irving Trust Company shows, a high percentage of the discrepancies that occur involve a rather short list of common errors. In order of descending importance, here are the 10 most common mistakes as adapted from an article by Arthur Bardenhagen and Joseph Colleran of Irving Trust:

1. Exporters present documents late, after the letter of credit has expired. Even if documents are only one day late, the letter of credit is no longer valid. Usually the exporter starts preparing documents too late and finds out that such items as consular invoices take much longer to obtain than anticipated.

2. Exporters ship their goods later than the credit allows. Again, even if shipment is made only one day later than specified in the letter of credit, the letter of credit is invalid.

3. Exporters try to draw more money than the letter of credit allows for. This often happens in cases where the letter of credit allows partial shipment, and the final shipment is for more money than there is left in the letter of credit. Often this is done by mutual agreement between exporter and importer; however, the letter of credit must be amended accordingly.

4. Exporters delay presenting documents for an undue period. Even though a letter of credit might not be near expiration, many letters specify that documents must be presented to the bank within a certain number of days of shipment. If no cutoff is specified, the rules of the UCP 500 apply, which stipulate that the exporter must present documents within 21 days after the goods are shipped (the transport document date).

5. Exporters make unallowed partial shipments. Usually the exporter did not study the letter of credit carefully enough and hopes to receive early partial payment if part of the shipment is made early.

6. Exporters present invoices that do not describe the merchandise exactly as it is described in the credit. Since the bank does not inspect the merchandise but only the documents covering shipment of same, it must report any discrepancy between the wording on the invoice and the wording on the letter of credit. This applies even if the wording is very similar, such as "cartons" versus "boxes," or a partial description, such as "equipment" instead of the specific type of equipment.

7. Exporters do not supply all the documents called for in the letters of credit. This could simply be an oversight or inability to obtain documents or certifications in time. Sometimes it is also the desire to avoid

paying for these documents. While the documents usually can still be furnished, the exporter does not get paid and runs the risk that the letter of credit will expire before the discrepancies are corrected.

8. Exporters do not have documents legalized. Sometimes documents must be either notarized or must be visaed or legalized by a consulate of a foreign nation. It takes time to correct this oversight, which can be difficult if the consulate wants to see other related documents.

9. Exporters fail to obtain completed onboard bills of lading. Some bills of lading lack an onboard stamp or contain a stamp that is undated or unsigned. Sometimes this omission is caused by a last-minute switch of the shipment to another vessel and this again takes time to correct.

10. Exporters fail to obtain insurance coverage soon enough. Even though many exporters have an open-ended arrangement with their insurance company, allowing them to write their own policies, such policies might not get approved until a few days after the vessel sailed. This violates the UCP. To correct this error, the exporter only need take the policy back and have it altered. However, there is the possibility that the goods might be damaged before the insurance takes effect or, worse yet, that the vessel might sink.

If anything is not in order when presented for negotiation after shipment, a discrepancy will result. If the discrepancy is not correctable, an amendment must be requested from the buyer, who may or may not respond. The response may depend entirely on whether the buyer has any reason to regret the purchase, and how much and how soon the import buyer still wants to become a "holder in due course" of the negotiable shipping documents and thereby take the goods by now on the dock. If the buyer declines to waive the discrepancy or amend the letter, the exporter retains title and possession, but still must make a disposition of the goods now being charged with demurrage. In the ordinary course of events, the buyer wants the merchandise and the amendment is forthcoming, but with a delay in payment and some extra costs and fees.

Personally, I used to feel that if our export letter of credit department could manage to negotiate in excess of 85 percent of our letters without discrepancies they were doing an excellent job. If clean negotiations fell below 75 percent, a careful review would be made concerning competency. At various times, some dependency on a given freight forwarder was permitted, but our own personnel were responsible for the final review of documents before presenting for negotiation. Even if you might be the sole negotiator, a good freight forwarder is your first line of defense against discrepancies so long as the forwarder is fully informed, has a copy of your letter, and receives the goods for shipment in a timely fashion.

(Continued)

One hard and fast rule then was that if the discrepancy was not correctable, the decision about how to handle the next step must be mine. If I felt we had any ground to stand on, I would discuss the alleged discrepancy with the head of the bank's export letter department, and if I had my facts straight and argued with some persuasion, I often won. A bank's documentary clerk is often justifiably proud of having found a discrepancy, that being a key element in his or her job. But just as often, the clerk has simply been overzealous, and a reasonable case can be made for accepting the document as it was presented so long as the mistake is not a material error or patently unarguable, such as a late date or wrong bill of lading. The chance for success improves considerably when it is a local bank, or better yet, your own bank. This is one good reason to try to control, or at least suggest, the advising or confirming bank whenever possible.

When Discrepancies Arise.   There are six major discrepancies, three of which cannot be corrected under any circumstances. They are:

1. Late shipment
2. Late presentation
3. Expired letter of credit

The remaining three can sometimes be corrected, but only in certain circumstances and with some difficulty. They are:

1. Incorrect bill of lading
2. A draft in excess of credit amount remaining
3. A freight insurance policy bearing a date later than the bill of lading

Be careful of suggestions to invoice in excess of the balance of the L/C, stating that the excess will be "settled outside the letter of credit." Many banks will not accept this. The new UCP 500 changes several of the former UCP 400 rules of negotiation, so be sure to be familiar with the current rules.

Keeping in mind that the goods are already en route, if a discrepancy is not correctable, one of three actions must be taken:

1. Ask the negotiating bank to contact the issuing bank and request that the buyer waive the discrepancy. This is often the best and fastest course.

2. Send the documents for collection, which means that usually nothing will happen until the shipment arrives in the buyer's country. Left to its own devices, this is what the negotiating bank will probably do as a routine matter, and in all likelihood the buyer will still want the merchandise, so he or she will authorize payment and accept the merchandise. Sometimes it is wise to proceed with both this action *and* the

first, and go with whichever works first, as time is critical and demurrage charges must be minimized.

3. If cashflow is a problem and you are confident the discrepancy will be waived, *and* if the beneficiary also has a good credit standing with the negotiating bank, you might ask the bank to pay and send the documents for collection. The beneficiary will first have to sign an indemnity agreement that gives the lender recourse, with interest, should the issuing bank refuse to reimburse the negotiating bank.

Standby Letters of Credit

There are circumstances under which the conventional letter of credit requiring shipment of goods or provision of services can be troublesome in its detail or too expensive to be practical (in the case of small, routine, or frequent orders) for both the seller and the buyer. To overcome these problems and still provide the seller with the complete protection of a letter of credit, a *standby* letter of credit is used. This type of L/C, which neither buyer nor seller really hopes will be negotiated, can effectively function as security for its beneficiary without requiring the expense and trouble of the negotiation and collection process involved in transactional letters of credit. Besides being used to protect the seller, the standby letter of credit finds frequent use in providing security for the buyer in terms of performance, warranties, or advance and progress payments. (See Figure 14-4 for a sample standby letter and accompanying point-by-point explanation.)

Standby Letters as Security for Open Account Terms. A standby letter can substitute for an operating letter of credit from the buyer when used in conjunction with open account terms. This type of standby letter is designed so that if the buyer fails to pay an outstanding open account in a timely fashion (usually within a brief specified grace period), the beneficiary can draw on the letter merely by certifying in a statement to the issuing bank that the party opening the standby letter has not paid within the predetermined number of days past due as specified in the letter. Little or no documentation is required beyond a signed statement concerning the overdue payments and perhaps a copy of the unpaid invoices to induce the issuing bank to pay without question. As a matter of courtesy and customer relations, the buyer should be advised in advance of such action to permit the buyer to first correct the late payment voluntarily.

Standby Letters in Lieu of Bid or Performance Bonds. The standby letter of credit may also be issued by a seller (exporter or contractor) at the buyer's (importer's) request to function as a bid or performance bond to protect the buyer from the possibility of a seller's failure to perform where advance payments, specifications, completion dates, or warranties are concerned, or where the contractor wins the bid but refuses to perform or sign the stipulated contract.

Bid bonds are a commonplace part of the tender offer process usually associated with responding to various government bids. The purpose is to assure the party requesting bids that when a bid *is* awarded, the bidder will proceed with the undertaking or accept the amount of the bid bond as a penalty. If the bidder fails to sign the contract, which typically requires a *performance bond,* intended to assure ultimate performance under the contract, the bond is forfeited and the funds are supposedly used to offset the added cost of rebidding or accepting the second-best bid. Typically, bid bonds are for about 3 percent of the contract value. Since most small businesses have no capacity to provide bonding from major surety companies, the only alternative is to have the bank provide a standby letter of credit that performs the same guarantee function.

Performance bonds are used in conjunction with construction or custom manufacturing projects and are frequently in the range of 5 percent of the contract value, but they can run as high as 10 percent. Here the purpose is to assure the party paying for the goods or project that the contractor or manufacturer will perform according to the terms of the contract, and that the final product will meet the contract specifications. If not, the bond or standby letter will be available in whole or in part to compensate the buyer for the deficiency.

Standby Letters in Lieu of Advance Payment Guarantees. When advance or down payments are necessary, the buyer, for its part, is likely to ask for a guarantee in the form of a standby letter to guarantee that the work or goods paid for in advance will be delivered. The standby letter is used for this purpose because if timely delivery is not forthcoming, the buyer merely needs to state that fact and draw on the standby letter to reclaim its advance. Occasionally, a letter of guarantee is requested, but U.S. banks are not authorized by our banking system to issue this particular instrument. In such cases, the U.S. bank provides a standby letter to a foreign bank which then issues the letter of guarantee.

When down payments under a contract are being negotiated, the buyer may agree to advance payments but will usually request in return the opening of a standby letter in a like amount to protect the advance. In view of most banks' usual practice of requiring cash collateral for standby letters, the down payment does not provide any additional working capital.

In each of the above cases, your bank will be happy to provide a standby letter of credit but, as mentioned, they will usually want it to be 100 percent collateralized with cash unless the exporter's credit is exceptionally strong. The reason for this requirement is the inherent and arbitrary burden of risk that standby letters represent and that banks cannot readily assess. Standby letters serve their purpose to protect the beneficiary very well—so much so that many times the party requesting the guarantee will demand a standby letter rather than a bond. This is because the bank issuing the standby letter is not supposed to consider the merits of the demand or "calling" of the letter, whereas the surety company providing a bond may look into the merits of a questionable claim before paying because it is not bound by the UCP 500 and functions as an insurer, rather than a guarantor, of credit.

If you are called upon to open a standby letter, be sure you discuss the consequences with a knowledgeable party and understand the special risks that may be incurred. The beneficiary of a standby letter is empowered to take very arbitrary actions that may be difficult to defend. The issuing bank is obliged to act on the basis of the demand documents before them, regardless of any other underlying or mitigating circumstances (which they are neither empowered nor willing to investigate). Thus, in the case of a contractor's standby letter securing performance, the beneficiary could submit a statement that the contractor had not performed certain tasks when, in fact, the obligation had been fulfilled. It would then be necessary for the contractor to take court action to recover the funds fraudulently demanded by the beneficiary and paid by the issuing bank to the beneficiary. In the case of a standby letter used to secure open account terms, if payments were declared to be past due, resulting in a drawing against the standby letter, the bank might pay even before the buyer had had a chance to present documents showing that timely payments had been made. Under such circumstances, restitution would probably be achieved with relative ease, however.

One potential abuse of standby letters is referred to as the threat to "extend or pay." In this case the beneficiary holding the letter requests that the standby serving as a performance bond be extended in order to provide what is, in effect, a longer warranty. If the contractor refuses to extend it, the contractor is then advised that an arbitrary demand or "unfair calling" may be made, which virtually blackmails the contractor into accepting the request. In some Third-World countries, such abuses can be real, though rare, problems. But with most of our regular trading partners, standby letters are a very normal part of project bids and government tender offers and are to be expected. Regardless of risks, standby letters as bid or performance bonds are often necessary, even though they can tie up large amounts of credit.

The Downside of Letters of Credit

Some exporters become so devoted to letters of credit that they fail to recognize when L/Cs may actually have little or no value. A customer who wishes to make small but frequent purchases is one example. Another might be a situation in which, though there is minimal commercial or political risk, the buyer is forced to open letters of credit and includes so much detail or such strict time frames and other conditions as to make it more trouble than it is worth to either buyer or seller. In fact, while letters of credit for shipments valued in the $5000- to $10,000-range are questionable, L/Cs for smaller shipments become completely impractical unless one can add enough to the price to cover the large minimum fees. Even then, the result is a higher price for the product and, inevitably, smaller sales. Also to be considered are higher negotiation costs that can easily rise into the 3 to 5 percent range as compared with a more reasonable .75 to 1.5 percent range for larger letters of credit. While discretion must be used in offering more generous terms, there are many cases in which, if the export effort is justified, so is the risk associated with more lenient terms, because much of your competition here and abroad is offering documentary collection or open account terms. Another alternative might be standby letters of credit, as already suggested.

Wire Transfers and Advance Payment

Wire Transfers

For high-risk or first-transaction situations, or when documentary collections or letters of credit cannot be negotiated, there is a hybrid sort of term falling somewhere between open account and absolute payment in advance, yet safer in many situations than documents against payment. We refer to *wire transfer payments* between banks on notification of the arrival of the merchandise at the dock of embarkation. A dock receipt can be issued for proof, if necessary, and the buyer's agent can even be invited to examine the goods before they are loaded aboard ship. Other variations can call for wire transfer at the time of shipment or some other trigger, but these latter variations become a matter of timing rather than risk abatement because in these cases, the merchandise is irretrievably bound for an overseas destination.

Payment in Advance

To round out the chapter, I'll conclude with the safest of all terms: receipt of full cash payment prior to any action by the seller. Actually, *payment in advance* is not really a "selling" term, but rather an excuse for the lack of one. It is appropriate in certain instances, however: as a partial security advance; for production installment payments in projects; or to overcome the obvious difficulties of assuring payment for sample shipments to unknown parties for whom a letter of credit or a determination of creditworthiness is impractical in view of either shipment size or time considerations. As a condition for payment in the normal course of business, however, it is usually a means of assuring that there will be no such business.

15
An Introduction to Export/Import Finance

In contrast to import financing, export financing can be a problem because the lender sees what would normally be collateral for the loan being exported and going outside the lender's control. In fact, many banks virtually ceased export-related lending during the trade and currency problems of the 1980s and confined any international financing they undertook to imports. But now, memories of the beating banks took a decade ago from inopportune international loans are fading and, as they watch international trade become one of the fastest-growing segments of our economy, they are once again interested in financing exports.

Export finance and *import finance* are broad terms that include all borrowing or financing for either venture. They refer to working capital needs for a single transaction, for a "bundle" of transactions, or for purposes of carrying the export receivables resulting from a continuing series of transactions. Much of this form of export finance is described as *supplier credit* because the funds are used by the supplier to pay for labor and materials to prepare the shipment; the resulting buyer obligation appears on the books of the supplier/exporter as a receivable until paid. In other words, the supplier, the manufacturer, or the exporter may be providing short-term financing to the import buyer, and this requires working capital.

Working capital financing, an important element to the financing of businesses of all sizes, is likely to be especially critical for start-up businesses and new-to-export businesses. Generally, a new-to-export business is not as likely to seek buyer credit–oriented forms of export financing. Buyer credit financing often involves negotiable documents arising from larger transactions and falls into a category of *trade finance* which is typically utilized by larger companies with medium- to long-term financing needs and that have access to substantial credit, thanks to a healthy balance sheet. You should be aware of trade finance fundamentals, nevertheless, to have an idea of the opportunities and techniques it represents, for the need and the opportunity may come up sooner than you think.

Working Capital Financing

If, because of a demonstrably good track record, the lender has confidence in an exporter's ability to perform, it might extend credit to a business with a balance sheet of somewhat less than acceptable financial ratios and profit margins, given the extra support of an assignment of letter-of-credit proceeds or even foreign accounts receivable proceeds. Alternatively, considerable export financing is provided by original suppliers or manufacturers rather than from lenders using assigned or transferred letters of credit. The main problem with this source of financing is that the supplier often hesitates, in the case of an assigned letter, to put much reliance on the exporting middleman's performance, or, in the case of a transferred letter, to burden itself with the duties of shipping and other arrangements.

In the case of imports, the lender extending credit for an import letter of credit knows it can have a lien on the imported merchandise and even the receivables subsequently generated from its sale. The lender's primary concern here is the ability of the importer to sell the goods, since the last thing a lender wishes to do is worry about disposing the merchandise collateral, but it nevertheless represents a hard asset for collateral. The importer, however, may have greater demands for funding up front for the purpose of opening import letters of credit, and often must allow more lead time than the exporter.

The banks welcome support for export financing from an assigned letter of credit because they have the additional advantage of negotiating the L/C and earning the fees that arise from those activities. Other lenders will consider lending against insured foreign receivables or payments flowing from sound project contracts. For further protection they can seek support from the U.S. Export-Import Bank or the Small Business Administration's working capital guarantees, as well as from some state programs. (See Chapter 18.)

The more active international banks may even consider issuing back-to-back L/Cs. A true back-to-back letter of credit is just what it sounds like: a domestic letter of credit issued as a mirror image to the incoming export letter. It differs only in naming a new beneficiary and a new applicant, which would be the original beneficiary or exporter, and in changing the dollar amounts (less the exporter's margin, of course), plus earlier shipping and/or validity dates. Seldom can this be done so perfectly that the bank has absolutely no exposure except for the credit of the original issuing bank. If proper documents are submitted under a perfect back-to-back letter, the bank can use those documents to negotiate the original letter even if the first beneficiary is nowhere to be found. Perfection being rare, banks more often consider the back-to-back approach as an extension of credit that requires minimal supporting assets from the exporter. Many banks, however, do not have sufficient confidence in their operational department—or "back room," as it is often called—to approve a true back-to-back transaction. As a result, such transactions are not commonly available. Asian banks seem more willing than most to engage in this activity, but they are still very selective.

Trade Finance

Trade finance, while forming an essential part of export or import finance, is not well understood because it relies entirely on the underlying transaction as represented by the transaction documents themselves, coupled with the credit of the buyer and/or third-party bank or sovereign guarantees. Often the documents will be negotiable instruments in their own right. For this reason, trade finance usually revolves around the credit of the buyer or the buyer's guarantor, who may have signed notes for purchase of the export/import or the export project. Depending on the circumstances, the exporter or the financial intermediaries involved can sell the paper with full recourse, limited recourse, or nonrecourse to the seller from the "holder in due course." An example of *full recourse* might be the case of a lender extending credit on the basis of assigned account receivables. *Limited recourse* occurs in situations where the lender is willing to take the full risk of the signed buyer obligations, usually in some form of note, but reserves the right to go against the exporter if there later proves to have been fraud or fault on the part of the exporter whose sale led to the creation of the paper. *Nonrecourse* is usually acceptable only in the case of obligations where there is no question that the buyer unconditionally accepted the goods as fulfilling the specifications or the performance standards prior to signing the paper, so that there is little or no opportunity for fraud. Within these broad parameters are a several basic types of trade finance, each subject to many variations.

Banker Acceptances

Banker acceptances (BAs) have been previously touched upon, but in this case the exporter receiving the acceptance sells it to the maker or a third party at what is usually a very favorable discount rate to improve cashflow. Acceptances can include banker's "clean" acceptance financing. This is more common in import transactions than in connection with exports, but offers borrowing at the most favorable rates. It is only available to financially strong businesses, however. Clean acceptances do not stem from a letter of credit transaction, but rather are created by a draft representing a promise to pay against a specific transaction or group of transactions.

Receivables Financing

Receivables can be financed by placing a lien on the receivables to serve as collateral, which the lender can then control through an assignment of proceeds and/or a lock box arrangement. Typically the lender wants the foreign receivables to be insured, and to be issued an assignment of any claims paid under the insurance policy. Otherwise, the bank is likely to reserve the right to individually accept the highest-quality accounts only. Alternatively, the receivables can be sold at a discount to the lender with full or limited recourse against the borrower on delinquent accounts. Regularly selling receivables is seldom a viable alternative for the smaller business since a conventional lender would want to see only quality accounts of substantial size that had been extended by a credit manager experienced in foreign credit. Similar arrangements could be made for domestic receivables arising from import activity.

Factoring

Factoring is a more readily available version of selling the receivables to a lender. This method of financing foreign receivables, depending on the factor and the options selected, can be a version of either selling the receivables or borrowing against them. Long established domestically in industries featuring undercapitalized companies such as apparel manufacturing, it is becoming an increasingly popular way of financing foreign receivables and sometimes permits active commercial accounts in countries where that would otherwise be impossible. The factor typically handles the credit research of the proposed account and reserves the right to approve or deny the proposed open account credit. The factor also usually receives payment directly from the buyer and remits the payment, less the factoring fee, to the exporter on receipt of payment. Alternatively, after an established maximum collection period (which is often 90 days), the factor pays the exporter for the account less the factoring fee, and proceeds with the bad debt collection effort for its own account. If the exporter or importer needs cash while the collection cycle is pending, it can borrow from the factor up to a certain percentage of the outstanding accounts. Again, some minimum volume of open account transactions is required to make an export business attractive to a qualified international factoring organization. Some exporters believe that factors' fees are too high. But they may not in fact be unreasonable for the services of well-organized foreign factor specialists, when considering all the costs of credit checking, follow-up costs, collection costs, and bad debt write-offs.

One of the largest international factoring groups is Factors Chain International (FCI) in Amsterdam, which links together about 95 independent factoring companies in 35 countries. FCI can be contacted directly by fax in the Netherlands at 31 20 625-7628. For contacts with U.S. banks offering links with international factoring organizations, check with the free AXCAP program offered by the Bankers Association for Foreign Trade (BAFT), which is discussed in detail in Chapter 3.

Forfaiting

Forfaiting is a classic form of trade finance and has been a major factor in supporting East/West trade in Europe since World War II. It is being used today in many countries where it is otherwise difficult to offer medium-term credit in the three- to five-year range. It is most frequently used for sales of between $250,000 and $10 million. The exporter makes a deal with a forfait house which, in cooperation with the importer, finds a strong guarantor. The latter is most often a bank in the country of the buyer. The sale amount financed is usually divided into notes of roughly equal value, each coming due at six month intervals for the term of the forfait agreement. The exporter is then paid in full without recourse. The advantage of forfaiting is a firm commitment for 100 percent of sale value at fixed rate financing for the buyer that can be speedily arranged. Understandably, it is often relatively expensive, given the sort of Third-World applications for which it is used. For the names of forfaiters active in the area you are selling, contact your international banker or AXCAP.

International Leasing

Leasing is a form of financing conducted through specialized firms and some international bankers. For U.S. exporters it would be called cross-border leasing and could be arranged as an operational lease or as a financial lease. The *operational lease* is like a typical lease, with a meaningful value remaining in the equipment at the end of the lease which can be reclaimed by the lessor or sold to the lessee depending on the agreement. Therefore, both political risk and commercial risk factors need to be considered.

A *financial lease* is merely a substitute for the relatively long-term financing of equipment and is constructed so that only a nominal value remains in the leased equipment at the end of the term. One of the prime advantages of such leasing is the absence of a down payment on a deal tailored to the needs of the importing lessee (buyer). Another advantage to the lessee is that the obligation is not reflected on the lessee's balance sheet as a liability, thereby improving the lessee's financial ratios to support other borrowing. The exporter or seller does not usually carry the lease but is paid directly for the equipment by a leasing specialist.

Buyer Credit

Larger foreign transactions and projects are traditionally financed with buyer credit. With or without the assistance of the exporting manufacturer, medium- or long-term credit is arranged for the foreign buyer. This enables the contractor or exporter to be cashed out by means of guaranteed bank credit extended directly to the buyer, usually with a federal agency—such as the U.S. Export-Import Bank (EXIM), the Overseas Private Investment Corporation (OPIC), the Agency for International Development (AID), or the Commodity Credit Corporation (CCC)—serving as the guarantor. Alternatively, some of these agencies can make a direct loan to the buyer. Forfaiting and leasing can also be forms of buyer credit if the seller is taken out of the deal, as in forfaiting, or if a third-party leasing agency buys out the seller. Direct extensions of credit to the buyer, often combined with guarantees or loans from the agencies just mentioned, are common means of financing trade, especially for larger or extended-term deals. Note that the federal agencies mentioned only support U.S. exports. It is public policy to support exports that create trade surpluses, but it is definitely not a policy to support imports, which create trade deficits. In other words, it is the country of the seller or contractor that offers the public support. An importer would therefore need to seek public sector support from domestic financial agencies such as the Small Business Administration's 7a loan-guarantee program.

Countertrade

Countertrade is its very own world. Although statistics vary wildly as to the percentage of world trade it represents, there is more of it than one would imagine. It goes back to the ancient trade concept of barter and is mostly used for trade with Third-World countries where foreign exchange availability is a major obstacle to transactions and with sovereign governments wishing to gain an advantage in return for doing business with a certain party or country. That advantage is most often in the form of assurance of future sales to offset lost foreign exchange dollars or technical expertise. For many transactions in parts of Eastern and Central Europe and Latin America, it is a necessary fact of life. In other cases it is simply a trade facilitator or marketing device. Some traders seem to make it a profession unto itself. Countertrade is vital in certain trade areas for four principal reasons. It helps one, or both, of the parties to the deal:

1. Substitute for scarce hard currency
2. Acquire more advanced technologies
3. Enter emerging markets
4. Minimize a negative balance of trade (a sovereign strategy)

While no two writers seem to agree on the names for countertrade in its various forms, I believe five forms best describe countertrade in all its varieties. These are (1) barter; (2) compensation; (3) counterpurchase; (4) buyback; and (5) offset.

Barter

Barter, the earliest form of trade, is still in use today, both domestically and internationally. It is characterized by a direct exchange of goods of equal value.

Compensation

Compensation is a modernized version of countertrade in which both of the products exchanged are valued in specified currencies and invoiced in those currencies. Thus, the transaction may be of unequal value for each side and payment may be partly in product and partly in currency. Even though the transactions need not take place simultaneously, they are all covered by a single contract, which enjoys a factor of simplicity for smaller businesses but which can also make the deal a bit unwieldy.

Counterpurchase

Counterpurchase, also known as *parallel barter,* accounts for the largest dollar volume of countertrade today, but it is better designed for medium to large corporations or established countertrade firms than it is for smaller businesses. Two contracts are signed and delivery, invoicing, and payment are carried out independently for each transaction. The arrangements sometimes cover periods of as much as five years. The initial purchase might be a substantial project or service, with the counterpurchase that subsequently takes place having little or nothing to do with the first segment of the transaction.

Buyback

Buyback is similar to counterpurchase and best describes many turnkey projects, though it is not necessarily limited to large projects. The manufacturer-installer of the equipment or plant agrees to buy back for sale to other customers in other countries a portion of the product resulting from the installed turnkey project over a period of time. An important consideration in such arrangements is the quality of the product the turnkey project's plant will produce. It is important that the contractor-builder retains some control over supervision of the plant or equipment operations and over employee training to ensure the quality of the product it will later be obliged to sell.

Offset

Offset is a product of World War II and is sometimes called *cooperation* by Europeans. It normally relates to sales of military equipment or defense systems to less-developed countries. The sovereign government involved wants to be sure that, in exchange for buying certain equipment, it will acquire opportunities for trade and development through the seller's obligation to transfer certain technologies, or to arrange advantageous joint ventures in the developing country.

Countertrade for Small Business

To begin with, do not seek out countertrade unless you wish to make a profession of it, for it will inevitably find you, especially if you trade with underdeveloped countries and emerging democracies. Under the right circumstances, some of the deals proposed may be well worth considering if you have the time to spend on them. A major problem is the considerable time countertrade consumes, linked with the relatively low percentage of deals finally consummated. On the other hand, if just the right fit is found for products you know and have a means of trading, it can be an effective marketing tool. Unless the fit *is* just right, however, you would be wise to share the profit by engaging a countertrade firm with experience and ongoing operations in the target territory to take on your share of the countertrade obligations.

Countertrade is of enough interest to the International Trade Administration that a countertrade division exists within its trade development unit to track countertrade's growth and techniques. Its level of activity seems to have lessened. There is also a wealth of books and articles on this specialized and rather difficult form of trade.

16

Insuring Your Export/Import Business

Every business has its risks and its rewards, but in the export/import field, profits and growth come only with great effort—too much effort to squander by taking unnecessary risks. Many risks can be eliminated or at least minimized through insurance and prudent examination of the degree of risk. The primary hazards addressed here are:

- Commercial foreign credit risks
- Political or country risks
- Transportation risks

These risks loom large in international trade and require specialized policies similar and yet quite different from those that one would carry in the normal course of business. In addition, there are many other risks that are very similar to the risks you would expect to face in doing regular domestic business, but that require special coverage when the exposure is overseas rather than in the United States. These might include health and accident insurance for overseas traveling or living, basic liability insurance (including auto and property damage), and product liability and personal property insurance (including such things as rental autos and samples).

Commercial Risks on Foreign Accounts Receivable

Commercial risk refers to the risk of buyer nonpayment due to insolvency or other financial problems—in other words, a bad debt. Nonpayment because of a legitimate buyer dispute is not covered by insurance and is not considered a commercial risk, but rather a quality or performance problem inherent in the business process that must be corrected or otherwise resolved. Payment problems caused by government regulations or similar actions beyond the buyer's control are part of political risk and will be discussed shortly. The term *accounts receivable* as used here includes all payments pending and due the seller under any terms, including negotiated letters of credit pending collection.

In the case of letters of credit, it is the issuing bank on which the letter of credit's value depends, and that bank must pay so long as the conditions of the letter are fully met and the letter is negotiated correctly and in a timely manner. There are special policies to cover letters of credit that focus primarily on country stability and currency convertibility risks, although when there is concern of this kind it is usually best to have the letter confirmed by a U.S. bank. When a confirming bank cannot be found, Eximbank cover is the next likely step, rather than private sector cover.

It should not be overlooked that, even though the transaction terms are letter of credit, there can be commercial risk in the form of the buyer's ability to open the promised letter of credit. Therefore, under many circumstances, credit information on the buyer proposing to provide an as-yet-unopened letter of credit can be important where there is to be an ongoing relationship or series of orders, or when there is to be a delay between start of production and opening of the letter. It is important to know whether the buyer has the financial capacity to open the promised future letters, for letters never opened can be as damaging to a small firm that has already invested in the preparation of an order as unpaid open accounts.

Political Risks on Foreign Accounts Receivable

Political risk on foreign accounts receivable, sometimes better described as *country risk,* is used in the broad sense of the word for this purpose and includes war, revolution, civil unrest, cancellation of the import or export license, and currency inconvertibility—all quite specifically defined. Most of these events and risks describe an unstable country or threatened hostilities between countries. There are companies that specialize in analyzing the likelihood of such instabilities for every country and for both short term and intermediate term. For some destinations these are very imminent risks and a small exporter should usually not consider extending credit without political risk cover to such areas. By contrast, it would be an excess of caution to worry about this cover for areas like most of Western Europe or Canada. Eximbank's political risk cover is automatically included when commercial risk insurance is purchased, but political risk cover is available alone. Private sector insurance usually covers only commercial risk and the insurers we will mention do not write even commercial insurance in the more unstable political areas. Other insurance companies specialize in political risk but offer little or no cover for commercial risk. If political risks seem remote to you, consider the expropriation risks realized with Iran in 1979, and Zaire's appropriation of oil company assets in 1992; to say nothing of the civil wars raging around the world today, some of which broke out almost overnight. Consider also the numerous occasions in recent U.S. history when the export licensing rules have been changed or embargoes have been imposed that suddenly prohibit an export regardless of the terms.

Sources of Foreign Credit Information

With or without insurance coverage—and sometimes even if the terms are letter of credit—the first step is to assess the risks. The second step, depending on that risk assessment is to qualify the account for insurance with adequate credit information on the buyer. Obtaining reliable financial and payment history information can sometimes be a difficult task even though there are a surprising number of credit information and reporting sources throughout the world. One such source, a household name for credit in this country, is *Dun & Bradstreet*, which has a large international credit reporting division with offices in every major city. It is headquartered in New York (phone 800/234-3867). Because of the high cost of its single reports, access to D&B effectively requires an annual contract, separate and apart from any domestic contract you may have. This makes it quite costly for a small export business anticipating only limited use. Incidentally, D&B also has an overseas bad-debt collection service. Another familiar name is *TRW Business Credit Services* of Orange, California (phone 714/385-7661), which has recently gone global with its credit reporting services. TRW will combine an international contract with domestic use, but a contract is essential, and the minimum is in the $3000 area. Two other less familiar sources for foreign credit information in the U.S. are *Owens OnLine, Inc.* in Clearwater, Florida (phone 800/745-4656), and *Graydon America* in New York City (phone 212/633-1434), a U.S. subsidiary of a large European credit service. Although small itself, Owens has a worldwide service with a special focus on Latin America. It provides an on-line service and offers a research and update service—at a somewhat higher price—as well. Owens serves the small or single user on a case-by-case basis as well as offering special rates with an annual contract. Graydon is much larger, but can provide reports on an case-by-case basis, too, and offers a credit collection service. Its special focus tends to be on Europe. Both firms do their own analysis in certain countries and contract with appropriate in-country credit services for the rest of the world. It would not be economical in terms of annual contracts and minimums for the small business to contract directly with a variety of foreign services unless its export sales were targeted strictly in one or two countries. On average, individual foreign credit reports range from $65 to $300 each, depending on the speed of reporting required, the country involved, and the need for a most recent report. A median cost might be $150, with lows of $50 and highs of $600.

The U.S. International Trade Administration provides another useful tool for exporters through its *World Traders Data Reports* (*WTDR*). The *WTDR* are provided at a reasonable cost through the DOC's Commercial Service offices around the world. Unfortunately, they can sometimes be quite slow in delivering the information unless there is a current report in the files. The emphasis in the *WTDR* is on the subject company's history, activities, and general reputation as a trade contact, with little financial detail or credit reporting information.

Finally, if your transaction is big enough it may be wise or even necessary under the terms of a credit insurance policy to request the firm's current and prior year's financial statements. This is common practice in this country when establishing substantial credit facilities, but for some reason many firms are hesitant to request such information from an overseas firm.

Credit Insurance on Foreign Accounts Receivable

If you wish to finance your accounts receivable, the probability is that the lender will insist that they be insured unless they are unusually high-grade corporate accounts known around the world, or government and quasigovernment accounts in "safe" countries. The alternative to bank financing, especially if you resist the idea of credit insurance, is to finance your account receivables by using a factor (see Chapter 15). This is possible because, in place of insurance, the factor has information sources, collection services, correspondents, agents, and/or branches established in the relevant countries or territories and will work through them to preapprove an individual account prior to soliciting or shipping to the account.

It is not only for financing reasons, however, that you may wish to insure your receivables. Insurance can take much of the risk out of offering unsecured terms, thereby permitting you to be more competitive—depending on your business and your competition. The dollar amount of the individual accounts relative to your overall volume is a major factor in considering the need for insurance because large accounts concentrate risk to the point that one or two bad credit decisions can seriously threaten your business. Ideally, you will have a "spread of risk," with many smaller accounts spread over a number of stable countries and territories, thereby minimizing the possibility that bad economic conditions in one territory will adversely affect a majority of your accounts.

Private Sector Credit Insurance Policies

For small businesses, the most common source for credit insurance is the United States Export-Import Bank (Eximbank) because it offers two credit insurance programs especially designed to serve small and new-to-export businesses, featuring zero or very small minimum annual premiums and no first-loss deductible. Because of the historically large minimum annual premiums demanded by private sector credit insurers (some as much as $30,000 or more), small exporters once had few choices. Today, however, the picture has changed, with at least three private companies recently entering the commercial-coverage-only field, offering small-business insurance policies having minimums as low as $1000 and $2500. Although neither of these directly offer cover for political risk, foreign business failures resulting from political unrest may still be covered. If rioters torch the buyer's business, thereby leaving the buyer insolvent, might be one example of this effect. The three private sector insurance companies that have recently entered the field are American Credit Indemnity (ACI) of Baltimore, Maryland; Fidelity and Deposit of Baltimore, Maryland; and Continental Insurance of Cranbury, New Jersey. ACI restricts itself to Western Europe, but Continental and Fidelity will cover a larger territory. Trade Underwriters for Reliance Insurance and FCIA for Great American Insurance offer policies that include political cover, but also with $10,000 minimum annual premiums, as in the case of ACI. Lloyds of London also offers commercial/political risk, in addition to special, defined risks in custom-tailored policies on a case-by-case basis. Some of these policies can be very useful to the international trader in areas such as contract repudiation. All figures are compared to each other and to Eximbank insurance in terms of features and cost in Figure 16-1.

For some exporters, private sector insurers have an advantage over Eximbank in not imposing restrictions as to the origin of the export. Eximbank will only insure products that are at least 51 percent U.S. origin. For companies selling to foreign firms that place multiple or repeat orders during the year, resulting in substantial accounts receivable that turn over several times each year, the private insurers may have another advantage. Eximbank's insurance rates are based on selling value, whereas ACI, Fidelity and Deposit, and Continental Insurance charge a much higher rate but base it on the maximum or average value of the receivables resulting

COMPARISON CHART OF FOREIGN CREDIT INSURANCE PROGRAMS
COMMERCIAL COVERAGE ONLY

	FIDELITY AND DEPOSIT	AMERICAN CREDIT INDEMNITY	CONTINENTAL INSURANCE COMPANY
RESTRICTIONS	Product may be 100% foreign content. No coverage to government buyers. Insolvency must occur while policy is in force	Product may be 100% foreign content. No coverage to government buyers. Insolvency must occur while policy is in force	Product may be 100% foreign content. No coverage to government buyers. Insolvency must occur while policy is in force
COVERAGE	Defined Insolvency and protracted default in eligible countries. Excludes insolvency due to war. Normally 85% coverage	Defined insolvency and protracted default in eligible countries. Excludes insolvency due to war. 100% insolvency coverage, 85% protracted default	Defined insolvency and protracted default in eligible countries. Excludes insolvency due to war. 100% insolvency coverage, 75% protracted default
COUNTRY ELIGIBILITY	List of eligible countries, primarily developed countries.	List of eligible countries, primarily developed countries.	List of eligible countries, primarily developed countries.
CREDIT APPROVALS	F&D gathers information and establishes credit limits for each buyer.	ACI gathers information and establishes credit limits for each buyer.	Continental gathers information and establishes credit limits for each buyer.
DEDUCTIBLE	No deductible.	Per policy year deductible.	Per policy year deductible.
PREMIUM PAYMENT	Prepayment, with year end adjustment. Determined as a percentage of insured sales.	Prepayment with adjustments for changes in buyer credit limits. Premium based on approved credit limits, endorsements, face value of policy. Premium charged per credit limit approved, based on quality of each buyer's credit rating	Prepayment with adjustments for changes in buyer credit limits. Premium based on approved credit limits, endorsements, face value of policy. Premium charged per credit limit approved, based on quality of each buyer's credit rating
MINIMUM PREMIUM	$1,250per policy year.	$10,000.	$2,500
CLAIM FILING	Insolvency claims can be filed at any time during policy period as soon as practicable after acquiring knowledge. Protracted default 180 days after due date.	Insolvency claims can be filed at any time during policy period but must be within 2 0 days after acquiring knowledge or 90 days from date of insolvency, whichever date is earlier. Past due claims must be filed within 3 months after due date. May have collection charges. 1 year waiting period for past dues	Insolvency claims can be filed at any time during policy period but must be within 2 0 days after acquiring knowledge or 90 days after date is from date of insolvency, whichever date is earlier. Past due claims must be filed within 3 months after due date. May have collection charges.

PLEASE NOTE THAT THIS CHART IS ONLY AN ADMINISTRATIVE GUIDE AND CONVEYS NO PERSONAL NOR AGENCY LIABILITY ON BEHALF OF

INTERNATIONAL INSURANCE ASSOCIATES.   (FCCOMP)

8202 FLORENCE AVENUE, SUITE 200

DOWNEY, CA 90240-3937

Figure 16-1. Comparison chart of foreign credit insurance programs.

COMPARISON CHART OF FOREIGN CREDIT INSURANCE PROGRAMS

COMPREHENSIVE COVERAGE (COMMERCIAL AND POLITICAL)

	FCIA (GREAT AMERICAN INSURANCE COMPANY)	EXPORT IMPORT BANK	TRADE UNDERWRITERS (RELIANCE INSURANCE CO.)	LLOYDS OF LONDON
RESTRICTIONS	No U.S. content restriction. Product may be 100% foreign content.	Products must be 51% U.S. content on cost basis. Military goods and/or services not eligible. Must be shipped from U.S.	No U.S. content restriction. Product may be 100% foreign content.	No U.S. content restriction. Product may be 100% foreign content.
COVERAGE	Commercial and Political Option 1: 95% for monthly reporting policy Option 2: 90% for country limits policy with a % refund for no claims bonus	Commercial and Political Option 1: 95% for both commercial and political. Option 2: 90% commercial and 100% political.	Commercial and Political 95% coverage a 5% refund for no claims bonus	Commercial and Political 90% coverage
COUNTRY ELIGIBILITY	All countries can be considered. Determined by each country's economic and political climate. Can include domestic sales Policy endorsed for countries covered	Dependent on U.S. government foreign policy. Specified by country limitation schedule.	All countries can be considered. Determined by each country's economic and political climate. Can include domestic sales Policy endorsed for countries covered	All countries can be considered except domestic sales. Determined by each country's economic and political climate. Policy endorsed for countries covered
CREDIT APPROVALS	Flexible Discretionary Credit Limits giving insured option to approve accounts to approved limits.	Discretionary Credit Limits giving insured option to approve accounts to approved limits.	Flexible Discretionary Credit Limits giving insured option to approve accounts to approved limits.	Flexible Discretionary Credit Limits giving insured option to approve accounts to approved limits.
DEDUCTIBLE	Policy year deductible, but one policy deductible can apply to shipments made to a buyer within 90 days of each other even if shipments were made in two policy years.	Per policy year deductible, based on date of shipment.	Policy year deductible, based on date of shipment.	Policy year deductible, based on date of shipment.
PREMIUM PAYMENT	Monthly or pre pay, determined as a percentage of insured sales. Requires spread of risk normally whole turnover	Monthly determined as a percentage of insured sales. Requires spread of risk normally whole turnover	Pre pay determined as a percentage of approved country limits. Requires spread of risk normally whole turnover. May be eligible for 5% refund.	Pre pay or quarterly installments, determined as a percentage of insured sales. Requires spread of risk or key accounts
MINIMUM PREMIUM	$10,000 per policy year. Minimum insured volume of $3,000,000.	$500 per policy year.	$10,000 per policy year. Minimum insured volume of $3,000,000.	$2,500 per policy year.
CLAIM FILING	90 days after due date.	90 days after due date	90-360 days after due date	180 days after due date

PLEASE NOTE THAT THIS CHART IS ONLY AN ADMINISTRATIVE GUIDE AND CONVEYS NO PERSONAL NOR AGENCY LIABILITY ON BEHALF OF INTERNATIONAL INSURANCE ASSOCIATES. (FCCOMP)
8202 FLORENCE AVENUE, SUITE 200
DOWNEY, CA 90240-3937

Figure 16-1. (Continued)

from credit sales in the course of a year. This figure is substantially less than total sales in an active short-term account with good turnover.

All the private sector policies include a first-loss deductible in a range of roughly 0.5 percent of anticipated foreign credit sales. But another advantage that all these insurers provide is that they do their own analysis of buyer credit, with the probability of applying greater experience and skill at no cost or a relatively low cost, before accepting the account for cover. This can be a substantial saving when the cost of credit reports is considered.

Eximbank Credit Insurance for Small Business

It is highly probable that if you are new to exporting and/or a small business, the best place to seek insurance is with one of Eximbank's two small-business short-term credit insurance policies. *Short term* is considered to be up to 180 days, extended somewhat in special circumstances but never longer than 360 days. The first alternative is the Umbrella Policy, offered through export associations, state agencies, and brokers specializing in international risk insurance on behalf of multiple exporters. Each Umbrella Policy is administered by experienced export credit insurance personnel whose participation, among other advantages, ensures that proper actions are taken and the paperwork maintained to keep each individual exporter's coverage valid and in force. The second alternative, called the Small Business Policy (formerly known as the New-to-Export Policy), is issued to individual businesses. They themselves are then wholly responsible for seeing that all records and responsibilities are properly taken care of in a timely fashion to keep the policy valid and in force.

The Umbrella Policy and the Small Business Policy share most of the characteristics that are designed to help small business get started exporting:

- 100 percent coverage of political risks and 95 percent coverage of commercial risk.

- No commercial risk first-loss deductible (unlike Eximbank's other insurance policies for larger exporters and private sector insurers).

- A "hold harmless" clause availability for lenders relying on the insured receivables, to assure the lender that any loan made against the receivables insured will not be invalidated due to exporter performance faults. This document is issued on request by the lender.

- Extended expiry dates of up to two years on creditworthy buyers, which provides the confidence necessary to invest in the work-in-process for project work or orders requiring extended production cycles. This is a recent improvement.

- Eligibility based on average annual export credit sales of less than $3 million. Once this level of sales is achieved, the export business is required to graduate to Eximbank's standard export credit policy, the Short-Term Multibuyer Policy.

However, there are also distinct differences between the two policies. The Umbrella Policy's special features include the following:

- No minimum fee for the exporter as it is paid by the administrator.
- Substantial administrative and clerical follow-up, which assures the new exporter that the policy is in force and that claims will be paid. As might be expected, this creates an overhead expense that must be compensated for, so the Umbrella Policy has a substantially higher rate—in the range of 35 to 50 cents per hundred. Administrative oversight can be very helpful, however, to an operation that is not yet organized, when it comes to tracking necessary details.

The Small Business Policy's special features include:

- A new enhancement providing for some discretionary Special Buyer Credit Limits (SBCL) which, until recently, were only available in the regular Multibuyer master policy. The convenience and effectiveness this feature can give an active policyholder with a number of accounts is hard to estimate.
- An annual minimum fee of $500.

In both policies, it should be emphasized, the hold harmless feature is a major incentive to lenders, encouraging them to offer foreign accounts receivable lending to smaller business. The caveat is that when a lender is paid off under the hold harmless clause, the liability of an exporter remains *if* insurance coverage was invalidated by virtue of fraud or failure to maintain and report proper records or complete the required timely actions remains. Eximbank will pursue such an exporter for restitution of the payment made to the lender. For the exporter, the absence of a first-loss deductible in either policy is equivalent to a major reduction of the effective cost of insurance compared to all other policies, public or private, and makes it well worthwhile to stay with one of these two special policies as long as eligible.

Other Eximbank Credit Insurance Policies

Qualified businesses that do not meet the $3 million limit can still obtain special advantages from Eximbank's insurance division, so long as they qualify under SBA's definition of "small"—which gets pretty big. The special breaks for the "small" category are built into several of their policies, including the Multibuyer and Single Buyer policies. If your company's products include equipment meant to improve the environment, it is worth checking the details of the Environmental Export Insurance Policy for the attendant special benefits.

Multibuyer Master Policy.   Eximbank's standard Short-Term Multibuyer Master Policy also has some advantages for those who qualify. The rates are substantially lower than the new-to-export policies unless the export business specializes in high-risk countries. Another valuable feature is the greater discretionary freedom allowed for adding new accounts to be covered without first obtaining a special buyer credit limit (SBCL) and for expanding the limits of existing SBCL accounts as the buyer's business increases. On the minus side, there is a larger minimum annual premium, and the first-loss deductible may be in the range of 0.5 percent to over 1 percent of annual export credit sales. The Multibuyer Policy may also be obtained as a medium-term or combination policy.

Single Buyer Policies.   If you are an exporter needing only occasional insurance for larger sales or even one having a multibuyer policy but with a unique and perhaps larger-than-usual sale opportunity, there are short-term single buyer policies. These can solve many problems, but there are substantial minimum premiums that vary with the circumstances, so it must be a substantial sale to warrant considering. For small businesses (those with export credit sales of less than $3 million), the minimum premium is $1000; for all others, the minimum is $10,000 for private sector buyers, $5000 for letters of credit or nonsovereign public buyers, and $2500 for public buyers.

   With single buyer policies, there is no need to insure other transactions or buyers that you feel do not need to be insured. That option is somewhat restricted in the case of the small-business policies and the Multibuyer Policy, for Eximbank does not want an exporter to cherry-pick the accounts to be insured within a general world territory; Eximbank, like most insurers needs some "spread of risk." If the business qualifies as a "small business" by SBA's definition, the single buyer minimum premium may be only $1000. Environmental equipment exporters get the same break on single buyer policies.

Medium-Term Policies.   The duration of medium-term cover is considered to be one to seven years for values of under $10 million and, once again, Eximbank is often the only game in town for anything but very substantial businesses. Eximbank has recently expanded and enhanced its medium-term cover and is therefore getting a great deal more use. The prime enhancements are a coverage increase to 100 percent for both commercial and political risk and the availability of Eximbank's hold harmless protection to the lender. Because of these two features, this new medium-term version is now being used in relation to bank lending that formerly would have required Eximbank's credit guarantee program. The bank's credit guarantee and lending activities relative to buyer credit will be explained briefly in Chapter 19.

Special Eximbank Insurance Coverage. Eximbank has many other policies for special purposes. Among them are policies banks can use to insure the exporters they lend to; letter-of-credit insurance; lease financing polices; service industry policies; and special policies constructed for specific trade associations. Similarly, there is special coverage to be added by amendment to some policies, such as preshipment coverage, nonacceptance coverage, consignment sales coverage, and even a foreign exchange endorsement.

In summary, if you have reason to think about credit insurance, you should at least first review what Eximbank has to offer. Eximbank's headquarters address is United States Export-Import Bank, 811 Vermont Avenue NW, Washington, D.C. 20571. Call the bank's automated information number at 800/565-EXIM, or contact its regional offices in Chicago; Houston; Long Beach, California; New York; or Miami. The regional offices are well equipped to discuss all of Eximbank's small business programs, especially insurance. In the case of insurance they can either sell you a policy directly or refer you to a qualified specialty broker. Most general insurance agents do not write or understand the Eximbank policies.

Overseas Private Investment Corporation Insurance

The Overseas Private Investment Corporation (OPIC) is a source of both political risk and commercial risk insurance for those dealing with less-developed countries as contractors or investors. Through OPIC's offices, you can insure against such problems as expropriation, political violence, or inconvertibility and protect equipment and unfinished work as well as ongoing overseas investments. The list of countries for which OPIC offers support is specific and changes from time to time. (Additional details about this interesting, self-sustaining quasigovernmental organization in Washington, D.C. may be found in Chapter 17.)

Transportation Risks

Transit risk is the second prime risk in international trade. It can be managed and insured in such a way that even a major misfortune need not threaten your business except in the most extreme circumstances.

When considering transportation insurance, many people seem to think that there is little to worry about unless a plane crashes or a ship sinks, but Barry Tarnef of CIGNA, writing in the May 1993 issue of *Export Today*, put that myth to rest with some illustrative horror stories. One concerned a very costly yacht that had been stored on deck next to a huge crane that was welded in place for the voyage. All went well until arrival, when the stevedores tried to "protect" the yacht with what proved to be a flammable tarp when they torched the weld prior to the crane's removal. Another story concerned a valuable load of antiques shipped in midwinter in a 20-foot container that proved to be a bit leaky. On arrival the antiques were discovered frozen in a solid block of ice. Pilferage is a major danger, typified by the shipment of a famous women's sportswear brand from its manufacturing point in Turkey to New York via Paris, where a transfer by local cartage truck was necessary between Orly Airport and Charles DeGaulle Airport. The brand name was clearly displayed on the shipping boxes in large letters and as a consequence much of the shipment never left Paris.

The first transit coverage we'll explore is marine insurance, for it is the oldest form of transit insurance and has traditions and history that have impacted the development of insurance for other modes of transportation.

Open Cargo Policies

The most common form of transport policy a shipper might carry is the open cargo policy, usually providing all-risk, warehouse-to-warehouse marine insurance. It might also include comparable insurance for air-freight and parcel post and the several other modes of transportation that can be involved in today's growing multimodal shipping systems. In multimodal shipping, two, three, or even four transport modes may be involved, sometimes one on top of the other, as in rail/truck piggyback shipments, and every form of transit is covered under one bill of lading. Most open cargo policies include insurance and rates for air cargo and should be utilized accordingly. Otherwise, the liability of the airline is restricted to a $1 value per pound, as in domestic trucking, and it is rarely sufficient to cover full value. For a valuation charge, however, flight-by-flight coverage can be obtained.

A step up from the open cargo policy is the blanket policy, which is a negotiated policy covering all of a shipper's needs with substantial deductibles. It is normally used only by larger shipping operations.

Alternatives to an Open Cargo Policy

An alternative to the open cargo policy is a shipment-by-shipment policy specifically tailored to the risks perceived and often somewhat less comprehensive. This approach is fairly convenient, and adequate coverage can be obtained on this basis from the air carriers. Single-voyage marine policies are available from brokers with varying degrees of risk protection, including all-risk. A more likely solution for the start-up or occasional exporter would be to piggyback on the freight forwarder's open cargo policy for either air or marine shipments. You buy the risk protection at retail, so to speak. But the forwarder probably has a good policy which, because of the forwarder's volume, experience, and wide spread of risk has lower base rates than those applied to a start-up export operation.

Special Coverages

Contingency insurance coverage is something to consider when the buyer is taking responsibility for insurance, for if the shipment is damaged, the buyer will have little interest in paying for it in case the buyer's insurance was inadequate or absent altogether. Contingency coverage reimburses the shipper for any omission or inadequacy in the buyer's coverage. It costs a fraction of regular coverage, so even though the cost must be borne by the shipper, it is well worth it, especially when no regular relationship has yet developed between buyer and seller.

Another special policy coverage to consider is war-risk coverage. This is not part of regular marine insurance or an all-risk open cargo policy. When the buyer requests a *cost, insurance, and freight* (CIF) or *carriage and insurance paid to* (CIP) quote, this coverage is not included according to the Incoterms definition, unless specified. Many shippers take it anyway as a matter of course because it is inexpensive, as long as the carrier's route does not enter or approach a war zone. The problem is, when there *is* a real and present danger, the coverage can become very expensive, sometimes even prohibitive, and the cost can fluctuate greatly within a matter of a few days. Once issued, however, the rate is firm as of the date of shipment. Therefore, it is advisable to make specific arrangements with your buyer as to this coverage and its cost if you are shipping into an area of conflict. Be sure to ask specifically that this policy be attached to the marine policy, for it cannot be added by endorsement.

Determining How Much
Coverage to Get

In determining what minimum insurance coverage you must have, review again the Incoterm definitions of the shipping terms agreed upon. The insurance required is clear-cut in the case of CIP, CIF or any of the "delivered" terms, because the shipper is fully responsible for obtaining insurance and without a certificate or policy to submit with the documents, would presumably be unable to negotiate the letter of credit. With *free on board* (FOB) or *free carrier* (FCA) and similar terms, the risk of loss lies with the shipper until the goods are delivered into the hands of the carrier or its agent, or until they cross the ship's rails for ocean shipments. An FOB or FCA endorsement to an open cargo policy will cover this transit-risk exposure from the point of origin until the risk transfers. It is wise to consider this coverage, because truck and cartage responsibilities are minimal and do not begin to cover most valuations.

The norm for the dollar amount of coverage is 110 percent, which is intended to cover miscellaneous transaction costs or minimal profit. Unless otherwise advised, consider 110 percent of value as the benchmark. For special coverages other than all-risk and warehouse-to-warehouse, which have become standard cover today, consult your forwarder or insurance agent regarding the general average clause. *Average,* as used in marine insurance, refers to "loss less than total," and is used in calculating losses over and above your own, including damage to the ship itself and to other cargo. Coverage referred to as with average (WA) cover and free of particular average (FPA) cover, the narrowest of the coverages, is most often used in the case of bulk cargo. An example would be nonperishable cargoes, such as scrap iron, for which a maritime loss incident would either be total or no loss at all.

The general average concept for marine insurance is difficult to understand, but its impact can result in an additional financial obligation to the shipper. If unpaid, this obligation results in the sacrifice of the salvaged cargo owned by the shipper. For a full explanation of marine insurance policies and background, ask your agent for a copy of the excellent booklet prepared by The Insurance Company of North America (a CIGNA company) entitled *Marine Insurance: Notes and Comments on Ocean Cargo Insurance.*[1]

Endnote

1. The Insurance Company of North America, *Marine Insurance: Notes and Comments on Ocean Cargo Insurance,* 1986.

PART 5

Public Sector Programs

17
Government Support for Export Marketing

There are many government agencies, most of them federal, whose mandate is to encourage U.S. businesses to export and thereafter to help them get started, obtain commercial intelligence on overseas opportunities, insure their overseas risks, and sometimes help them finance the sale or project. This is accomplished with differing levels of efficiency, depending on the agency, its current budget, and any special focus or emphasis currently dominating the federal or state government's interest. With so many governmental budgets seemingly in a crisis state, times can be difficult for these agencies. However, there also exists a strong realization, in both the public and private sectors, of a national need to increase exports and develop jobs. This realization tends to preserve, or even expand, the spending authority of the entities charged with export support. In this chapter we will explore that support, with an emphasis on export research and export marketing.

Once again, however, I must call to your attention the dramatic changes proposed at this moment in the federal public sector regarding certain departments and agencies and their budgets as a result of the 104th Congress's efforts to shrink government. Such efforts usually also involve greater "cost recovery" in the form of higher fees for government services. Nowhere have the changes in government been as dramatic as in the case of the Department of Commerce, which may be the first cabinet-level department ever to be disbanded—and possibly in fairly short order. If so, as I explained in Chapter 2, most of the functions and programs of Commerce will continue to go forward, but under the masthead of some other agency or department. There is support for most of the assistance the Department of Commerce provides to international traders, so here the problem will be to find out exactly where things have been moved, rather than whether they still exist. Most of Commerce's international functions are carried out within its International Trade

Administration (ITA), which includes the U.S. and Foreign Commercial Service (US&FCS), even now in the process of informalizing its name to the Commercial Service. It has been proposed that both agencies might be moved in their entirety to the U.S. Trade Representative (USTR) and be known as the International Trade Office (ITO), but the possibility of this happening is beginning to seem less likely.

In view of the slowdown of the most aggressive proposals and the House Appropriations Subcommittee's positive recommendations of a continued emphasis on export assistance and support (as the final editing was being done on this book in early 1996), it is reasonable to believe that the ITA's international functions will escape excessively severe cutbacks. In fact, *increases* were recommended insofar as ITA's Commercial Service's overseas offices and operations were concerned. I feel fairly secure, therefore, in assuming that the international trade activities covered by ITA programs, as revised and upgraded in 1994 and 1995, will continue to function for at least the next few years, even if some names, agencies, or even departments change. I will summarize them as they existed in late 1995, with the caveat that the reader keep a lookout for possible new locations of these functions should the 104th Congress succeed in its efforts.

International Trade Administration

The International Trade Administration (ITA) is divided into four units:

1. The Import Administration
2. International Economic Policy
3. Trade Development
4. The U.S. and Foreign Commercial Service, or Commercial Service

The Import Administration unit is not actually germane to this book. Its involvement with imports is mostly through its focus on the victims of unfair trade practices and its administration of trade restraint agreements and foreign trade zones.

International Economic Policy

The International Economic Policy unit's primary value to an export company would be via its "country desks" located in Washington, D.C. Each country desk is staffed by an officer who specializes in the affairs and activities of a major country, or cluster of smaller countries, as it might affect or influence the activities of an exporter to that area. These desk officers can be a useful source of information before you travel overseas or when you need the most current possible answer to a specific question and you can't find it in the usual statistics or country background information.

Trade Development

The Trade Development unit is also organized by "desks" to focus on specific industries and their trade problems and to facilitate those industries' trade promotion efforts. Industries are divided into five broad industry groups:

1. Technology and aerospace
2. Basic industries (including automotive, machinery and chemicals, energy, and infrastructure)
3. Textiles, apparel, and consumer goods industries
4. Service industries and finance
5. Environmental technology exports

U.S. Foreign and Commercial Service

By far the most important unit and the one most used by exporters is the U.S. Foreign and Commercial Service (US&FCS), now more commonly known as the Commercial Service. This organization maintains overseas Commercial Service trade specialists, augmented by local experts in 69 U.S. embassies and consulates in major export markets around the world. It also maintains close contact with another 96 embassies and 36 consulates not covered by US&FCS staff. In cooperation with several other agencies, including the Department of Agriculture's Foreign Agriculture Service (FAS). The organization is the source of much of the commercial intelligence available to exporters. The Commercial Service has a domestic presence through its U.S. staff of Trade Specialists in 47 district office locations, plus 22 branches in 69 U.S. cities.

The trade specialists assist export-ready U.S. firms continue or expand existing export operations with planning and research activities. Although the Commercial Service exists for all exporters, there is so much demand for its trade specialists' time that the concept evolved of having them focus on "export-ready" firms. Today's smaller, new-to-export firms and individuals gain part of their support from The Small Business Administration, which also has international trade specialists and SCORE advisors with international experience. The SBA is well equipped to help small firms with basic business advice and counseling.

Other ITA and DOC Related Offices or Units of Exporter Interest

In addition to the four major units or divisions of the ITA there are other, special offices of interest to exporters. Some of them are administered by ITA and some fall under other jurisdictions. One of the ITA-administered offices is the Office of Export Trading Company Affairs, which can offer certain industry groups or coalitions protection from antitrust charges when they engage in cooperative export efforts or promotions. Another is the Multilateral Development Bank Operations (MDBO) office. The MDBO helps exporters utilize the opportunities that are generated either by the World Bank, which functions on a global level, or by the various public sector banks that fund infrastructure projects in specific regions around the world.

There are still other ITA offices or bureaus not under the ITA's supervision that nevertheless are vital to exporters. One is the Bureau of the Census, which collects and disseminates much of the government's international trade statistics. The Census Bureau can provide you with detailed figures on a wide variety of export-related matters, such as how much of any product range, as defined by the Schedule B commodity code, the United States is exporting to or importing from any given country in the world. This detailed information is available directly from the Census Bureau through its Trade Data Services. Census statistics also play an important role on the National Trade Data Bank (NTDB) CD-ROM discs. In addition, there is the National Institute for Standards and Technology (NIST), which provides both domestic and foreign product standards information; the National Technical Information Service (NTIS), which is an archive and clearinghouse of research and technical information; the U.S. Travel and Tourism Administration, which promotes the export of U.S services in the form of tourism and travel marketing; and the National Oceanic and Atmospheric Administration, which provides the seafood industry with market access. The Bureau of Export Administration's management of export controls and licensing is a vital component of technology and other special exports. (It is discussed further in Chapter 19.) Within DOC there are also a number of special programs for manufacturing and technology sharing.

Office names, programs, and activities mentioned in the 1992 DOC *Basic Guide to Exporting* have continued to change since its last official publication in 1992. I remind you again of the most current alternative, the free booklet from the Trade Information Center (TIC), *Export Programs: A Business Directory of Government Services*, which is now printed annually.[1] The TIC is the central clearinghouse for sources of export assistance from many agencies and departments of the federal government and has a very easy-to-remember TIC number, 1-800/USA-TRADE (800/872-8723). Call it to order the booklet or obtain it from your nearest DOC District Office. The TIC itself is an invention of the relatively new Trade Promotion Coordinating Committee (TPCC). This interagency group increases the usefulness of all the federal export-support programs by coordinating their activities to improve efficiency. The TIC is an example of this coordinated effort. The TIC phones are manned by trade specialists in Washington, D.C., who can answer your questions or refer you to other offices or agencies that can help. For a book detailing the application of DOC programs and those of other agencies as they might apply to export marketing, insuring, and financing, consider *Exporting: From Start to Finance* by L. Fargo Wells and Karin B. Dulat, the 1995 edition.[2] Another book is *Inside Washington: Government Resources for International Business* by William A. Delphos.[3] Though published in 1992, and thus not reflective of recent changes, Delphos's book is an exhaustive catalog of international trade help from all areas of government.

International Trade Administration Services and Information

Following is a list briefly describing the various ITA services and information sources. Many of these facilities have previously been described relative to a particular phase of the export process, but here we relate them as a family of services by provider. They are subject to change, and a few are not mentioned because of their questionable value to the reader. Your DOC trade specialist or SBA trade officer will be able to help you focus on the services most useful for your purposes.

Export Counseling. Export counseling services are those that offer advice or assistance on a one-to-one basis. These services are particularly useful for exporters with some experience who need to resolve a special problem or plan a new campaign. In the case of newer exporters, they should work with their SBA and/or Commercial Service trade specialist after formulating a focused start-up plan and seek the specialists' suggestions as to which of the following sources of assistance will be of most help.

Trade Information Center. If you can be quite specific as to your needs, calling the Trade Information Center, at 800/USA-TRADE, is an excellent idea, but is not a substitute for a working relationship with a trade specialist in your nearest DOC district office or SBA office.

U.S. Export Assistance Centers. The U.S. Export Assistance Centers (USEAC) constitute another interagency device in selected major cities. Designed by the TPCC to facilitate ready access to both marketing and financing help, the centers include staff from the DOC district offices, SBA, and Eximbank, plus such other organizations as the Agency for International Development (AID) when available. By the end of 1995 or early 1996, there should be 15 major cities with USEAC facilities. Ask your nearest DOC district office for the location in your area.

DOC District Office.   At this time, this office remains the heart and soul of the federal government's export marketing support system. If your first experience with the district office is not all you would like it to be vis-à-vis any of its counseling agencies or overseas Commercial Service offices, do not fail to try again. Some members of the staff are always better qualified than others, and you may find better communication and rapport the second or third time around. It is a person-to-person relationship that depends on each party's ability to relate to the other. Remember, too, that its staffers are often overworked, due to peak demand or short staffing. Incidentally, I am told the DOC district offices are renaming themselves District-Export-Assistance Centers (DEACs). This does seem a more apt name and parallels the new USEACS, so I hope this change at least stands firm.

Export Counseling from Regional Business Centers.   Regional business centers are typically focused on especially dynamic areas of economic opportunity or on economies in transition that the ITA terms as "big emerging markets." The centers are called American Business Centers, but some of the newer big emerging markets have what are called U.S. Commercial Centers, including São Paulo, Brazil, and Jakarta, Indonesia. The TIC information number, 800-USA-TRADE, can update you on active American Business Centers or U.S. Commercial Centers and their location and provide whatever special information and assistance is available relative to an area of your particular interest. Most also have parallel fax retrieval systems, permitting you to obtain prepared information on the area or subject of a very current nature. The regional centers currently operating are:

- U.S.–Asia Environmental Partnership (US-AEP)
- Business Information Service for the Newly Independent States (BIS-NIS)
- Eastern Europe Business Information Center (EEBIC)
- Japan Export Information Center (JEIC)

Fee-Based Custom Information Services.   The following services involve a specific fee per service, but in most cases it is very modest relative to the requirements and, hopefully, the results. These are frequently used and usually very useful sources of information that have been greatly enhanced in terms of being current and fairly accurate as a result of the DOC electronic databases and information transfer systems.

Agent/Distributor Service.   The Agent/Distributor Service (ADS), a customized service based on Commercial Service staff research to help exporters identify up to six reputable prospects—including agents, distributors, and foreign representatives—who have been provided with the requesting firm's product literature and have expressed an interest. The current price, subject to change, is $250.

World Trader Data Reports. A function handled by the Commercial Service for checking buyer credibility, reputation, and general financial status is the *World Trader Data Report (WTDR)*, which gives the year established, size, number of employees, products handled, and a recommendation as to suitability as a trading partner from the overseas field officer. The current price is $100 per report.

Export Contact List Service. A current and customized database retrieval of buyer contacts, including names, addresses, contact, size, products handled, and other relevant information on prospective foreign buyers. The names are collected by the Commercial Service personnel in the district offices and commercial officers in overseas posts, with the Foreign Traders Index database as a starting point.

Customized Sales Survey. This micromarket research service is also conducted by the Commercial Service overseas staff and provides marketing information about specific products in given countries to help exporters define their distribution strategies, representation, pricing, competition, trade practices, trade barriers, and the most applicable trade events. It is only available for major trading countries with well-staffed Commercial Service offices. The current price is from $800 to $3500 per country and product.

DOC/ITA Computerized Databases and Fax Retrieval Systems. The fax, floppy disk, CD-ROM, and computer networks have almost taken over the job of disseminating information, statistics, and new developments. The federal network is FEDWORLD, which can be accessed through the Internet or by direct dial. Following are some of the chief sources.

National Trade Data Bank. The National Trade Data Bank (NTDB) is the star of the new information age. It is also an interagency effort supplied by 17 agencies, including several divisions of Commerce, in addition to ITA, the Department of Agriculture, the Department of State, the Department of Energy, the Department of Labor, the Bureau of Export Administration, the Federal Reserve, the U.S. Trade Representative, the Bureau of the Census, the Export-Import Bank, the Overseas Private Investment Corporation, and the Small Business Administration. Each monthly edition contains approximately 100,000 updated documents (about two libraries' worth), covering 49 programs besides the CIA's *World Factbook,* the monthly edition of *Business America,* and the *Basic Guide to Exporting.* Included among this myriad of reports are most of the current import/export statistics by commodity and country needed for market research; the new and current *Country Commercial Guides,* which combine eight interagency reports into one comprehensive and detailed report; the Foreign Traders Index of 55,000 foreign firms that have inquired about U.S. products from our overseas offices or from the DOC (listed together with names, addresses, and other details, including products handled); and software programs to assist in browsing. The NTDB comes on two updated CD-ROM discs each month at a cost of $360 per year, or $40 for any individual month's issue. Alternatively, the CD-ROMs may be reviewed at any of the nearly 900 Federal Depository libraries around the country, as well as at various world trade centers and the Commercial Service offices or the USEACs and Small Business Development Centers (SBDCs). See Figure 17-1 for an index of the NTDB's contents.

Country Commercial Guides. The *Country Commercial Guides* represent such a useful tool to the average exporter for quickly obtaining current information on any given country or region that they are listed here again as a separate entity although at this time they can only be accessed through the NTDB disc mentioned above. Since these reports can be very long, running to well over 100 pages, most users download for printing only those portions of a guide pertinent to their needs. Each guide's table of contents is divided into nine subjects:

1. Commercial Overview
2. Leading Trade Prospects for U.S. Business
3. Economic Trends and Outlook
4. Political Environment
5. Marketing U.S. Products and Services
6. Trade Regulations and Standards
7. Investment Climate
8. Trade and Project Financing
9. Business Travel

Foreign Traders Index. The Foreign Traders Index (FTI) is another database that is available by itself or as part of the NTDB. It is an excellent tool, and is particularly useful for a start-up export process and therefore deserves special mention. The FTI is in large part the underlying database for the Export Contract List Service. The index contains over 55,000 names, is categorized by country and commodity, and provides the company address, telephone, contact name, year established, number of employees, relative size, date of their U.S. inquiry, and products handled by name and harmonized code.

Economic Bulletin Board. The Economic Bulletin Board (EBB) is a PC-based electronic bulletin board offered as an on-line (or by fax) source for up-to-the-minute Trade Opportunities Program leads virtually the day an overseas inquiry is received. In addition, the EBB provides the latest statistics from the Bureau of Census, Economic Analysis, Department of Labor, and other agencies. The annual registration is $45, plus modest on-line charges,

U.S. Department of Commerce
Office of Business Analysis
HCHB Room 4885
Washington, D.C. 20230

Tel (202) 482-1986
Fax (202) 482-2164

❑ **Board of Governors of the Federal Reserve**
Foreign Spot Exchange Rates
Foreign Three-Month Interest Rates
Stock Price Indices for the G-10 Countries
U.S. Three-month CD Interest Rates
Weighted Average Exchange Value of the Dollar

❑ **Central Intelligence Agency**
Handbook of Economic Statistics
The World Factbook

❑ **Export-Import Bank of the United States**
Export-Import Bank of the United States, Quarterly Report

❑ **Office of the U.S. Trade Representative**
National Trade Estimates Report on Foreign Trade Barriers
North American Free Trade Agreement
Trade Projections Report to the Congress

❑ **Overseas Private Investment Corporation**
OPIC Program Summaries

❑ **Department of State**
Background Notes
Key Officers of Foreign Service Posts
Resource Guide to Doing Business in Central and
  Eastern Europe
Country Reports on Economic Policy and Trade Practices

❑ **U.S. International Trade Commission**
Trade Between the U.S. & Non-Market Economy Countries

❑ **U.S. Small Business Administration**
Small Business and Export Information System

❑ **University of Massachusetts (MISER)**
State of Origin of Exports

❑ **Department of Agriculture, Foreign
Agricultural Service**
Foreign Production, Supply & Distribution of Agricultural
  Commodities

❑ **Department of Commerce/ Economics &
Statistics Administration (ESA), Bureau of
Economic Analysis**
Fixed Reproducible Tangible Wealth Estimates
Foreign Direct Investment in the U.S.: Balance of
  Payments Basis
International Services
National Income & Product Accounts, Annual Series
National Income & Product Accounts, Quarterly Series
Operations of U.S. Affiliates of Foreign Companies
Operations of U.S. Parent Companies & Their Foreign Affiliates
U.S. Assets Abroad & Foreign Assets in the U.S.
U.S. Businesses Acquired & Established by Foreign Direct
  Investors
U.S. Direct Investment Abroad: Position, Capital, Income
U.S. Expenditure for Pollution Abatement & Control (PAC)
U.S. International Transactions (Balance of Payments basis)
U.S. Merchandise Trade (Balance of Payments basis)

❑ **Department of Commerce/Bureau of Export
Administration (BXA)**
BXA Today
Bureau of Export Administration Annual Report
Export Licensing Information

❑ **Department of Commerce/ ESA, Bureau of
the Census**
Exports from Manufacturing Establishments
Merchandise Trade-Imports by Commodity
Merchandise Trade-Exports by Commodity
Merchandise Trade-Imports by Country
Merchandise Trade-Exports by Country
Total Mid-Year Populations & Projections through 2050
Trade and Employment

❑ **Department of Commerce/International
Trade Administration**
Business America
A Basic Guide to Exporting
Domestic & International Coal Issues and Markets
Eastern Europe Looks for Partners
EC 1992: A Commerce Department Analysis of EC Directives
Europe Now: A Report
Export Programs: A Business Directory of U.S.
  Government Resources
Export Promotion Calendar
Export Yellow Pages
Foreign Direct Investment in the U.S. - Annual Transactions
Foreign Traders Index
Investment Guides
Market Research Reports: Country Marketing Plans; Industry
  Subsector Analyses; Foreign Economic Trends
North American Free Trade Agreement (NAFTA) Information
Trade Promotion Coordinating Committee Calendar of Events
Understanding U.S. Foreign Trade Data
U.S. Foreign Trade Update - Monthly Analysis
U.S. Industrial Outlook
U.S. Manufacturers Trade Performance - Quarterly Report

❑ **Department of Commerce/National Institute
of Standards & Technology**
GATT Standards Code Activities of NIST
Organizations Conducting Standards-Related Activities
National Standards & Metric Information Programs

❑ **Department of Commerce/ESA, Office of
Business Analysis**
NTDB BROWSE Manual
Sources of Information and Contacts

❑ **Department of Energy/Energy Information
Administration**
International Energy Annual

❑ **Department of Labor/Bureau of
Labor Statistics**
International Labor Statistics
International Price Indices

(Contents are listed as they appear in the NTDB and are subject to change)

Figure 17-1. Index of NTDB's contents.

with the first $20 of use covered by the registration fee. Alternatively, you can participate in the EBB by fax on demand at no subscription fee but at the higher cost of 65 cents per minute. Call TIC for details.

Trade Opportunities Program. The Trade Opportunities Program (TOP) provides companies with current trade leads from international firms seeking specific American products or services. The new arrivals are posted daily and can be accessed through the EBB mentioned above or can be found daily in leading commercial newspapers, most notably the *Journal of Commerce.*

Regional Fax Retrieval Systems. Although no staff is on hand for personal counseling, these are excellent databases that contain very current information in sharp focus relative to the region involved. The current list of offices to contact, besides those already mentioned relative to the regional business centers, includes:

- Office of NAFTA and the Office of Latin America and the Caribbean Business Development Center (Amerifax)
- Office of the Pacific Basin
- Office of Africa, Near East, and South Asia

Trade Fair and Exhibit Activities. These events can be of enormous help to you if you want to get fully involved in export activities. They help put you and your product directly into a region, lessen the need for advance planning and logistics, and offer qualified help at the show or event for guidance and even translation. Participation in them is also less expensive than independent participation in private sector shows, because Commerce normally provides special U.S. pavilions to create attention and to share costs. Your district trade specialist will have a calendar of events around the world and can help you select the most appropriate events. The ubiquitous NTDB disc also contains a current calendar of trade show events planned for about one year ahead. These exhibit activities are divided into five categories:

1. *Foreign buyer shows.* U.S. shows that attract a high level of foreign buyer attendance. The Commercial Service publicizes the event overseas and provides staff to facilitate direct contact and meeting with the foreign buyers registering at the show.

2. *Catalog and video exhibitions.* A very inexpensive, but not always effective, way of pictorially presenting your product overseas under the supervision of the Commercial Service staff or an industry expert hired for the occasion. Often one such show is organized to display in a series of countries in a region.

3. *Trade missions.* Business development events focused on a single industry, organized to introduce the overseas market to U.S. firms so they can gain advance contacts and publicity and develop a well conceived entry strategy.

4. *Matchmaker trade delegations.* Similar to missions, but with a broader focus and at a lower cost. Discuss these with your trade specialist to be sure the event will fit your objective in light of the other firms attending and the overall itinerary.

5. *Trade fairs and exhibitions.* These are the prestige events for presenting your products and making new sales contacts. About 80 to 100 trade fairs each year are selected by the DOC to include a U.S. pavilion and for which the ITA assists in organizing and recruiting U.S. exhibitors. The basic fee, before other costs, is in the range of $2500 to $12,000. The ITA also certifies additional events as good opportunities but does not become involved in their organization or recruitment except to provide field officers from the area to be on hand for assistance.

ITA Trade Publications. Once again the line between printed and electronic dissemination of trade news and information becomes blurred. For instance, the long-standing monthly magazine, *Business America*, can now be accessed from the NTDB discs at no extra cost. The magazine follows the DOC party line on trade policies, but it is useful for keeping up with developments in Commerce and provides good information on the part of the world each particular issue focuses on. The *Export Yellow Pages* is an annual directory of 18,000 U.S. manufacturing firms, banks, export service providers, and export trading companies. It is distributed to 275 embassies, consulates, and overseas posts in quantity, and redistributed by them to qualified buyers in the country. Free copies are available from your DOC district office and it is included in the NTDB discs.

One particularly effective publication is strictly oriented to foreign buyers. It is called *Commercial News U.S.A.*, and is published 10 times a year to display and promote the services and products of U.S. firms at a very modest cost. It is said to reach 125,000 business readers and government officials in 155 countries, where it is distributed free, plus many more through bulletin board subscribers. Contact TIC at 800/USA-TRADE for more details.

In addition to these publications, there are hundreds of pamphlets, books, and reports on the subject of international trade available from the Government Printing Office (GPO). Catalogs are available at no charge or the GPO can send a list specifically listing publications covering international trade. Call the GPO at 202/512-1800.

Department of Agriculture

The Department of Agriculture (USDA) has its own export priorities and programs, with far greater budget support and subsidization than does the DOC's International Trade Administration that handles manufactured goods, especially when one considers that agriculture accounts for only 10 percent of total exports. This is a distortion that will probably become even greater when the 104th Congress completes its work. Exporting, importing, and all overseas activities of the USDA are administered by the Foreign Agricultural Service (FAS). Thanks to the Trade Promotion Coordinating Committee (TPCC) and its National Export Strategy, there is now better interagency cooperation between the DOC and USDA in terms of pooling information and reports—as in the case of the *Country Commercial Guides*—and somewhat less overlap of programs as well.

Foreign Agricultural Service

The Foreign Agricultural Service (FAS) is broken into five areas, each with deputy administrators, of which the last three named are of special interest to the agricultural exporter. The five areas are:

1. *International Trade Policy.* This unit deals with policy at the level of the General Agreement on Tariffs & Trade (GATT), including subsidy issues. It makes U.S. policy known and reacts to the policies and trade practices of other nations.
2. *International Cooperation and Development.* This unit is responsible for international-organization affairs, research, and scientific exchange.
3. *Foreign Agricultural Affairs.* This unit is similar to the US&FCS in that it contains the overseas offices located in about 80 U.S. embassies and covering 100 countries. These offices are responsible for global reporting, market development and expansion, detection of trade barriers, and related activities.
4. *Export Credit.* This unit administers those export activities relating to USDA's wholly owned financing corporation known as the Commodity Credit Corporation (CCC).
5. *Commodity and Marketing Programs.* This unit, also known as C&MP, is the one of greatest immediate interest to exporters of agriculture. It administers programs that include subsidized support for market penetration or that offset foreign subsidized competition, always with a focus on specific commodities or commodity clusters. There is a director for each of six broad agricultural areas: grains and feeds; oilseeds and oilseed products; tobacco and cotton; horticultural and tropical products; dairy, livestock, poultry, and seafood; forest products.

FAS Counseling and Research Assistance

Many of the tools or programs for agriculture are very similar to the export programs and services for manufactured products or services and are therefore described very briefly here because of the similar descriptions found in the DOC section.

Trade Assistance and Promotion Office. The Trade Assistance and Promotion Office (TAPO) is the initial contact point within FAS for exporters seeking information and research on foreign markets. It might be compared to the DOC district office, although in this case the office exists only in Washington D.C. While the ubiquitous interagency TIC number can direct you to the appropriate personnel within the FAS, it would be better to approach TAPO directly, by calling 202/720-7420 (or fax 202/690-4374), to ask for specific assistance considering your problem or questions.

AgExport Connections. This program group offers four contact or prospect research services on a fee- or cost-recovery basis for exporters:

- *Trade Leads*. Similar to TOP leads in Commerce. Like TOP, it can be accessed daily through the Economic Bulletin Board (EBB) or in the *Journal of Commerce* and perhaps in other commercial newspapers and agriculture-oriented publications, or by fax on the AgExport polling system.

- *Buyer Alert*. A weekly overseas newsletter designed to introduce food products to foreign buyers. A small fee is charged to the exporter for the announcement or advertisement.

- *Foreign Buyer Lists*. A database of details similar to the DOC's Foreign Traders Index on over 20,000 foreign importers of food products. It can be ordered for a specific commodity worldwide or by named countries at $15 per list.

- *U.S. Supplier Contact Lists*. A domestic database of 6500 names for sourcing various food and agricultural products. It is similar to the *Export Yellow Pages* available by commodity at $15 per list.

USDA Research, Publications, and Databases. In addition to the statistics, research, and data available from Commerce and the Census Bureau, including the much-discussed NTDB and the National Technical Information Service (NTIS), agricultural exporters have certain specialized research and data available.

Food Market Briefs. Each brief is a country-specific description of one of over 50 primary overseas markets for consumer food products, including trends, competition, labeling, licensing requirements and U.S. market positions. The briefs are a focused version of the *Country Commercial Guides* found in the NTDB and come from the same sources and research. They, too, may be added to the NTDB in time.

Economic Research Service. The Economic Research Service (ERS) provides in-depth economic analysis on agricultural economies, their foreign trade policies, and their linkage with the U.S. food and fiber economy.

Agricultural Trade and Marketing Center.   The Agricultural Trade and Marketing Center encompasses the National Agricultural Library and its AGRICOLA database which includes on-line systems. Assistance in accessing the computerized database is available.

General FAS Publications.   The monthly magazine for agricultural exporters is called the *AgExporter* and can be ordered directly from FAS or through NTIS as the central information distribution for a host of specialized reports, including monthly circulars, fact sheets, and *Agricultural Trade Highlights*.

Trade Shows and Overseas Activities

Trade shows and exhibits do not play as key a role for agricultural products as they do for manufactured products, but processed foods must be displayed to be sold. Therefore, FAS sponsors or participates in a number of international food and beverage expositions around the world. It also conducts sales missions, targeting emerging markets for consumer-ready foods. To assist in these activities it maintains about 20 Agricultural Trade Offices in strategic locations—somewhat like the DOC's U.S. Commercial Centers for "big emerging markets." These usually include space for meetings and conferences, together with kitchens and trade libraries to help individual agricultural exporters explore a particular market.

Technical Support

The USDA coordinates activities and provides information pertaining to the technical aspects of food distribution in the regions of the world. Among its concerns are food safety regulations, including pesticides, additives, labeling, and similar issues. USDA also provides guidance relative to transportation problems and issues the inspection certificates so often necessary to food imports and exports.

Commodity and Marketing Programs

The FAS unit, collectively known as the Commodity and Marketing Programs (C&MP), administers a wide range of subsidized or partly subsidized programs developed to encourage overseas market penetration or to fight foreign subsidies.

Market Promotion Programs.   Marketing promotion programs (MPP) promote a wide variety of commodities and food products worldwide. They are based on proposals initially drafted in the private sector or through state groups and national associations related to the proposed product promotion. If approved, they are advertised in the federal register for participation. These are usually short-term promotions and sometimes create controversy because private, often large businesses use the USDA's cash assistance to promote their own brand names.

Foreign Market Development Programs. Through its Foreign Market Development Program (FMD)—also known as the Cooperator Program—the FAS enters into long-term agreements with trade associations or individual businesses and with them shares the cost of specified overseas marketing and promotion of generic and occasional brand-name products with the objective of long-term market-share development. Surplus commodity stocks from the Commodity Credit Corporation (CCC), as well as USDA funds, are used to partially reimburse the organizations or business.

Export Enhancement Program. The Export Enhancement Program (EEP) is a totally subsidized program funded through CCC but administered by the C&MP office to provide assistance to agricultural commodities suffering from unfair trade practices or foreign subsidies. The most recent list of eligible commodities consists of wheat, wheat flour, eggs and certain other dairy products, vegetable oils, sunflower seed oils, and cottonseed oils.

Commodity Credit Corporation Export Programs

Although the Commodity Credit Corporation (CCC) programs provide financial support to export, it is not the kind of support that would normally be employed in a start-up situation. Nonetheless, these programs should be mentioned here as part of the overall USDA activities. The CCC's guarantees are particularly relevant in cases where the buyer is operating from a less-developed country with problems of currency inconvertibility or political risk. In such instances, the CCC's guarantees permit U.S. agricultural exporters to accept a buyer's letter of credit with time or usance terms for which bankers' acceptances would not otherwise be discountable at U.S. banks. If the exporter could not discount such bankers' acceptances, he or she would have to carry the acceptances to term, which would require a burdensome and impractical level of working capital.

There are two broad areas for the export side of CCC activity, one consisting of commercial programs in which the terms of sale are within the prevailing world market prices, and one that is concessional. All CCC activities related to export are administered by the Export Credit unit of the FAS.

GSM-102 Program. Of the commercial programs, the largest by far is known as GSM-102. It assists in letter-of-credit transactions by permitting extended terms of six months to three years for buyers whose countries may be experiencing currency restraints or political instability. For a modest fee, CCC provides a guarantee for 98 percent of the FAS or FOB commodity value to the bank accepting the letter-of-credit transaction and assumes that the bank will thereupon take the exporter out of the transaction altogether. The program only applies to certain listed commodities and countries, although others can be applied for. Most often the foreign government has already made application for a GSM-102 guarantee and its use is advertised as part of the bidding parameters.

GSM-103 Program. The GSM-103 program is similar to GSM-102 but is designed for terms of three to seven years and carries higher guarantee fees because it is intended for even less stable countries.

Public Law 480 Program. The Public Law 480 (PL 480) program is on strictly concessional terms for needy countries. In emergencies it may even be on a U.S government–gift basis, with the commodity procurement under competitive bids from the private sector; it is sometimes taken from CCC surplus stocks. The exporter clearly has no control over this government-to-government program except for the bidding and shipping process itself.

Small Business Administration

The Small Business Administration (SBA) has a wide range of programs for its broad definition of a small business (making most businesses eligible), but only a few of its programs are designed especially for exporters. The nonfinancial international programs are the only SBA programs to be discussed here, even though a small business may well find application for other SBA advisory programs that are not export-oriented but that will nevertheless assist a business in its export efforts. The SBA's entry into the international arena has at times been painful, both as to its export marketing and counseling programs and in terms of its export-targeted financial programs (the latter will be discussed in Chapter 18). Once again, the 104th Congress may play a role in SBA's future. Given SBA's past experience of dodging bullets and given the political impact of small business, the agency will largely survive, but there will be a smaller number of SBA branch offices, making physical access to SBA international programs more difficult. Even so, the SBA will have more offices, than the DOC has district offices, and where financing is involved, SBA will be more accessible than Eximbank in Washington, D.C.

Because many of the SBA's international programs so plainly overlap DOC's, on the marketing and promotion side, and Eximbank's, on the working capital side, its role has often been unclear. Now, however, a division of labor seems to have emerged: DOC trade specialists will focus on providing market and promotion assistance to the more export-ready firms, and SBA will specialize in assisting the really new-to-export companies and individual entrepreneurs just starting up in export. Of course, SBA can make any of the necessary research and statistics of both SBA and ITO available to the SBA exporter.

SBA Assistance and Outreach Programs

The SBA has been especially effective in organizing and partially funding export seminars, conferences, and expositions, and in securing shared support from the private sector. The SBA is also a natural for providing sound business advice and counsel to small business of whatever nature. Below are the SBA programs related to international business:

Small Business Answer Desk.   No one seems to be able to do without a tricky name for an all-purpose, automated-menu 800 number these days and SBA is no exception. It is designed to provide answers to some specific questions on domestic or international programs and refers the caller on to the department or desk best qualified to help the caller. The number is 1-800/U-ASK-SBA (800/827-5722).

Export Counseling and Training

SBA Office Counseling.   International trade specialists for individual counseling are offered in the district SBA offices and a few additional key offices. The 800-plus volunteer members of the Service Corp of Retired Executives (SCORE) with international experience are also available to help in any of the offices. They are aided by the 2500 members of the parallel Active Corp of Executives (ACE) who also have international experience.

U.S. Export Assistance Centers.   SBA staff are participants in approximately 15 interagency export assistance centers (USEACs) for advice and counseling in both finance and marketing. (They were described in the previous discussion of ITO programs.)

Small Business Development Centers.   These Small Business Development Centers (SBDC) are usually established by the state government or local area associations or other participants, in cooperation with the SBA. Many have some specialists in international trade, and a very limited number are exclusively oriented to export training. SBDCs can offer a very effective way to learn and do research at the same time. Some also serve very well in place of a DOC district office which may not be as conveniently located, even though DOC research and other assistance can still be used to supplement the SBDC efforts electronically.

Small Business Institute Programs.   Small Business Institute (SBI) programs are joint efforts with selected colleges and universities in some 450 locations. They can be helpful both in understanding export and in gaining assistance to accomplish the necessary research for an export project. They utilize business students to help in making feasibility studies and surveys and, depending on demand at the center's location, may be well equipped for international trade work. This program, however, seems to be a special target for demolition by the Office of Management and Budget.

Export Legal Assistance Network Organized by the SBA, The Export Legal Assistance Network (ELAN) is a nationwide group of attorneys with solid international experience who have volunteered to provide free initial consultations to small businesses on export-related matters. Working with ELAN is an excellent means of determining just what your legal problems might be and what your options are. Its volunteers may even review a proposed agreement and point out the pitfalls, but do not expect them to draw new agreements or take on your legal problems unless you should decide to retain them otherwise.

Agency For International Development

The Agency for International Development (AID) has for decades been a regular target of criticism by the handling of its humanitarian objectives and the objectives themselves, and for its international political positions, to say nothing of its budget. Its destruction has been a primary goal for many of its enemies. Certainly today is no exception, considering the introspective, isolationist, and anti-foreign-aid mood of the current Congress. AID's task has always been to administer American foreign aid programs throughout the world in cooperation with the State Department. The aim of these programs has been to promote economic and political stability, encourage the development of creditworthy trading and investment partners, and reduce poverty and hunger for humanitarian purposes. The Clinton Administration has broadened and colored these traditional aims by layering in the additional goal of sustainable development. In any case, there has been a consistent effort in recent years to make the programs somewhat more self-serving to American interests by considering how the AID dollars can be spent with an eye to U.S. business opportunities and by providing the U.S. investor or trader with some special advantages.

The 104th Congress is at work here as well, seeking both to trim foreign aid and to shrink government by removing AID's status as an independent agency and returning it to the Department of State with a much reduced budget. The extent to which Congress will be successful in this effort is yet to be determined, but almost surely the agency will be affected to some degree. In all the talk about cutting U.S. foreign aid, it should be noted that U.S. foreign aid has already been cut. It once constituted more than 50 percent of all foreign aid provided by developed nations; today it provides less than 17 percent of that aid and now amounts to less than 0.5 percent of the federal budget. U.S. foreign aid today, in terms of percentage of the gross national product, represents the smallest percentage of foreign aid of any fully developed industrialized nation in the world.

Regardless of what is being spent and the philosophical compass of how it is being spent, AID outlays still represent a serious opportunity to sell goods or provide services based on a significant dollar expenditure under U.S. control. AID business is not necessarily an easy source of business. It requires some research and study to understand how to seek it efficiently and exactly what the opportunities might be for a given business or service provider.

Types of AID Business Opportunities

A worthwhile first step in checking out AID possibilities is to obtain *The Guide for Doing Business with AID* from the Government Printing Office (GPO) or nearest GPO bookstore.[4] (A nearby SBA office may also have one available.) The reference to "commodities" in the *Guide* is used to include equipment, material, foods, and virtually anything except services and consulting, which are dealt with separately. AID is not permitted to assist in procurement of certain items, such as unsafe or ineffective products, luxurious or frivolous products, surplus or used products, or items intended for military or police use. To determine whether your product qualifies for commodity eligibility, check the AID Commodity Eligibility Listing, published according to Schedule B numbers and available from AID through their Office of Small and Disadvantaged Business Utilization/Minority Resource Center or from the AID quarterly CD-ROM. If your commodities do qualify, you can apply to be placed on the AID mailing list to receive descriptions of desired commodities with a lead time of 30 to 60 days.

Through the Commodity Import Program (CIP), AID provides U.S. dollars in the form of loans or grants to host countries to finance a wide variety of products to help keep the economy moving or meet urgent needs. The funds are allocated and paid out by the foreign government's own agencies. The purchases must be negotiated by the host country and the exporter is paid by that country according AID regulations. Usually— but not always—the commodities must be of U.S. origin. The means for announcing such opportunities are discussed later in this section, but the acquisition might be made through the public sector or through the host countries' private sector, and it might be arranged through negotiation or bid, depending on the circumstances.

AID-financed contracts for projects, loans, or grants to finance specific projects, facilities, or undertakings are arranged through the public sector of the host country. Such contracts are subject to the laws of the host country as well as to AID's conditions and the resident AID mission. These undertakings—including such things as irrigation projects, rural health care facilities, and small electrical generating plants—are advertised in the paper *Development Business* as well as in AID's regularly used media.

Consultants and firms offering services that AIDs might be interested in should register with the Consultant Registry Information System (ACRIS) at no charge. Today service industries are in considerable demand by AID. In addition to such traditional consultants and services as architects/engineers and construction firms, there is a focus on such areas as telecommunications, environmental-related services, education, management, information, transportation, water and sanitation, nutrition, and both rural and urban development services.

Accessing AID Business Opportunities and Information

Naturally AID is based in Washington, D.C., and, like many denizens of the area, it is a many-headed monster. To make it easier for companies seeking to do business with it, the Center for Trade and Investment Services (CTIS) was recently established as the central point of contact for free-of-charge inquiries and information about business opportunities in AID-assisted nations. Call 800/872-4348 and begin with a statement as to the AID country or world region of your interest, because CTIS is staffed by trade specialists according to region.

You might consider asking CTIS for more details about the following sources of information:

- The *Environmental Technology Network for Asia (ETNA)*. Operates in conjunction with the U.S.–Asian Environmental Partnership and focuses on nine Asian countries. Faxes leads within 48 hours of their being received.

- The *Procurement Information Access System*. An early alert of AID-financed procurement opportunities operated through the DOC's Economic Bulletin Board.

- *Commerce Business Daily*. A publication for firms doing business with many areas of the government, including AID.

- *AID Procurement Information Bulletins (PIB)*. Bulletins from SBA targeted at small and minority firms. Announce informal negotiated procurement by the public and private sectors. Cover both trade and general procurement opportunities.

- *The Office of Small and Disadvantaged Business Utilization/Minority Resource Center (OSDBU/MRC)*. Perhaps AID's best small business initial contact point for detailed information on AID export opportunities and notification of bid and contract invitations. It distributes at no cost the *Guide to Doing Business with the Agency for International Development.*

- *Consultant Registry Information Service (ACRIS).* A computerized database profiling providers of technical and professional services for future AID-financed projects.

Trade and Development Agency

The Trade and Development Agency (TDA) is the smallest of all federal agencies and is the only agency now providing feasibility study grants for overseas projects. Not surprisingly, therefore, TDA is also a target for the current conservative Congress. According to the present budget bill, it will suffer the largest percentage budget cut of all the export-support organizations. The TDA works closely with AID and with OPIC because all three specialize in the world's less-developed areas. The objective of TDA is to increase U.S. exports and jobs through studies that result in substantial projects for U.S. firms in less-developed countries. The host country receives the feasibility study grant but must select a U.S. firm to conduct the study, with the presumption that the study and subsequent engineering will feature U.S. equipment. This tends to give U.S. suppliers a substantial edge in seeking the resulting project contracts and supplies. For TDA to be involved, it must be assured that:

1. The project is a developmental priority of the host country
2. The project will provide export potential for U.S. suppliers
3. Financing will be available
4. U.S. companies face strong competition in the relevant product and geographical areas

Of more immediate interest to consultants might be the Definitional Missions. These are smaller grants, averaging just over $300,000, that are directly negotiated by the TDA to determine whether a project's feasibility study should be funded. The TDA will look into suggestions for appropriate projects and studies if they are advanced by U.S. suppliers or consultants, but the host country must express its own interest for the suggestion to be pursued.

To track TDA activities and opportunities, watch *Commerce Business Daily* or call for on-line computerized information, or subscribe to TDA's publications. The TDA "hotline" is 703/875-7447. If grants for studies and projects interest you, you can find out more about them in two books by William Delphos: *Inside Washington: Government Resources for*

International Business[5] and *Capitol Capital: Government Resources for High Technology Companies.*[6] The latter covers both domestic and foreign grants and financing sources.

Assistance from State and Nonfederal Governmental Units

Most states provide export encouragement and support in some form and to some degree. Almost all have some export promotion support or trade lead services. A majority of states have one or several overseas offices to support both exporters and efforts to bring foreign investment into the state. Almost half belong to Eximbank's City/State Program, by which means they can help package loan guarantee applications for Eximbank's and SBA's export working capital program as well as help with other financial programs offered by Eximbank, OPIC and others. Some states, such as California, have very active export working capital programs of their own. (See Appendix D.)

But nonfederal export support does not end with the states. A number of port authorities offer programs, as in the case of the Port of New York/New Jersey, which offers XPORT, a trading company, as well as trade missions. Local universities may have a Center for International Trade program, or a Small Business Institute (SBI) program, as mentioned in the SBA section. Other organizations offer Small Business Development Centers (SBDC) in cooperation with the SBA. Some individual cities even have their own programs. Ask your local chamber of commerce and check with the state trade development or economic development agency to find out what your state can offer you.

Endnotes:

1. *Export Programs: A Business Directory of Government Services*, U.S. Government Printing Office: 1995—385-142.

2. *Exporting: From Start to Finance*, L. Fargo Wells and Karin B. Dulat; 3rd Edition, 1996, McGraw-Hill, N.Y.

3. William A. Delphos, *Inside Washington: Government Resources for International Business*, Venture Publishing, Washington, D.C., 1992.

4. *The Guide for Doing Business with AID*, Government Printing Office, Washington, D.C.

5. William A. Delphos, *Inside Washington: Government Resources for International Business*, Venture Publishing, Washington, D.C., 1992.

6. William A. Delphos, *Capitol Capital: Government Resources for High-Technology Companies*, Venture Publishing, Washington, D.C., 1994.

18
Government Export Finance Support

The Small Business Administration

As you know from discussion in Chapter 17, the Small Business Administration (SBA) plays an active role in export consulting and business counseling and works closely with the ITA's Commercial Service agency in that area. Strangely enough, the role of the SBA in export *finance* solidified only recently and has yet to be fully validated. Unfortunately, just as the SBA finally appeared to be making progress in establishing a functional export working capital guarantee program, Congress reduced the percentage of the total loan SBA is allowed to guarantee. This will have a major impact on lenders' acceptance of the SBA guarantee on export working capital loans (especially relative to Eximbank's comparable guarantee), and it will undoubtedly have some effect on all SBA guarantees. The SBA guarantee is now reduced to 80 percent for loans under $100,000 and 75 percent for loans over that amount. SBA guarantee fees have also been increased.

SBA International Loan Guarantee Programs

As you review SBA's export loan guarantee programs, keep in mind that there are domestic SBA programs that may accomplish the same end. All are briefly summarized here:

Export Working Capital Program, Section 7(a)14. SBA's Export Working Capital Program (EWCP) has the advantage of relying mostly on the underlying transaction (depending on the loan officers involved). This permits the exporter to take greater advantage of documentary credits like L/Cs, making it easier to obtain short-term bank credit with a weaker balance sheet or credit standing. The SBA and Eximbank have established a protocol whereby the SBA will do transaction-based export working capital guarantees, harmonized as to format and conditions with those of Eximbank up to $750,000 (covering a maximum loan of $833,000), with Eximbank handling all guarantees over that limit. On its own, Eximbank continues to handle its well-established buyer credit loans and guarantees. But where a bank has Eximbank's delegated guarantee authority, it will be able to use it on loans of less than $750,000 when such loans might otherwise have been handled by SBA.

The EWCP is a revised and updated version of an earlier SBA program inspired by the outstanding success of California's Export Finance Office (CEFO). Because it is transaction-based, it requires less emphasis on the company's net worth and profit-and-loss statement, so long as the exporter can prove its ability to perform the transaction being financed and that there is very positive assurance of ultimate payment by the buyer, coupled with an assignment of the proceeds.

As mentioned, the guarantee to the lender is now for 75 to 80 percent of the loan, which compares to 90 percent for the similar, and formerly harmonized, Eximbank guarantee. The proceeds of the loan must be for preexport purposes, such as acquiring inventory, goods, or services for the transaction. It can also be for supporting standby letters of credit that serve as bid bonds, performance bonds, or payment guarantees if one of the latter is required to comply with the export transaction(s) conditions. Finally, it can be used for postshipment needs to carry export receivables, if the usual terms do not exceed one year. An advantage of the SBA guarantee over the Eximbank guarantee is that SBA can support transactions in which the product is of less than 50 percent U.S. origin. A 60-day preliminary commitment is available to help in finding a lender. The SBA guarantee fee on loans for under a 12-month term for this program only, was an exception to the general increase in SBA fees. It stands at 0.75 percent, which is still less than Eximbank's, at least for now. For loans over 12 months, however, the general increase to the 2- to 3-percent range applies. This increase, combined with the reduced percentage of guarantee, probably means that the EWCP's recent increased acceptance within SBA will once more decline. Combined with Eximbank's improved delegated authority for lenders, the lion's share of the EWCP guarantees will probably be undertaken by Eximbank instead of SBA.

International Trade Loan Guarantee Program. The International Trade Loan provides long-term financing to help small business compete overseas more effectively and to expand or develop export markets. If the purpose of the loan is for the acquisition or modernization of facilities for export production, the SBA 7(a)16 program applies. It has a maximum term of 25 years for the facilities or equipment portion of the loan. In the case of the longer-term International Trade Loan, the overall SBA guarantee limits are expanded because the maximum international trade loan is $1 million, which is $250,000 over the SBA's normal maximum. In addition, a further working capital loan may be allowed, up to $250,000, which provides for substantially more borrowing than the usual SBA program limits.

Domestic SBA Loan Guarantee Programs

The basic SBA loan guarantee is the 7(a) Program, which can be used for medium- or long-term needs for working capital or asset acquisition. SBA facilities for revolving loan guarantees have been enhanced by the Greenline program, which permits the loan level to fluctuate according to need based on inventories or accounts receivable levels. The new Low Documentation Loan Program (LowDoc) is suited for very young or small, growing companies (including exporters) for loans up to $100,000. It is designed to put more emphasis on character, management experience, and credit history and less on collateral and net worth. As the name implies, it also minimizes documentation and paperwork, which results in speedier approval. The 504 Loan Program is available for loans up to $2.5 million, of which the SBA can guarantee as much as $1 million. The purpose of the loan should be to acquire long-term fixed assets. Such loans are handled through a private or quasiprivate Certified Development Company, whose identities SBA will gladly provide.

The Export-Import Bank of the United States

The U.S. Export-Import Bank—known as EXIM or Eximbank—is the primary agency charged with providing financing support for U.S. exports, but it has nothing to do with imports, despite its name. Eximbank's four functions or activities include:

1. Foreign credit insurance
2. Exporter working capital loan guarantees
3. Foreign buyer loan guarantees
4. Direct loans to foreign buyers

The activity most used by smaller exporters is Eximbank's foreign credit insurance, which permits U.S. exporters to offer competitive selling terms to foreign buyers. While credit insurance represents the greatest area of Eximbank's activity in terms of transactions and the second-greatest in terms of dollar volume, Eximbank's working capital loan guarantee represents by far the smallest part of its activity in dollar volume. Buyer loan guarantees and direct loans are usually involved in larger transactions or for the project finance aspect of international trade finance. With the exception of the exporter working capital guarantee, all Eximbank guarantee and insurance programs cover commercial risk as well as every type of political risk. Insurance may be taken out for political risk only, but the savings are relatively small and Eximbank discourages this practice.

Eximbank's headquarters are at 811 Vermont Avenue, NW, Washington, D.C. 20571; its hot line number is 800/565-EXIM (800/565-3946). There are five regional offices—in New York, Miami, Chicago, Houston, and Los Angeles—for which the addresses can be found in Appendix C.

Foreign Credit Insurance

Eximbank foreign credit insurance has more competition from the private sector today, especially in the case of small and midsize businesses. As explained in Chapter 16, the once-high minimum premiums for foreign credit insurance made private sector insurance impractical except for the very largest exporters, but today that has changed, and other credit insurance might well be considered. However, depending on the levels of political risk in the countries you do business in, the type of customer you deal with, and the regularity of your export activities, Eximbank short-term (180 days or less, or 360 days for agriculture) or medium-term (to five years) insurance facilities can be an important key to your export strategies and to your overall competitiveness. They will very likely be at least your initial choice. An important qualifying factor, however, is Eximbank's insistence that the insured goods must be of at least 50 percent U.S. origin and not for military purposes.

As previously noted, under the two special small business policies a hold harmless clause can be added that protects the lender from any performance deficiencies on the part of the exporter, such as failure to properly report or pay according to the terms of the policy. The Eximbank insurance policies of greatest interest to small business are explained in Chapter 16.

Exporter's Working Capital Guarantee Program

The working capital guarantee is a small part of Eximbank's activity, in 1994, representing 155 guarantees authorized for a total of $181 million, but critical to the exporter requiring extra working capital for inventory, labor, or other preshipment needs to permit it to take advantage of an export opportunity or to help it carry foreign receivables. This is the only program in Eximbank's repertoire that is usable before an export actually occurs; it is called *supplier credit* as compared to *buyer credit*. It is intended for short-term loans and is similar to the SBA export working capital program except that it can guarantee 90 percent of any export loan (a higher percentage than SBA), and is primarily intended for guarantees exceeding $750,000 (under that amount, the exporter might be referred to SBA). There is a stipulated exception to this general rule: If the bank has Eximbank's delegated authority and chooses to use it to accommodate an established, good customer needing a smaller loan, the guaranteed minimum limit need not apply. Another difference from the SBA facility is that Eximbank must apply the 50 percent U.S. origin rule. Eximbank, like SBA, can provide a preliminary commitment that permits the exporter to shop for a suitable lender.

Foreign Buyer Loan Guarantees

Buyer credit risk protection comprises the third Eximbank function and the largest with $7.4 billion guaranteed in 1994. The purpose is to make it possible for the foreign buyer to obtain credit from U.S. or foreign lenders to pay for the U.S. export. The foreign buyer can apply through its lender or may be assisted in seeking this help by the exporting seller involved. The guarantee can be used for medium- or long-term loans. Medium-term would be one to five years for capital goods or related services (under some circumstances, seven years) and for less than $10 million. Long-term is considered to be for five years or more and for a guaranteed or financed value of more than $10 million. The buyer's cash payment must be at least 15 percent, leaving no more than 85 percent to be financed, but the guarantee then applies to 100 percent of the financed amount. The guarantee is unconditional as to risks of nonpayment due to political and/or economic reasons and is transferable. There are variants of this program that permit the lending banks to bundle several smaller transactions together to create lines of credit.

Foreign Buyer Direct Loans

The fourth function—once Eximbank's prime activity, but now of declining importance—is the foreign buyer direct loan. These are fixed-interest-rate loans at the lowest rates allowed by agreement of the member countries of the Organization for Economic Cooperation and Development (OECD) and are extended to buyers of plant and equipment. They too, have a prerequisite 15 percent cash down payment, and otherwise the conditions are very similar to those of the loan guarantee.

Project Financing

Not truly a separate function, but rather a distinct and important technique, project financing is now identified and used more intensively by Eximbank to help finance overseas projects. This can be guaranteed or direct loan financing, which gives as much consideration to the current stream of revenue from a project and from future profits as it does to the present liquid assets of the borrower, or sovereign, or other financial institution guarantees. On a much larger scale, it is more like the transaction-based lending of the preexport working capital guarantee. Most developed countries also engage in similar types of export support, and there are occasions when a U.S. exporter can take advantage of export-import banks of another country to obtain financing for products or projects that have a high percentage origin content from that country.

Overseas Private Investment Corporation

The Overseas Private Investment Corporation (OPIC) is an important resource for exporters involved in Third-World countries, especially if some form of temporary investment is involved in the export or project, as in the case of heavy construction equipment. OPIC is the one U.S. agency that has paid back the original capital invested in it and is organized as a self-sustaining corporation that consistently operates at a profit. Its purpose is to promote growth in undeveloped countries and emerging democracies and to help U.S. contractors and investors operate in such countries, and especially to provide cover when political risk is involved. OPIC can only function in those countries that empower it to function by means of a treaty therefore.

OPIC's activities include insurance, loans, loan guarantees, and a variety of investor services, plus a special program to protect contractors and exporters. Investment insurance is OPIC's largest program and covers risks such as currency inconvertibility, expropriation, and political violence. The coverage can include loss of income as well as tangible property loss and frequently involves project financing as well as cross-border leasing. While most OPIC activities relate to medium- or long-term activities, the Contractor and Exporter Insurance program is specialized to help these parties in the case of wrongful government actions, such as disputes pertaining to the underlying contract and payments for same, wrongful calling of standby letters of credit for performance or bid bonds, or loss of assets due to inconvertibility, confiscation, or political violence. In all of the above, OPIC's coverage is for 90 percent of the loss.

OPIC does not provide concessional financing because it is oriented to the private sector and to projects that amortize themselves on an economic basis, however creative. It also encourages joint ventures with local citizens or corporations and may even participate on an equity basis, although it will only insure or guarantee the American citizen's interest, which must be no less than 50 percent. Participation may include direct loans in the case of projects sponsored by small business up to a maximum of $10 million.

There is one important feature of OPIC policies that anyone considering making use of this excellent tool should know: Investors, contractors, and exporters who hope to use OPIC facilities must advise OPIC of their interest *before* they make any irrevocable commitment to a contract for the project. If OPIC considers the request a valid use of its facilities, it will send a letter confirming that it is aware of the interest and will consider participation. After receipt of this letter, final negotiations can proceed. OPIC's purpose is to provide, *during negotiations,* advice as to the nature of the construction or investment contracts to ward off unnecessary problems or risk and thus make it easier for OPIC to participate. It is also important for prospective investors, contractors, and exporters to determine which less-developed countries OPIC is currently working with, for the list is fluid. A notable exception to that list is Mexico, because it refuses to agree to one of OPIC's basic requirements for dispute settlement concerning arbitration in the U.S.

OPIC's offices are in Washington, D.C. and they have an Infoline at 202/336-8799. (See Appendix E for address.)

Foreign Sales Corporations

A foreign sales corporation (FSC) does not represent financial support in the form of credit insurance, loan guarantees, or loans but does represent a financial incentive in the form of reduced income taxes. Furthermore, in any one of its several variations it is the only financial incentive to exporters offered by the United States. Designed to help export companies take advantage of the tax benefit, the basic FSC enables the manufacturer or exporter to set up something of a shell subsidiary corporation offshore in a qualified foreign country to allow a 15 to 32 percent permanent tax savings on income from the export of U.S.–produced goods. There are certain costs included in setting up, maintaining, and managing the foreign corporation, so that minimum export volumes and profits must be maintained to make it worthwhile.

For this reason, a slightly more lax set of rules, called a *Small FSC,* was set up for smaller companies. A Small FSC makes the FSC concept potentially attractive for a company with foreign sales of as little as $1 million and a gross margin for tax purposes of 20 percent, providing tax savings in the area of 15 percent, or $30,000. Another alternative for the smaller firm is the *Shared FSC,* in which a state export development agency, a trade association, accounting firm, or similar umbrella group combines up to 25 even smaller firms into one regular FSC even though each business maintains its own identity and privacy. The other variation is what is called an interest charge domestic international sales corporation (IC-DISC). This can be useful in certain situations, but 95 percent of its sales must be for export. The tax savings in IC-DISCs are greater, but they are only deferred, rather than permanent, savings as in the FSC. You might wish to discuss these two tax vehicles with your accountant.

Details and information can also be obtained from the FSC/DISC Tax Association at P.O. Box 748, FDR Station, New York, New York 10150. This association can also advise you of appropriate shared FSCs and books or manuals for further details.

State-Based Export Finance Support

As mentioned in Chapter 17, several states have active export finance programs, many of them modeled on the California program or Eximbank's working capital program. Over half the states participate in Eximbank's City/State Program to varying degrees. Still others are currently attempting to set export finance programs in motion. Some states have economic development and small business loan programs that they did not originally intend for export purposes, but that they are now quite willing to use for those purposes. In such instances, there may be less willingness to rely as much on the underlying transaction because of lack of export knowledge or other restrictions, but this need not necessarily prohibit an exporter's effective use of the program.

The states currently offering such programs are California, Georgia, Florida, Kansas, Maryland, Minnesota, and the Port of New York/New Jersey. Alaska and Virginia, among others, are also interested in starting such a program. Check with your state's economic development agency to find out whether there is or will be such a program in your state.

19

U.S. and International Trade Regulations

This chapter covers regulations, prohibitions, and responsibilities relative to exporting and importing. The subjects covered include intellectual property rights (trademarks, patents, etc.); export licenses; boycott requests; and foreign corrupt practices (especially relating to foreign agents or representatives). You will be able to determine, as you read these pages, which areas have particular relevance to your business and call for further investigation and research on your part, or perhaps a talk with your attorney. Use this chapter and the government entities it mentions to direct you to additional documents and publications that discuss these issues at greater length. My book, *Exporting: From Start to Finance,* also reviews and explains these regulations and responsibilities in more detail.

Intellectual Property Rights

Intellectual property rights (IPR) is an umbrella term describing patents, trademarks, copyrights, and "know-how" or trade secrets. This subject deserves *very* important consideration—with all due attention to research, detail, and an orderly approach—because seemingly minor or innocent actions can strip you of valuable rights in an important market for all time. If the problem can be rectified at all, it is often only at a substantial cost. There are even areas of the world where, depending on the product and the laws of the land, it may be wiser to forgo pursuing the market at all because of extensive problems or expenses related to IPRs. In general, trademarks and patents should be obtained *before* marketing in a target country. Some products, while not lending themselves to patenting, can readily be trademarked for consumer identification. This process often provides protection from copying.

In almost all cases, the first step to maximize the value of your rights is to seek protection under the applicable U.S. rules and then set up an IPR calendar to make sure you remain aware of the specific deadlines you have to meet to protect your IPR interests under the various deadline dates relative to your IPR interests concerning the various property rights treaties and conventions to which the U.S. is a participant.

Copyrights

Copyrights are the easiest of all the intellectual property rights to secure in at least 75 countries. It is done with a single application to the Universal Copyright Convention. The material is thereafter protected by indicating:

- The symbol *c* in a circle (in some countries the word *copyright* in a circle is equally acceptable)
- Name
- Year of publication

The Buenos Aires Copyright Convention specifies that authors in the United States and 17 Latin American countries who have obtained copyrights in their own country gain protection automatically in all other 17 countries merely by indicating "all rights reserved." Because the United States is now also a member of the Berne Convention, one no longer needs to publish in a second country simultaneously with publishing in the United States to be eligible for protection in the member countries. Copyrights anywhere are very inexpensive to obtain and last for the life of the author plus 50 years after death.

Computer software is readily protected under United States copyright laws, but it is a far from settled issue in many other countries. China is the most current notable example of software piracy in spite of a 1995 agreement. The problem is so serious that it has had an impact on U.S.–China relations. Copyrights were a very contentious issue in the recently concluded GATT treaty, as well as in various bilateral negotiations. As a result of these discussions, the climate for protection should vastly improve, although there are still many countries that must ratify the treaty and many uncertainties remain. For up-to-date information, contact the U.S. Copyright Office, Library of Congress, Washington, D.C. 20559.

Trademarks

The United States and about 88 other countries belong to the most important international treaty in the IPR field: the Paris Union International Convention for the Protection of Industrial Properties, covering both patents and trademarks. An important provision of the convention is that foreign filings in one of the member countries made within six months of the original U.S. filing will date back to the U.S. filing. The United States also belongs to the General Inter-American Convention for Trademark and Commercial Protection of 1929 and to several other bilateral agreements. Most of them adhere to the "national treatment" concept, meaning that foreign firms receive the same treatment under a member country's patent and trademark laws as do its own citizens. Contrary to popular impression, there is no means by which a trademark can be registered with a central authority of one of these conventions in order to obtain protection from signatories to the convention. Protecting your foreign rights in this area is an essential element of your global marketing plan and will require competent legal counsel.

Unfortunately, it is not uncommon to find that another party has registered your trademark, because prior use is not a prerequisite for registration in most countries. The only restrictions are on names that sound similar to descriptive common words, geographic names, or brand names already registered or in use in that country. This concept can be stretched quite far.

> I recall trying to register the well-known trademark and name for Olga Lingerie in Japan in the 1970s. It was determined that *Olga* sounded too much like *organ* which was used in connection with the Fender brand of organs. The potential for confusion lay in the way the Japanese pronounce *l* and *r*. The problem was never resolved, even though millions of dollars of Olga lingerie was sold to Japan. Finally Japan's largest lingerie company purchased one-third of Olga and took over my distribution rights. Thereafter, the matter was swiftly resolved.

Others will register your trademark in hopes of selling it back to you someday when your company decides to expand into the market. Similar trademark problems can stem from a misconception based on the practice in this country that a company can have exclusive use of a trademark by being the first to use it under common law. Registration can come later, but the trademark must remain in use. Once registration occurs it is valid for 10 years.

Even though going through the patent process in a number of countries may be too expensive for your budget, a registered trademark can often provide a substantial level of protection in place of patents. People relate to the first- and best-identified product, even though the products that follow it may otherwise be equal. The trademark process does not happen all at once and does not need to be paid for all at once, but rather as the process unfolds over two, three, or even four years, with the initial cost ranging from $150 to $500 per country. This gives the trademark applicant a chance to see how the product is being accepted and how the market is developing. There are several strategic decisions involved in selecting the countries in which to register. An ideal candidate, for example, would be a country with large potential demand but few facilities for the product's manufacture. The choice also depends, of course, on your plans and opportunities for licensed manufacturing; the manufacturer should be sure to maintain control of the trademark.

As to form, the *TM* indicates the trademark is claimed, while *R* in a circle indicates that it has been registered in the respective country; otherwise, the use of the circled *R* is prohibited. For more information on trademark protection and laws, contact the Foreign Business Practices Division, Office of International Finance and Investment, Bureau of International Economic Policy, in the ITA at Commerce. Official journals of foreign patent offices providing trademark information are maintained by the U.S. Patent and Trademark Office, Crystal Plaza, 2021 Jefferson Davis Highway, Arlington, Virginia 22202.

Patents

Filing patents is by far the most difficult and expensive procedure in the intellectual rights protection process. Foreign patents are expensive, and it is usually neither economical nor practical to file in each country to which you hope to export. To decide which countries should be considered, a formula similar to the one you have worked out for trademarks can be used, but it must be even more restrictive. Naturally, you begin by filing for the U.S. patent, at which point the clock starts ticking. In 1994, the validity period for U.S. patents became 20 years from filing date to conform to international GATT standards. Previously, the validity period had been shorter, but it did not start until the patent was awarded, which sometimes has the effect of reducing the time frame for patent validity.

There is no way to have the U.S. patent automatically recognized abroad, although the process was somewhat simplified in 1978 by the Patent Cooperation Treaty the United States signed with 35 other countries. The treaty allows one patent application to be filed with the U.S. Patent Office as a central source, but has the effect of a filing in each member country the applicant designates. Thereafter, each country proceeds under its own regulations and schedule. Some real time and money is saved by means of that first step, however.

More streamlined still is the European Patent Convention, under which a U.S. national can file a single application at the European patent office in Munich and name those countries for which the European Union patent is desired. If granted, it becomes a national patent in the designated countries. The United States belongs to many other treaties and conventions, most notably the Paris Union International Convention of 88 countries and the Inter-American Convention of 12 countries. These basically allow the "national treatment" previously mentioned. However, under the Paris Convention, you must file for foreign patents within 12 months of the U.S. filing date to establish, in other countries, a patent that dates back to the U.S. filing and provides maximum protection.

How soon you file your U.S. patent before any public use or publication of the process or invention improves the status of your foreign application, even though in the United States you have one year to file after earliest publication or use. Use, sales, or advertising activities concerning the patented product in the United States or in any other country before filing may weaken the foreign patents obtained subsequent to the American patent. Keep in mind that in most countries, patents are issued on the basis of "first to file," which is contrary to the U.S. standard of "first to invent."

If you cannot or did not file within 12 months of the U.S. filing, it is still possible to file, under some circumstances, up to the time the U.S. patent is issued, as long as there has been no publication (or sale, in some cases) of the invention. You are not, however, entitled to the priority treatment dating back to the U.S. filing as mentioned. Most industrial countries will not issue a patent after the U.S. patent has been issued. A few countries will issue confirmation or importation patents, but such patents must be filed before any use of the product in that country. For further sources on patent information, contact the same organizations that were mentioned in the discussion of trademarks on pages 296–298.

It's essential to consult a competent attorney for patent-filing procedures. The cost of obtaining a patent in foreign countries is typically about $2000 per country for English-speaking countries, $4000 for the initial filing in the European Union, and $6000 to $7000 for filing in Japan and Brazil. Additional costs for translation must be added in in almost any non-English-speaking country. In practice, little patent registration is done by smaller firms in the countries of Latin America except in Brazil and Argentina. In the European Union, in addition to the "front-door" joint EU filing fee required on completion of the patent process, there are final registration costs of $1000 to $2000 per country. It is not necessary, however, to register in each of the 15 EU countries, for some will probably not be critical to the product's patent protection. For most countries, achieving a patent is at least a two-year process. Thereafter, in almost all countries, maintenance fees of $200 to $500 will be required every other year.

Trade Secrets

According to U.S. common law, trade secrets are any "formula, pattern, device, or compilation of information which is used in one's business, and which gives an opportunity to obtain an advantage over competitors who do not know or use it." In the United States proprietary information is protected by law indefinitely—so long as that information remains a secret. Many states will enforce noncompetition agreements against ex-employees and make misappropriation of trade secrets a criminal offense. Trade secret protection abroad is both rare and limited. Even in the case of well-drawn licensing agreements or contracts, there is often no effective legal remedy to prevent or punish misappropriation of trade secrets.

The GATT Uruguay Round and IPR

The lengthy Uruguay Round of international trade negotiations finally concluded in 1994 and resulted in the creation of the World Trade Organization (WTO) to replace the GATT framework, effective January, 1995. One of the major achievements of the negotiations was an agreement on Trade-Related Aspects of Intellectual Property Rights (TRIPS). All members of the WTO made the provisions of the Berne Convention and the Paris Convention the minimum standards. Copyright protection will be extended to software and audiovisual works (a major achievement). Trademarks are less likely to be revoked for nonuse and more readily renewable. And trade secrets may receive better protection.

In January 1996, the industrialized members of the WTO will begin enforcing the TRIPS regime. Developing countries will have an extra four-year grace period to establish procedures called for under the agreements, while the least-developed countries may delay full implementation for a maximum of 10 years. During the next few years, the laws and practices of many countries will be extensively changed in favor of owners of intellectual property. And hopefully, China will be among them, as a result of recent bilateral negotiations, even though it is not currently a member of the WTO.

Sources of Help and Information

There are four government offices available to answer questions concerning intellectual property rights overseas:

1. Patent and Trademark Office 703/557-3341
2. International Trade Administration (ITA) 202/482-4501
3. U.S. Customs Service 202/566-5765
4. Copyright Office, Library of Congress, Subcommittee on Intellectual Property 202/395-6161

Export Licensing

Those new to export often think of an export license as a "business license" similar to the license often required by local city governments in order to legally do business. This is not the case regarding export licenses. Rather, an export license is a U.S. government authorization to engage in an export *transaction* which, according to the U.S. agency responsible for that product's regulation or licensing, requires an export license because of the nature, end-use, end-user, and/or destination of the product. You do not need an "export license" just to be in the business of exporting.

In recent years the need for a license has somewhat diminished as many products have been removed from the list of controlled commodities and a number of countries, especially in Eastern Europe, have ceased to be as closely surveilled. In fact, between typical quarterly periods in 1993 and 1995 the number of exports requiring licensing dropped from $6.1 billion to $1.5 billion—about 75 percent. That trend is expected to continue, together with revised and streamlined procedures and requirements. But it will not disappear altogether. Quite rightly, there will always be technology and defense products we do not want to get into the hands of certain countries. In fact, our understandable fear of terrorist actions by irresponsible small governments or sect leaders make certain controls all the more important. In many ways it was easier to establish export restrictions during the Cold War than it is in the context of today's more loosely defined and recognized threats.

The focus of today's controls is on nuclear weapons and materials, of course, but also on chemical and biological weapons and materials, missile delivery systems, and various other crime and terrorist materials. Exercising these controls is a complex task, because the authorities consider the components as well as the finished products. As we saw with the blast in Oklahoma, even common fertilizer can become a deadly bomb. In the Cold War days the Western nations and their allies made a cooperative effort to control exports through an organization called COCOM. Today, although that group has been disbanded, a less formal international and multilateral organization is in operation, pursuing similar goals and in agreement as to the emphasis on terrorists and rogue nations.

For these reasons, even though the dollar value and number of license-controlled exports has been sharply reduced, it remains extremely difficult to determine what is controlled and what must be licensed. The task is made even harder because of the need to control the possibilities for dual-use or even multiple-use of materials that might be employed to build or maintain terrorist weapons. It is nevertheless the responsibility of the exporter to be knowledgeable regarding the export license regulations and the changes that regularly take place within those regulations. While it is outside the scope of this book to fully analyze and detail the regulations or the licensing process, I will try to explain them in broad outline so that you can better understand the export licensing burdens and how to determine when to investigate further.

An Overview of Export Controls

The Export Administration Act is the basis for governmental control of designated U.S. exports and pertains to a wide range of products—or *commodities* as they are termed in the act—including technology and software, transported by whatever means or carrier. Insofar as technology is concerned, all forms of transfer overseas—including verbal, written, fax, and computer data transfer—are considered to be exports. This control extends beyond the initial export to include reexport by the original consignee to a third party, and applies whether the export is comprised all or in part of domestic or foreign origin. The right to export is considered a privilege by the U.S. government and it places the burden and responsibility on the exporter to be informed, to understand, and to adhere to the export regulations as they are today and as they change or are affected by ongoing administrative rulings.

Agencies Involved in Export Control and Licensing

The Bureau of Export Administration (BXA) controls by far the larger part of the regulated exports. Its Export Administration Regulations (EAR), covered in the U.S. Code of Federal Regulations, CFR 15, define all the rules and regulations for those products. However, depending on the item to be exported, its intended use and the country of destination, other agencies have sole jurisdiction or share jurisdiction with BXA. Some of these commodity areas are:

- *Defense services and defense articles* (including the U.S. Munitions List as defined and governed by the Arms Export Control Act). These are controlled by the U.S. Department of State, Office of Defense Trade Controls (DTC), covered under CFR 22.
- *Foreign assets and transactions.* These are controlled by the Department of Treasury, Office of Foreign Assets Control, covered under CFR 31.
- *Narcotics, dangerous drugs, and their processing equipment.* These are controlled by the Drug Enforcement Administration, covered under CFR 21.
- *Natural gas and electric power.* These are controlled by the Department of Energy, covered under CFR 10 and 18.
- *Nuclear equipment, materials, reactor vessels, and other specifically designated commodities; and nuclear technical data for nuclear weapons/special nuclear materials.* These are controlled by the Nuclear Regulatory Commission, covered under CFR 10.
- *Patent filing data sent abroad.* These are controlled by the Patent and Trademark Office, covered under CFR 37 and 15.
- *Watercraft* (U.S. Coast Guard documented watercraft of five net tons or

more, for export or transfer to a foreign interest). These are controlled by the U.S. Maritime Administration, App. U.S.C. 808, 839.

- *Certain agricultural plants and products.* These are controlled by the U.S. Department of Agriculture.

- *Endangered fish and wildlife, dead or alive.* These are controlled by the U.S. Fish and Wildlife Service.

Understanding Export Controls

To find out for sure whether there is or is not a need to obtain an export license for any given export, you must first find out whether the product falls within an Export Control Classification Number (ECCN) from the Commodity Control List (CCL) (EAR Part 774, Supplement No. 1) and determine if any export restrictions apply. The restrictions are applied on a country-specific basis, which can be determined by studying the Commerce Country Chart (EAR Part 738, Supplement No. 1) and the Country Group Chart (EAR Part 740, Supplement No. 1).

To understand BXA's areas of licensing concerns, it helps to understand the composition of the ECCN number. The CCL is divided into 10 functional categories. The categories form the first digit of the ECCN number, and the list makes apparent where the emphasis in licensing is. The categories are:

1. Materials
2. Materials processing
3. Electronics
4. Computers
5. Telecommunications
6. Sensors
7. Avionics and navigation
8. Marine technology
9. Propulsion systems and transportation equipment
10. Miscellaneous

The second item in the ECCN number is a letter indicating one of five types of a commodity within the category:

A. Assemblies and components of equipment
B. Testing equipment
C. Materials
D. Software
E. Technology

These designations provide a further idea of the export licensing parameters. To round out these parameters, the last two digits of the ECCN differentiate the item itself and are developed within five clusters of 20, each intended to group the primary reasons for control. The associated numbers and principal reasons are:

1. 0–19: National security

2. 20–39: Missile technology

3. 40–59: Nuclear nonproliferation

4. 60–79: Chemical and biological weaponry

5. 80–99: Miscellaneous, which includes crime, antiterrorism, United Nations sanctions, and short supply, among others

Help can be obtained from the BXA headquarters in the U.S. Department of Commerce, 14th Street and Pennsylvania Avenue NW, Washington, D.C. 20230; or from one of its two branch offices on the West Coast in Newport Beach or Santa Clara, California. If there is any doubt as to the need for obtaining a license, get an opinion in writing from the BXA. Verbal opinions are unofficial. Adequate technical data is required as part of the request, and a response can be expected in about two weeks. The trade specialist at the DOC district office may be of some help, but don't count on it in very technical areas and any opinion expressed would be strictly one of a casual observer. If a number of your products are subject to licensing and you have highly technical or sensitive products, or if the BXA response seems less than definitive, retain the services of a qualified export licensing consultant.

When considering the EAR regulations, keep in mind the other areas of regulation by other agencies or departments already mentioned, especially for those products that could be used in chemical and biological warfare or terrorism, nuclear proliferation, or missile technology. This includes commodities that might be used to research, manufacture, or store such products. Theoretically, if you plan to export paper clips (which clearly would not ordinarily need a license) and you know, or have reason to know, that they are going to be used in the assembly of a nuclear weapon in a country that the U.S. has imposed nuclear weapon export controls on, your planned export may be in violation of the EAR.

Keeping up With the EAR.   If your export activities do seem to involve licensing requirements, it is vital that you keep up with changes in the EAR, which take place continually. This can be done through the Federal Register and the monthly updates on the NTDB disks, by downloading from FED-WORLD to your computer, and by supplementing this data with a subscription to the BXA quarterly newsletter. If you have any questions, contact a BXA officer or the FEDWORLD staff by voice mail, at 703/487-4608, or contact one of the West Coast branches I mentioned.

Antiboycott Regulations

Antiboycott regulations are actually part of the EAR under the title Restrictive Trade Practices or Boycotts, CFR 15, Part 760. The initiating legislation, however, has nothing to do with the Export Administration Act in terms of time frame, purpose, or applications, so it is helpful to treat them as a separate issue. The single thing both sets of regulations have in common is that both represent an administrative problem to the exporter and a potential threat in terms of both civil and criminal penalties.

While the antiboycott regulations prohibit various actions, they also require that the exporter report certain boycott requests even though the exporter has no intention of accepting, much less complying with, the proposed boycott terms. The Act was put into effect in 1965 in response to the practice of the Arab League, which was blacklisting firms that had dealings with Israel. These regulations were intended, not only to prevent such secondary and tertiary boycotts, but also to make it possible to learn which Arab firms and countries were attempting such activities through the reporting feature of the Act.

Violations of the boycott regulations are much less frequent today than they were in the 1960s and 1970s, although apparently not substantially different from what there were in 1989. It appears that the major portion of the Arab League that wants to do business with the United States has learned to sidestep or omit provisions in their contracts, letters of credit, and orders that run contrary to the regulations.

However, the regulations should pose no problem to you if you understand them in a very general way. You will learn to check further when you sense that there might be exposure to violations. In such an event, any bank with an experienced international department or your forwarder can advise you as to illegal clauses contained within a letter of credit, shipping and insurance instructions, or the like. If, however, the Middle East is a primary target marketing area for you, become acquainted with the regulations firsthand. Also, keep in mind that while it was the Arab League's efforts to boycott Israel that created the regulations, at some future date the Arab League could choose to apply the boycott provisions against other nations.

Be sure you understand the difference between a primary boycott and a secondary or tertiary boycott action, and also between a negative versus a positive request. The United States does not and could not object to any nation refusing to do business with Israel. This is a primary boycott and this country has some of its own in effect. Everything else is a secondary or tertiary boycott, and it does not matter which of the two it is—the intent is to prohibit both. A positive request, which is likely to be acceptable, would ask you to certify that the merchandise was of U.S. origin. A negative request or order, usually unacceptable, would request certification that it was not made in a boycotted country.

The essence of the secondary and tertiary boycott is the blacklist onto which a person or firm, often without their knowledge, can be placed. The prospective Arab buyer advises the exporter that he cannot do business with the blacklisted party relative to any given transaction—or possibly, that he cannot do any business with it whatsoever. To do so could mean being blacklisted in turn. Such advice can be made in any form—verbally or through correspondence, purchase order, letter of credit, or shipping and insurance instructions.

The distinction between "positive" and "negative" can be misleading, and therefore the intent and purpose must be considered. An example is that a *whitelist*, which is a list of those firms or persons with whom you *can* do business, is in effect, advising you whom *not* to do business with. Such a list can therefore be just as illegal as a blacklist. Enforcement is particularly strict concerning letters of credit, but your banker is especially qualified to give you advice in this area.

The antiboycott regulations are analyzed in detail in the book by Leibman and Root entitled *United States Export Controls*.[1]

Foreign Corrupt Practices Act

The Foreign Corrupt Practices Act (FCPA), 15 USC Section 78, might have been more carefully and fairly drafted in today's export environment. However, when the FCPA became law, it was a different world, and the United States was the largest creditor nation in history with a trade surplus. Consequently, when congressional hearings revealed that more than 400 American companies were regularly engaging in bribery, Congress felt that something had to be done to maintain the ethical image of the United States abroad; never mind that the United States was not alone in that practice or what the competitive consequences might be.

Always inherently unfair for its ambiguous definitions of what is illegal and the degree of vicarious liability imposed, the FCPA is clearly seen today as another export disincentive, even though some improvements have been made as to its fairness and clarity. While aimed primarily at the multinationals, it excludes no one and no type of business, individual, or association. Employees are made liable as well as the company, and it provides that the company cannot directly or indirectly pay fines on behalf of the guilty employee.

The act sets forth certain accounting standards and describes various penalties. But at this juncture the most important point for the smaller exporter or business to know concerns bribery to influence the foreign government to buy or to act in a certain way. On this issue it is far more likely that one of your agents or representatives for business in the Middle East would be involved in such activities on your behalf than you or your company might be. If you *know* (a term broadly defined) of bribery or related activity, you could be liable without realizing it. Extremely high commissions in the range of 20 to 30 percent can be a clue and one cause for a federal investigation, followed by a claim that you "knew" and thereby incurred a "vicarious liability." This alone serves as an incentive for some firms to make use of independent distributors in the Middle East.

Endnote

1. John R. Leibman and William Root, *United States Export Controls*, Aspen Law & Business, Gaithersburg, Maryland, 1991.

Appendix A
Export Help
800 Numbers

DOC Trade Information Center 800/USA-TRADE. Operated by the U.S. Department of Commerce for information on export assistance offered by the 19 federal agencies comprising the Trade Promotion Coordinating Committee. Trade Specialists advise exporters on how to locate and use government programs and guide them through the export process.

Small Business Foundation of America Export Opportunity Hotline 800/243-7232. Answers questions about getting started in exporting. Offers advice on product distribution, licensing and insurance, export financing, distribution options, export management firms, customs, currency exchange systems, and travel requirements.

Small Business Administration (SBA) 800/U-ASK-SBA. The SBA answer desk is available for information on SBA export and financial assistance, as well as information on minority programs.

Agency for International Development 800/USAID-4-U. This number at the Center of Trade and Investment Services provides country-specific information.

Export-Import Bank of the United States 800/424-5201. Provides information on Eximbank's financing programs, including the export credit insurance and working capital guarantee programs for small and midsize firms.

Overseas Private Investment Corporation 800/424-OPIC. OPIC has information on its programs to promote economic growth in developing countries through U.S. private investment in those countries.

Export Hotline 800/USA-XPORT. A corporate-sponsored, nationwide fax retrieval system providing international trade information for U.S. businesses.

Metric and English Equivalents

Metric and English Equivalents

LINEAR MEASURE

English Unit	Metric Unit
1 inch =	{ 25.4 millimeters { 2.54 centimeters
1 foot =	{ 30.48 centimeters { 3.048 decimeters { 0.3048 meter
1 yard =	0.9144 meter
1 mile =	{ 1609.3 meters { 1.6093 kilometers
0.03937 inch	= 1 millimeter
0.3937 inch	= 1 centimeter
3.937 inches	= 1 decimeter
39.37 inches } 3.2808 feet } 1.0936 yards }	= 1 meter
3280.8 feet } 1093.6 yards } 0.62137 mile }	= 1 kilometer

SQUARE MEASURE

English Unit	Metric Unit
1 square inch =	{ 645.16 square millimeters { 6.4516 square centimeters
1 square foot =	{ 929.03 square centimeters { 9.2903 square decimeters { 0.092903 square meter
1 square yard =	0.83613 square meter
1 square mile =	2.5900 square kilometers
0.0015500 square inch	= 1 square millimeter
0.15500 square inch	= 1 square centimeter
15.500 square inches } 0.10764 square foot }	= 1 square decimeter
1.1960 square yards	= 1 square meter
0.38608 square mile	= 1 square kilometer

LIQUID MEASURE

English Unit	Metric Unit
1 fluid ounce =	29.573 milliliters
1 quart =	{ 9.4635 deciliters { 0.94635 liter
1 gallon =	3.7854 liters
0.033814 fluid ounce	= 1 milliliter
3.3814 fluid ounces	= 1 deciliter
33.814 fluid ounces } 1.0567 quarts } 0.26417 gallon }	= 1 liter

CUBIC MEASURE

English Unit	Metric Unit
1 cubic inch =	{ 16.387 cubic centimeters { 0.016387 liter
1 cubic foot =	0.028317 cubic meter
1 cubic yard =	0.76455 cubic meter
1 cubic mile =	4.16818 cubic kilometers
0.061023 cubic inch	= 1 cubic centimeter
61.023 cubic inches	= 1 cubic decimeter
35.315 cubic feet } 1.3079 cubic yards }	= 1 cubic meter
0.23990 cubic mile	= 1 cubic kilometer

WEIGHTS

English Unit	Metric Unit
1 grain	= 0.064799 gram
1 avoirdupois ounce	= 28.350 grams
1 troy ounce	= 31.103 grams
1 avoirdupois pound	= 0.45359 kilogram
1 troy pound	= 0.37324 kilogram
1 short ton (0.8929 long ton)	= { 907.18 kilograms { 0.90718 metric ton
1 long ton (1.1200 short tons)	= { 1016.0 kilograms { 1.0160 metric tons
15.432 grains } 0.035274 avoirdupois ounce } 0.032151 troy ounce }	= 1 gram
2.2046 avoirdupois pounds	= 1 kilogram
0.98421 long ton } 1.1023 short tons }	= 1 metric ton

Eximbank Regional Offices

Export-Import Bank of the United States
811 Vermont Avenue NW
Washington, D.C. 20571

Export Financing Hot Line 800/424-5201

Divisions at above address or FAX 202/566-7524:

Public Affairs and Publications	Tel: 202/566-4490
Marketing and Programs Development Division	Tel: 202/566-8860
Export Insurance Division	Tel: 202/566-8197

Eximbank Regional Offices

Chicago	19 South LaSalle Street, Suite 902
	Chicago, Illinois 60603
	Tel: 312/641-1915, FAX 312/641-2292
Houston	88050 Dairy Ashford, Suite 585
	Houston, Texas 77077
	Tel: 713/589-8182, FAX 713/589-8184
Los Angeles area	One World Trade Center, Suite 1670
	Long Beach, California 90831
	Tel: 310/980-4550, FAX 310/980-4561
Miami	80 SW 8th Street, Suite 1800
	Miami, Florida 33130
	Tel: 305/372-8540, FAX 305/372-5114
New York	6 World Trade Center
	New York, New York 10048
	Tel: 212/513-4292, FAX 212/513-4277

Appendix D
Eximbank City/State Programs

Contacts	Programs
Arkansas Development Finance Authority P.O. Box 8023 100 Main Street, Suite 200 Little Rock, Arkansas 72203 Tel. 501/682-5909, Fax 501/682-5939	Export trade finance counseling, packaging of federal assistance program, and WCGP
California Export Finance Office 6 Centerpointe Drive, Suite 760 La Palma, California 90623 Tel. 714/562-5519, Fax 714/562-5530	Eximbank umbrella policy, pre/post shipment loan guarantee, and SBA packaging
Florida Department of Commerce 107 West Gaines, Suite 366 Tallahassee, Florida 32399 Tel. 904/922-8830, Fax 904/487-1407	WCGP packaging and insurance counseling
Georgia Department of Industry, Trade, and Tourism Trade Division 285 Peachtree Center Avenue, Suite 1100 Atlanta, Georgia 30303 Tel. 404/656-4504, Fax 404/656-3567	Six-city network for counseling and packaging of WCGP, Eximbank insurance, and SBA
Hawaii International Business Center City Financial Tower 201 Merchant Street, Suite 1510 Honolulu, Hawaii 96813 Tel. 808/587-2797, Fax 808/587-2790	Export trade finance counseling, packaging of federal assistance programs, and WCGP
Illinois Development Finance Authority 2 North LaSalle, Suite 980 Chicago, Illinois 60602 Tel. 312/793-5586, Fax 312/793-6347	Trade finance structuring, fixed asset financing, and WCGP packaging

Contacts	Programs
Indiana Department of Commerce Indiana Finance Authority/Trade Division One North Cal Street, Suite 700 Indianapolis, Indiana 46204 Tel. 317/233-4337, Fax 317/232-4146	Trade finance structuring, insurance counseling, and WCGP packaging
Louisiana Economic Development Corporation 101 France Street Baton Rouge, Louisana 70802 Tel. 504/342-5675, Fax 504/432-5389	Trade finance structuring, fixed asset financing, and WCGP packaging
Maine Office of Business Development International Commerce Division State House Station 59 Augusta, Maine 04333 Tel. 207/287-2656, Fax 207/287-5701	WCGP packaging, insurance, and counseling
Maryland Industrial Development Bank Financing Authority The World Trade Center, 7th Floor 401 East Pratt Street Baltimore, Maryland 21202 Tel. 410/333-8189, Fax 410/333-4302	Trade finance structuring, Eximbank umbrella policy, and preparation of applications for all Eximbank programs
Massachusetts Industrial Finance Agency 75 Federal Street Boston, Massachusetts 02110 Tel. 617/451-2477, Fax 617/451-3429	WCGP packaging
Michigan International Trade Authority Keesee and Associates 540 South Glenhurst Birmingham, Michigan 48009 Tel. 313/540-8476, Fax 313/540-2250	Trade finance structuring, insurance, and WCGP packaging
Nebraska Dept of Economic Development Office of International Trade 301 Centennial Mall South Lincoln, Nebraska 68509 Tel. 402/471-4668, Fax 402/471-3778	Counseling, technical assistance, and financial packaging
Nevada Commission on Economic Development Howard Hughes Parkway, Suite 295 Las Vegas, Nevada 89158 Tel. 702/486-7282, Fax 702/486-7284	Counseling, loan packaging, and referral service for Eximbank programs

Contacts	Programs
New Hampshire Office of International Commerce 601 Spaulding Turnpike, Suite 29 Portsmouth, New Hampshire 03801 Tel. 603/334-6074, Fax 603/334-6110	WCGP packaging, insurance, and counseling
New Mexico Border Authority 505 South Main, Suite 145 Las Cruces, New Mexico 88001 Tel. 505/525-5622, Fax 505/525-5623	Counseling, loan packaging, and referral service for Eximbank programs
Ohio Department of Development International Trade Division P.O. Box 1001 Columbus, Ohio 43266 Tel. 614/466-5017, Fax 614/463-1540	Technical assistance, agent/distributor searches, marketing information, and WCGP packaging
Oklahoma Department of Commerce Export Finance Program 6601 Broadway, P.O. Box 26980 Oklahoma City, Oklahoma 73126 Tel. 405/841-5259, Fax 405/841-5142	Trade financing, WCGP packaging, Eximbank umbrella policy, and foreign accounts receivable financing
Pennsylvania Department of Commerce Office of International Development 486 Forum Building Harrisburg, Pennsylvania 17120 Tel. 717/787-7190, Fax 717/234-4560	WCGP packaging
South Dakota Export Trade Administration Governor's Office of Economic Development 711 East Wells Avenue Pierre, South Dakota 57501 Tel. 605/773-5735, Fax 605/773-3256	Full service export support, WCGP packaging, and insurance counseling
Texas Department of Commerce P.O. Box 12728 Austin, Texas 78711 Tel. 512/320-9662, Fax 512/320-9452	WCGP packaging
Vermont Department of Economic Development 109 State Street, Suite 200 Montpelier, Vermont 05609 Tel. 802/828-3221, Fax 802/828-3258	WCGP packaging and counseling for export trade structuring

Contacts	Programs
Virginia Small Business Financial Authority 1021 East Cary Street, P.O. Box 798 Richmond, Virginia 23206 Tel. 804/371-8255, Fax 804/225-3384	WCGP packaging, Eximbank umbrella policy, and trade finance structuring
Washington Export Assistance Center 2001 6th Avenue, Suite 2100 Seattle, Washington 98121 Tel. 206/464-7123, Fax 206/587-4224	WCGP packaging, SBA packaging, and trade finance structuring
West Virginia Economic Development Authority Building 6, Room 525, Capitol Complex Charleston, West Virginia 25305 Tel. 304/558-3650, Fax 304/558-0206	WCGP packaging, Eximbank umbrella policy, and trade finance counseling services
Puerto Rico Economic Development Bank Credit Analysis Division 437 Ponce de Leon Avenue, 15th Floor Hato Rey, Puerto Rico 00919-5009 Tel. 809/766-4300, Fax 809/756-7875	WCGP packaging, SBA loans, insurance, trade finance counseling, and consulting services

Appendix E
Public and Private Export-Related Organizations

U.S. Government Agencies

Agency for International Development
Center for Trade and Investment Services
320 21st Street NW
Washington, D.C. 20523

Bureau of Export Administration (BXA)
Office of Export Licensing
HCH Building Room 1099
Washington, D.C. 20230

Customs Service
1201 Constitution Avenue NW
Washington, D.C. 20229

Department of Agriculture
Foreign Agricultural Service
14th Street and Independence Avenue SW
Washington, D.C. 20250

Department of Commerce
14th Street and Constitution Avenue NW
Washington, D.C. 20230

Eastern European Business and Information Center
Department of Commerce
ITA Room 5341 HCHB
Washington, D.C. 20230

Export-Import Bank of the United States
811 Vermont Avenue NW
Washington, D.C. 20571

International Executive Service Corps
333 Ludlow
Stamford, Connecticut 06902

Overseas Private Investment Corporation
1100 New York Avenue NW
Washington, D.C. 20527

Private Export Funding Corp. (PEFCO)
747 Third Avenue
New York, New York 10017

Small Business Administration
409 Third Street SW
Washington, D.C. 20416

Superintendent of Documents
U.S. Government Printing Office
Washington, D.C. 20402

U.S. Patent and Trademark Office
International Affairs
Box 4
Washington, D.C. 20231

U.S. Trade Representative
600 17th Street NW
Washington, D.C. 20506

International Trade Organizations

American Association of Exporters and Importers
11 West 42nd Street
New York, New York 10036

American Society of International Law
2223 Massachusetts Avenue NW
Washington, D.C. 20008

Bankers Association for Foreign Trade (BAFT)
1600 M Street NW, Suite 7F
Washington, D.C. 20036

Chamber of Commerce of the United States
1615 H Street NW
Washington, D.C. 20062

Export Managers Association of Southern California
110 East 9th Street, Suite A-761
Los Angeles, California 90079

FCIB-NACM Corporation
100 Wood Avenue South, Metro Center One
Iselin, New Jersey 00830

Federation of International Trade Associations
1851 Alexander Bell Drive
Reston, Virginia 22091

ICC Publishing Corporation
156 Fifth Avenue
New York, New York 10010

International Chamber of Commerce
38, Cours Albert
75008 Paris, France

National Association of Export Companies
P.O. Box 1330, Murray Hill Station
New York, New York 10156

National Association of State Development Agencies
444 Capitol Street NW, #345
Washington, D.C. 20001

Small Business Exporters Association
4603 John Taylor Court
Annandale, Virginia 22003

Small Business Foundation of America
1155 15th Street NW
Washington, D.C. 20005

World Trade Centers Association
1 World Trade Center, 55th Floor
New York, New York 10048

Export
Reference Books

Export Marketing and International Trade

The Arthur Young International Business Guide, Charles F. Valentine, John Wiley, New York, New York.

A Basic Guide to Exporting, Superintendent of Documents, U.S. Government Printing Office, Washington, D.C.

Building an Import/Export Business, Kenneth D. Weiss, John Wiley, New York, New York.

Capitol Capital: Government Resources for High-Technology Companies, William A. Delphos, Venture, Washington, D.C.

Developing Skills for International Trade, JuDee Benton, TEAM Export, Merced, California.

Elements of Export Marketing, John Stapleton, Woodhead-Faulkner, Dover, New Hampshire.

Expanding Your Business Overseas, Deloitte Haskins & Sells, Washington, D.C. 20004.

Exporting from Start to Finance, L.F. Wells & Karin Dulat, 3rd Edition, McGraw-Hill, New York, New York.

The Export Operation: Putting the Pieces Together, Unz & Co., Jersey City, New Jersey.

Export Sales and Marketing Manual, John R. Jagoe, Export USA Publications, Minneapolis, Minnesota.

A Guide to Export Marketing, International Trade Institute, Dayton, Ohio.

A Guide to Expanding in the Global Market, Ernst & Young, John Wiley, New York, New York.

Exporters Guide to Federal Resources for Small Business, U.S. Government Printing Office, Superintendent of Documents, Washington, D.C.

Exportise (No. 2), Small Business Foundation of America, Boston.

Export Trading Company Guidebook, U.S. Government Printing Office, Superintendent of Documents, Washington, D.C.

Foreign Commerce Handbook, Chamber of Commerce of the United States, Washington, D.C.

Going Global: Strategies and Techniques for New Multinations, Business International Corp., New York, New York.

Getting to Yes, by Fisher and Ury, Houghton-Mifflin,

The Global Edge: How Your Company Can Win in the International Marketplace, Sondra Snowdon, Simon & Schuster, New York, New York.

Going International, Griggs and Copeland, Random House and New American Library, San Francisco, California.

Inside Washington: Government Resources for International Business, William A. Delphos, Venture, Washington, D.C.

The International Business Woman: A Guide to Success in the Global Marketplace, Marlene L. Rossman, Greenwood Press, Westport, Connecticut.

International Marketing Handbook, Gale Research, Detroit, Michigan.

Management Export Information Manual, Southern California District Export Counsel, Los Angeles, California.

Cultures and Customs and Negotiations

The Art of Negotiation, Gerald Nierenberg, Cornerstone Books, Division of Simon and Schuster, New York, New York.

Culture Grams, Center for International Studies, Brigham Young University Publications, Provo, Utah.

Do's and Taboos Around the World, Roger Axtell, John Wiley, New York, New York (also available in video format).

Doing Business in and with Latin America: An Information Sourcebook, E. Willard and Ruby Miller, Oryx Press, Phoenix, Arizona.

Doing Business in....Series, Matthew Bender, International Division, Albany, New York.

European Markets, Washington Researchers, Washington, D.C.

Funding for Research, Study and Travel: Latin America and the Caribbean, Karen Cantrell and Denise Wallen, Oryx Press, Phoenix, Arizona.

Getting Your Yen's Worth: How to Negotiate with Japan, Inc., Robert T. Moran, Gulf Publishing, Houston, Texas.

How to Do Business with Russians, Misha G. Knight, Greenwood Press, Westport, Connecticut.

How to Do Business with the Japanese, Mark Zimmerman, Random House, New York, New York.

International Business Practices, U.S. Department of Commerce, International Trade Administration, U.S. Government Printing Office, Washington, D.C.

International Exporting Agreements, Matthew Bender & Co., Albany, New York.

National Negotiating Styles, edited by Binnendijk, Foreign Service Institute, U.S. Department of State, Washington, D.C.

Japanese Business Etiquette: A Practical Guide to Success with the Japanese, Diana Rowland, Warner Books, New York, New York.

Managing Cultural Differences, Philip R. Harris and Robert T. Moran, Gulf Publishing Houston, Texas.

The Traveler's Guide to Asian Customs and Manners, Kevin Chambers, Simon & Schuster, New York, New York.

The Traveler's Guide to European Customs and Manners, Elizabeth Devine and Nancy Braganti, Simon & Schuster, New York, New York.

The Traveler's Guide to Latin American Customs and Manners, Elizabeth Devine and Nancy Braganti, St. Martin's Press, New York, New York.

Understanding Cultural Difference: German, French, and American, Edward T. Hall and Mildred Reed Hall, Intercultural Press, Yarmouth, Maine.

Letters of Credit, Documentation and Shipping, and Contracts

Export Documentation Handbook, Dun & Bradstreet International, Mt. Lakes, New Jersey.

Export Documentation and Procedures, Unz, Jersey City, New Jersey.

Export/Import Procedures and Documentation, Second Edition, Thomas E. Johnson, AMACOM, Saranac Lake, New York.

Export Shipping Manual, Bureau of National Affairs, Distribution Center, Rockville, Maryland.

Guide to Incoterms, International Chamber of Commerce, ICC Publishing, New York, New York.

Harmonized System Reference Library, Unz, Jersey City, New Jersey.

INCOTERMS 1990, ICC Publishing, New York, New York.

INCOTERMS for Americans, Frank Reynolds, International Projects, Holland, Ohio.

Letters of Credit, Methods of Payment and Export Finance, Center for International Trade and Development, Boulder, Colorado.

Ports of the World: A Guide to Cargo Loss Control, CIGNA, Philadelphia, Pennsylvania.

Exporting from Start to Finance, L.F. Wells & Karin Dulat, 3rd Edition, McGraw-Hill, New York, New York.

Trade Finance, Insurance, and Countertrade

Countertrade Guide for Exporters, Project and Export Policy Division, Department of Trade and Industry, 1-19, Victoria St., London SW10ET, England.

The Countertrade Handbook, Dick Francis, Greenwood Press, Westport, Connecticut.

Countertrade: Practices, Strategies and Tactics, C. G. Alexandaides and Barbara L. Bowers, John Wiley, New York, New York.

Financing and Insuring Exports: A User's Guide to Eximbank and FCIA Programs, Export-Import Bank of the United States, Washington, D.C.

International Countertrade: A Guide for Managers and Executives, Superintendent of Documents, Pittsburgh, Pennsylvania.

International Countertrade: Individual Country Practices, Superintendent of Documents, Pittsburgh, Pennsylvania.

The Fundamentals of Trade Finance: The Ins and Outs of Import-Export Financing, Jane Kingman-Brundage and Susan A. Schulz, John Wiley, New York, New York.

Up Your Cash Flow, Harvey Goldstein, Granville, Los Angeles, California.

Research and Statistics

Findex: The Directory of Market Research Reports, Studies & Surveys, Cambridge Information Group, Bethesda, Maryland.

Guide to Foreign Trade Statistics, U.S. Department of Commerce, Superintendent of Documents, U.S. Government Printing Office, Washington, D.C.

High-Tech Exporter's Sourcebook, Land Grant, LGC Publishing, Brooklyn, New York.

Inside Washington: The International Executive's Guide to Government Resources, William A. Delphos, Venture Marketing Corp., Washington, D.C.

World Bank Atlas, World Bank Publications Department, Washington, D.C.

World Factbook, U.S. Government Printing Office, Superintendent of Documents, Washington, D.C.

Dictionaries, Directories, and Encyclopedias

Bergano's Register of International Importers, Bergano, Connecticut.

Dictionary of International Finance, Julian Walmsley, John Wiley, New York, New York.

Dun & Bradstreet Exporter's Encyclopedia, New York, New York.

The Export Yellow Pages, Delphos International, Washington, D.C.

Exporters Directory/U.S. Buying Guide, Journal of Commerce, Phillipsburg, New Jersey.

Exporters' Encyclopedia, Duns Marketing Service, Parsippany, New Jersey.

Foreign Sales Corporation Annual Directory, FSC/DISC-Tax Association, New York, New York.

Manufacturers' Agents National Association, European Distributors, Laguna Hills, California.

Partners in Export Trade Directory, Superintendent of Documents, U.S. Government Printing Office, Washington, D.C.

Registry of Export Intermediaries, National Association of Export Companies, SPC Marketing Co., Northport, New York.

Reference Book for World Traders, Croner Publications, Inc. Queens Village, New York.

Trade Directories of the World, Croner Publications, Inc. Queens Village, New York.

Trade Shows Worldwide, Gale Research, Detroit, Michigan.

Trading Company Sourcebook, International Business Affairs Corp., Bethesda, Maryland.

Export Periodicals, Magazines, and Publications

American Shipper
P.O. Box 4728
Jacksonville, Florida 32201

Business America
Superintendent of Documents
U.S. Government Printing Office
Washington, D.C. 20402

Commerce Business Daily
U.S. Government Printing Office
Superintendent of Documents
Washington, D.C. 20402

Development Business (U.N.-sponsored)
P.O. Box 5850, GCPO
New York, New York 10163-5850

The Exporter
Trade Data Reports, Inc.
34 West 37th Street
New York, New York 10018

Export Today
733 15th Street NW
Washington, D.C. 20005

Foreign Trade Magazine
6849 Old Dominion Drive #200
McLean, Virginia 22101

Global Trade Magazine
  North American Publishing Company
  401 North Broad Street
  Philadelphia, Pennsylvania 19108

International Business
  P.O. Box 50286
  Boulder, Colorado 80323

International Trade Reporter
  Export Shipping Manual
  The Bureau of National Affairs
  1231 25th Street NW
  Washington, D.C. 20037

Journal of Commerce
  Two World Trade Center, 27th Floor
  New York, New York 10048

Pacific Shipper
  560 Mission, Suite 601
  San Francisco, California 94105

Semiconductor International Magazine
  1350 East Towhy Ave.
  Des Plaines, Illinois 60018

Shipping Digest
  Geyer-McAllister Publications
  51 Madison Avenue
  New York, New York 10010

Trade and Culture
  7127 Hartford Road
  Baltimore, Maryland 21234

World Bank Publications
  1818 H. Street N.W.
  Washington, D.C. 20433

World Trade
  30 Broad Street
  Denville, New Jersey 07834

Index

Access to Export Capital (AXCAP), 32
Accounting, 29
ACRIS (*see* Consultant Registry Information Service)
Africa, trade with, 50, 104–113
Agency for International Development (AID), 100, 102, 248, 272, 284–287
  AID programs, 285, 286
Agent/Distributor Service (ADS), 145, 272
Agriculture, Department of (USDA), 146, 147, 171, 190, 200, 210, 277–282
  AgExport Connections, 279
  Commodity and Marketing Programs, 280
  Export Enhancement Program, 281
  Foreign Agricultural Service (FAS), 278
  Foreign Market Development Program (FMP), 281
  GMS-102 Program, 281
  GMS-103 Program, 282
  market promotion programs, 280, 281
  Public Law 480 Program, 282
  research, publications, databases, 279, 280
  Trade Assistance and Promotion Office, 146
  trade shows, 280
Agricultural Trade and Marketing Center, 280
Airway bill, 186, 187
  (*See also* Shipping Documents)
Albania, trade with, 99
Andean Pact Group, 85, 86
Antiboycott regulations, 27, 307, 308
Arab League, 307
Arbitration, 24, 43, 47, 295
Argentina, trade with, 83
Asia-Pacific Economic Cooperations (APEC), 133
Assessment of Resources, 48–52
Association of Southeast Asian Nations (ASEAN), 74, 130
Australia, trade with, 134, 135

Baltic states, trade with, 92, 99
Band/banker selection, 31–34

Bankers acceptance, 231
Bankers Association for Foreign Trade (BAFT), 32, 247
  Access to Export Capital (AXCAP), 32
Barter, 249
  (*See also* Financing: countertrade)
Belize, trade with, 80
Bills of lading, 185–188, 204, 217, 226, 231–235, 238, 262
  (*See also* Shipping documents)
Blacklist, 308
Business Information Service for the Newly Independent States (BISNIS), 100, 101, 103, 272
Bookkeeping, 29
Boycott, antiboycott regulations, 307, 308
Brazil, trade with, 83
Bureau of Export Administration (BXA), 212, 304–306
Business plan, 52–55
Buyback, 247
  (*See also* Financing: countertrade)
Buyer Alert, 147, 279
Buyer credit, 248

California Export Finance Office (CEFO), 32, 290
Canada, trade with, 9, 75
  NAFTA, 12, 76
Caribbean Basin Initiative (CBI), 82, 202
Caribbean Community (CARICOM), 82
Caribbean, trade with, 81
Catalog and video exhibitions (*see* Commercial Services)
Catalog missions (*see* Commercial Services)
Census, Bureau of, 39, 270
  analysis of exporters, 39
  FT925, 9
Center for Trade and Investment Services (CTIS), 286
Central Africa, trade with, 111–112
Central Europe, trade with, 97–101

Certificate of origin, 184
  (*See also* Shipping Documents)
Checklist:
  for agent consideration, 62, 63
  for business plan, 53–55
  for distributor consideration, 63–65
  for letters of credit, 193, 194, 234, 235
  for license contracts, 45
China, trade with, 50, 123–126
  special economic zones, 124
Clean acceptances (*see* Bankers
  Acceptances)
Commerce, Department of (DOC):
  Customized Sales Survey, 145, 273
  DOC district offices, 144, 272
  DOC export assistance, 16–20
  International Trade Office (ITO), 18, 268
  (*See also* International Trade
    Administration)
Commercial invoice, 183, 204, 206
  (*See also* Shipping Documents)
Commercial risk, 198, 258
Commercial risk insurance, 251–263, 292
Commercial Service (*see* U.S. & Foreign
  Commercial Service)
Commodity Control List (CCL), 305
Commodity Credit Corporation (CCC), 278,
  281
Commodity Import Program (CIP), 285
Commonwealth of Independent States
  (CIS), 101
Compensation, 249
  (*See also* Financing: countertrade)
Congress, 104th, 4, 17
Consortia of American Businesses, 103
Consular invoice, 183, 230
  (*See also* Shipping Documents)
Consultant Registry Information Service
  (ACRIS), 286
Contingency insurance, 263
Contract manufacturing, 48, 120
Contracts for the International Sales of
  Goods (CISG), 195
Convention/treaties, 298–302
Coordination Council for North American
  Affairs, 129
Copyright office (*see* Library of Congress)
Copyrights, 297, 298, 302
Costa Rica, trade with, 79
Counterpurchase, 249
  (*See also* Financing: countertrade)
Country Commercial Guides, 273, 274
Country risk (*see* Risk Management, Degree
  of Trading Difficulty)

Credit report (*see* World Traders Data
  Report)
Custom house broker, 181, 202–206, 211–213
Customs Service, U.S., 199–206, 211–212,
  302
  American goods returned (AGR), 202
  bond, 205
  drawbacks, 210, 211
  duties, 201, 202
  fines and levies, 199
  formal entries, 204–206
  informal entries, 206–208
  laws and regulations, 199–201
  restricted products, 210
Customized Sales Survey, 273
Customs broker (*see* Custom house broker)
Czech Republic, trade with, 99

Degree of Trading Difficulty, 50, 126
  in Africa, 105–106 (table)
  in Asia, 116–118 (table)
  in Europe 90–91, 92 (table)
  in Western Hemisphere, 70–71, 72 (table)
Direct loans, 291, 293
Direct mail, 142, 169
Discrepancies (*see* Letter of Credit)
Distribution strategies, 56–66
  in centralized countries, 75
  dealing with end user, 56
  in decentralized countries, 75
  direct mail, 142
  through agent/representative, 59
  through distributors, 61–66
  through retailers, 57
District office (*see* Commerce, Department
  of)
District Export Assistance Center (DEAC),
  272
District Export Council (DEC), 19
DOC (*see* Commerce, Department of)
Documents (*see* Shipping documents)
Documentary collections, 190, 197, 217–219
Domestic intermediaries, 41
  (*See also* Export intermediaries)
Drawbacks, 210

EAR (*see* Export Administration
  Regulations)
East Africa, trade with, 111
Eastern Europe, trade with, 50, 101–104
Eastern European Business & Information
  Center (EEBIC), 100, 272

Economic Bulletin Board (EBB), 145, 274–276, 279
Economic Cooperation Organization (ECO), 118, 121, 123
Egypt, trade with, 108
EMC (*see* Export Management Company)
EMC/ETC (*see* Export Management/Trading Co.)
Enterprise for the Americas Initiative (EAI), 80, 87
Enterprise funds, 48, 100
Environmental Technology Network for Asia (ETNA), 286
ETC (*see* Export Trading Company)
Europe, trade with, 89–104
European Community (EC), 89
European Free Trade Association (EFTA), 74, 89, 92, 93, 97
European Patent Convention, 300
European Union (EU), 89
Eximbank, 18, 31, 71, 78, 100, 102, 104, 118, 244, 248, 252, 255, 258–261, 272, 282, 288, 291–294
   City/State Program, 288
   credit insurance, 258–261
   foreign buyer direct loans, 293
   foreign buyer loan guarantees, 293
   foreign credit insurance, 292
   project financing, 293, 294
   Working Capital Guarantee Program, 292
Export Administration Act, 304–308
Export Administration Regulations (EAR), 27, 29, 190, 304–307
Export Assistance Centers (USEAC), 18, 271, 272
Export Contact List Service (ECLS), 145, 273
Export contracts, 193–195
Export control classification number (ECCN), 305, 306
Export finance, 243
   (*See also* Financing)
Export Hotline, 101
Export information, sources of, 16–21
Export intermediaries:
   advantages/disadvanteages of, 41, 42
   domestic intermediaries, 41
   export management companies (EMC), 36, 37
   export management/trading companies, 43, 44
   export trading companies (ETC), 37, 38
   general trading companies, 39, 40
   selection, 42, 43

Export Legal Assistance Network (ELAN), 30, 284
Export licenses/controls, 188, 253, 302–307
   CCL categories, 305
   government agencies involved, 304, 305
   overview, 304
   understanding controls, 305, 306
Export management companies, 36, 37, 41–44, 50, 51, 156
Export management/trading companies, 43, 44
Export potential, 5–11
   largest export customers, 9
   products with, 6–9
   top 30 products with, 8 (table)
Export trading companies, 37, 38, 41–44, 50, 51, 156
Export Working Capital Program, 32, 297, 298
Exporting directly, 44
Exporting distributors, 35
Exporting manufacturers, 35

Factoring, 246, 247
Financing:
   bankers acceptance, 245, 246
   buyer credit, 248
   countertrade, 248, 250
   factoring, 246, 247
   forfaiting, 247
   international leasing, 247
   receivables financing, 246
   transaction based, 33
   working capital, 244, 245, 289–291, 318
   (*See also* Trade finance)
Foreign Agricultural Service (FAS), 278–282
   [*See also* Agriculture, Department of (USDA)]
Foreign buyer direct loans, 293
Foreign buyer loan quarantees, 293
Foreign Buyers List, 147, 279
Foreign Corrupt Practices Act (FCPA), 308
Foreign Sales Corporation (FSC), 295, 296
   ICDISC, 296
   shared FSC, 295
   small FSC, 295
Foreign traders index, 144, 274
Forfaiting, 247, 248
Formal entry, 204, 205
Fourth World, 74
Franc Zone, 105, 106
France, trade with, 9

Franchising, 44–47, 84, 104, 131
  (*See also* Licensing)
Freight forwarder, 27, 181, 182

General Agreement on Tariffs and Trade
    (GATT), 78, 128, 134, 202, 278, 298, 300,
    302
General trading company, 39–41
Generalized System of Preferences (GSP),
    202
Geographic World Order Tables, 72–73,
    90–92, 105–106, 116–118
Germany, trade with, 9, 95, 96
Greece, trade with, 92
Greenland, trade with, 89
Guatemala, trade with, 79
Gulf Cooperation Council (GCC), 119

Harmonized Tariff Schedule of the US
    (HTSUS), 201–203, 205, 209, 213
"hold-harmless" clause, 258, 259
Home office, 15
Hong Kong, trade with, 129, 130
Human resources, 4
Hungary, trade with, 99

Import finance, 243, 244
  (*See also* Trade Finance)
Import/export:
  combined activities for, 12
  drawbacks, 210
Import process, 199–213
  classifying product, 202
  clearance costs, 200
  computing duty, 202
  formal entry, 204–206
  import licenses, 200, 210
  informal entry, 206, 207
  marking and labeling, 199–201
  preimport preparation, 199–203
  quotas, 208, 209
  restricted products, 210
  surety bond collateral, 203
Importer's identification number, 200
Incoterms (*see* Shipping Terms)
Inspection, preshipment, 196
Inspection certificate, 191
Inspection services, 196, 197
Insurance:
  commercial risk, 251, 252
  contingency, 263

Insurance (*Cont.*):
  country risk, 252, 253
  credit (accounts receivable), 31, 216,
    255–261
  Eximbank, 258–261
  foreign accounts receivable, 254
  marine/air cargo, 31, 182, 190, 262–264
  multibuyer, 259, 260
  open cargo, 262, 263
  OPIC, 261
  political risk, 252, 253
  private sector, 255–258
  special coverage, 263
  transit, 261, 262
  umbrella policy, 204, 259
Intellectual property rights (IPR), 297–302
  copyrights, 298
  patents, 300, 301
  trademarks, 298–300
  trade secrets, 301, 302
International Chamber of Commerce (ICC),
    226
International Economic Policy Unit, 268, 269
International leasing, 247
International Monetary Fund (IMF), 108,
    132
International Trade Administration (ITA),
    17, 18, 39, 66, 144, 171, 268, 270–273,
    277, 289, 300, 302
  (*See also* Commerce, Department of)
International Trade Office (ITO), 18, 268
ISO 9000 requirements, 95

Japan, trade with, 9, 126–129
Japanese External Trade Organization
    (JETRO), 127
Joint venture, 48

Korea, South, trade with, 9, 126
Kuwait, trade with, 119

Latin America, trade with, 10, 73–81
Latin American Integration Association
    (LAIA), 87
Legal assistance, 23, 30, 284
Legal structure:
  corporation, 25, 26
  general partnership, 24, 25
  limited partnership, 25
  sole proprietorship, 23
  sub chapter S corporation, 26

Less developed countries, 81, 131
Letter of credit (L/C):
  about/approximate, 230
  advised through, 230
  amendment to, 228, 229
  assignment of, 229
  checklist, 193, 194, 234, 235
  common errors in, 235–238
  confirmed, 230
  discrepancies in, 228, 238–239
  expiry, 231
  irrevocable, 219–225, 230
  negotiation, 230, 235
  parties to, 226–228
  sight, 231
  standby, 219, 239–241
  straight, 230
  transactional, 219, 226
  transferable, 229, 230
Library of Congress, 298, 302
Licenses and permits, 27–29
  city requirements, 29
  county requirements, 28
  federal requirements, 27
  state requirements, 28
Licensing, 44–47, 84
  (*See also* Franchising)

Maastricht, Treaty of, 89
Mandated preshipment inspection program,
  196
Market Development Cooperator Program,
  103
Matchmaker events, 277
Mercorsur, 83–87
Mexico, trade with, 9, 75–79
Middle East, trade with, 114–120
Morocco, trade with, 108
Multilateral development banks, 48

NAFTA (*see* North American Free Trade
  Agreement)
National Institute of Standards and
  Technology (NIST), 270
National Technical Information Service
  (NTIS), 270, 279, 280
National Trade Data Bank (NTDB), 144, 147,
  270, 273, 274, 276, 277, 279, 288, 306
Netherlands, trade with, 9, 93
New-to-export policy, 258, 259
Newly Independent States (NIS), 101–103,
  115, 121–123

New Zealand, trade with, 134, 135
Nicaragua, trade with, 79
Nonvessel Operating Common Carrier
  (NVOCC), 185, 188
North Africa, trade with, 106–108
North American Free Trade Agreement
  (NAFTA), 12, 76–78, 80, 85, 94, 126, 134,
  184, 187, 202, 276
NTDB (*see* National Trade Data Bank)
NVOCC (*see* Nonvessel Operating Common
  Carrier)

Ocean bill of lading, 185, 186
  (*See also* Shipping Documents)
Oceania, trade with, 135, 136
Office of Small and Disadvantaged Business
  Utilization/Minority, Resource Center
  (OSDBU/MRC), 286, 287
Offset (*see* Financing: countertrade)
Open Account (*see* Payment terms)
Open cargo policy (*see* Insurance)
Original equipment manufacturers (OEM),
  35, 39, 44
Overseas Private Investment Corp (OPIC),
  100, 102, 261, 287, 294, 295

Packing list, 184
  (*See also* Shipping documents)
Panama, trade with, 80
Paraguay, trade with, 84, 85
Patents, 300, 301
Payment terms, 214–242
  advance payments, 242
  documents against acceptance, 218
  documents against payment, 217, 218
  letters of credit (*see* Letters of credit)
  open account, 214–217
  wire transfers, 242
Performance standards, 43, 196, 245
Phytosanitary certificate, 190
  (*See also* Shipping Documents)
Poland, trade with, 97, 98
Political risk, 31, 71, 76, 87, 88, 241, 252, 253,
  255, 258, 261, 281, 292, 294
Political World Order tables, 72–73, 90–92,
  105–106, 116–118
Post sales service, 197
Preshipment inspections, 196, 197
Procurement Information Access System,
  286
Procurement Information Bulletin (PIB),
  286

Product promotion:
  audiences to consider, 142
  through catalog shows, 171
  communication skills needed, 139–141
  via direct mail, 139, 169
  via fax, 142, 143
  finding leads, 144, 146
  by media advertising, 170, 171
  through overseas trade fairs, 172–174
  with private sector assistance, 149
  with samples, 150, 151
  through trade missions and exhibits, 171, 172
  by traveling, 169
Pricing strategies, 155–160
  caveats, 161, 162
  determining landed cost, 157
  discount structuring, 158
  export invoicing, 158
  price lists, 158
  pro forma invoice, 159
Private sector insurance, 255
Project financing, 293
Public sector guarantor, 180

Quotas, import, 201, 208, 209

Receivables financing, 246
  (*See also* Financing)
Resources, assessment of, 48–52
Restricted import products, 210
Risk Management, 31, 32
  commercial risk, 198, 251, 252
  country risk, 252, 253
  country risk levels, 99, 100
  political risk, 252, 253
  transportation risk, 261–264
  (*See also* Insurance)
Romania, trade with, 98
Russia, trade with, 50, 91, 94

Samples, 150, 151, 167–169
Saudi Arabia, trade with, 10
Scandinavia, trade with, 92, 93
Schedule B, 202, 270, 285
Selling through retailers, 57
Service Corps of Retired Executives
  (SCORE), 19, 54, 71, 270, 283
Services, export of, 8
Shipper's export declaration (SED), 12, 181,
  188, 190, 198

Shipping documents, 183–190
  airway bill, 186, 187
  bill of exchange, 190
  bill of lading, 185–188, 204, 217, 226,
    231–235, 238, 262
  certificate of origin, 184
  combined transport bill of lading, 187
  commercial invoice, 183, 204, 206
  consular invoice, 183, 230
  dock receipt, 191
  drafts (bill of exchange), 190
  house bill of lading, 188
  inspection certificate, 191
  insurance certificate, 190
  NVOCC bill of lading, 188
  packing list, 184, 195
  postal forms, 191
  phytosanitary certificate, 190
  rail bill of lading, 187
  shipper's export declaration, 188, 189
  truck bill of lading, 187
  warehouse receipts, 191
Shipping Terms (incoterms), 152–155
  CFR—Cost and Freight, 154
  CIF—Cost, Insurance and Freight, 154
  CIP—Carriage and Insurance Paid to, 154
  CPT—Carriage Paid to, 154
  DAF—Delivered at Frontier, 154
  DDU—Deliver Duty Unpaid, 154
  DDP—Delivered Duty Paid, 154
  DES—Delivered Ex Ship, 154
  DEQ—Delivered Ex Quay, 154
  EXW—EX Works, 152
  FAS—Free Alongside Ship, 153
  FCA—Free Carrier, 153
  FOB—Free on Board, 153
Singapore, trade with, 9, 130
Single Internal Market Information Service
  (SIMIS), 95
Small Business Administration (SBA),
  17–19, 34, 53–55, 269, 270, 282–284, 286,
  288, 289–291
Small Business Development Centers
  (SBDCs), 17–19, 274, 283, 288
Small Business Insurance policy, 258
Society for Worldwide Interbank Financial
  Telecommunication (SWIFT), 226
Soft currencies, 100
Southern Africa, trade with, 112–113
Southern Common Market, 84
Southern Cone Group, 84
Standard Industrial Trade Classification
  (SITC), 8
Standby letter of credit (*see* Letter of Credit)

State based export finance support, 296
Strategic alliance, 48
Sub-Saharan Africa, trade with, 108, 109
Suitability for export:
  adaptability of product, 11
  potential export conditions, 5
  potential export products, 6–9
  prime target countries, 9
  types of export people, 4
  utilitarian value of product, 11
Supplier credit, 243, 292

Taiwan, trade with, 9, 129
Target countries, 9, 50, 74, 163, 164
Trade acceptance, 218
  (*See also* Payment Terms)
Trade Assistance and Promotion (TAPO),
  146, 279
Trade and Development Agency (TDA), 102,
  287
Trade blocs, 12, 73, 74
Trade Data Services, 270
Trade Development Unit, 269
Trade fairs, 98, 127, 129, 166, 171, 172, 277
Trade Information Center (TIC), 4, 95, 100,
  146, 167, 270–272, 276, 277
Trade finance, 32, 33, 38, 243, 245–248, 292
  (*See also* Financing)
Trade missions, 173, 276, 288
Trade Opportunity Program (TOP), 144, 145,
  276
Trade Promotion Coordinating Committee
  (TPCC), 271, 278
Trade Representative's Office (USTR), 18,
  85, 98, 120, 127, 131, 268
Trade secrets, 297, 301, 302
Trademarks, 45, 46, 131, 169, 210, 297,
  298–302
Transaction-based financing, 33
Travel overseas, 163–169
  budget, 166, 167
  first trip, 164
  travel tips, 164, 165
  which staff member, 163
  with samples, 167–169
  world holidays, 165
Treaties/conventions:
  Berne Convention, 298
  Buenos Aires Copyright Convention, 298
  European Patent Convention, 300

Treaties/conventions (*Cont.*):
  General Inter-American Convention,
    299
  Inter-Amereican Convention, 300
  Paris Union International Convention,
    298
  Patent Cooperation Treaty, 300
  Treaty of Rome, 94
  Vienna Sales Convention, 195
Tunisia, trade with, 108

U.S. Agency for International Development
  (AID) (*see* Agency for International
  Development)
U.S. Bureau of Export Administration (BXA)
  (*see* Bureau of Export Administration)
U.S. Census Bureau (*see* Census, bureau of)
U.S. Customs Service (*see* Customs Service)
U.S. Department of Agriculture (USDA) (*see*
  Agriculture, Department of)
U.S. Department of Commerce (DOC) (*see*
  Commerce, Department of)
U.S. Export Assistance Centers (USEAC)
  (*see* Export Assistance Centers)
U.S. Export-Import Bank (*see* Eximbank)
U.S. & Foreign Commercial Service
  (US&FCS), 17, 18, 268, 269
U.S. Trade Representative (*see* Trade
  Representative USTR)
Umbrella policy (*see* Insurance)
Uniform Commercial Code (UCC), 195
United Arab Emirates (UAE), trade with,
  119
Uruguay, trade with, 84, 85

Venezuela, trade with, 83

West Africa, trade with, 109–110
Western Europe, trade with, 89–97
Working capital financing, 243–245,
    289–291, 318
  (*See also* Financing)
Working capital loan guarantee, 291
World Bank, 100, 104, 108, 132, 133, 270
World price, 196
World Trade Organization (WTO), 302
World Traders Data Report (WTDR), 58, 59,
  62, 150, 254, 273

About the Author

L. Fargo Wells has been a leader in the international trading community for over 20 years. He is currently a sought-after consultant on exporting and travels the world on assignments. He is also a director of several corporations to which he lends his international trading expertise. Mr. Wells is the founder and former director of the California Export Finance Office, and, with Karin Dulat, is the coauthor of *Exporting: From Start to Finance*.